Conception, Reception, and the Spirit

Conception, Reception, and the Spirit

Essays in Honor of Andrew T. Lincoln

Edited by
J. Gordon McConville
and Lloyd K. Pietersen

CASCADE Books • Eugene, Oregon

CONCEPTION, RECEPTION, AND THE SPIRIT
Essays in Honor of Andrew T. Lincoln

Copyright © 2015 Wipf and Stock Publishers. All rights reserved. Except for brief quotations in critical publications or reviews, no part of this book may be reproduced in any manner without prior written permission from the publisher. Write: Permissions, Wipf and Stock Publishers, 199 W. 8th Ave., Suite 3, Eugene, OR 97401.

Cascade Books
An Imprint of Wipf and Stock Publishers
199 W. 8th Ave., Suite 3
Eugene, OR 97401

www.wipfandstock.com

ISBN 13: 978-1-62032-746-3

Cataloguing-in-Publication Data

Conception, reception, and the Spirit : essays in honor of Andrew T. Lincoln / edited by Gordon McConville and Lloyd Pietersen.

xxii + 352 p. ; 23 cm. Includes bibliographical references.

ISBN 13: 978-1-62032-746-3

1. Lincoln, Andrew T. 2. Bible—Criticism, interpretation, etc. 3. Bible—Hermeneutics. I. McConville, J. G. (J. Gordon). II. Pietersen, Lloyd. III. Title.

BS511.3 M433 2015

Manufactured in the U.S.A.   07/30/2015

Contents

Contributors | vii
Abbreviations | ix
Introduction | xiii
   —J. Gordon McConville and Lloyd K. Pietersen

Part I: Exegesis

1. Figures in Isaiah 7:14 | 3
   —J. G. McConville

2. Rival Group Identities in the Matthean Gospel: Evidence from Matthew 1–2 and 23 | 19
   —Philip F. Esler

3. Let John be John (2) | 36
   —James D. G. Dunn

4. Worlds of Judgment: John 9 | 48
   —L. Ann Jervis

5. Another Look at "Lifting Up" in the Gospel of John | 58
   —Catrin H. Williams

6. John, Jesus, and "The Ruler of This World": Demonic Politics in the Fourth Gospel? | 71
   —N. T. Wright, with J. P. Davies

7. Land, Idolatry, and Justice in Romans | 90
   —Sylvia C. Keesmaat

8. A New Translation of Philippians 2:5 and Its Significance for Paul's Theology and Spirituality | 104
   —Michael J. Gorman

9 Wine, Debauchery, and the Spirit
   (Ephesians 5:18–19) | 123
   —Lloyd K. Pietersen

10 The Metaphor of the Face in Paul | 136
   —Stephen C. Barton

Part II: Theological Interpretation

11 Born of a Virgin? The Conversation Continues | 157
   —David R. Catchpole

12 Historical Criticism, Theological Interpretation, and the
   Ends of the Christian Life | 173
   —Stephen Fowl

13 What Makes New Testament Theology "Theology"? | 187
   —Robert Morgan

14 Who and What is Theological Interpretation For? | 210
   —Angus Paddison

15 The Use of the Old Testament in the Work and Preaching
   of F. W. Robertson of Brighton | 224
   —John W. Rogerson

16 ὑπὸ πνεύματος ἁγίου φερόμενοι ἐλάλησαν ἀπὸ θεοῦ
   ἄνθρωποι: On the Inspiration of Holy Scripture | 236
   —John Webster

Part III: Theology and Embodiment

17 Good Sex, Bad Sex: Reflections on Sexuality
   and the Bible | 253
   —Loveday Alexander

18 Spirituality, Ethics, and Memory | 274
   —John Goldingay

19 Pacing the Cage: Biblical Resonance
   and Embodied Testimony | 289
   —Brian J. Walsh

Bibliography | 309
Ancient Documents Index | 331
Author Index | 347

Contributors

Loveday Alexander, Emeritus Professor of Biblical Studies, University of Sheffield, UK.

Stephen C. Barton, Honorary Fellow, Department of Theology and Religion, University of Durham, UK.

David R. Catchpole, Emeritus Professor of Theological Studies, University of Exeter, UK.

Jamie P. Davies, Teaching Fellow in Biblical Studies, School of Divinity, University of Edinburgh, UK.

James D. G. Dunn, Emeritus Lightfoot Professor of Divinity, University of Durham, UK.

Philip F. Esler, Portland Chair in New Testament Studies, University of Gloucestershire, UK.

Stephen Fowl, Professor of Theology, Loyola University, Maryland.

John Goldingay, David Allan Hubbard Professor of Old Testament, Fuller Theological Seminary, California.

Michael J. Gorman, Raymond E. Brown Professor of Biblical Studies and Theology, St. Mary's Seminary & University, Baltimore, Maryland.

L. Ann Jervis, Professor of New Testament, Wycliffe College, University of Toronto.

Sylvia C. Keesmaat, Biblical Scholar in Residence for the Anglican Deanery of Victoria-Haliburton, Diocese of Toronto, and Adjunct Professor of Biblical Studies, Trinity College, University of Toronto.

J. Gordon McConville, Professor of Old Testament Theology, University of Gloucestershire, UK.

Contributors

Robert Morgan, formerly Reader in New Testament Theology and Fellow of Linacre College, Oxford; priest-in-charge Sandford-on-Thames.

Angus Paddison, Reader in Theology, University of Winchester, UK.

Lloyd K. Pietersen, Honorary Research Fellow, The Centre for Anabaptist Studies, Bristol Baptist College, and Visiting Research Fellow, Newman University, UK.

John W. Rogerson, Emeritus Professor of Biblical Studies, University of Sheffield, UK.

Brian J. Walsh, Christian Reformed Campus Minister, and Adjunct Professor of Theology of Culture, Wycliffe and Trinity Colleges, University of Toronto.

John Webster, Professor of Divinity, University of St. Andrews, UK.

Catrin H. Williams, Reader in New Testament Studies, University of Wales Trinity Saint David, UK.

N. T. Wright, Professor of New Testament and Early Christianity, University of St. Andrews, UK.

Abbreviations

AB	Anchor Bible
ABD	*Anchor Bible Dictionary*
AGJU	Arbeiten zur Geschichte des antiken Judentums und des Urchristentums
AYB	Anchor Yale Bible
BAR	*Biblical Archaeology Review*
BDAG	*Greek-English Lexicon of the New Testament and Other Early Christian Literature.* 3rd ed.
BDF	*A Greek Grammar of the New Testament and Other Early Christian Literature*
BECNT	Baker Exegetical Commentary on the New Testament
BETL	Bibliotheca ephemeridum theologicarum lovaniensium
BJRL	*Bulletin of the John Rylands University Library of Manchester*
BNTC	Black's New Testament Commentaries
BWANT	Beiträge zur Wissenschaft vom Alten und Neuen Testament
CBQ	*Catholic Biblical Quarterly*
CSR	*Christian Scholars Review*
ExpTim	*Expository Times*
HBT	Horizons in Biblical Theology
HBS	Herders biblische Studien
HTR	*Harvard Theological Review*
ICC	International Critical Commentary

IDB	*The Interpreter's Dictionary of the Bible*
Int	*Interpretation*
IVPNTS	IVP New Testament Commentary Series
JBL	*Journal of Biblical Literature*
JSNT	*Journal for the Study of the New Testament*
JSNTSup	Journal for the Study of the New Testament: Supplement Series
JSOTSup	Journal for the Study of the Old Testament: Supplement Series
JSPL	*Journal for the Study of Paul and His Letters*
JTC	*Journal for Theology and the Church*
JTI	*Journal of Theological Interpretation*
LNTS	Library of New Testament Studies
NCB	New Century Bible
NHL	*Nag Hammadi Library in English*
NIB	*The New Interpreter's Bible*
NIBCOT	New International Biblical Commentary on the Old Testament
NIGTC	New International Greek Testament Commentary
NICOT	New International Commentary on the Old Testament
NovT	*Novum Testamentum*
NTOA	Novum Testamentum et Orbis Antiquus
NTS	*New Testament Studies*
OBO	Orbis biblicus et orientalis
OTL	Old Testament Library
PG	Patrologia graeca
SBLSymS	Society of Biblical Literature Symposium Series
SE	*Studia evangelica*
SJT	*Scottish Journal of Theology*
SNTSMS	Society for New Testament Studies Monograph Series
TDNT	*Theological Dictionary of the New Testament*
TDOT	*Theological Dictionary of the Old Testament*
THNTC	The Two Horizons New Testament Commentary

TRu	*Theologische Rundschau*
TS	*Theological Studies*
VCSup	Vigiliae Christianae Supplements
VT	*Vetus Testamentum*
WBC	Word Biblical Commentary
WMANT	Wissenschaftliche Monographien zum Alten und Neuen Testament
WUNT	Wissenschaftliche Untersuchungen zum Alten und Neuen Testament
ZTK	*Zeitschrift für Theologie und Kirche*

Introduction

J. GORDON MCCONVILLE
and LLOYD K. PIETERSEN

WE ARE DELIGHTED TO present this *Festschrift* in honor of our esteemed friend and colleague, Professor Andrew T. Lincoln, on the occasion of his retirement. The title of this volume reflects Andrew's lifelong interests in Christian origins, the reception of biblical texts in believing and scholarly communities, and the embodiment of the gospel in believing communities made possible by the Spirit. Furthermore, his commitment to careful exegesis of biblical texts, combined with a sensitivity to theological interpretation of those texts and a passionate desire to see such theological interpretation worked out in the life and practice of believing communities, result in the threefold division of this volume: exegesis, theological interpretation, and theology and embodiment.

THE LIFE AND WORK OF ANDREW LINCOLN

Andrew was born on 17 May 1944; he was an undergraduate at Trinity College, Cambridge from 1963–66 where he obtained a BA Honours in Modern Languages followed by an MA in 1971. After obtaining his BA he studied Theology at Westminster Theological Seminary in Philadelphia, culminating in receiving a BD summa cum laude in 1971. From there he went on to do his PhD at Cambridge and his doctoral dissertation was accepted in early 1975. This dissertation was revised and subsequently published as the very well received *Paradise Now and Not Yet* (1981). Andrew was Assistant Professor in New Testament at Gordon-Conwell Theological Seminary in

Massachusetts from 1975 to 1979 and then Lecturer in New Testament at St. John's College, Nottingham from 1979 to 1985 (where he also taught at the University of Nottingham between 1982 and 1983). He became Lecturer and then Senior Lecturer in Biblical Studies at the University of Sheffield, where he taught from 1985 to 1995. During his time at Sheffield, his *Ephesians* Word Biblical Commentary was published (1990) as was *The Theology of the Later Pauline Letters*, jointly authored with A. J. M. Wedderburn (1993). Andrew returned to North America in 1995, where he was Lord and Lady Coggan Professor of New Testament at Wycliffe College, University of Toronto until 1999 and a Visiting Professor of New Testament at Fuller Theological Seminary in California for the summer session of 1998. In 1999 Andrew became Portland Professor of New Testament at the University of Gloucestershire, a position he held until 2013. Since September 2013 he continued to work part-time at the University of Gloucestershire until his eventual retirement in March 2015. He is now Emeritus Professor of New Testament there. As well as being an outstanding researcher and teacher, Andrew has been an excellent doctoral supervisor. His research students have always been very important to him and to date he has successfully supervised twenty-seven PhDs.

During his tenure at the University of Gloucestershire Andrew published a number of significant works: *Truth on Trial* in 2000; *Colossians* in *The New Interpreter's Bible*, Vol XI, also in 2000; a commentary on *The Gospel according to St. John* (BNTC) in 2005; and *Hebrews: A Guide* in 2006. He co-edited with Angus Paddison the volume *Christology and Scripture: Interdisciplinary Perspectives* in 2007, and co-edited with J. Gordon McConville and Lloyd K. Pietersen the volume *The Bible and Spirituality* (2013). His latest monograph, *Born of a Virgin?*, was published in 2013.

Andrew has also published numerous articles in scholarly journals and edited volumes. These articles are wide-ranging and cover Matthew, Mark and John, Luke-Acts, the Pauline corpus, Hebrews, theological interpretation, and spirituality. He served as General Editor of the monograph series New Testament Guides, published by Sheffield Academic Press and then T & T Clark International, and was a member of the Editorial Board for the journal *Biblical Interpretation*. He was president of the British New Testament Society from September 2006 to September 2009.

Andrew's research has also contributed to bridging the gap between academic biblical studies and popular understanding in the church and society, as readers turn to his work on New Testament texts and issues to find ways to integrate the challenges of critical reading with an appreciation of the contemporary significance of the Bible for theological thinking and the religious imagination. His work on John has led to a number of invitations to address audiences beyond academia as diverse as workshops and lectures for German Baptist leaders in Hannover and videos on John for A-level students. With an eye on present disputes in the Anglican Communion, the Church of England's Council for Christian Unity commissioned Andrew to write a paper on the concept of *koinonia* or communion in Paul's letters. The implications of his research on the concept of *koinonia* in Paul's letters were presented as a keynote address to the Porvoo Conference (a consultation between the Church of England and the state churches of Northern Europe) on Ethics and Communion in January, 2008. It also led to participation in the Church of England's further consultation with the German State Lutheran Church under the Meissen Agreement in Düsseldorf in November, 2008. Furthermore, the interest generated by the publication of *Truth on Trial* led to the invitation to give the only New Testament paper at a February 2012 conference on the Divine Courtroom in Comparative Perspective at the Yeshiva University Center for Jewish Law and Contemporary Civilization, New York, where the sessions were open to rabbis, students, and members of the public.

THIS VOLUME

Andrew's wide-ranging interests, and the esteem in which he is held, are reflected in the contributions to this volume. Gordon McConville begins, fittingly, given Andrew's latest monograph, with an examination of Isa 7:14. Given Matthew's use of this text, McConville is interested in the ways in which a text "can be said to mean something entirely different in a new [setting], far removed from it in time and circumstance." After considering various problems surrounding העלמה (or ἡ παρθένος in LXX), McConville goes on to examine Isa 7:14 in the immediate context of 7:1—9:1 before considering both redactional and figurative, or metaphorical, explanations for the perplexities surrounding this text. He concludes with a discussion of the role of imagination aided by the work of both Paul Ricoeur and Sandra Schneiders to argue that the relationship between OT text and NT reception requires the responsible exercise of human imagination.

Philip Esler also works with the Matthean infancy narrative, as well as Matt 23. Esler uses the foundational work of Fredrik Barth on ethnic identity together with the research of John Hutchinson and Anthony Smith on ethnicity to suggest that Ἰουδαῖοι should be construed in terms of Judean ethnic identity rather than as "Jews." He illustrates this with reference to Matt 1–2. Esler contrasts this with Matthew's construal of a different type of group entity, which Esler designates as "the Christ movement." In this group boundaries between ethnic identities have been relaxed and Matthew uses the language of fictive kinship to describe membership in it. Matthew 23 focuses on the conflict between these two group identities and seeks to subvert Judean ethnic identity rooted in Abrahamic descent "by presenting Judeans as a threat to Christ-followers."

Four essays on John follow. James Dunn focuses on John's christology as the Fourth Gospel's greatest contribution to Christian theology. Dunn argues that John goes beyond the Pauline language of texts such as Rom 8:3; Gal 4:4; and Phil 2:6–7 to articulate "that the Son acted as the Father's plenipotentiary in the fullest sense." Dunn notes that John's christology is so radical that it comes close to, but does not amount to, gnosticizing the gospel. Dunn argues that John succeeds in maintaining the "both-and of flesh and glory." Ann Jervis pays detailed attention to John 9. She examines this chapter in close conversation with Andrew's *Truth on Trial*. Following a close reading of the narrative Jervis concludes that the "worlds of judgment" of her chapter title include not only the creation of believers and nonbelievers, but also a different kind of judgment which involves the giving of life and light rather than the apportioning of blame. The challenge for contemporary followers of Jesus, therefore, is similarly "to live with our eyes open to the world of life and light that he has brought into our darkness." Catrin Williams takes another look at the concept of "lifting up" in John. Williams is interested in whether this saying amounts to a Johannine expansion of the resurrection-ascension motif to include crucifixion or whether it amounts to a transference of that motif onto crucifixion exclusively. She proceeds by examining the use of ὑψόω in a variety of texts outside John before analyzing its function within the Fourth Gospel. In doing so she turns especially to its use in connection with the Isaianic Servant. This enables her to draw out links between John and Isaiah—not only in connection with "lifting up," but also in connection with "seeing." Williams is thus able to conclude that John's portrayal of Jesus' physical "lifting up" on the cross signifies, in fact, for those "with eyes to 'see,'" "his exaltation to the Father's presence." Finally, Wright and Davies examine John's use of "the ruler of this world" language. Following a brief survey of recent work on John and empire, they turn to a close examination of John 12:20–36 in which "the ruler of this world" suddenly appears. In considering whether this refers naturally and only to Satan they turn to the end of chapter 14 where the phrase again occurs and ask what it would mean to speak of Satan as "coming" in this context. They argue that the closest parallel is found in Revelation, where the imperial force and satanic power are found in close association (e.g., Rev 13:2). In their concluding section they turn to the trial narrative in John and suggest that a close examination of John 12:30–36, the farewell discourses of chapters 13–17, and the trial narrative of chapters 18–19 point to "the ruler of this world" as both Satan and Caesar.

Sylvia Keesmaat employs Brueggemann's categories in his *Prophetic Imagination* to argue that Romans is engaged in prophetic critique of the environmental degradation wrought by the Roman empire. She draws on Paul's description of idolatry in Rom 1 and the language of Rom 8 to argue that "creation is groaning for the same reason that believers groan: because it is suffering under the exploitative economic practices and violent militarism of Roman imperial rule." Keesmaat goes on to demonstrate ways in which Romans also embodies a vision of hope evident in Paul's language of resurrection and glory. For her, "embodied faithfulness can't help but impact the land as well."

Michael Gorman provides a new translation of Phil 2:5: "Cultivate this mindset—this way of thinking, acting, and feeling—in your community, which is in fact a community in the Messiah Jesus." The key element here for Gorman is the relative clause "which is in fact . . . ." After surveying the two prevailing interpretive options for Phil 2:5, which Gorman calls the "imitative" and "locative" perspectives, he continues by examining some key exegetical questions. His detailed exegetical conclusions lead him to the view that "Paul is not describing an ethic of imitation, but a spirituality of participation."

Lloyd Pietersen turns to a letter that Andrew Lincoln has written extensively on—Ephesians. He re-examines the injunction against drinking wine to excess in Eph 5:18 in the light of the consensus, endorsed by Andrew, that the text is not addressing a particular problem of alcohol abuse in the congregation. After examining the three main solutions on offer as to why drunkenness is mentioned at this point in the letter, Pietersen rejects the recent renewed emphasis on the Dionysian cult and concludes that excess wine drinking in the context of *symposia* is the most likely background for this prohibition. Noting the link between wine and "the good life" in the ancient world Pietersen suggests that the "good life for our author is manifested not in the 'obscene, silly and vulgar talk' (Eph 5:4) so characteristic of excess drinking but in thanksgiving . . . expressed in song inspired by the Spirit."

Stephen Barton considers the metaphor of the face in Paul, recognizing that in speaking of the face we are dealing with issues of the self in relation. Following a survey of the face in the biblical world, Barton turns to Paul's use of the metaphor, focusing on 1 Cor 13:12; 2 Cor 3:18; and 2 Cor 4:6. Through a detailed analysis of these texts he demonstrates that the face is not only a relational metaphor for Paul but is also "a metaphor of revelatory encounter, liberation, and eschatological transformation." Barton concludes with some reflections on the significance of the metaphor for spirituality, liturgy, and moral formation and social life.

David Catchpole opens the second section of this volume dealing with theological interpretation and interacts extensively with Andrew's latest book, *Born of a Virgin?* He notes that the Gospels provide support for three possibilities concerning Jesus' parentage: (A) that he had no human father; (B) that Joseph was his normal human father; and (C) that his human father was a person unknown. Andrew argues that (C) has considerable merit but ultimately rejects it. Catchpole argues the case for a reconsideration of (C) by a close examination of the relevant passages in the Synoptic Gospels. He concludes that although there is much support within the Gospel traditions for the view that Jesus was Joseph's son, pre-Matthew provides us with our best evidence and the likelihood is that the tradition would move from an unknown father to Joseph, but not the other way round. For Catchpole, therefore, the identity of Jesus' father remains unknown.

Stephen Fowl documents the failure of historical criticism to produce *the* meaning of a biblical text. The failure to achieve a grand unified theory of textual meaning may be considered by some to be a crisis, but, for Fowl, this provides the opportunity to reinvigorate genuinely theological forms of biblical interpretation such as abounded in the pre-modern era. Fowl notes that scriptural interpretation was seen as a central task of theology and not a separate discipline distinct from it in the pre-modern period. Theological interpretation should be marked by a commitment to keep theological concerns primary, but this does not mean that the theological interpreter cannot make use of other interpretive methods. Fowl concludes with a plea for the moral and intellectual formation of theological interpreters by cultivating the virtues of charity and practical reasoning. For him the question of such formation is far more pressing than debates about the nature and definition of theological interpretation.

Robert Morgan provides a survey of the field of New Testament theology and reflects on how "theology" is understood. He contends that it has a strong sense of articulating and perhaps advocating a religious stance, and a secondary sense which is descriptive and analyzes the faith commitments of others. The secondary sense has been prevalent in that the discipline of New Testament theology has been a sub-division of New Testament scholarship, rather than of systematic theology. Morgan notes the influence of Wrede here in the latter's insistence that the discipline should exclude the interpreter's own theological interests. For Morgan, Wrede's position has had serious consequences for religious faith and practice. On the one hand, theological faculties associated with the church could engage in sophisticated forms of theological interpretation, whereas in secular universities scholarship had to be non-confessional. Morgan's essay carefully advocates a recovery of the strong sense of "theology" in "New Testament theology" and suggests that the phrase is "better reserved for a scholarship that wants to engage in (Christian) theology in the primary sense of expressing something of a Christianity that is credible today and true to the biblical witness."

Angus Paddison continues the theme of theological interpretation and notes that proponents of such interpretation have not sufficiently engaged with both practical and public theologians. Paddison's essay consists of two parts. In the first, he examines the nature of theological interpretation and, by focusing on Stanley Hauerwas and John Webster, suggests there are two prevailing approaches: the "ecclesiocentric" and "theocentric" respectively. In the second part, Paddison addresses the question as to what theological interpretation would look like if it were to prioritize practical and public theological concerns. He offers three theses in the light of this. First, that theological interpretation should encourage intensive forms of both living with the text and engaging with the world. Second, such interpretation should be alert to the risks of ecclesiocentric approaches. The focus on public theology prioritizes regard for the world ahead of the church's self-interest. Third, a focus on practical theology would shift attention from abstract notions of "church" to the actual church in its diversity and to actual readers "in their non-negotiable concreteness."

John Rogerson examines the nineteenth-century Anglican churchman F. W. Robertson and his use of the Old Testament. Rogerson draws on Robertson's lectures on Genesis and twelve other Old Testament sermons. He notes that "Robertson did not shrink from confronting the results of biblical criticism and scientific discoveries." For Robertson there were two revelations: one in creation and understood by means of scientific investigation and the other in Scripture and written according to the knowledge available at the time of composition. But Robertson's appropriation of biblical criticism was far from negative and Rogerson draws attention to some of the profound insights Robertson's sermons have on Old Testament narratives. For Rogerson, Robertson's example highlights ways in which one can embrace biblical criticism and engage imaginatively with biblical texts.

John Webster tackles the issue of the inspiration of Scripture. Webster notes that the doctrine of inspiration is one element in a comprehensive theology of Scripture. Furthermore, such a theology of Scripture has to begin with the doctrine of God and, in particular, with the economy of divine instruction rooted in God's knowledge, goodness, and communicative action. Webster continues with a discussion of the authorship of Scripture and maintains that God is the primary author whose first causal work in this connection is the calling and sanctification of the human authors. He is clear that God's causal work does not constitute the human authors as mere artefacts, but as agents to whom tasks are assigned. For Webster inspiration can be arranged into three distinct acts which are nevertheless co-inherent and may be concurrent. First, is the illumination of the biblical author—a "vivification of intelligence." Second, is the Spirit-given impulse to write. Webster recognizes that this process is complex and involves the writer's own will and understanding. Third, "the Spirit provides both the *res* of the biblical writings and *verba* by which that matter is expressed," but not in a way that renders the biblical writers as wholly passive. Webster thus agrees with Rahner that a biblical author is "a true human author whose authorship remains whole and inviolate at the same time as it is permeated and embraced by that of God."

The third section of this volume—theology and embodiment—begins with Loveday Alexander's essay on sexuality and the Bible. Alexander advocates a "this is that" hermeneutic that is essentially dialogical—a process of exploration. Beginning with the present context ("this"), one goes back to Scripture to find a correspondence ("that"). This then provides a framework for better understanding what is happening now and for interpreting what to do in the future. Alexander then examines the biblical material on same-sex relations, briefly looks at sex and marriage in the Gospels, and then turns to a discussion of "good sex" and "bad sex" with reference to 1 Cor 5–7. Finally, she considers the pastoral consequences for the church today and concludes that many examples of both homosexual and heterosexual practices today fall under Paul's concept of "bad sex." However, "a permanent, faithful, stable relationship that is legally sanctioned by the law of the land" would fall under Paul's definition of "good sex" and this applies to both heterosexual and homosexual relationships.

John Goldingay outlines four aspects of the relationship between spirituality, ethics, and memory. First, spirituality involves remembering the story on which the faith is based. Second, spirituality and ethics require people to remember the ways in which God has related to them personally in the past. Third, living a good life requires remembering the obligations that the past imposes on us—there is thus an ethics of memory. Finally, spirituality and ethics involves remembering that God remembers, and Goldingay suggests that this "may be the most important aspect of the link between spirituality and memory."

In the final essay Brian Walsh draws upon a Bruce Cockburn song, "Pacing the Cage," to suggest that Andrew Lincoln "has found himself, more than once, pacing the cage in his struggle to be a faithful interpreter." Walsh interacts extensively with Andrew's *Truth on Trial* and particularly with Andrew's insistence that "testimony is known to be true when it takes on flesh and moves into the neighborhood." Walsh illustrates this from his own personal encounter with John's Gospel and with his experience of a worshipping community he founded at the University of Toronto called Wine Before Breakfast. He concludes with a sermon given in the community at the end of a year spent studying the Fourth Gospel.

The essays within this volume are wide-ranging and reflect Andrew's extensive interests. All the contributors are immensely grateful to him as a friend and colleague and we offer this volume to him in honor of his work.

Part I

Exegesis

I

Figures in Isaiah 7:14

J. G. MCCONVILLE
University of Gloucestershire

THE MEANING OF "IMMANUEL"

IN MATTHEW 1:23 WE read: "Behold, a virgin shall conceive and bear a son, and his name shall be called Immanuel" (RSV), in a formula that is immediately recognizable as a central element in Christian liturgy and theology about Jesus Christ. There are curiosities about the passage, not only in its announcement of a virgin birth, but also in the fact that the child that is born is called not Immanuel, but Jesus, a first indication (in our present enquiry) that texts do not necessarily say exactly what they mean. This oblique connection between text and meaning is evident in the story of interpretation that leads up to this appropriation of biblical prophecy in the Gospel of Matthew. The point applies to Matthew's use of the Old Testament generally, but in the present case he is referring to Isa 7:14, a text that pre-dates the birth of Christ by some seven centuries, and has its context in a political crisis involving several minor states in Syria-Palestine. The question is by what hermeneutical pathway a text that meant something in one setting can be said to mean something entirely different in a new one, far removed from it in time and circumstance.

Part I: Exegesis

In 735–33 BC, King Ahaz of Judah is under pressure from an alliance of two near neighbors, the kingdoms of Israel, to the immediate north, and Syria (or Aram). These appear to want to de-throne Ahaz and force Judah into an alliance for defensive purposes against the current local superpower, Assyria (centered farther east on the River Euphrates). The crisis raises political and theological issues, rooted in Judah's identity as a people in covenant with Yahweh, under a king in Jerusalem who is successor to King David, and thus heir to Yahweh's promise to David of national integrity and continuity (2 Sam 7:11b–16). That promise is variously conditionalized in the tradition, and it underlies the encounter in Isaiah 7, in which Ahaz is twice referred to by the metonymy "House of David" (7:2, 13).

The "figures" in Isa 7, therefore, as the stage is set, are the king and the prophet Isaiah, with the kings of Israel and Syria ominously in the wings, a pretender to the throne of Judah, "the son of Tabeel," and Isaiah's son with the double-edged symbolic name, Shear-Jashub, or " a remnant shall return" (7:1-6). In the religio-politics of the ancient world, kings conventionally consulted prophets or other intermediaries in the hope of rightly discerning the will of God or the gods in relation to urgent matters. In this case, the prophet is sent by Yahweh to confront Ahaz "at the end of the conduit of the upper pool on the highway to the Fuller's Field" (7:3), where presumably the king is personally inspecting the city's water supply in view of the impending crisis. Ahaz is doing what kings and governments do—that is, he is preparing a political and military strategy for confronting the crisis. According to the account of the same crisis in 2 Kgs 16, his plan involves an embassy to the King of Assyria himself, accepting vassalage to that king, to secure him against the threat from his immediate neighbors. Isaiah's message to Ahaz is that he is to trust Yahweh for a good outcome of the crisis. "If you will not believe, surely you will not be established" (7:9b RSV). Reading Isa 7 along with 2 Kgs 16, this appears to mean that Isaiah is warning him not to put his trust in alliance with Assyria, but rather in Yahweh. The "sign" in 7:14, as explained in vv. 15–16, supports this message: before a child who is shortly to be born is very old, the kingdoms that now seem so threatening will lie in ruins. It is Yahweh, not great powers, who knows and governs outcomes.

I have already suggested that the narrative context of the sign opens up a line of interpretation. But what do the terms of the sign actually mean? Isaiah's words are:

הנה העלמה הרה וילדת בן וקראת שמו עמנו אל

It introduces two important new "figures," a young woman and her son, who is yet to be born. It is not said who the young woman is, nor is the child identified with any figure known otherwise from the book of Isaiah or elsewhere. There are further unclarities arising from the form of the words. First, the Hebrew is capable of various translations, as a glance at a range of standard English versions shows. Should we translate it "the young woman," or perhaps "this young woman," taking the definite article ה as demonstrative? Or is it "*a* young woman," since the article can have the quite different function of denoting one of a kind? So whether she is someone who is known to the small circle who hear the prophet's words or not is impossible to determine.[1] Secondly, is she already pregnant, or shortly about to be? This cannot be immediately determined from the adjective הרה, but has to be inferred from the context. As the verb וילדת is a participle, a present tense may be suggested for both, hence "she is pregnant."[2] Yet there is obviously a future reference in the naming of the child and the effect of the sign, and the adjective and participle could equally be a vivid depiction of an event shortly to happen. The LXX puts both the pregnancy and the birth in the future:

ἡ παρθένος ἐν γαστρὶ ἕξει καὶ τέξεται υἱόν.[3]

Thirdly, what does the word העלמה actually mean? It is variously taken in the standard English translations as "virgin" or "young woman." In the few occurrences of העלמה in other Old Testament texts it undoubtedly refers to young women who may be presumed to be virgins, in that they are not married,[4] but this does not make it a *terminus technicus* for "virgin,"[5] and therefore the text cannot bear the sense that the conception will be a virginal conception. Watts meets the translation problem thus: "The common meaning [of *'almâ*] signifies one who is sexually mature. It is difficult to find a word in English that is capable of the same range of meaning. 'Virgin' is too narrow, while 'young woman' is too broad"; and he translates: "A *young*

---

1. Seitz, however, thinks that "the young woman is one of the king's own consorts, who is known by him," Seitz, *Isaiah 1–39*, 79.

2. Childs, *Isaiah*, 66.

3. There are variations in the LXX tradition, but not on the point of the future tense.

4. The singular form עלמה occurs only three times elsewhere in the Old Testament: Gen 24:43 (Rebekah), Exod 2:8 (Miriam), and Prov 30:19; see Blenkinsopp, *Isaiah 1–39*, 233. The last case concerns "the way of a man with a young woman," and refers presumably to the "wonder" of awakening sexual awareness.

5. So Childs, who expresses the common view that the technical term for *virgo intacta* is בתולה, *Isaiah*, 66. The point has been challenged by Wenham, "*betûlāh*: A Girl of Marriageable Age," who thinks that it is בתולה that denotes a woman of marriageable age. See to the contrary, Locher, *Die Ehre einer Frau in Israel*, who cites Babylonian marriage laws in support. It is possible that neither term has the force to express *virgo intacta*, but would generally convey an assumption of virginity because the woman is not yet married.

woman who is . . . not yet married (i.e., a virgin) will in due course bear a child."⁶ LXX, as we have seen, translates העלמה with ἡ παρθένος, the term which Matthew then cites in Matt 1:23. This does not make a significant difference to our understanding of עלמה, however, for as Andrew Lincoln has shown, παρθένος has the same range of meaning as the Hebrew term; that is, it can denote a young woman of child-bearing age who is not yet married.⁷ The term παρθένος in itself, therefore, whether in Isaiah LXX or in Matthew, is not sufficient to denote a virginal conception. Lincoln contends that it is not absolutely clear that Matthew had an actual virginal conception and birth in mind in his annunciation narrative; rather, the idea of Christ's virgin birth took time to establish itself in early Christian thought, with the work of Justin Martyr in the second century CE playing a decisive part.⁸ Daniel Harrington, commenting on Matthew 1:23, also thinks that while LXX presumes the young woman was a virgin at the time of the oracle, both texts (MT or LXX) assume a natural mode of conception.⁹

There are, therefore, a range of obscurities for the modern reader in Isa 7:14. The sign concerns a young woman who cannot be identified, who may or may not be already pregnant, who will give birth to a son, who also cannot be identified, at a time in the future that cannot be determined. It is possible that Isaiah's words were clearer to his contemporary hearers, but any such clarity has been lost in their committal to text.

Modern readers have attempted to penetrate behind the obscurities. Among those who think it is possible to identify whom Isaiah had in mind in his sign of Immanuel, the two leading contenders are the son of King Ahaz, who would become King Hezekiah,¹⁰ and the son of the prophet himself. In favor of Hezekiah is the way in which the underlying "narrative" of the book of Isaiah unfolds from this giving of the sign (of which more in a moment). Against it is the likelihood that, at the time of the encounter between Isaiah and Ahaz, Hezekiah was already several years old (though the biblical chronology is admittedly difficult to reconstruct on this point).¹¹

---

6. Watts, *Isaiah 1–33*, 97, 99. Childs expresses a similar view, and translates: "A maiden (*'almāh*) is with child and she will bear a son"; *Isaiah*, 61, 65.

7. Lincoln, *Born of a Virgin?*, 75.

8. Ibid., 177–80.

9. Harrington, *Gospel of Matthew*, 35.

10. This identification is ancient, being represented by Justin Martyr's Jewish interlocutor Trypho in Justin's *Dialogue with Trypho*.

11. Commentators point to the chronological difficulties involved in identifying the child with Hezekiah. Blenkinsopp adjudicates, on the grounds of the confused biblical chronology of the period, that "a conclusion cannot be reached on chronological grounds alone either permitting or excluding identification of Immanuel with

In favor of the prophet's son is the fact that two other sons of the prophet feature in the immediate context (chs. 7–8), namely Shear-Jashub and Maher-Shalal-Hash-Baz, both having symbolic names rather like Immanuel. The similarities of structure and meaning between 7:14–16 and 8:1–4 in this regard are particularly striking, and might be taken to imply the same parentage of both children.[12] Yet against this is the resistance of the text itself (7:14–16) to be read in this way with any certainty. Brevard Childs is right therefore, in my view, when he says:

> The reader is simply not given enough information on the identity of the maiden, or how precisely the sign functions in relation to the giving of the name Immanuel. It is, therefore, idle to speculate on these matters; rather the reader can determine if there are other avenues to understanding opened up by the larger context.[13]

This is not a counsel of despair regarding the possibility of understanding ancient texts in general, or this one in particular, but rather is part of an intractable problem entailed in the (essential) historical dimension of biblical study. This is frankly expressed by H. Utzschneider, who opens his monograph on conceptions of God in the Old Testament with a section entitled "Die Uneindeutigkeit biblischer Texte als hermeneutisches Problem," and says of the Bible reader's inevitable experience of this, together with the proliferation of attempts at explanation: "Sie ist auch eines der hermeneutischen Grundprobleme der historisch-kritischen Bibelwissenschaft."[14] For him, the meaning of texts is inseparable from their aesthetics, and thus the forms in which they have been received.

My concern, therefore, is not only with the fact that the text is in certain respects obscure to us, but also with the ways in which such a text comes to us in a form in which it has already been subjected to reflection from a standpoint, or standpoints, later than the time when it was delivered, in this case to King Ahaz. This entailment of retrospect in the sign seems to be there at the outset, since it is given to Ahaz only after he has refused to

Hezekiah"; Blenkinsopp, *Isaiah 1–39*, 233–34.

12. Some think Immanuel actually *is* Maher-Shalal-Hash-Baz; Wolf, "A Solution to the Immanuel Prophecy in Isaiah 7:14—8:22"; Oswalt, *Isaiah 1–39*, 213; Keener, *Matthew*, 58. But this is not the natural reading of the texts.

13. Childs, *Isaiah*, 66. Cf. also Moberly on the Immanuel sign: "The initial setting fades from view: what follows lacks any clear setting, and the train of thought becomes increasingly difficult to follow"; Moberly, *Old Testament Theology*, 150. Seitz is among those who identify Immanuel with Hezekiah, arguing that the well-known chronological difficulties are not fatal to this reading: Seitz, *Isaiah 1–39*, 60–71.

14. Utzschneider, *Gottes Vorstellung*, 17.

ask for it (v. 12), or in different terms, to "enquire of the LORD," and so with the implication that he refuses to heed it when it comes. If it can function for Ahaz only in retrospect, this accords well with the logic that operates in Isa 8:16, where a prophetic word is formally witnessed and sealed in order to be produced at an appropriate later time. The sign may, indeed, be uttered by way of a word of judgment. In that case, the real audience of the sign is not Ahaz, but other hearers or readers. This leads us, next, to consider what happens to Isaiah's words to Ahaz in what follows in the remainder of Isa 7:1—9:1.

THE TEXT IN CONTEXT (7:1—9:1)

The immediate sequel to the narrative of the Immanuel sign is perplexing. It begins with 7:17, which seems to be a non sequitur from vv. 14-16. That is, the words that declare the threat to Ahaz to be void—making it formally an oracle of salvation—are followed directly by a judgment saying. Syria and Israel are not a problem: but Judah will be laid low by Assyria! And the remainder of the chapter follows suit.

The oddities continue. In 8:1-4 we have a new sign remarkably similar to the one in 7:14-16: a child is conceived and born, receives a pregnant name, the imminent demise of the Syro-Israelite alliance is reiterated, again within a short time as measured by the child's period of early maturing, and the child's name is seen as a token of this. Differently, both the mother and father of this child are identified, namely Isaiah and "the prophetess"—who we suppose, for propriety, is his wife. Curiously therefore, several of the aspects of the Immanuel sign that were obscure are clear in this one, and it seems as if the element of reassurance in Isa 7:14-16 is reinforced by this.

Yet there is a new twist in 8:5-8. While in 8:4 Assyria is introduced as the nemesis of Syria-Israel, it now turns (again) against Judah ("this people" in 8:5)—in an oracle that culminates in a dramatic address to *Immanuel*! God-with-us becomes a word of judgment. Even this is not the end, however, for a new oracle of salvation follows in vv. 9-10, this too culminating in the word *Immanuel* (v. 10). *Immanuel* is once again "good news." The double possibility of *Immanuel* is realized throughout this redacted whole. There is also, in this culmination, a certain intensification or overflow of meaning, in the extension of the original oracle of salvation from the context of an immediate threat from two enemy nations to a more generalized threat from "all you far countries" (NRSV), or better, "all remote places of the earth" (NAS; Hebrew כל מרחקי ארץ). The taunting invitation to these to "take counsel together" in futile conspiracy recalls Ps 2, with its images of Yahweh's rule from Zion after the conquest of his enemies.

Yet the section (to 8:23a) changes gear twice more. In 8:11–15 the prophet himself is addressed with a plea to fear Yahweh, and a declaration that he will become a "stone of offence" (etc.) to *both* houses of Israel. Judgment for Judah is thus rolled into judgment on Israel. *Many* shall stumble on it—so perhaps not all, in an echo of "remnant," and 1:27–31. And in 8:16–23a, Isaiah affirms his own intention, with his children (including Immanuel?), to put his trust in Yahweh, and be "signs and portents" (לאתות ולמפתים—elsewhere "signs and wonders," v. 18) in Israel from Yahweh. The "testimony" heralds a time of judgment—followed by salvation! The sign given to Ahaz, therefore, has become the occasion of theological development in the context. There is little that is obviously logical or natural, however, about the relationship between the terms of the sign and the lines of development from it.

REDACTIONAL EXPLANATIONS

Redactional approaches to interpreting the Immanuel sign look for its possible meanings in terms of those readings of it that have themselves become part of the received tradition, both in the immediate context as just outlined, and in the book of Isaiah more widely. This means considering the stages of the text's composition against the backdrop of historical changes. There is evidence of this within Isa 7–8, since the setting of the Syro-Ephraimite threat to Judah in the 730s, when according to Isaiah Ahaz's decision might yet affect the course of events, is evidently overlaid by a perspective which knows that Judah would become a victim of Assyria. While the "reach" of the original oracle runs to 722 BCE (the fall of the northern kingdom, and thus fulfillment of Isaiah's vision about the alliance), the Assyrian "overwhelming" of Judah points at least to Sennacherib's invasion in 701 BCE. The idea of the book as "redaction" pays attention to the attempt perceived in it to understand the meaning of prophetic words in ever new contexts. Isaiah 1–12, as a sub-unit of the book, evidently aims to weave together words of judgment and salvation, presumably from a point of view that has tried to make sense of Yahweh's work in history, and inherited prophetic words about the fate of Israel and Judah. Isaiah 1 illustrates this perspective, not least in 1:21–26, which contains in brief compass a theological concept and logic that knows of judgment on Jerusalem followed by its restoration. (Isa 1:21–26 has been likened to Isa 1–55 in this respect, while 1:27–31 makes a parallel with chs. 56–66).

Kings Ahaz and Hezekiah also function in contrastive relation to each other within a certain conception of the book, which has as its theological focus the notion of Zion's inviolability (cf. 29:1–8; 31:1–5). Ahaz refuses to listen to Isaiah and declines to accept a sign, while Hezekiah listens to the prophet, prays for deliverance, and sees the salvation of Jerusalem (Isa 37; it might be said, in the terms of 7:9, that "he believes and is established"). Ahaz in contrast fades out of focus, and sees no benefit from the word of assurance given him—instead, the notes of hope and assurance that feature in chs. 7–8 are re-directed. Thus, 9:5–6[6–7] is often taken of Hezekiah; and 14:28 opens an oracle against Philistia and in favor of Zion with the telling words, "in the year that King Ahaz died"! The respective fates of the two kings become a paradigm of faith in relation to the divine providence. This paradigmatic approach to historical representation is typical of the book, in which Assyria and Babylon can serve successively as types of the oppressor of Yahweh's people, and in which Cyrus of Persia can appear as his "anointed" (Isa 45:1).

The series of non-logical articulations in Isa 7–8 can thus be explained partially in terms of a redactional process, whose result is a series of distinct theologoumena arising out of ever new situations. The theological layering includes: Judah need not fall victim to an enemy if it is faithful, for "God is/will be with her" (7:1–16; 8:1–4); Judah (presumably having been unfaithful) will succumb to an enemy in its turn (i.e., after Syria and Israel)—for "God will be with her" in judgment (7:17–25; 8:5–8); God will punish nations that conspire to come against Judah, for "God is with us" (8:9–11); both houses of Israel are equally under judgment—*many in them* shall fall because they have not trusted Yahweh (8:11–15); a judgment is coming (or has come) that will be followed by salvation (8:16–23a). This layering, and juxtaposing, of distinct theologoumena becomes a new theological reflection in itself, an attempt to understand what "God with us" can mean when brought to bear on the vicissitudes of the history of the chosen people.

Redactional study is based on the form of historical enquiry that aims to understand the meanings of texts in their original contexts. Yet it also shows that the individual texts come to point beyond themselves and their putatively original scope. More importantly, it shows that in principle the meaning of a text is not confined to what might be taken to be its meaning in the specific context of its conception, and of its first utterance or committal to writing.

FIGURATIVE (METAPHORICAL) EXPLANATIONS

Redactional explanations go part of the way towards an explanation of the perplexities of Isa 7:14, but there is more to be said. A text's redactional history can be something like an updating, a re-application in a new situation, an adjustment of understanding and expectation. But it does not necessarily explain things that are puzzling in themselves, as several features of Isa 7:14 are. What do we make of the fact of elusiveness here? The text's elusive quality is made the more conspicuous by comparison with its Doppelgänger, 8:1–4. The latter case notably provides answers to the sort of questions 7:14 casts a veil over: the father of the child is Isaiah and the woman is "the prophetess" (the theoretical doubt about whether she is his wife is a minor uncertainty); there is no question about whether she is already pregnant or not, and the validity of the process as a "sign" is strengthened by the writing of the name beforehand in the presence of witnesses. Even the measure of the child's age at the time when the prophecy would be fulfilled (before he could say "my father" or "my mother") is relatively clear compared with the more gnomic 7:15–16. The comparison of the two passages might lead us to think of it as a disambiguation of 7:14–16, that is, to suggest, when taken together with 8:18, that Isaiah is also the father of Immanuel, thus creating a coherent narrative in which the prophet's sons, with their eloquent names, serve as signs.[15] Yet even if this represents some level of intentionality in the text, it does not answer the question why Isa 7:14 needs to be rescued from ambiguity in the first place. Just as plausible a reading of the comparison between the texts is that the latter throws the imponderables of the former into relief. Isaiah 8:1–4, though it has similarities with "exegetical" texts,[16] does not function by simply telling us what Isa 7:14–16 actually meant. Rather, it produces a juxtaposition that poses a question about the limits of a text's meaning.

The common scholarly belief that Isa 7–8 is part of the prophet's "memoir" does not entirely answer the question about how it functions as a text. On the surface it is a sequential account of things that Isaiah said and did, but this is somewhat undermined by the perplexing relationship of 8:1–4 to 7:14–16. The nature of the text is helpfully illuminated, I think, by a discussion by Joel Rosenberg of what he calls "allegorical" texts. He enters the caveat that allegory is not best understood as a "genre," but is hard to

---

15. Thus with Ibn Ezra, Rashi, and "a host of modern interpreters," Seitz, *Isaiah 1–39*, 62.

16. I have in mind the way in which Genesis 20, in a quasi-midrashic fashion, apparently answers questions left unanswered by the more reticent Genesis 12:10–20; see Westermann, *Genesis 12–36*, 319.

define so as to include all cases of it, and he carefully distinguishes between texts that are allegorical in a sustained way and others that employ allegory in some measure as part of their rhetorical strategy.[17] Texts can be seen as allegorical if they contain signals that undermine their surface impression of coherence. Allegory, he says, "[spreads] out along the axis of an imaginary time in order to give duration to what is, in fact, simultaneous within the subject."[18] And he goes on:

> Yet the allegorical text must somehow, by the details or contradictions of its own unfolding, invert or destabilize that succession, providing the clues to the sense of disjunction and otherness that eventually awakens in the mind of the reader. Such clues can often be quite faint and obscure—a word, a turn of phrase, an invasive discourse, any small linchpin of temporal structure whose enunciation loosens and collapses the temporality into the ruin (one could say, rune) of allegorical insight.[19]

This applies well, in my view, to the process by which the reader makes sense of Isa 7–8. Rosenberg suggests that meanings can be inflected in the words of a text in ways that differ from the ordinary interrelationships of grammar, syntax, and logical progression. There is a resonance here with the kinds of studies of Old Testament texts that find pointers to meaning in compositional structures and patterns, such as chiastic or concentric forms. It is evident that Isa 1–12 (or 2–12) has been organized into a pattern in which oracles of judgment alternate with oracles of salvation. The culmination in ch. 12, a song of thanksgiving that knows of a divine anger that is now past (12:1), has echoes of Isa 40, which also proclaims a time of punishment now ended. There is a sense in chs. 1–12, therefore, of a meaning of texts that goes beyond the particularity of their individual, immediate contexts. One striking attempt to reckon with this dimension of Isaiah is Andrew Bartelt's analysis of Isa 2–12 based on a count of lines and syllables and the comparative length of sub-units. Bartelt claims that the words "she shall call his name Immanuel" (וקראת שמו עמנו אל) lie at the exact center of the Isaiah *Denkschrift*, with 844 syllables both before and after this line. As the *Denkschrift* forms the center structurally of Isa 2–12, the Immanuel sign, and the name of the child, consequently are at the exact center of Isa 2–12.[20]

---

17. He follows Northrop Frye who sees it, not as a genre, but as "a structural principle in literature," or in his words, "in the broadest sense, as a process of signification"; Rosenberg, *King and Kin*, 12.

18. Ibid., 17.

19. Ibid., 18.

20. Bartelt, *Book around Immanuel*, 256. The success or validity of Bartelt's

The implication of this analysis, if accepted, is that Isa 2–12 is an extremely sophisticated compositional performance, demonstrating that "Immanuel" is illuminated by, and gives meaning to, the full range of Yahweh's actions towards Israel and the nations exhibited in that part of the book. The teasing echo of 7:14–16 in 8:1–4, therefore, is a clue to look more carefully in the larger context for what the Immanuel sign might mean. The reception of the sign within Isaiah itself opens the way for new readings of what "God with us" might mean in ever new situations.

This, of course, is precisely what has happened to the text in its larger reception history, beginning with LXX and the Gospel of Matthew. Matthew zooms in on the promise of a child whose name is Immanuel, and applies it to the birth of Jesus, who is "God with us" in a way that transcends the horizons of Isaiah. His interpretation leans heavily on his rendering of the Hebrew העלמה הרה וילדת בן as ἡ παρθένος ἐν γαστρὶ ἕξει καὶ τέξεται υἱόν. In taking העלמה as ἡ παρθένος he follows the wording of LXX, but with his own purpose of using the text to support his announcement of Jesus' virginal conception. For him, the issues surrounding Isaiah, Ahaz, and Hezekiah are no longer in view, though his interpretation presumably rests on a perception of some relationship between the meaning of "God with us" for Ahaz (and Hezekiah) and its meaning in relation to the birth of Jesus.

This is only the beginning of the hermeneutical question as to how the Old Testament text can be read in the context of the two Testaments, and especially in the light of specific New Testament appropriations. If the meaning of a text is not enshrined within its "original" historical setting, as far as that can be determined, nor within an authorial intention contingent on such a setting, what process is involved in establishing its meaning?

The issue is the relationship between "literal" meanings of Old Testament texts and their meaning in the context of the two-Testament witness to Jesus Christ. The present section is headed "figurative (metaphorical) explanations" (sc. of the way in which Isa 7:14–16 becomes meaningful beyond its immediate context), but this has to be set in the context of time-honored attempts to conceptualize the relationship. Rosenberg took a cue from the history of reading Old Testament or Hebrew Bible texts. Early Jewish and Christian interpretations each had a version of a "four-fold sense," distinguishing "literal" readings from several kinds of non-literal.[21]

---

analysis cannot be adjudged here; my point is to suggest the significance of this kind of approach to the text for an understanding of how its language works.

21. Rosenberg, *King and Kin*, 12–15. There are close correspondences between the Christian version, traceable to Nicholas of Lyra (literal, spiritual, moral, anagogical/ eschatological), and the Jewish PaRDeS. This acronymic term, meaning "Paradise," is formed from the initials of "*peshaṭ* (simple, literal, or historical sense), *remez* (allusive,

The fundamental distinction for ancient interpreters, however, lay between "literal" and non-literal, or "figurative" meanings. There was a recognition, in these approaches, of a complex relationship between the literal, or plain, sense of a text and its wider possibilities of interpretation, especially when located in a canon, which implied some ultimate meaning relationship among all the texts that composed it.[22] This recognition gave rise to a hermeneutical language that included a range of terms such as allegorical, typological, spiritual, and *sensus plenior*. Differences among the meanings of these terms could be exaggerated. For example, the Antiochene hermeneutical tendency broadly affirmed the "literal," historical meanings of texts, and its version of the relationship between literal and non-literal meanings has often been characterized as "typological," on the grounds that this formula protects the close relationship between the two. Alexandrian "allegory," on the other hand, has been thought to allow meaning to float freer of the literal and historical. Yet this distinction is now widely acknowledged to be an over-simplification.[23] For the Alexandrian Origen, according to Childs, "the difference between the literal and the allegorical was not absolute, but lay within a spectrum"; and again:

> The move from the literal to the spiritual is not an alien transference to bridge a double meaning, but rather a generalization to a universal scope of the historical particularity, because the literal sense has already opened up the one spiritual reality.[24]

Childs, citing a work by Otto Pesch, finds that the discovery of levels of meaning—here with reference to a "four-fold sense"—was far from being merely a reflection of contemporary Hellenistic philosophy, but "the method relates organically to the Christian faith."[25] And for Seitz, "figural" interpretation, while fully respecting the plain sense of the original, is essential to an understanding of the Old Testament as part of the two-Testament witness

---

conceptual, or allegorical), *derash* (homiletical, exemplary, or moral), and *sod* (esoteric, mystical, or eschatological" (ibid., 13).

22. On this, Aichele comments: "The texts in the intertextual mechanism [in this case in the biblical canon] resonate, interfere with, or otherwise contact each other in various and complex ways"; *Control of Biblical Meaning*, 19. For Aichele, the canon exerts a constraint on what would otherwise be limitless meaning possibilities, a constraint which he thinks can be understood as ideological control. The canon can also be regarded as "a process . . . of accommodation and compromise," Brueggemann, *Theology of the Old Testament*, 710, following Rainer Albertz.

23. Childs, *The Struggle*, 65–66.

24. Ibid., 68–69.

25. Ibid., 149. He refers to 1 Cor. 10:11 for New Testament warrant, and to Pesch, "Exegese."

to Christ. This he contrasts with the brand of historical enquiry that he calls "historicism," in which meanings of texts from the past have in principle no bearing on modern concepts, including concepts of God.[26]

Terminology can obscure the issues at stake here. Rosenberg expressly dissociates his concept of "allegory" from what he calls "allegoresis," in which alternative meanings are assigned to the words and phrases of a text.[27] His allegory moves subtly between literal and non-literal meanings, and is based on pointers within the form of a text that precisely arise from the extent to which it succeeds in making meaning in an ordinary or "literal" sense. As, for Origen, the relationship between literal and allegorical "lay within a spectrum," so Rosenberg also spoke of degrees in which texts might be regarded as allegorical. Childs deploys the term "metaphorical" to express a kind of relationship that is neither "allegorical" nor "typological," where "typology" is taken to entail a historical relationship between the literal and non-literal. Rather, metaphorical interpretations attempt to catch a real relationship or resonance between the literal and the figurative.[28] Childs' case study for this kind of interpretation is Theodoret of Cyrus, who cites Immanuel and Maher-Shalal-Hash-Baz as an example of metaphorical extension.[29] The advantage of this approach is that it does not require some logical or necessary connection between the two Isaiah passages, but allows room for an imaginative construal of the meaning of their relationship.

REDACTIONAL AND FIGURATIVE READINGS

There are some similarities between modern redactional and traditional Christian figurative interpretation. Both look beyond the immediate (putative) reference of the text (of Isa 7:14–16) to elucidate its meaning. Both assume that the meaning of the text (beyond the "literal") can be found in relation to a reality that transcends the immediate situation of the text. In redaction criticism, it is supposed that the redaction pushes beyond Isaiah's word to Ahaz, in order to express something about God's activity in judgment and salvation to Israel on a broad historical canvas. In this sense, it perceives a relationship between the word (the text in its immediate context)

---

26. Seitz, *Figured Out*, 6–10.

27. Rosenberg, *King and Kin*, 13. In his view, "allegory" describes a kind of text, while "allegoresis" is an "allegorical *criticism*" (emphasis original).

28. Childs, *The Struggle*, 143.

29. Theodoret gives as an example, besides the two characters in Isaiah, Heb 7:4–10, on Levi paying tithes to Melchizedek, as it were, while still in the loins of Abraham; Childs, *The Struggle*, 143. Childs sees in Theodoret's take on Maher-Shalal-Hash-Baz "an ontological move in the interpretation of Immanuel" (ibid.).

Part I: Exegesis

and a reality that transcends that situation and word-event. A similarity with patristic hermeneutics may be found in this. There are significant differences too, however. In modern thinking, the relationship between word and reality is not intrinsic. Individual words are contingent, and can be regarded as simply wrong, or of limited value in relation to truth. Texts that are difficult or obscure, moreover (such as Isa 7:14), do not become occasions for appeal to special spiritual knowledge, nor are they assigned definitive *literal* meanings on the grounds of their New Testament usage.[30] The difference between traditional Christian and modern interpretation can become a chasm, as (for example) the different approaches of Childs and Walter Brueggemann show. Brueggeman (as a self-styled "postmodern" Christian Old Testament/Hebrew Bible scholar) is at pains to deny any overarching theological narrative comprising the Old and New Testaments, on the grounds that this is in principle hegemonic and anti-Jewish.[31] There is nothing in OT texts that pushes in the direction of Christian theological interpretation. Rather, the NT and early church imaginatively adopted OT texts in the interests of their belief in Christ. In Childs' critique of Brueggemann on Isaiah, he focuses on Brueggemann's deployment of this idea of the "imagination": for Brueggemann, "the biblical text serves to provide a potential for the endless generation of new meanings."[32] Childs, in contrast, affirms that the OT is indeed part of a two-Testament witness to Christ, and his account of the ways in which the church has attempted to understand this, in relation to the stubborn particularities of the OT, is part of his attempt to articulate it. The disagreement between these two has at its heart the same dilemmas over the "literal" understanding of the OT that have always attended the Christian reception of it (though Childs thinks Brueggemann's hermeneutical position "offers a serious break with the entire Christian exegetical tradition."[33])

I think, however, that this difference does not turn on the place of the imagination in interpretation as such. Rather, there is an indispensable role for the human imagination in the reading of Isa 7:14-16 as Christian Scripture, in a way that does not entail the radical disjunction of meanings

---

30. Some commentary on Isaiah still understands the meaning of עלמה in the light of Matthew's reading of the sign. Oswalt thinks the term is such that it can speak truly about a natural birth in the time of Ahaz and also the supernatural birth of Jesus. Regarding Isaiah's choice of it, rather than another term such as אשה, he argues that it made the sign capable of being fulfilled in a miraculous birth; Oswalt, *Isaiah 1–39*, 210–11. Goldingay in contrast simply cuts the connection between the literal meaning of Isa 7:14 and its ("inspired") re-application in Matthew; Goldingay, *Isaiah*, 67.

31. Brueggemann, *Theology of the Old Testament*, 707–20.

32. Childs, *The Struggle*, 294–95. He refers to Brueggemann, *Isaiah* and *Theology of the Old Testament*.

33. Childs, *The Struggle*, 294–95.

between OT and NT advocated by Brueggemann. This is evident from the outset in the surmises that are bound to arise from the non-disclosures of the text that we have observed. Its assimilation into a redactional nexus testifies to an act on the part of the biblical writers that involves what may be called "theological imagination." This is not the unbridled imagination of postmodernism, but tutored by what the redactors know and think about God. The redactors' use of theological imagination is offered to readers, who must use theirs. The early Christian interpreters of the OT were equally employing intellectual powers that included the human imagination.

I call Paul Ricoeur in aid on this. For him, the imagination is "the power of giving form to human experience," or differently, of "redescribing reality."[34] In biblical narrative and its reading, he finds the fusion of a type of imaginative production that follows certain conventions characteristic of narrative, and a type of "heuristic" imaginative creativity in which the reader re-contextualizes what they read in their own world.[35] In relation to texts within texts (in "The Bible and the Imagination" he is writing about Jesus' parables), he shows how the individual story (here, the "narrative-parable") both illuminates and is illuminated by the encompassing context. The dynamic that exists between narrative and context he sees as a "metaphorization process," where "metaphorization" is understood as a "transformation of meaning."[36] The role of the imagination, for him, is inherent in the reading process.

In Ricoeur's analysis, where history belongs to the subject matter of the narrative, the narrative is nevertheless fictive: "Narratives, in virtue of their form, are all fictions."[37] This is not a skeptical point, but one about the nature of literature and reading. It means that there is an imaginative quality in the text that engenders in the reader the activity of imaginative interpretation, involving both thought and action.[38] In theological context, however, the specific characteristic of Christian reading of the biblical text is that Jesus Christ is at the center of the reality within which the reader's imaginative activity takes place.[39]

---

34. Paul Ricoeur, "The Bible and the Imagination," 144. He used the term first in his *The Rule of Metaphor*, 216–56.
35. Ricoeur, "The Bible and the Imagination," 144–45.
36. Ibid., 147, 150–51.
37. Ibid., 145.
38. Ibid., 147.
39. Ibid., 146–47.

Somewhat similarly, Sandra Schneiders speaks of the "paschal imagination," or "the Christian theological/spiritual imagination."[40] This is a form of the "constructive imagination" that we have encountered above,[41] meaning "our capacity to construct our world."[42] For her, the Gospels (which are her immediate focus) are "works of the imagination appealing to the imagination," in a formula that echoes Ricoeur. Here too, the point is not historically skeptical; indeed, for her, the reader whose objective is spiritual transformation must also read for certain "information" that is required for the text to make sense, and upon which the spiritual reading is predicated.[43] The paschal imagination integrates historical experience with faith experience:

> The gospels, in short, are the product of the paschal imagination. What they give us is the Jesus-image, or the proclaimed Jesus who actually lived and died in first-century Palestine, who now reigns gloriously as savior of the world, who indwells his followers in this and every age, and who is the Christ in whom God is definitively and salvifically revealed.[44]

The "imagination," understood thus, recognizes that the language of the Bible (especially the OT with its poetry and narratives, its "gaps," and its heavy dependence on appeals to human experience through metaphor), is often not of the sort that can closely determine meaning. This seems to me to be a gain of modern hermeneutics broadly speaking. It follows, I think, that the relationship between OT text and NT reception cannot be a simple matter of seeing that "this is that." Even where one says that "this is analogous to that," an effort of the imagination is entailed in expressing why it is so. We are still in the business of understanding what it means to say "Jesus Christ is Immanuel," Son of God, Savior, Messiah, Lord. If it ever mattered in the scheme of things whether or not a small Near Eastern people should be overwhelmed by its enemies—if this had anything to do with the belief that "God is with us"—there remains a great deal to think about in working out the meaning of confessions of faith, and the human imagination has a role to play in it.

---

40. Schneiders, *The Revelatory Text*, 102.

41. She refers to the work of Kaufman, *Theological Imagination*. She also cites Hart, *Unfinished Man and the Imagination*, and Tracy, *Analogical Imagination*; Ibid., 129.

42. Ibid., 103.

43. Ibid., 14.

44. Ibid., 107.

2

Rival Group Identities in the Matthean Gospel

Evidence from Matthew 1–2 and 23

PHILIP F. ESLER

University of Gloucestershire

Throughout his career Andrew Lincoln, happily now my colleague in the University of Gloucestershire and predecessor in the named chair I hold, has undertaken the most perceptive and detailed interpretation of a wide range of New Testament texts, especially on John, Ephesians, and Hebrews. He has also written important thematic studies of Pauline eschatology and theology and the virgin birth of Jesus. It is, accordingly, a great privilege to be able to contribute this essay on Matthew to his *Festschrift*, which, in its focus on the Matthean infancy narrative, connects with a passage on which he has written at length and with great insight.

GETTING GROUP IDENTITIES RIGHT

Recent decades have witnessed a strong upsurge of interest by scholars in issues of identity in biblical texts. In part this reflects the impact of events in our contemporary setting. The title of a recent book on ethnic and sectarian conflict, *Identity Matters*,[1] taken with verbal force, makes excellent sense in a world where one's ethnic or religious identity can easily get one killed. The long history of intergroup violence in Northern Ireland, the mass killings in Rwanda in 1994 and during the break-up of Yugoslavia in the early 1990s, ethnic violence in Kenya after the disputed 2007 presidential elections,[2] the ongoing succession of deaths in Israel/Palestine, and the recent onslaught by "Islamic State" against various non-Muslim minorities and even other groups of Muslim faith in Syria and Iraq illustrate the issue quite sharply. Sometimes the group to which a person belongs will be the dominant factor in his or her existence. Not only do we owe it to individuals to take such identities seriously, but in the resolution of intergroup conflict we need to understand the nature of the identities and that their significance for those who bear them may be of primary and paramount importance.

For some time now I have been concerned that many areas of New Testament interpretation are detrimentally affected by a failure to pay due attention to the two dominant identities we encounter in the twenty-seven texts of this corpus: the Ἰουδαῖοι/Ἰσραηλῖται and those who had come to have faith in Christ. Many scholars still speak of "Jews" and "Christians," of "Judaism" and "Christianity" as if the two identities in play were religious in nature, with a symmetrical relationship existing between them. This perspective is reflected in the metaphor (a very misleading one, in my view) of the "parting of the ways," with its image of two entities of the same type, two religions, coming to a fork in the road and each, sorrowfully perhaps, heading off in a different direction.

An alternative view, that I have explored in a number of studies,[3] is to recognize that the Ἰουδαῖοι/Ἰσραηλῖται are best regarded as an ethnic, not a religious group, while Christ-followers bore an identity of a very different kind. Their identity was certainly not ethnic, but to call it a religion introduces the risk that we will import modern notions, where religion can be a stand-alone institution separate from other institutions, unlike in the ancient Mediterranean world where a strong case can be made that our notion of religion did not exist.[4] In the ancient world what we recognize as religious phenomena were usually embedded in familial or political structures.[5] It is difficult to find any single word that encapsulates

1. Peacock et al., *Identity Matters*.
2. On this see, Kanyinga, "The Legacy of the White Highlands."
3. See Esler, "Paul's Contestation" and "From *Ioudaioi* to Children of God."
4. See W. Smith, *The Meaning and End of Religion*.
5. See Malina, "Religion in the Imagined New Testament World" and "Mediterranean Sacrifice."

Christ-movement identity. It certainly involved a new vision of the God-human relationship; it was located in small informal settings, often but not always houses;[6] its members (at least in the first generation) experienced ecstatic phenomena at meetings;[7] it had a distinctive set of group beliefs and group norms;[8] it came into conflict with other groups; and so on. "Socio-religious" is the best word I have been able to come up with for this type of identity, but it is barely adequate.

We must recognize that nearly all of the evidence we have for understanding the respective identities of, and the relationship between, Ἰουδαῖοι/ Ἰσραηλῖται and Christ-followers in the first century CE comes from the latter. The tendency in Christian tradition to look at Ἰουδαῖοι/Ἰσραηλῖται and misunderstand them and their identity originates in the New Testament itself. There is a revealing example in John 9. When the man whom Jesus has cured of blindness asks those who are interrogating him, "Do you too want to become his disciples?" (v. 27), they reply, "You are his disciples, but we are the disciples of Moses" (v. 28). There is vanishingly little evidence for Judean teachers portraying themselves as "disciples of Moses." John, on the other hand, is very fond of the word "disciple" (with seventy-five occurrences in his gospel). Here he has mistakenly projected the notion of discipleship onto the Ἰουδαῖοι. By equating the relationship they had with Moses with the relationship Christ-followers had with Christ, he has fallen into the error of interpreting their identity through the prism of his group's identity.[9] Christians have been making the same mistake ever since. To avoid this error, it will be useful first to model ethnic identity. An important aspect of this will be the role of what we must, for lack of a better word, call the "religious" dimensions of ethnic identity. I will then consider Matthean evidence for the nature of the group identities of Judeans and Christ-followers against that model.

MODELLING ETHNIC IDENTITY

The recent understanding of ethnic identity starts with a programmatic essay by Fredrik Barth published in 1969.[10] Barth was reacting against the

---

6. Adams, *The Earliest Christian Meeting Places*.

7. See Esler, *The First Christians in Their Social Worlds*, 37–51.

8. On group beliefs, see Bar-Tal, *Group Beliefs* and "Group Beliefs."

9. See the argument in Esler, "The Early Christ-movement in Its Mediterranean Context," 188–91.

10. Fredrik Barth, "Introduction." For a recent discussion on the current lively debate on the subject of ethnicity, see Phoenix, "Ethnicities."

"primordial" approach that understood ethnic groups as being constituted by their possession of a set of cultural features. Instead, he argued, their sense of themselves as a group interacting with other groups came first and that cultural *indicia* (which frequently changed over time) were employed, as a boundary, to express that group identity. So understood, ethnic identity was a field of self-ascription and identification used by certain groups to organize their relationships with other groups. The continuing analytical power of this self-ascriptive approach is evident in a recent article on the concept of ethnicity in social psychology research.[11] In taking this line, Barth was viewing ethnic identity as constructed rather than essentialist. This sharply differentiated ethnic identity from the biologically determinist notion of "race," with its (fanciful and vicious) postulation of categories among human beings based on observable physical characteristics, where those categories were inevitably ranked in a hierarchical order, with "white" Europeans at the top and Irish, Jewish, Asian, and African "races" beneath them. Yet although ethnic identities in the Barthian sense are constructed, Hanna Zagefka has correctly noted that "they are 'real,' in the sense that they form an important part of people's *psychological* realities." She continues:

> While the notion of ethnic groups as consisting of members that share a common descent has to be rejected, it should be acknowledged that a *myth* of common descent is a powerful part of people's social realities (as opposed to objective empirical reality).[12]

In this issue of descent we confront an important question that Barth's approach inevitably left hanging: what distinguished ethnic groups from other groups? Barth provided some help on this issue when he noted that an ascription of someone to a social category was ethnic in character "when it classifies a person in terms of his basic, most general identity, *presumptively determined by his origin and background*."[13] Yet this was still very general and applied to a family as much as to an ethnic group. A limited repertoire of features is needed that must, to accord with Barth's ascriptive and interactive approach, be diagnostic and not constitutive of ethnic identity. John Hutchinson and Anthony Smith provided just such a repertoire in 1996:

(a) a common proper name to identify the group;

(b) a myth of common ancestry;

---

11. See Zagefka, "The Concept of Ethnicity," at 231 (even though she does not cite Barth as the originator of this approach).

12. Ibid., 231 (italics original).

13. Barth, "Introduction," 13 (emphasis added).

(c) a shared history or shared memories of a common past, including heroes, events, and their commemoration;

(d) a common culture, embracing such things as customs, language, and religion;

(e) a link with a homeland, either through actual occupation or by symbolic attachment to the ancestral land, as with diaspora peoples; and

(f) a sense of communal solidarity.[14]

While a claim of common ancestry (feature [b] in this list) is a frequently cited element of ethnic identity, at other times it might be a homeland (as with today's Kurds currently living on land that straddles Iraq, Syria, and Turkey) or language or culture, and so on. To repeat, these are diagnostic, not constitutive, features of ethnicity. But such malleability does not affect the reality of ethnic identity itself. According to Hanna Zagefka, "It is considerably more common for people to kill members of a different ethnic group over some intergroup dispute than it is for people to kill members of a different tennis club."[15] Stefan Wolff, moreover has observed: "Empirically, it is relatively easy to determine which conflict is an ethnic one: one knows them when one sees them."[16]

Of particular importance for this essay is feature (d): a common culture that includes customs, culture, and religion. I note "religion" is appropriate for our modern world where it is a separate institution, but for the ancient world it is safer to speak of "religious phenomena." In the Hutchinson and Smith formulation religion is part of a much larger ethnic identity; indeed, it forms merely one of three factors in one of six features. Strong support for this approach appeared in 2006 in an important essay by sociologist Claire Mitchell entitled "The Religious Content of Ethnic Identities."[17] With a focus on Northern Irish Unionism and Nationalism, Mitchell argues that the religious dimensions of ethnic identities have been under-theorized and that the religious content of ethnic boundaries may be more important than is commonly assumed. She outlines a number of possibilities, with the role religion plays in the relevant ethnic identity increasing in each case. First, religion can serve as an ethnic marker, in that religion provides the labels of identity but no content or values, for example, where claimed shared

---

14. Hutchinson and Smith, *Ethnicity*, 3–14, at 6–7.

15. Zagefka, "The Concept of Ethnicity," 232.

16. Wolff, *Ethnic Conflict*, 2. He then cites, as cases in point, Northern Ireland, Kosovo, Cyprus, the Israeli-Palestinian dispute, Rwanda, the Congo, Kashmir, and Sri Lanka.

17. Mitchell, "The Religious Content of Ethnic Identities."

descent or a homeland is dominant. Secondly, religion can support ethnicity, with its symbols, rituals, and organizations serving to boost ethnic identity. Thirdly, religion can function as the fabric of ethnicity: "The content of a specific religion may have an important impact on how a certain ethnic group thinks of itself and what its core values are."[18] Such an impact can occur by religion evoking a sense of the sacred, or providing ideological concepts useful for the ethnic group in question (I would suggest here the former use of the book of Joshua by South African Boers), by transmitting communal identity and by facilitating a sense of community.

So far, so good. At the end of this article, however, in seeking to show "the two-way relationship between religion and ethnicity," she refers to her study of twenty "conservative evangelical Protestants in Northern Ireland" who have moved away from affinity with Britain and also oppose affinity with a united Ireland.[19] Many of her interviewees believed they were living in "the end times," with some having lost interest in politics to focus on "saving souls, evangelism and conversion." She concludes from this material that "ethnic identity is reconfiguring and religion is playing an active role in this."[20] But a better interpretation of her data is that these interviewees have abandoned their ethnic identity altogether and have adopted instead one that is purely religious, eschatologically so in particular. Other evidence exists for the possibility that a religious identity will take the place of an ethnic identity. Early Christians in the Roman Empire came close to this, as do, perhaps, some modern Muslims who live in European countries but feel so alienated from them as not to claim (or even have attributed to them) the ethnic identity of the country in which they live.[21]

Still, even granted my different interpretation on this last point, Mitchell has valuably shown that ethnic identity and religion are separate but can be related, with religion often featuring in wider ethnic identity. At a pragmatic level we can see the wisdom in acknowledging the distinction between them by noting, for example, that to be Serbian does not necessitate being Serbian Orthodox (when some Serbians are Catholics or atheists), to be Sinhalese does not necessitate being Buddhist (when some Sinhalese people are Christian), and to be Northern Irish Unionist does not necessarily mean being Protestant (since some Catholics are Unionists and some

---

18. Ibid., 1143.
19. Ibid., 1147.
20. Ibid., 1148.

21. For a study of various permutations of ethnic, national, and religious identities among Muslims living in the Netherlands, see Verkuyten and Yildiz, "National (Dis)identification and Ethnic and Religious Identity."

Nationalists are Protestant). It is therefore unwise to blur the distinction between ethnicity and religion.[22]

JUDEAN ETHNIC IDENTITY AND RELIGION IN THE FIRST CENTURY CE

In the *Contra Apionem* of Josephus, we have very good evidence that first-century-CE Judeans regarded themselves as what we would call one ethnic group among others.[23] All fifty or so peoples of the Mediterranean world mentioned by Josephus in this text were named with respect to the territory they come from (except for a couple of anomalies like the Hycsos). Josephus actually notes Aristotle's view that the Ἰουδαῖοι were named after Judea (1.179). Phenomena aligned with most, if not all, of Hutchinson and Smith's indicators of ethnic identity are attributed to the Judeans and other ethnic groups by Josephus. The line Josephus takes is not to argue that the Judeans were an exceptional social group in their world. Rather, his point is that they are a λαός, an ἔθνος and a γένος just like all the others, but a very good example of those categories. Josephus calls his people Ἰουδαῖοι many times in the text. As John H. Elliott has pointed out,[24] this was the way foreigners referred to Judeans and the way they referred to themselves when foreign peoples were in the frame (as in the *Contra Apionem*). But this people also had an ingroup appellation for themselves, as Israel, or the sons of Israel, or Ἰσραηλῖται, after their glorious ancestor Jacob, who acquired the name Israel in Gen 35:10. Josephus does not even once refer to his people as Ἰσραηλῖται in the *Contra Apionem*, no doubt because this was a work involved with how his people compared with other ethnic groups in his world.

As mentioned above, good grounds have been presented for the view that "religion" as a stand-alone phenomenon was unknown in the ancient world. To develop this idea a little here, there is no ancient Greek equivalent for what we mean by "religion." Λατρεία and its verbal form λατρεύω, for example, refer to the organized cultic service to a god. The verb is found in Matt 4:10, but the noun does not occur in this gospel.[25] The word θρησκεία, which is not found in Matthew, but occurs in Acts 26:5, Col 2:18, and Jas 1:26 and 27 refers to worship of a god, especially in cultic rites. The word

22. As David G. Horrell appears to do in "'Race,' 'Nation,' 'People.'"
23. See Esler, "Judean Ethnic Identity in Josephus' *Against Apion*."
24. Elliott, "Jesus the Israelite Was Neither a 'Jew' Nor a 'Christian,'" 148.

25. The noun appears at John 16:2; Rom 9:4 and 12:1, and Heb 9:1 and 6, while the verbal form appears nineteen times (including in Matt 4:10).

δεισιδαιμονία means a concern with the divine realm, especially in the form of religious rites and customs.[26] This word appears once in the New Testament, at Acts 24:19 and its cognate, δεισιδαίμων, meaning "superstitious," also appears once, in Acts 17:22. Yet there were phenomena we can reasonably designate as "religious" or "socio-religious," usually associated with the state (and its permitted cults) or the household, or with other groups, such as trade associations, or mystery cults. I will argue below that the identity of the Christ-movement as Matthew understands it can reasonably be labeled "social-religious." It most certainly was not ethnic in character.

ETHNIC IDENTITY AND MATTHEW 1–2

To establish the relevance of ethnic identity in interpreting the Matthean gospel I will now briefly consider its first two chapters, with the aim of showing the extent to which the entity that the evangelist portrays as the context for the appearance, and hence the later ministry, of Jesus is very definitely an ethnic group and not a religion.

Ethnic identity emerges as early as Matt 1:1. Ulrich Luz reasonably takes the view that βίβλος γενέσεως, the first two words of the Gospel, relate to the genealogy, the line of physical descent, plus the rest of Matthew 1, and translates the phrase "Register of the Origin."[27] We observe the same phrase in a similar sense in Gen 5:1 (LXX), while the operative verb throughout the genealogy, ἐγέννησεν, appears in Gen 5:6 and other places. Although Matthew's genealogy (1:1–17) serves to illustrate the ascribed honor that accrues to Jesus from having illustrious ancestors such as these,[28] its main function is to connect Jesus with the core Judean myth of common ancestry—that traced their descent back to the glorious ancestor who was Abraham. For most first-century-CE Judeans, this ancestry must have been a physical reality, not a myth. The ancient Greeks (Hellenes, living in Hellas), similarly, regarded themselves as descended from an eponymous ancestor, Hellen. The Ethiopic (*Ge'ez*) version of Matthew strengthens the link between Abraham and Jesus by adding at the end of v. 17: "Now all the generations from Abraham to Christ numbered forty-two generations."[29] Yet this is not just any genealogy, since it runs from Abraham *through David* to Jesus. It follows from this that not only was Jesus a descendant of Abraham but

---

26. Danker, *A Greek-English Lexicon of the New Testament*, 216.

27 Luz, *Matthew 1–7*, 103–4.

28. Malina and Rohrbaugh, *Social-Science Commentary on the Synoptic Gospels*, 23–26.

29. *Wa-kwellonkē tewled 'em-'Abrehām 'eska Kerestos tewled 'arbe'ā wa-kelētu.*

also of David the king, even though that descent came through Joseph, the adoptive, not the natural, father of Jesus. Whether real or fictive, as noted above, claims of succession, or biological descent from some great person in the past, are very common among the diagnostic indicators of ethnic identity, as was highlighted by Fredrik Barth, with the latter acknowledging, even from his anti-primordial perspective, that ethnicity was presumptively determined by one's origin and background.

It should not be forgotten, however, that Matthew introduces into his genealogy four women, the first three of them non-Judean and the fourth married to a non-Judean: Tamar (v. 3), Rahab and Ruth (v. 5), and Bathsheba, described as the wife of Uriah (v. 6), he being a Hittite.[30] Yet the mention of these four women, which in each case disturbs the usual formulaic structure of the genealogy, does not in any sense negate its ethnic character.[31] Rather they convey the implication that the descent of Jesus was ethnically diverse, that there were among his forebears Judeans and non-Judeans. This does not break the patrilineal chain, however, since the ancient world had no concept of genetic mixing as do we, in that the father was regarded as providing a *homunculus* that was nurtured in the mother's womb (a view evident in Heb 7:9-10). It is possible, in my view, that these women were added to an earlier form of the genealogy that lacked them when the audience to whom Matthew was writing welcomed non-Judeans into their midst.

After the genealogy Matthew provides his description of the conception and birth of Jesus Christ (1:18-25) and then the dramatic events that occurred thereafter: the visit of the μάγοι, the response of Herod, the flight of the holy family to Egypt and their return to Nazareth (2:1-23). Although the religious dimension of the culture of this group is prominent throughout Matt 1:18—2:23, we noted above that there is nothing problematic about an

---

30. Bathsheba herself is probably to be understood as a Judean. Not only, as Mark Bredin has noted ("Gentiles and the Davidic Tradition in Matthew"), is she the daughter of Eliam, probably the man mentioned in 2 Sam 23:34, himself the son of Ahitophel, a councilor of David and therefore a Judahite (2 Sam 15:12), but she is also described as "purifying herself from her (menstrual) uncleanness" (2 Sam 11:4), which seems to indicate adherence to Israelite law.

31. While I favor an ethnic identity rationale, other reasons for the inclusion of the four women have been proposed. For example, see Davies and Allison, *Matthew*, 170-72; Humphries-Brooks, "The Canaanite Women in Matthew;" McKinlay, *Reframing Her* (chapter 3 [37-56] is "Reading Rahab and Ruth" and there is also relevant material in chapter 6 [96-111], "Further Framings"). One common element that has been suggested is that the additional people were righteous. This view is espoused by Amy-Jill Levine, "Matthew," 253, followed by Bredin, "Gentiles and the Davidic Tradition in Matthew," 97.

ethnic group having a pronounced religious dimension, *while still remaining an ethnic group*.

In Matt 1:18–25, first of all, we see data comparable to diagnostic feature (d) of an ethnic identity, a common culture. The story is told from the perspective of Joseph, Jesus' stepfather, who is on the verge of acting in relation to the customs of a patrilineal and patrilocal society in divorcing his betrothed when she is discovered to be pregnant before they have come together. Actually, however, he does not intend on acting as might be expected in this society of someone in his position,[32] here by publicly divorcing and hence shaming Mary. Instead, Joseph seeks to divorce her quietly, for which he is described as "righteous" (δίκαιος). He is the first person in the Gospel to whom this important epithet is attached. Yet he is dissuaded from this course by the advice he receives from an angel in a dream (1:20–21), an angel who addresses him as "Joseph son of David," which designates him with respect to his descent from an illustrious ancestor in a manner typical of ethnic identity. Joseph is instructed to name the child Jesus, "because he will save his people (λαός) from their sins" (1:21). This is the first of fourteen instances of λαός in Matthew. According to Strathmann, in the LXX this word has the meaning of "the people as a union"[33] and it may have that connotation here. In Matt 1:21 λαός comes close to meaning Israel, although we must wait till Matt 2:6 for the first of the twelve appearances of that word in this gospel.

The use of λαός in Matt 1:21, coming so soon after the assertion of the physical descent that has led to Jesus, also suggests that the group we are concerned with here is not a "religion," but an ethnic group. Admittedly it is an ethnic group with a strong religious character, similar to cases where Claire Mitchell has suggested religious dimensions provide fabric for ethnic identity. For in these verses we encounter conception by God under the guise of the Holy Spirit, a warning from an angel of the Lord, a mission to save from sins, and an assertion that all this fulfilled what the Lord had predicted through a prophet. For Matthew, however, Judean ethnic identity embraces features other than these. Matthew's perspective, in fact, is very similar to that of Josephus in the *Contra Apionem*. Judea/Israel is in the same broad category as other peoples, like the Ῥωμαῖοι, the Αἰγύπτιοι, and the *Hellenes*, but they are a distinctive example of that category, especially by reason of their customs that surround their relationship with their God (even though other peoples also had relationships with theirs). This

---

32. On this issue see Marohl, *Joseph's Dilemma*.
33. Strathmann, "laos," in *Theological Dictionary*, 33.

impression is confirmed beyond possibility of contradiction by the way the λαός in question is described in chapter 2.

At the outset we learn that Jesus was born in the town of Bethlehem in Judea (2:1). Judea was the homeland (see ethnic indicator ([e] above) of Judeans—whether they actually lived there or in diaspora communities—who were named after that land just like all other ethnic groups in the Mediterranean world of the time. Moreover, this is an ethnic group organized into the political configuration of a kingdom, with its king, Herod, who is to be found in his capital, Jerusalem (2:1). There he is visited by wise men (μάγοι) from the east looking for the one who has been born "king of the Judeans (τῶν Ἰουδαίων)" (2:2). As we have seen from the *Contra Apionem*, ethnic groups were known from the land from which they derived, so the *magoi* come from the east to Judea to find the king of the Judeans. As expected, they employ the group designation used of this people by foreigners or by themselves when other ethnic groups were in the frame: οἱ Ἰουδαῖοι. This is indicator (a) of ethnic identity, a proper name for the group.

Herod is troubled by this news, as would be anyone in his position, for reasons I have explored elsewhere,[34] and all Jerusalem with him. Having gathered all the chief priests and scribes of the people (τοῦ λαοῦ), Herod enquires of them whence the Messiah will come. They tell him (2:5) "in Bethlehem of Judea" (τῆς Ἰουδαίας), that is, in a nearby town in the ethnic homeland, their view being evidenced by the citation of a version of Mic 5:1. In its Matthean form, this verse predicts that out of Bethlehem of Judah, which is not at all least among the rulers of Judah, will come a ruler who will shepherd "my people Israel (τὸν λαόν μου τὸν Ἰσραήλ)." In this quotation "Judah" in Micah is equivalent to "Judea." But here we also have the *other* proper name for this people (= indicator [a]), its *ingroup* designation, "Israel." The application of Micah also illustrates another indicator of ethnic identity, namely (c), a shared history and shared memories, here embodied in the written prophetic tradition. After they have visited Jesus the μάγοι returned into their own land (εἰς τὴν χώραν αὐτῶν). By implication, this involves a return from the χώρα (land/homeland) of the Judeans. Later, when Herod is dead, Joseph is advised (2:20) by an angel to return "into the land of Israel" (εἰς γῆν Ἰσραήλ). So he brought the child and his mother back "into the land of Israel" (εἰς γῆν Ἰσραήλ; 2:21). These verses reflect the second use of Israel, as the ingroup name for the ethnic homeland, rather than of the people itself. Since Archelaus has taken the place of his father as king of Judea (Ἰουδαία), an angel advises them to settle in Nazareth instead (2:22–23).

---

34. Esler, "Beware the Messiah!"

MATTHEW AND A NEW CHRIST-MOVEMENT IDENTITY

We have now demonstrated that the first two chapters of the Matthean gospel convey an unambiguous picture of the group from which Jesus came as ethnic Judeans, or ethnic Israel. This understanding is presupposed and affirmed throughout the work. When Jesus later says (15:24), "I was sent only to the lost sheep of the house of Israel" (οἴκου Ἰσραήλ), he is acknowledging ethnic Judeans/Israelites as the focus of his ministry. This statement, indeed, endorses two predictions made concerning him in Matt 1–2: "He will save his people from their sins" (1:21) and he will be a leader who "will shepherd my people Israel" (2:6), as just discussed. This is also the context in which we must understand his direction to his twelve disciples, "Do not go upon the road of the foreigners (εἰς ὁδὸν ἐθνῶν), and enter no town of the Samaritans, but go rather to the lost sheep of the house of Israel" (10:5–6). The Matthean Jesus also expected many Judeans/Israelites to enter the kingdom, some from every tribe at least, since he later tells his disciples that, when the Son of man shall sit on his glorious throne, those who have followed him will "sit on twelve thrones, judging the twelve tribes of Israel" (19:28). There is even an echo of the μάγοι designating Jesus as "the king of the Judeans" (2:2) in the sarcastic remark of the chief priests, with the scribes and elders at the foot of the cross: "He saved others; he cannot save himself. He is the King of Israel; let him come down now from the cross and we will believe in him" (27:42).

Yet at the same time Matthew presents a narrative in which a very different type of group identity makes its appearance, one characterized by the acceptance of people from other ethnic groups. We should not underestimate the significance of this. A group that encompasses people from two or more ethnic groups, at least without making all the members acquire only one of the ethnic identities represented, is no longer an ethnic group. It is something very different, for the boundaries between the ethnic identities in question have been relaxed so as to permit the creation of a new superordinate group identity that the members now share. This is not to say that the original ethnic identities have disappeared.[35] Perhaps outside the confines of the new movement the members seek to maintain links with co-ethnics. But the situation is a potentially unstable one, especially if those co-ethnics who have not joined the new movement and adopted its identity refuse to accept that those who have are still truly members of their ethnic group. This is what we find in Matthew.

---

35. On this issue, see Esler, *Conflict and Identity in Romans*, 24–33.

Matthew presents a Jesus who is moved through encountering faithful non-Judeans in the course of his mission to acknowledge their ultimate inclusion in the kingdom, after his death and resurrection. Initially capable of remarkable ethnophobic derision of non-Judeans as ἐθνικοί (5:47; 6:7), it is through meeting the centurion of Capernaum (8:5–13) and the Canaanite woman (15:21–28), that the Matthean Jesus realizes that the kingdom will also include non-Judeans.[36] Thus this gospel presents a two-stage process, a mission to Israel alone (with two exceptions) in the lifetime of Jesus and a subsequent period when the movement will be opened to non-Judeans. Table-fellowship between Judeans and non-Judeans (forbidden to Judeans in the first century CE)[37] will characterize this second stage, as Jesus predicts in Matt 8:11. In addition, the entry requirement will be baptism (not circumcision), as Jesus directs in the programmatic mandate to make disciples of all peoples (ἔθνη), baptizing them in the name of the Father and of the Son and of the Holy Spirit, that closes this gospel (28:18–20). It is worth noting that this development had been foreshadowed earlier in the Gospel (12:17–21).

While it is convenient for us to refer to this new group as "the Christ-movement" (avoiding "Christianity" as being very anachronistic in this context), Matthew himself does not offer any particular designation for it. In chapter 18 (vv. 15–20), however, when he is talking about discipline within the assembly (ἐκκλησία; v. 17) in such a way that he is clearly referring to the post-Easter situation of the movement, he uses the word "brother" (ἀδελφός; v. 15) to refer to a member. So a fictive family is being invoked to provide a manner of designating group membership. This is extended in other parts of the Gospel (see below) to the idea that the members are jointly sons of God. He makes an even more daring move in Matt 21:43 when his Jesus says, "Therefore I tell you the kingdom of God will be taken away from you and given to a people (ἔθνος) producing its [sc. the kingdom's] fruits." Since on every one of the thirteen other occasions in this gospel when ἔθνος is used it bears the meaning of "people" in the sense of ethnic group,[38] its fictive employment here (in relation to a group that will embrace people from various ethnic groups and thus not be ethnic) is very striking.

RIVAL GROUP IDENTITIES IN MATTHEW 23

Yet the differences between Judean and Christ-movement identities in Matthew are hardly exhausted by the evidence for both being represented in

---

36. This is the thesis of my essay "Judean Ethnic Identity and the Matthean Jesus."
37. See Esler, *Galatians*, 93–116.
38. Matt 4:15; 6:32; 10:5, 18; 12:18, 21; 20:19, 25; 24:7, 9, 14; 25:32; and 28:19.

this gospel. Matthew goes much further than this, in particular, by lauding the identity of the Christ-movement, by subverting Judean ethnic identity, and by presenting Judeans as a threat to Christ-followers. To illustrate these social dynamics I will refer to evidence in Matthew 23.[39]

In Matt 23:8–12 the evangelist sets out two carefully balanced mini-essays on the identity of the Christ-movement (and I have numbered the stichoi to bring out the careful parallels Matthew has produced here, in what must have been a conscious redactional exercise):

1a. But as for you, do not be called "Rabbi,"
    1b. for you have one teacher.
        1c1. You are all brothers
        1c2. And do not call anyone on earth your father,
        1c3. For you have one father, who is in heaven.

2a. Neither be called "Guides,"
    2b. because you have one guide, the Christ.
        2c1. He who is the greatest among you will be your servant.
        2c2. Whoever exalts himself will be humbled,
        2c3. And whoever humbles himself will be exalted.

I will only reflect on selected issues here. The first thing to note is that this whole sequence is prompted by the criticism that (Judean) Pharisees and scribes loved being called "Rabbi" (23:7). Matthew urges the opposite of this behavior, that his audience (Christ-followers) should not be called "Rabbi." He is defining the ingroup identity of his audience as the opposite of that of the Judean outgroup. This then leads to the statement that they have one teacher and that they are all brothers under their heavenly Father (23:9). As already noted in relation to Matt 18:15–20, "brother" is a word used for a fellow member of the Christ-movement and here we find an explication of this thought to the effect that they are brothers under a heavenly father. The idea here is very similar to that expressed by John in 1:12. Thus Matthew implies that which John, in 1:13, specifies—that membership of this group does not depend upon any kind of physical descent. The evangelist is reminding them of the very foundation of their identity, shared sonship under God. This notion found explicit expression earlier in the Gospel. One of the beatitudes asserted that the peacemakers will be called "sons of God"

---

39. For a full account of my views on this matter in Matt 23, see Esler, "Intergroup Conflict and Matthew 23."

(5:9). In like vein, those who love their enemies and pray for those who persecute them (= values central to the new movement) will become "sons of your Father who is in heaven" (5:45).

With the second mini-essay in Matt 23:10–12, the evangelist illuminates distinctive ways of relating to one another that are characteristic of the identity of the Christ-movement. The balanced two clauses of Matt 23:12 entail a radical rejection of modes of conduct prevalent in the honor and shame culture of the ancient Mediterranean. While they reflect what it means for a leader ("Guide"), the "greatest" among them, to act like a servant, they go far beyond this one issue and occupy the entire domain of the attitudes and behavior Christ-followers should adopt in relation to one another. These attitudes and behavior thus become powerful identity-descriptors of the movement. We are not dealing with humility but with the much broader notion of the new identity of the Christ-movement.

Later on in this chapter the Matthean Jesus moves from an endorsement of the identity of Christ-followers to an attack on that of Judeans, an attack directed at the scribes and Pharisees, but of its very nature embracing other Judeans. The most notable example comes in the Seventh Woe (23:29–36). Jesus initially expands upon the Sixth Woe by mentioning the actions of the scribes and Pharisees in building tombs for the prophets and adorning the monuments of the righteous (v. 29), after which he stigmatizes the hypocrisy involved in doing so (vv. 30–32). These are highly suggestive verses from the perspective of ethnic identity. When Jesus attributes to them the sentiment (v. 30), "If we had lived in the days of our fathers, we would not have taken part with them in shedding the blood of the prophets," we again come up against the centrality of physical descent for Judean ethnic identity that we have discussed above. The Matthean Jesus recognizes that descent from male ancestors is a primary mode by which the scribes and Pharisees (like all Judeans) imputed Judean identity to themselves, but also attributes to them a likely attempt to separate themselves from a particularly abhorrent way that those same ancestors behaved—in killing the prophets.

In Matt 23:33 Jesus subjects one of the pillars of Judean ethnic identity characterizing the scribes and Pharisees to a savage reappraisal. He says to the scribes and the Pharisees, "You serpents, you brood (γεννήματα) of vipers, how are you to escape being sentenced to hell." In the Greek of this period one of the standard words for what we are calling an ethnic group was γένος often mistranslated as "race." The word appears, for example, in Josephus' *Contra Apionem*, along with λαός and ἔθνος, as a word to denote the various ethnic groups in the Mediterranean world of his time, including the

Judeans.⁴⁰ It is cognate with γεννάω, a transitive verb still usefully translated by the somewhat antique English word "beget." Thus a γένος is a descent group, a family or a people that traces its ancestry back through male ancestors generation after generation, a pattern evident in genealogies such as in Matt 1:2–17. As explained above, belief in such shared common descent, regardless of whether the physical lineage claimed was real or fictive, is often a central feature of ethnic identity. In this context of descent and ethnic identity, the Matthean Jesus' description of the scribes and Pharisees as the "progeny (γεννήματα) of vipers," a word also cognate with γεννάω and γένος, carries a very heavy rhetorical punch. The force of the expression is actually to re-define their ancestors not as "the fathers" now, but as vipers. This is savage invective: they are not really even Judean, but instead . . . ophidian. The Matthean gospel itself provides support for this interpretation. At Matt 3:7b–9 John the Baptist says to the Pharisees and Sadducees:

> You progeny (γεννήματα) of vipers! Who warned you to flee from the coming anger? Bear fruit worthy of repentance and do not presume to say to yourselves, "We have Abraham as our father"; for I tell you, God is able from these stones to raise up children to Abraham.

The critical point is that in describing the Pharisees and Sadducees as "progeny of vipers" (the same expression we have just seen Jesus apply to the scribes and the Pharisees in Matt 23:33) John appreciates that they are likely to respond by asserting their *Abrahamic* ancestry. That is, John assumes that they will reject the slur on their lineage that would flow from descent from snakes by asserting their descent from Abraham. John knows that they will interpret the slur as related to descent. So we are fully entitled to find this implication in Matt 23:33, and what an extraordinarily unpleasant implication it is!

CONCLUSION

I began this essay by noting the importance of group identities in social life and by criticizing the scholarly tendency to see in "Jews" and "Christians" exemplars of two religions standing in a symmetrical relation to one another. Using recent theory on ethnic identity, including the role of religious phenomena in such identity, I have sought to show that the Judean group identity that Matthew presents as the field for the appearance of Jesus in the world and his earthly ministry is very definitely an ethnic one, although

---

40. See Esler, "Judean Ethic Identity in Josephus' *Contra Apionem*," 78–80.

with a strong religious dimension. At the same time, however, the evangelist adumbrates a very different identity for the Christ-following ingroup for whom he is writing. This is an identity with an asymmetrical relationship to Judean identity, which has at its core the members' shared sonship under the heavenly Father. As sons of God they are brothers in a new fictive family. Rendering the contrast between these two identities even sharper are the lengths taken by the evangelist to subvert the very foundation of their identity, Abrahamic descent, and to propose in its place descent from snakes. In reading texts such as this, we must be very careful to emphasize the context-specific nature of what is being said and deny any application of such language to Jews of later periods.[41]

---

41. On this point, see a full argument in Esler, "Intergroup Conflict and Matthew 23."

3

Let John be John (2)

JAMES D. G. DUNN
University of Durham

Andrew is by no means a stranger to John's Gospel, as his great commentary thereon certainly confirms.[1] So I offer in congratulation this reflection on its distinctive christology, drawn principally from my current work on the subject.[2] For it is undoubtedly John's christology which constitutes his greatest contribution to the development of Christian theology. But our over-familiarity with it has probably diminished our perception of the radical transmutation that John in fact makes in his portrayal of Christ.

THE INCARNATE WORD

It is the prologue to the Gospel (John 1:1–18) that immediately grabs the reader's (or, originally, listener's) attention. The claim that John made was that the Logos had "become flesh" (John 1:14). That is, not just that the Logos was manifest in poetic metaphor to describe divine action,[3] not just

---

1. Lincoln, *John*.
2. For vol. 3 of my *Christianity in the Making* (Grand Rapids: Eerdmans, 2015, hopefully) project. I have taken the liberty of using a title here that echoes my earlier "Let John be John."
3. As in Wis 10–11 and 18:14–16.

as symbolized in the character of Israel's heroes and heroines (as in Philo),[4] and not just as a casual visitor like an angelic messenger in human appearance. But the Logos "*became* flesh," *became* a human being who had lived a full life from birth to death in first-century Palestine.[5]

John was fully aware of the immensity of the claim he was making. He did not introduce it in ways open to varied interpretation, as had Paul in Col 2:9. He did not refer to it allusively as could be said of Matthew's Wisdom christology in Matt 11:2, 19. He did not seek to distinguish the Logos from God, as an emanation somewhat distant from God, as in later gnostic systems; the Logos was not only with God in the beginning, but was God (John 1:1). Nor did he attempt to play down what the Logos had become: "that which is born of flesh is flesh" (3:6); "the flesh is of no value" (6:63); but the Logos "became *flesh*," its polar opposite.[6] The Johannine prologue relishes the paradox, what most thoughtful people of his time would regard as an absurdity, a nonsense, as inconceivable: that God could become a human being of flesh and blood, a man who would die; that the infinite gulf between creator and creation could be thus spanned. The Greeks could conceive of gods appearing on earth for a short time or in disguise. They could conceive of demigods, the offspring of a god with a human partner, or of humans being deified. But a god becoming material and corruptible flesh, a human being, and living a full human life? After all, the sages of Israel felt it both appropriate and necessary to identify divine Wisdom with the Torah[7]—Wisdom as inscripturated; but to claim that Wisdom/Logos had *become* a particular human figure—as incarnated?[8] And the later gnostic systems could only envisage the gap between creator and creation being bridged through a lengthy series of aeons of decreasing divinity. But the Johannine prologue sees the gap as bridged in one step: "the Word became flesh" (1:14).[9]

---

4. Particularly Sarah (*Leg.* 2:82; *Cher.* 9–10, 45, 49–50; *Det.* 124; *Congr.* 9, 13, 22, 79–80, 129; *Mut.* 79–80, 151–53; *Abr.* 100).

5. The *Prayer of Joseph* (first century CE?), in which Jacob/Israel is presented as designating himself as "the firstborn of every living thing to whom God gives life," "the archangel of the power of the Lord and the chief captain among the sons of God," and "the first minister before the face of God," is more a way of glorifying Israel in the person of its eponymous patriarch than a precedent for John 1:14.

6. Lincoln, *John* 103–4; cf. McHugh, *John 1–4*, 51–53.

7. Sir 24:23; Bar 4:1.

8. Jewish speculation moves in a different direction in Merkavah mysticism; see e.g., Gruenwald, *Apocalyptic*; Halperin, *Faces*; Orlov, *Heavenly*.

9. Schnelle, *Antidocetic Christology*, particularly 221–22; "here *sarx* cannot be understood as merely an irrelevant factor or a necessary medium" (227). Schnelle's principal thesis is that John's Gospel presupposes the conflict reflected in 1 John (1 John

The step that the Johannine prologue took moved the theology of divine/human relationships into new territory. In further expressions of the gospel of salvation it was a potential game changer of huge significance. Should John's bold identity, God-become-flesh, be regarded as a step too far and the essential difference and distance between divine and human be reasserted by denying the reality of the Logos-Christ's flesh? Or should the logic of John's concept of incarnation be pressed further, in claiming that the incarnation had complete soteriological significance as well—that by taking flesh into God (the Godhead) flesh itself was redeemed, incarnation as theosis (divinization)—the cross and resurrection becoming something of an afterthought—salvation gained by eating the flesh and drinking the blood of the Son of Man (John 6:53-58), no longer the body broken and the blood shed as a way of dealing with sin? Whatever John's intention in these matters, the die was cast and the theological discussion moved on to a different level.

THE SON SENT AND THE SON OF MAN DESCENDED

Just as deliberate was John's presentation of Jesus as the Son of God as a way of transforming earlier christological debates. The firm identification of the Messiah as "the Son of God" in describing the purpose of the Gospel (John 20:31) transformed the old debate as to whether Jesus was the Messiah, a debate still reflected in John. Even more striking is the way the Johannine prologue went out of its way to link the Logos-become-flesh assertion with the thought, evidently of equal importance, of the incarnate Logos as the Son of God. The glory evident in the incarnate Logos was "a father's/the Father's only (begotten) son/Son" (1:14). "The only-begotten (μονογενής) God[10] who is in the Father's close embrace has made him known" (1:18). This blending of the prologue's unique Logos christology with Son christology not only attached the former tightly with a christology firmly rooted in Jesus' own spirituality,[11] it also gave Son christology a new dimension.

---

predating the Gospel) and so the Gospel itself has to be understood as engaging in "a comprehensive theological combat with Docetism" (ibid., 228-29).

10. "God" is the more strongly attested reading for John 1:18; see, e.g., Barrett, *John*, 169; Metzger, *Textual Commentary*, 198. See also n.16 below; Ehrman, *Orthodox Corruption*, 78-82; McHugh, *John 1-4*, 69-70. "Though μονογενής means in itself "only of its kind," when used in relation to *father* it can hardly mean anything other than only(-begotten) son" (Barrett, *John*, 166).

11. See, e.g., my *Jesus Remembered*, §16.2.

This concept of the Logos-Son's intimacy with the Father, as revelatory of the Father, transforms what had been a powerful image into something still more powerful. "Son of God" is no longer simply a way of indicating that someone was especially favored by God.[12] "Sent" by God was no longer simply a way of denoting a divinely authorized commission.[13] In one of John's favorite ways of speaking of Jesus' mission, "the Father who sent me," a *commission* from heaven has been transformed into a *mission* from heaven. The Son came down from heaven (6:38); here is the source for the Nicene Creed's clause "he came down from heaven." What had not been clearly articulated in passages like Rom 8:3 and Gal 4:4, or Phil 2:6–7, was now openly expressed, and its full corollary drawn out — not only that the Son knew the Father's purpose to an intimate degree, but also that the Son acted as the Father's plenipotentiary in the fullest sense. The μονογενής and the Logos-who-is-God-and-who-has-become-flesh are two sides of the one coin for John.

It was no doubt in the same spirit that John advanced the earlier Son-of-Man christology by adding the thought of the Son of Man's descending and ascending (John 3:13; 6:62). What had been an apocalyptic image of Christ's triumph, "coming on the clouds of heaven," whether to heaven or from heaven, now becomes a further way of speaking of Christ's *initial* coming from heaven. The somewhat surprising assertion of 3:13 — "No one has ascended into heaven, except the one who descended from heaven" — may indeed be directed against the characterization of the patriarchs and prophets as those who in effect had ascended into heaven to hear (firsthand) what God said.[14] Here again the thought of the prophet as sent, that is commissioned by God, has been transformed into the claim that Jesus, as the Logos-Son, was in fact one, the only one, who had really been present in the heavenly assembly such as was envisaged in Job 1–2. It is this opening of heavenly reality — not so much by means of a heavenly journey and with the help of an interpreting angel, but an opening *on earth* in and through Jesus to those ready to receive it — that moves the Gospel of John on to a new plane.

---

12. See my *Christology in the Making*, §3.

13. See particularly Bühner, *Der Gesandte*.

14. Suggested originally by Odeberg, *The Fourth Gospel*, 72–98; see also Lincoln, *John*, 152.

THE REVEALER

Since for John, Jesus is the incarnate Word, the one who has made the unseen God seeable, it was a central concern for John to bring home to audiences the truth of this very fact. In a famous *bon mot* Rudolf Bultmann highlighted the role in John's Gospel of Jesus as the revealer; but all that he reveals is that he is the revealer![15] That was an inadequate summary of John's purpose. It is true of course that Jesus as the incarnate Word and Wisdom fulfils the role previously filled in Second Temple reflection on Word and Wisdom—not least their role as revealers. But the significance of Jesus as the divine revealer for John was that he revealed *God*, the Son revealed *the Father*, the uttered Word revealed the one who uttered the word. To know this was to know the reality which Jesus was, and thus to know God, the Father. "This is eternal life that they know you, the only true God, and the one you sent, Jesus Christ" (17:3).

This emphasis on Jesus as the one who reveals the true reality of God is a further key element in John's transmutation of the gospel into something more daring and challenging. Christ not only brought the word of God—"Thus says the Lord," in classic prophetic speech—he *is* the Word. He not only brought revelation from the Father, he *is* the revelation. "No one has ever seen God . . . (but) the only-begotten God[16] . . . has made him known" (1:18); "Whoever sees me sees him who sent me" (12:45); "Whoever has seen me has seen the Father" (14:9). He and the Father are one (10:30). He utters the divine "I am."[17] That is the claim that lifted Jesus from the status of one who might finally be reckoned on a par with Moses or Mohammed, and that makes the claims of Christianity seem so intemperate in inter-faith dialogue. But the claim is nonetheless at the heart of John's presentation of Christ.

---

15. Bultmann, *Theology*, 2.66—"Jesus as the Revealer of God *reveals nothing but that he is the Revealer*" (his emphasis); "in his Gospel (John) presents only the fact (*das Dass*) of the Revelation without describing its content (*ihr Was*)." The reformulation by Bultmann's pupil, Käsemann, *Testament of Jesus*—"Jesus is nothing but the revealer and . . . Jesus is the only revealer of God and therefore belongs totally on the side of God even while he is on earth" (11)—typifies Käsemann's misreading of John (see also n.27 below). Ashton reflects at length on Bultmann's *"blosses Dass"* ("naked 'that'") and concludes, "the medium is the message" (*Understanding*, 553 and ch. 14).

16. The text of 1:18 is not finally certain. The most probable reading is μονογενὴς θεός ("the only-begotten G/god"); μομογενὴς υἱός ("the only S/son") looks to be secondary, presumably on the ground that υἱός was the obvious correlate with μομογενής, not θεός. See above n.10. It should be noted that Philo did not hesitate occasionally to refer to the Logos as god—particularly *QG* 2:62—"the second God, who is his Logos."

17. Particularly 8:28, 58; 13:19.

As a corollary it should not be assumed that in his talk of the Son's dependence on the Father (as in 5:19), John was already caught up in the later debates about the relationships of the two persons of the Trinity, the Father and the Son. Rather, the point[18] is that to label 14:28 ("the Father is greater than I") as "subordinationist christology" is to read John against a much later background of theological discussion than the first century. The language used by John was more an expression of his Logos christology, as a way of expressing the *continuity* between the Father and the Son, the authority and definitiveness of the Son's revelation of the Father, the Son as the self-expression (Logos) of the Father. This is what John wanted to get over when he has Jesus asserting that he speaks the words of God (3:34), what he heard from God (8:26), what the Father commanded him to speak (12:49); the Son did not come of his own accord (7:28; 8:42) but as the Son sent to reveal the Father. The Logos expresses primarily continuity, oneness, not distinction.[19]

JOHN'S CHRISTOLOGY IN GNOSTIC PERSPECTIVE

The transmutation in christology that John achieved was so radical that it raised the question whether John had gone too far. In particular, had John gnosticized the gospel? The presentation of Jesus as the Son sent from the Father, of the Son of Man descending to earth, had striking parallels with the later gnostic redeemer myth, and could imply that the myth was already full blown, as some found suggested also in the Wisdom myth evidenced in Bar 3:37 and 1 *En.* 42. Likewise John's emphasis on Jesus as the divine revealer, who brings the truth,[20] and the characteristic Johannine light/darkness dualism,[21] would naturally carry the corollary that salvation was

18. C. K. Barrett, "'The Father is greater than I,'" 19-36; Stuhlmacher, *Biblische Theologie*, 2:225; Lincoln, *John*, 398.

19. See Barrett, "Christocentric or Theocentric?" 1-18; see also Appold, *Oneness Motif*: "John's christology leaves no room for even incipient subordinationism" (22). Relevant is also Theobald's observation that "The Johannine Jesus never says of himself in the passive: '*I* have been sent,' but speaks of his '*Father*, who sent him' or regularly only of 'the one who has sent him'" ("Gott, Logos und Pneuma," 366; he speaks also of "the Johannine mutation of Jewish monotheism" [358]). See also Meyer, "Father," 255-73; Schröter, "Trinitarian Belief": "it is possible to speak of a 'proto-Trinitarian thinking' in Johannine theology" (193).

20. Ἀλήθεια ("truth")—John 25x; other Gospels 7x. Ἀληθής ("true")—John 14x; rest of NT 12x. Ἀληθινός ("true, authentic")—John 9x; rest of NT (apart from Rev) 9x. Ἀληθῶς ("truly")—John 7x; rest of Gospels 8x.; e.g., John 1:14, 17; 8:32; 14:6.

21. Notably John 1:4-5; 3:19-21; 8:12; 12:36, 46.

ignorance being dispelled by new knowledge,²² those blind being given to see (particularly John 9),²³ and would almost inevitably imply that such knowing, such illumination, was the heart of the salvation being offered. The issue became acute in the twentieth century with Bultmann's drawing what for him was the obvious conclusion: that John's christology had in fact been shaped by the (pre-Christian) gnostic redeemer myth.²⁴ The summary of his conclusions expressed the claim unequivocally:

> The figure of Jesus in John is portrayed in the forms offered by the Gnostic Redeemer-myth which had already influenced the Christological thinking of Hellenistic Christianity before Paul and then influenced him. It is true that the cosmological motifs of the myth are missing in John, especially the idea that the redemption which the "Ambassador" brings is the release of the pre-existent sparks of light which are held captive in this world below by demonic powers. But otherwise Jesus appears as in the Gnostic myth as the pre-existent Son of God whom the Father clothed with authority and sent into the world.²⁵

Ernst Käsemann, Bultmann's leading pupil, was well enough aware that a closer parallel to the Johannine dualism was to be found in the Dead Sea Scrolls,²⁶ but he still found it impossible to avoid the conclusion that John's Gospel was already well on the way to portraying Jesus in gnostic terms.

> One can hardly fail to recognize the danger of his [John's] christology of glory, namely, the danger of docetism. It is present in a still naïve, unreflected form and it has not yet been recognized by the Evangelist or his community.²⁷

22. Cf., e.g., οἶδα ("know")—4:25; 7:28–29; 10:4–5; 14:7. Γινώσκω ("know")—6:69; 8:32; 10:14, 38; 14:17, 20; 17:3—though we recall that John does not use the noun γνῶσις itself.

23. See also R. Brown, *John*, 1:513–14; and on the verbs denoting seeing, 1:501–3.

24. Bultmann, "History of Religions," 27–46. Bultmann found the evidence for John's dependence on the gnostic myth chiefly in the Revelation-discourse source which he thought to underlie Jesus' discourses in the Gospel (*Theology*, 2:13). However, a significant course-correction in the quest for a pre-Christian gnostic redeemer myth was provided by the demonstration of MacRae that it was precisely the Jewish form of the Wisdom myth which the gnostics used—"Jewish Background," 86–101.

25. Bultmann, *Theology*, 2:12–13; the author's background was Judaism, but not "orthodox" Judaism, rather "a gnosticizing Judaism" (13).

26. Bultmann, in an early response to the Dead Sea Scrolls, saw in them proof that "a pre-Christian gnosticizing Judaism" already existed in Palestine (*Theology*, 2:13 n).

27. Käsemann, *Testament of Jesus*, 26, where his famous characterization of John's presentation of Jesus, as "naïve docetism," misses the subtlety of John's Logos/Wisdom

Käsemann's views were still well towards one end of the spectrum that characterized the second half of the twentieth century,[28] but his characterization of the dangers to which John's christology exposed itself would seem to be confirmed by the popularity that John's Gospel enjoyed among the various gnostic groupings, particularly the Valentinians. Heracleon (c. 160-180) wrote the first known commentary on John's Gospel.[29] We learn from Irenaeus and Epiphanius that Ptolemaeus offered an extensive exegesis of the Johannine prologue.[30] Irenaeus was well aware also that the followers of Valentinus made copious use of John's Gospel (*Haer.* 3.11.7). And the Nag Hammadi codices indicate influence from John at a number of places.[31] A curiosity is that the *Alogoi*, a Christian sect that flourished in Asia Minor around 170 CE, so named because they opposed Logos Christology, attributed John's Gospel to Cerinthus (Epiphanius, *Pan.* 51:3-4).

---

christology; note the protest of Thompson, *Humanity of Jesus*. Unsurprisingly Käsemann concluded that John's acceptance into the church's canon was a human error but by divine providence: "From the historical viewpoint, the Church committed an error when it declared the Gospel to be orthodox." But he saw the reception of the Fourth Gospel into the canon as "the most lucid and most significant example of the integration of originally opposing ideas and traditions into the ecclesiastical tradition," and a proof of his thesis that the NT canon is the basis not so much for Christianity's unity as for its diversity (*Testament of Jesus*, 74-76).

28. The transition from Bultmann's radical view is well demonstrated by Kümmel, that John "lays claim to the language of gnosis in order to show Christians that Jesus is the true revealer" (*Introduction*, 218-28, here 230), and H. Koester (Bultmann's last pupil), who argues strongly that John rejects a gnosticizing understanding of salvation (*Ancient Christian Gospels*, 263-67). For the debate, see also Schnackenburg, *John*, 135-49; R. Brown, *John*, 1.lii-lvi; Barrett, *John*, 81-82; and particularly Schnelle, *Antidocetic Christology*, with his more recent review in *History*, 504-9; and Zelyck, *John*. In British scholarship the transition from a dominant interest in the Greek/Hellenistic background of John to a focus primarily on its Jewish background was marked by the transition from Dodd's *Interpretation* (1953) to Barrett's *John* (1955); see Barret's own comments on the point (*John and Judaism*, 63-64). See also Charlesworth, "Dead Sea Scrolls," 65-97; and Lincoln, *John*, 59-64.

29. See Pagels, *Johannine Gospel*.

30. Irenaeus, *Haer.* 1:1.1-8; Epiphanius, *Pan.* 31:9.1-27; extensive selection in Foerster, *Gnosis* 1:127-45.

31. See R. Brown, *Community*, for example: "There is a Word (*Logos*) Christology in the *Tripartite Tractate*, and 'I AM' Christology in the *Second Apocalypse of James*; also in *The Thunder, the Perfect Mind*, and in the *Trimorphic Protennoia* (where it is joined with a docetic account of the death of Jesus)" (147-48). But the influence of John on the *Second Apocalypse of James* is minimal (cf., e.g., NHL 5:49.5-6 and 5:58.2-8). And *The Thunder: Perfect Mind* echoes not so much the "I am's" of John as the self-proclamation of Lady Wisdom (Sir 24), but in a sequence of antithetical and paradoxical contrasts which bemuse more than inform (*NHL* 295-303); cf. the *Acts of John*. See also Culpepper, *John*, 114-19.

What we find, however, when we consult the Valentinian exegesis of John (at least as it is available to us from Irenaeus, Clement of Alexandria, and Hippolytus) is that they recoil from John's explicit assertion that the Logos "became flesh," that is, from any thought that there could be such an immediate conjunction of God and the physical world.[32] Rather they bring to their reading of the prologue the assumption that the divine realm is much more complex than Jewish monotheism allowed[33] and that the transition from divine to human is much more tortuous than a surface reading of John 1:3[34] and 1:14[35] allowed. Thus, Ptolemaeus reads John 1:1-2 as distinguishing three—God, Beginning, and Logos. And when 1:3-4 and 14 are drawn in, it is to distinguish a first Tetrad (Father, Grace, the Only-begotten, and Truth). Linked with the second Tetrad (Logos and Life, humanity and church) they make up the Ogdoad, "the mother of all the aeons."[36] Again, when Heracleon reads "What was made in him was life" (John 1:3-4), he understood "in him" as meaning "for spiritual men" (pneumatics),[37] that is, reading into John's words the Valentinian presupposition that humanity was divided into three classes: pneumatics, psychics, and choics.[38] For other illustrations, we could note Heracleon's allegorical interpretation of John 2:13-20,[39] of 4:1-42 (the awakening of the spiritual essence), and of 4:46-54

---

32. "Gnostic critics claim that the basic error of 'the many' involves their preoccupation with the historical reality of Jesus" (Pagels, *Johannine Gospel*, 11). If John (in Ephesus?) was engaged in a wider debate with Greek mythology (cf. John 7:35; 12:20-26), as argued by George van Kooten in a paper given in Cambridge in 2014 ("Between Mythology and Philosophy: Rereading John's Notion of Being Begotten from God in a Greek Context—Engaging with C. H. Dodd's 'The Interpretation of the Fourth Gospel [1953]' Sixty Years On"), John 1:14 would be equally critical.

33. Ptolemaeus reads Isa 45:5 as the Demiurge, "too weak to know anything spiritual, (imagining) that he was himself the only God" (Irenaeus, *Haer.* 1:5.4).

34. Particularly Sophia submitting to an illegitimate passion from which matter was derived (Irenaeus, *Haer.* 1:2.2; 1:4.1; 1:5.1-6).

35. Ptolemaeus insisted that Christ "was endowed with a body which had a psychic substance.... He received nothing whatever material ... for matter is not capable of being saved" (Irenaeus, *Haer.* 1:6.1).

36. Irenaeus, *Haer.* 1:1.8.5; also 1:1.1-3 (Foerster, *Gnosis* 1:144-45). Similarly Clement of Alexandria, *Exc.* 1:6 (Foerster, *Gnosis* 1:223); and the *Tripartite Tractate*.

37. Fragment of Heracleon in Origen, *Comm. Jo.* 2:15; Foerster, *Gnosis* 1:163. See also Clement of Alexandria, *Exc.* 1:7; 1:41.3-4.

38. Irenaeus, *Haer.* 1:6.2, 4; 1:7.5. "The spiritual is saved by nature; the psychic, being possessed of free will, has an inclination towards faith and towards incorruptibility, but also towards unbelief and destruction, according to its own choice; but the material perishes by nature" (Clement of Alexandria, *Exc.* 55:3); and see also Irenaeus, *Haer.* 1:5.1; 1:6.1.

39. Foerster, *Gnosis* 1:166-68; though, as Pagels reminds us, Origen also practiced "spiritual exegesis" (*Johannine Gospel*, 66-67).

(the demiurge asking the Savior for help, as the human being created by the demiurge was about to die).[40] And Ptolemaeus maintains that Jesus' confessions in John 10:30 and 14:6 indicate that Jesus "was other than that which he assumed"; that John 19:34 indicated "the outflowing of the passions"; and that in references to the Son of Man in the passion predictions "he appears to be speaking of another person, namely, of him who experiences passion."[41] In the *Trimorphic Protennoia* the "I" speaks regularly of having come down to the world, as "Word, and I revealed myself in the likeness of their shape" (*NHL* 13:47.15-16); "As for me, I put on Jesus. I bore him from the cursed wood, and established him in the dwelling places of his Father."[42]

Such readings of John are typical of the gnostic exegesis reported by Irenaeus and Clement of Alexandria, characteristic of a mindset looking for arguments to support its given position rather than anything that might call the given in question—what is now regarded as eisegesis rather than exegesis.[43] By reading through the text to what they assumed was an underlying schema, the reading itself could come across as sophisticated, more appealingly subtle than a straightforward reading.[44] Irenaeus was able to refute such eisegesis by the much more straightforward exegesis of John 1:14: it was the Word of God that became flesh, the only-begotten Son of the only God; "the apostle certainly does not speak regarding any other, or concerning any Ogdoad, but respecting our Lord Jesus Christ[;] . . . flesh is that which was of old formed for Adam by God out of the dust, and it is this that John has declared the Word of God became."[45]

---

40. Dunderberg, "Valentinus," 80.

41. Clement of Alexandria, *Exc.* 61:1-4. We might add that the sense of alienation from the world indicated in John's Gospel (R. Brown, *Community*, 63-66) would likely resonate with the characteristic gnostic sense of alienation, an emphasis brought out particularly by Jonas, *Gnostic Religion*. It is not surprising that the interest in Gnosticism arose when Existentialism was a dominant force in European philosophy, since the existentialist sense of *Geworfenheit* ("thrownness") matched the gnostic's sense of "alienation" so closely; cf. Rudolph, *Gnosis*, 33-34.

42. *NHL* 13:50.12-15; cf. John 14:2.

43. Irenaeus provides good examples of Ptolemaeus' interpretation of other NT passages (*Haer.* 1:8.2-4).

44. Particularly significant here was the critique by Sanders, *Fourth Gospel*. Even Hengel, *Four Gospels*, thought that "for a long time it [the Fourth Gospel] was not regarded as 'on the same level' as the other Gospels" (137); but see also his *Johannine Question*. In contrast, the Apologists' Logos christology was much closer to and a more empathetic reading of the Johannine prologue. See further particularly Hill, "Johannophobia," who refers also to Nagel, *Die Rezeption*.

45. Irenaeus, *Haer.* 1:9.3; see also 3:11.2-3 ("according to the opinion of no one of the heretics was the Word of God made flesh"); 3:16.2, 5-8; 3:17.4; 3:18.1, 7; 3:19.1; 5:18.2-3.

Käsemann's argument was, in effect, similar to that of Ptolemaeus and may indeed be said to reflect what must have been the interpretative logic of many Valentinians:

> Does the statement "The Word became flesh" really mean more than that he descended into the world of man and there came into contact with earthly existence, so that an encounter with him became possible? Is not this statement totally overshadowed by the confession "We beheld his glory," so that it received its meaning from it.... Do not [the] features of his lowliness... represent the absolute minimum of the costume designed for the one who dwelt for a little while among men, appearing to be one of them, yet without himself being subjected to earthly conditions?[46]

But Käsemann was being equally unfair to John. For John "the Word became flesh" was *not* "totally overshadowed by the confession 'We beheld his glory.'" It was precisely that the glory was manifested *in and as flesh* on which John insisted.[47] The "glory" was not only the glory of the pre-existent Word or of the ascended Christ, but Jesus being glorified in his crucifixion; John retains the structure given to the Gospel by Mark.[48] To be sure, John sailed close to the wind, but he was never blown off course. Gnostic exegesis could only claim John's support by denying the both-and of flesh and glory, of glory-in-flesh, the both-and of death-and-resurrection. In emphasizing the immediacy and completeness of the conjunction in John 1:14, John subverted all attempts to pull him into the gnostic camp.[49] Irenaeus and Clement of Alexandria were right to claim that the gnostics abused John's Gospel and to insist that it remained a fundamental expression of Christian belief.

At the same time, Käsemann was right to emphasize that John did sail close to the wind, and to draw the corollary that the church's recognition of John's canonical authority amounted to a recognition that proclamation of the gospel has to be inventive and creative, at times dangerously so, if it is to speak effectively to generations with changing presuppositions and worldviews. The success of Irenaeus, then, in ensuring that Valentinian gnostics would be unsuccessful in their attempt to claim John and the Johannine

---

46. Käsemann, *Testament*, 9–10.

47. Bultmann had similarly missed the point in his insistence that "his incarnation is only a *means* to the revelation which he brings and not the revelation *itself*" (*John*, 65).

48. Contrast Käsemann, who notably, and surprisingly, claims that "apart from a few remarks that point ahead to it, the passion comes into view in John only at the very end" (*Testament*, 7).

49. See also Thompson, *Humanity*, chapter 2 ("Incarnation and Flesh").

prologue as their own, was something of a mixed blessing since John's Gospel includes within the NT canon a degree of adaptation and inventiveness in the proclamation of Jesus that those who prefer simply to retell the old gospel story without much variation will typically find unnerving.

There is a final irony which should not escape notice—that it was *John's* christology which made its most lasting effect on Christian theology, which shifted the focus in christology from cross and resurrection to incarnation; whereas its individualistic ecclesiology[50] was quickly passed over and survived or revived only on the fringes of a Christianity dominated by monarchical episcopacy and a strict doctrine of apostolic succession.

---

50. Dunn, *Unity and Diversity*, §31.1.

4

Worlds of Judgment

John 9

L. ANN JERVIS
Wycliffe College

THE FOURTH GOSPEL'S COSMIC lawsuit motif has been brilliantly elucidated by Andrew Lincoln.[1] In *Truth on Trial* Lincoln clarifies how the narrator of the Gospel of John presents the long-standing battle between light and darkness coming to a head in God's lawsuit with God's world.[2] In this lawsuit, Jesus is the witness and the judge, and those who believe the truth of Jesus' witness and judgment are liberated from darkness and death into light and life.

Lincoln rightly articulates the Fourth Gospel's conviction that the "lawsuit is not primarily about judging humans for their deeds and punishing them for not performing rightly."[3] Rather, the lawsuit is concerned with asking humanity to recognize God and God's work. Sin's "primary characteristic and the grounds for condemnation" is failure to believe in Jesus.[4]

---

1. A finer colleague and friend I cannot imagine. Through several years of working alongside him, and years since of friendship, I know Andrew Lincoln to exemplify commitment to living the reality Jesus brings.

2. Lincoln, *Truth on Trial*, 333.

3. Ibid., 188.

4. Ibid., 119.

One of the key passages in the Fourth Gospel's development of God's lawsuit with the world is, Lincoln notes, chapter 9. This chapter, which itself is framed as a trial, makes evident the clash between Jesus' witness and "what appears to be a straightforward interpretation of the Mosaic law."[5] Lincoln ponders the contrast between the Jewish law as the evidence for a "true judgment in a lawsuit about claims for God" and Jesus' witness which "requires a totally new assessment of the law."[6] He writes that "the law as used by Jesus' opponents has become an idol that needs to be judged."[7] For the Fourth Gospel, "the law is seen as providing the wrong categories for judging."[8] In other words, the witness and judgment of Jesus is in categories that are distinct from those of the law.

I wish to testify to the generative power of Lincoln's interpretation by looking again at John 9. Accepting Lincoln's view that the narrator presents the story of the man born blind as a trial (a trial both of the man[9] and of Jesus[10]), I suggest that the narrator also puts on trial the law and a reality-structure shaped by law and sin. Lincoln astutely points out that the closing of the episode, with Jesus' "verdict of judgment"[11] on the Pharisees, shapes the narrative. The narrative reveals the conflicting claims of Jesus and Moses.[12] It is plain that the implied audience[13] is directed to see that it is the man and Jesus who are vindicated.

I wish to flesh out how this vindication entails also the vindication of the categories by which and in which Jesus and his new disciple live. The narrator offers opportunity to see that sin and the law structure a reality that the implied audience should recognize as false. The narrative pronounces a verdict on sin and the law: they are part of the darkness. They do not belong in the reality of light and life that Jesus brings.

I propose, then, that in John 9 the revelation of the conflicting claims of Jesus and Moses is not only aimed at deepening faith in Jesus, but also at encouraging understanding of the *consequence* of such belief. Belief in Jesus means living a reality that is separate from the law and sin. It is not

5. Ibid., 232.
6. Ibid.
7. Ibid., 236.
8. Ibid.
9. Ibid., 96
10. Ibid., 99.
11. Ibid.
12. Ibid., 101.

13. Lincoln (and others, e.g., van Unnik, "Purpose," 382–411) rightly regards the Fourth Gospel as written to believers. I take it that the narrator's implied audience is also believers in Jesus.

just that Jesus' claims are true and the law's are not.[14] It is that belief in Jesus entails living in a world formed only by him. Believers are directed by this narrative to open their eyes to the new environment they inhabit by virtue of faith in Jesus.

Lincoln describes chapter 9 as "a narrative embodiment" of 3:19–21[15]—the judgment is that the world and people loved darkness rather than light. Indeed; and this narrative embodiment also fleshes out the *nature* of darkness. The darkness, which subsequent to Jesus' coming is based in failure to believe in Jesus, is a reality-structure in which people make sense of their world by means of sin and blame; in which they cannot let go of sin and sin's arbiter, the law.

I suggest that chapter 9 is at once an encouragement to followers of Jesus to hold firm to their confession, and a challenge to them to recognize that now their existence is to be structured by Jesus alone. As we will shortly see, it is the disciples of Jesus who are the first to seek to make sense of the man's condition with the category of sin. The narrator thereby signals to the implied audience of believers that they should critique their own use of this category.

THE NARRATIVE

Jesus is the one who sees the man blind from birth, after which his disciples ask him "Rabbi, who sinned, this man or his parents, so that he was born blind"? Immediately, Jesus reframes the conversation. It is not, Jesus says, a matter of sin. The man's blindness from birth has a purpose (ἵνα) and that is that God's works might be revealed in him (v. 3). In the context of the disciples' question about sin, the "works of God" are implicitly contrasted with the works of the law. There is here an echo of the prologue's programmatic statement: "the law was given through Moses; grace and truth came through Jesus Christ" (1:17).

At the outset of the narrative Jesus pulls the curtain open for his disciples on an alternative reality in which to regard the man's condition. With Jesus' presence, the man born blind is not a victim of sin, or a sinner himself, but a site for revelation—a person in whom and through whom Jesus

---

14. It is important to note here the fruit of Pancaro's full-scale study of the law in the Fourth Gospel. He concludes that John is not concerned to denigrate the law itself. The law is God's revelation, but, subsequent to Christ's coming, its function is to lead people to faith in Christ (*Law*, 528). It is not the law, but people's misunderstanding of its place, that is at issue in the Fourth Gospel.

15. Lincoln, *Truth on Trial*, 102.

reveals God's works. The narrator guides the implied audience to recognize that with Jesus there comes another structure for making sense of and acting in the world—one that is not determined by sin.

Jesus' disciples have tried to make sense of the man's blindness in legal categories. Jesus offers instead the categories of revelation and God's works, all of which are enveloped in Jesus himself who, while he is in the world, is the light of the world. Whatever this strange response is meant to indicate in its particulars, it is clear that Jesus does not accept the category of sin as explicative of the man's condition and that sin is excluded from the manner in which he perceives the man. Sin cannot be evoked as the reason the man was born blind nor as the framework for response to the man. Jesus places the man's condition—and himself and his disciples[16]—in a framework apart from sin and so in a framework not shaped by the law.

In the course of articulating this alternative framework Jesus performs the miracle that allows the man to see. The man's subsequent capacity to see confirms the revelation of the works of God and the form of life that may flow from that revelation. Jesus, the light of the world, has taken away the man's blindness. And in doing so has revealed that God acts outside a legal framework.

When the man born blind opens his eyes, the first thing the narrator recounts him seeing is the people accustomed to his being a blind beggar squabbling about his identity (vv. 8–9). Instead of celebration or support, the man sees distrust and hostility. However, despite their speaking about him and not to him, the man states forthrightly, ἐγώ εἰμί (v. 9).

The man's declaration, given just a few verses after Jesus' dramatic claim, "before Abraham was, I am" (8:58), invites the implied audience to ponder whether the man might be aware not only that he has gained vision but that he has also gained being. Does he recognize that he has been transferred by Jesus from the domain of darkness and non-being into the place of light and life? Using the same words as Jesus did during his debate with the Jews who had believed in him (8:31) but now seek to kill him (8:40)—a debate over Jesus' ability to free them from slavery to sin (8:34)—the narrator signifies that the man is now in Jesus' reality. The man's "ἐγώ εἰμί" suggests not only that he is in fact the man who used to sit and beg, but that he knows he now lives in a reality defined by Jesus, the light of the world.

On the other hand, the discomfort of the neighbors and others with the revelation of the works of God in the blind man signifies that they live in a separate landscape. Their inability to rejoice in the good thing that has

---

16. Note that Jesus includes his disciples along with himself as those who work the works of God, v. 4.

happened to the man, let alone to accept its truth, indicates the difference between their world and his.

Jesus is foreign to them. They nevertheless need to find him (v. 12), the implication being that they intend to domesticate him, fit him into their space. The man's miraculous vision—which is not a problem to him—is a problem only when encountered in a reality structured by sin and the law. Perhaps by finding Jesus they can resolve the "problem" on their terms. They never do find Jesus and, in the remainder of the narrative, it is only the Pharisees among the opponents who will again interact with him (v. 40).

Their question to the man ("how were your eyes opened?"; v. 10), which the man answered directly by naming Jesus and describing the miracle (v. 11), has not satisfied them. They need an answer that fits their categories. Consequently, they bring the man to the Pharisees; the legal framework is the one they know and trust.

The subsequent disagreement among the Pharisees is, of course, shaped by a legal framework. Some of the Pharisees determine that since Jesus broke the law by not keeping Sabbath, he cannot be from God, while others are willing to believe that Jesus made the man see, which must mean that he is not a sinner. The issue of sin—whether or not Jesus is a sinner—is central to the Pharisees' discussion.

The narrator of the Fourth Gospel does not say whether or not the Pharisees' dispute helped the neighbors and others. Instead, the narrator immediately features another group of interrogators—"the Jews."[17] These people doubt that the man had been blind. The event troubles them so much that they call the man's parents, asking them to identify the man as their son. The "Jews" then put to his parents the same question that the first group of inquisitors had asked of the man himself—how is it that he sees now (v. 19).

The parents are willing to identify the man as their son and to state that he was indeed born blind. But they refuse to answer the second question, telling "the Jews" to ask their son themselves. The narrator gives as the reason for their response that they feared "the Jews." The narrator's explanation, as J. L. Martyn famously highlighted, is that "the Jews" had agreed that if anyone confessed Jesus as the Christ, they would be put out of the synagogue (v. 22).[18]

Implied in the narrator's explanation is that the parents in fact know the identity of the person who healed their son. Yet they allow their response to be determined by the rule about not confessing Jesus as the Christ. They do

---

17. Lincoln describes the designation "the Jews" as the Fourth Gospel's name for those who are "hardened in opposition and unbelief" (*Truth on Trial*, 99).

18. Martyn, *History and Theology*. See the brief history of response to Martyn's proposal in Visotzky, "Methodological Considerations," 91–107.

not want to be on the wrong side of a community ruling—the punishment would be harsh. Their response directs the implied audience to condemn the reality structured by sin and the law: it is a life of such fear of blame and shame that parents will abandon their child.

Now the man born blind is called back for a second interrogation. The investigation intensifies. The man is threatened with the command to give God the glory[19] and with the expectation that he will acknowledge the judgment of his questioners—that "this man is a sinner" (v. 24). The interrogators have come to their judgment and now they want the man in the dock to confess. The confession they need from him is determined by their legal categories. They need him to agree that Jesus is a sinner, one who disobeys the law.

The man born blind responds from another place, a place shaped not by the law but by his experience of revelation, which the narrator has concretized and dramatized in the story of his receiving sight. The category of sin is irrelevant to the man—"whether or not he is a sinner, I do not know." What he does know is that he was blind but now he sees.

The man's eyes are opened and he sees more than the physical world. He sees that he does not need to be confined by the structure of the law—the structure that bounds his interrogators' existence. The trial initiated by his questioners only occurs because they think in the terms of the law. The man born blind does not need his experience to be tried. A trial is irrelevant and cannot make sense of what has been revealed in him and to him. His eyes are opened to a new reality—that life is found in learning from Jesus. He knows that he has become a disciple of Jesus—that Jesus now structures his existence (vv. 27–28).

Implied in the man's brilliant response to his interrogators—"do you also want to become his disciples?"—is that their obsession with Jesus means they are confronted with a choice. The interrogators' immediate response makes clear the choice they make—they remain disciples of Moses (v. 28). The law is their world and how they make sense of life: "God has spoken to Moses" (v. 29). Jesus, on the other hand, seems to them to come from nowhere. Their comment, "we do not know where he is from," is, of course, classic Johannine irony. It demonstrates to the implied audience how very ignorant the interrogators are. The narrator has told his implied audience repeatedly that Jesus is from God, and yet these interrogators are ignorant of this basic truth. They are sure of so much (note their repetition of "we know" in vv. 24 and 29) and yet they do not know the fundamental thing

---

19. The word δός is in the imperative mood. R. E. Brown notes that "give glory to God" was an oath formula used before taking testimony or a confession of guilt, e.g., Josh 7:19 (*John*, 374).

about Jesus. The narrator directs the implied audience to recognize that ignorance of where Jesus is from means being trapped in legal categories. At one level, in chapter 9 it is the man born blind and Jesus who are on trial. At another level, this chapter puts on trial the categories of law and sin.

The man responds by clarifying for his interrogators their dilemma—his eyes are opened and this is *sui generis*, for never has there been an incident like it (v. 32). This is the fact and their need to explain this marvel in the categories of sin is ridiculous—"we know that God does not listen to sinners" (v. 32). It is clear that the person who healed him is from God. Because they are trapped in a system of law, they cannot see this truth.

Their response proves the man's point—"you were born completely in sin" (my translation; v. 34). Their closing verdict is not only their judgment that the man is not a proper law observer, but also echoes the opinion of Jesus' disciples with which the narrative opened (v. 2). Despite the energy and intensity of their investigation, the interrogators are stuck in a position outside of Jesus' revelation.

The only explanatory category the interrogators have is sin. And they use it, not only as the explanation for the man's congenital blindness, but now also for his sight and his allegiance to Jesus. Their repetitive invocation of sin reveals the poverty of their reality. The weakness of their world is manifest when all they can do is to throw the man out (v. 34). They have judged him and punished him, but they have not solved their dilemma. How did this happen and what is the identity of the one who did it? They are still in the dark.

Jesus finds the man a second time. Now he gives him clearer vision. Jesus reveals his identity to the man—he is the Son of Man (v. 37). The man confesses his faith in Jesus and worships him. In clear contrast to the courtroom ethos of vv. 8–34, this interaction is structured not by interrogation but by conversation, confession, and reverence. An alternative way of knowing and being is in evidence—a way structured not by sin and the law, but by belief in Jesus.

Jesus then describes the reality he has come to create. His description of the reality created by his coming does not include sin or the law. It is rather "for judgment" (v. 39). The judgment for which Jesus comes is distinct from the judgments of the interrogators. It is not according to the law, with sin as an explanatory category. Rather, the judgment Jesus comes for transfers people from blindness to sight and sight to blindness.

Since the narrator could hardly have been more obvious about the meaning of sight as the ability to say "Lord, I believe" (v. 38), the implied audience is led to understand that Jesus' judgment creates believers and non-believers.[20] The reality Jesus brings is entirely structured by belief in him. The alternative way of being—the way of the world into which Jesus came—is structured by sin and the law.

The episode closes with the Pharisees' defensive challenge to Jesus. Again, taking on a courtroom style, the Pharisees who have overheard Jesus' conversation with the man ask "surely we are not blind, are we?" (v. 40).[21] Their response shows how utterly they have misunderstood and how deeply embedded they are in a way of being that is separate from the one Jesus brings. They have entirely missed the point. Why would they want to claim to be sighted when Jesus has said he is going to make the sighted blind?

Jesus replies, using the classifications of sight and blindness in a way that reveals the chasm between these observers of the law and himself— between the two realities. In fact, Jesus says, they are not blind, because in the reality that Jesus brings, the blind are those who do not have sin (clearly implying that they *do* have sin). In the context of Jesus' statement that he will give sight to those who do not see—making blindness the state with which Jesus wants to work (as evidenced in the story itself)—Jesus is judging that they are the ones he has warned about. They are those who see but who will become blind. When Jesus comes into the world, it is those who think they see already who in fact cooperate with sin.

Jesus says this outright in the next sentence: "Now you say you see, your sin remains" (v. 41). Jesus brings a reality separate from the law and sin. Those who think they do not need the reality he brings, who think they see already, will continue in an existence structured by the kind of distrustful and deluded interaction dramatized in the trial of the man born blind. Sin is not Jesus' category, it is theirs. Jesus came to save people precisely from the oppression of sin.

Jesus' judgment creates a new mode of existence from which sin is excluded—a mode of existence shaped by the divine life.

Chapter 9 is a narrative embodiment not only of 3:19–21, but also of 1:29[22] and 8:34–36.[23]

---

20. The problem of agency is not addressed, though it is raised by Jesus' words here. Do people have a choice about whether they are made sighted or blind? This theological problem raises its head at the beginning of the episode—it is Jesus who initiates the miracle of giving sight to the man born blind.

21. Lincoln's translation, *John*, 287.

22. "Behold the Lamb of God, who takes away the sin of the world."

23. "Truly, truly, I say to you, everyone who commits sin is the slave of sin. The slave does not remain in the house forever; the son does remain forever. So, if the Son makes you free, you will be free indeed."

WORLDS OF JUDGMENT

Jesus' judgment, which the narrator juxtaposes with the judgments of the opponents in the mini-trials of chapter 9, creates believers and non-believers. It also brings into the world a new world in which judgment means something other than determining fault and laying blame. It brings into the world a reality not built around sin; one in which the law is marginalized.[24]

Judgment in the context of Jesus' life—which is the divine life—is creative rather than destructive. It is not concerned with blame, but with the works of God—with the giving of light and life. Jesus' judgment exists in a reality that is of life and for life. It is a judgment that offers freedom from the sorts of judgments which are only about who is to blame.

The narrator of the Fourth Gospel seeks to dramatize the world Jesus brings by contrasting it with the world that informs the judgments of his opponents. On the one hand are those who are acclimatized to sin's presence and to the law as the only means of making sense of their experience. They have accepted that reality includes sin. Their extreme discomfort with the man's sight highlights how terrifying it is for them to have the structures of sin challenged. It was reassuring to daily walk by someone they thought of as sinner. Life made sense—blame and praise, based on the rubrics of the law, were meaning-makers.

On the other hand, there is Jesus who judges, not on the basis of the law, but as God—the one who is light and life. Jesus' judgment creates life and light. In the world of Jesus, meaning is made through life in him.

The narrator of the Fourth Gospel tries in chapter 9 to accomplish what Paul seeks to articulate through poetry and discourse—a demonstration of the difference between existence in, to use Paul's words, "the flesh," which sphere includes sin and the law; and life in the Spirit. The implied audience of John 9 is directed to see that belief in Jesus Christ means life apart from sin and the law—life lived in the light of the world. The narrative pronounces a verdict on sin and the law—they are part of the darkness.[25]

---

24. Interpreters of the Fourth Gospel need to be extremely wary of perpetrating anti-Semitism. Particularly since chapter 9 begins as a critique of the disciples' misunderstanding, we might hear references to the law as to more than the Mosaic law. Legalism of all sorts may blind us to life in Christ. See Visotzky, who advises thinking of the Fourth Gospel in terms not only of a two-level drama, as did Martyn and Brown, but as a four-level one. Interpreters cannot ignore the "long history of (mis)interpretation"—the third level; and "our own current biases"—the fourth level ("Methodological Considerations," 104).

25. Pancaro rightly points out the distinction between Paul and John in regards to the law (*Law*, 528). Paul opposes faith in Jesus and works of the law, whereas John does not. However, as Pancaro also notes in passing, both Paul and the Fourth Gospel claim

This is a message that believers in Jesus need to hear repeatedly, for it remains tempting to make sense of our lives by accepting sin's presence—for instance, that beggar we pass by daily. It seems straightforward to make meaning by following the rules that structure our lives—whether they be those authorized by church, family, or society. Jesus' challenge to his disciples is instead to live with our eyes wide open to the world of life and light that he has brought into our darkness; to know that our belief in him means we live in his world.

---

that there is a "way to life" (ibid., 528) that Jesus brought—a way distinct from the way directed by law.

5

Another Look at "Lifting Up" in the Gospel of John

CATRIN H. WILLIAMS
University of Wales Trinity Saint David

One of the distinctive ways in which John's Gospel communicates Jesus' identity as God's heavenly revealer on earth is by attributing to him a profoundly enigmatic mode of speech. Figurative vocabulary and riddles feature prominently in the discourses of this "stranger from heaven," not least in the cluster of declarations whose verbal building blocks consist of words to which more than one level of meaning can be ascribed (e.g., John 3:3–4; 4:10–11). Among the most well known, and baffling, of these Johannine cases of *double entendre* is the use of the verb ὑψόω to describe Jesus—in his capacity as the Son of Man—being lifted up on the cross, which, ironically and at the same time, is also his exaltation (3:14; 8:28; 12:32, 34).

Most commentators agree that John deliberately plays on the literal and figurative associations of ὑψόω and that it relates in some way to Jesus' death. It is also widely recognized that his three "lifting up" sayings function as the Johannine counterpart of the threefold Synoptic predictions of the suffering, death, and resurrection of the Son of Man (Mark 8:31; 9:31; 10:33–34). Where there is less agreement is *how* and *why* Jesus' death and exaltation came to be telescoped together in John's Gospel. What does it mean to combine the physical act of lifting up Jesus through crucifixion with an understanding of that act as pointing, in some way, to his exaltation? Does John's (re)positioning of the exaltation motif, which in some NT texts (Acts 2:33; 5:31; cf. Phil 2:9) is linked to Jesus' resurrection-ascension, amount to its *expansion* so that Jesus' crucifixion is now included within the integrated "event" of his death, resurrection, and return to heaven? Or is it a *transference* of that motif to convey Jesus' death exclusively as his moment of exaltation?

These are far from insignificant questions for the interpretation of John's Gospel, particularly for determining the significance it attaches to the death of Jesus,[1] and for establishing what is means to describe Jesus' death, narratologically, as "the resolution to the Johannine narrative plot," and, theologically, as the revelation of God's glory, as testimony to the truth, as the means of the gift of eternal life.[2] While Johannine scholarship on the "lifting up" sayings has centered largely on whether Jesus' exaltation is fulfilled *in part* or *in full* on the cross, this essay focuses on another set of interpretative questions and perspectives. It firstly examines the use of ὑψόω in a variety of texts outside John's Gospel before analyzing its function within the Gospel narrative, particularly with reference to the immediate literary context of the three passages in question (3:13–15; 8:28–29; 12:31–34). The essay concludes by considering the likely implications of the progressive explication of Jesus' "lifting up" within the narrative, and the extent to which its gradual elucidation can shed light on what it means, from a Johannine perspective, to speak of "Jesus' exaltation to glory by means of his death by crucifixion."[3]

ELEVATION, EXALTATION, AND CRUCIFIXION

Though relatively rare, the verb ὑψόω can mean "lift high/raise up" and "exalt/elevate" in classical Greek.[4] A similar semantic range is attested in the various Septuagint translations, although surprisingly, given the frequent occurrence of ὑψόω in the LXX (around 200 times),[5] this evidence has not been subjected to much systematic treatment,[6] even by Johannine scholars.

1. See Frey, "*Die 'theologia crucifixi*,'" 169–238, especially 176.
2. Lincoln, "'I Am the Resurrection and the Life,'" 123–24.
3. Lincoln, *Truth on Trial*, 89; cf. Lincoln, *John*, 269.
4. See LSJ, 1910.
5. See the entry on "ὑψόω" in Lust et al., *Lexicon*, 498.
6. See Bertram, "ὑψόω, ὑπερυψόω," *TDNT* 8: 606–7; and, most recently, Mardaga, "Repetitive," 105–7.

There are some examples of ὑψόω to denote upward movement, either for the lifting of the head (e.g., IV Kgdms 25:27) or voice (e.g., IV Kgdms 19:22; Isa 37:23) or even for the raising of the ark by water (Gen. 7:17: ὑψώθη ἀπὸ τῆς γῆς). However, in the majority of cases where the referent is God, the emphasis falls upon status or position, not movement. God is frequently acclaimed as "exalted" within the context of judgment, particularly in the Psalms (e.g., 17:47; 45:11; 96:9) and also the prophecies of Isaiah (cf. 2:11; 30:18), whose use of ὑψόω will be subjected to closer treatment in the next section of this essay.

Both the literal and figurative use of ὑψόω is attested in other Jewish texts composed in, or translated into, Greek during the late Second Temple period.[7] It is striking, therefore, that the extant New Testament evidence centers primarily on the notion of exaltation.[8] Of particular interest is the possible wordplay between the various connotations of ὑψόω in Jesus' oracle to Capernaum in Matt. 11:23//Luke 10:15. The oracle refutes the possibility that the city will be exalted/lifted up to heaven (ὑψωθήσῃ) and, though rhetorically phrased, it conjures up the image of spatial elevation as well as change in status, as indicated by Jesus' subsequent announcement of abasement: "You shall be brought down (καταβήσῃ) to Hades." Nevertheless, the three New Testament passages that have received most attention in this connection—even sometimes functioning as the lens through which the Johannine "lifting up" sayings are interpreted—are those in which ὑψόω denotes the post-resurrection exaltation of Jesus. If Peter, in his first speech in Acts, declares that Jesus has been raised (2:32: ἀνέστησεν) and exalted (2:33: ὑψωθείς) to God's right hand, he is attributed the same expression for the same purpose after his subsequent reference to God "raising up" (ἤγειρεν) Jesus (5:30). The emphasis in Paul's declaration about Jesus' super-exaltation (Phil. 2:9: ὑπερύψωσεν) is also on resurrection-ascension as *resulting from* (διὸ καὶ) Jesus' death on the cross.

This rich depository of Jewish and early Christian evidence provides significant comparative material for assessing the five occurrences of ὑψόω in the Gospel of John. The fact that none of this evidence relates specifically to "lifting up" in death has occasioned several attempts at identifying

---

7. The verb is used figuratively in the sense of "exalt" (e.g., *Let. Aris.* 263; *Pss. Sol.* 1:5; *Sib. Or.* 3.583; *T. Jud.* 21:8) and literally as "lift high/raise up" (e.g., Josephus, *B.J.* 2.219; 5.523).

8. Of the fifteen NT occurrences of ὑψόω outside John's Gospel, all connote exaltation rather than physical movement, with ten occurring in connection with the motif of exalting vs. humbling (Matt. 23:12 (x2); Luke 1:52; 14:11 (x2); 18:14 (x2); 2 Cor. 11:7; Jas 4:10; 1 Pet 5:6). Cf. also Matt 11:23; Luke 10:15; Acts 2:33; 5:31; 13:17 (Phil 2:9: ὑπερυψόω).

a possible link between the Johannine sayings and examples of the double connotation of being "raised up" and "impaled/crucified" in Aramaic (אסתלק or אזדקף)⁹ and Hebrew (נשׂה; cf. Gen 40:13, 19, 20).¹⁰ However, what undoubtedly warrants a more prominent place in the discussion of traditio-historical questions is the intriguing cluster of possible parallels in *Oneirocritica*, a second-century-CE compendium of dream interpretations by Artemidorus of Daldis.¹¹ This text is of interest because its interpretation of certain dreams of crucifixion as predictions of the future "elevation" of the one crucified demonstrates how a cross, with the aid of ὑψόω and its cognates, can be "transformed from an instrument of execution to one of exaltation."¹² Artemidorus states:

> It is also auspicious for a poor man [to dream of crucifixion]. For a crucified man is raised high (καὶ γὰρ ὑψηλός ὁ σταυρωθείς) and he nourishes <many birds>. But it [a dream of crucifixion] means the exposure of what is hidden. For a crucified man can be seen (ἐκφανής) by all. (*Oneirocritica* 2:53).

Admittedly, this passage does not provide a precise verbal parallel to the Johannine evidence (ὑψηλός is used, rather than a form of ὑψόω), and it centers on transformation rather than recognition of the actual status of the one who is "lifted up" through crucifixion, the latter arguably being the case with the Johannine Jesus. Nevertheless, it suggests that the semiotic potential of ὑψόω would have been culturally familiar to John and his first readers/hearers.¹³ This is a form of dream interpretation which highlights the possibility of viewing a highly positioned cross as a symbol of honor and a corpse as a symbol of nourishment/wealth.¹⁴ And whatever the actual sociopolitical reasons for placing those crucified in such an elevated position,¹⁵ Artemidorus indicates that the *visual display* achieved through crucifixion is an effective way of bringing what is hidden to light (2:53: ἐκφανής). The

---

9. E.g., McNamara, "Ascension," 450–59.
10. See Hollis, "Root," 475–78.
11. See Harris McCoy, *Oneirocritica*.
12. Meggitt, "Artemidorus," 204. See also Labahn, "Bedeutung," 452–55.
13. Meggitt, "Artemidorus," 206–7, demonstrates how dream interpretations in *Oneirocritica* probably already belonged to a "popular cultural context" in a wide variety of locations in the first century CE.
14. Cf. Labahn, "Bedeutung," 453–54. See further Harris McCoy, *Oneirocritica* 4:49: "So, for example, someone dreamt of being crucified, which signifies honor and wealth (δόξαν καὶ εὐπορίαν)—honor, because the crucified person is in a very high position (ὑψηλότατον), and wealth, because he provides food for many birds."
15. On associating (ironic) high elevation on a cross with the public shaming of those who had sought self-elevation, see Marcus, "Crucifixion," 77–80.

symbolic interpretation of crucifixion emerging from this wordplay points to the close link that can be forged between death and exaltation—that is, a "lifting up" not *from* the cross, but *on* the cross.

"LIFTING UP" AND THE ISAIANIC SERVANT

The association between ὑψόω and the Servant of the Lord (Isa 52:13 LXX) requires separate discussion, not least because the influence of this Isaianic passage on the Johannine "lifting up" sayings is already widely acknowledged.[16] If the texts surveyed in the previous section enable one to appreciate the broad semantic range of ὑψόω within John's cultural repertoire, the primary contribution of LXX Isaiah is its capacity to supply a theological impetus for the presentation of Jesus' "lifting up" as an event of revelation and salvation. Of particular relevance is God's opening declaration in the fourth servant song: "See, my servant shall understand, and he shall be exalted and glorified greatly" (52:13 LXX: ἰδοὺ συνήσει ὁ παῖς μου καὶ ὑψωθήσεται καὶ δοξασθήσεται σφόδρα). The juxtaposition of ὑψόω and δοξάζω is a distinctive characteristic of LXX Isaiah,[17] and the fact that the same verbal pattern is used with reference to the future exaltation (ὑψωθήσεται) and glorification (δοξασθήσεται) of Yahweh (5:16; 33:10) points to an intentional alignment of God and his servant.

Other features, particularly in the first divine oracle of the song (Isa 52:13-15 LXX), yield valuable clues as to why this passage, above all others, could have motivated John to describe Jesus' death as his exaltation and glorification. First, and in contrast to the Hebrew text (cf. 52:14, 15 MT), all of God's introductory speech is orientated towards the future. The future tense is used not only to express God's promise regarding the exaltation and glorification of his servant (52:13), but also to describe the servant's dishonoring among people (52:14)[18] and the amazement of nations and kings when they finally see and understand him.[19] Secondly, the casting of all these different facets of God's speech as future "events" means that they lend themselves to mutual interpretation. The most widespread estimation of the introduction

---

16. E.g., Bauckham, *God Crucified*, 47-51, 64-65; Tang Nielsen, "Lamb of God," 228-33, 244-49.

17. The three-part declaration in Isa 52:13 MT (ירום ונשא וגבה מאד) becomes a twofold formulation in 52:13 LXX. The same correlation, but with the remnant of Israel as referent, occurs in Isa 4:2, 10:15.

18. This involves interpreting the oracle as shifting from a statement *about* the servant (52:13) to one addressing him directly (52:14: σε and σου).

19. For further details, see Ekblad, *Isaiah's Servant Poems*, 170-71, 179-94; Schwindt, *Gesichte*, 81-83.

to the oracle (52:13 MT and LXX) is that it offers an anticipatory outline of the exaltation that will *follow* the servant's suffering and death, as described in the main part of the song (53:1–11). Another proposal is that John reads this particular verse (52:13) as a summary assessment of the message of the song in its entirety: the exaltation of the servant is "the whole sequence of humiliation, suffering, death, and vindication beyond death which chapter 53 describes."[20] However, in view of the consistently future-orientated focus of 52:13 LXX *and* of what follows in 52:14–15 LXX, it can be argued that the "humiliation-as-exaltation" pattern is in fact already established in the LXX version of the oracle, or at least that it has the potential to be read in this way: although the servant's appearance and "glory" (δόξα) will be "deglorified" (ἀδοξήσει) in the eyes of other people, he will, at the same time, be exalted and greatly glorified by God.

Given that the LXX version of Isa 52:13–15 points to a twofold "vision" of the servant—one that characterizes those who see him in a physical sense (52:14) and the other centered on the divine perspective on "seeing" (52:13)—this passage attests a motif already encountered in the dream interpretation of Artemidorus, namely their shared interest in the *visual* aspect of "lifting up" to focus, more specifically, on the unveiling of that which has so far been hidden.[21] This is already firmly established in the opening call of Isaiah's song (ἰδού) and then receives affirmation and fulfillment when they—to whom it was not previously announced about the servant—will finally see (52:15: ὄψονται) and understand. A much stronger connection is thus forged in LXX Isaiah between the divine challenge to "see" the exaltation and glorification of the servant and the eventual "coming to see" attributed to the nations. The relevance of these features for understanding how John perceives the "lifting up" of Jesus will be considered after the sayings in question have been examined.

"LIFTING UP" AND JESUS' DEATH

The first occurrences of ὑψόω in John's Gospel bind together one of its many explanations of the significance of Jesus' mission, in this case through a comparison of the lifting up (ὑψωθῆναι) of the Son of Man (3:14b) and the wilderness incident in which Moses lifted up (ὕψωσεν) the bronze serpent (3:14a)—an act intended to heal the Israelites from the bites of the fiery snakes (Num 21:4–9). John's framing of this correspondence (καθὼς . . .

---

20. See especially Bauckham, *God Crucified*, 64. Cf. also Dodd, *Interpretation*, 247.
21. On the focus on visuality in Isa 52:13—53:12, see now Heath, *Paul's Visual Piety*, 228–31.

οὕτως) establishes a tight correlation between two events now regarded as mutually illuminating. The elevation of the serpent acts as a kind of type or foreshadowing of Jesus' "lifting up," whereby the scriptural incident is compressed to include only essential components for the comparison and its vocabulary harmonized with that of the "present" event through the deliberate use of ὑψόω (not ἱστάναι of Num 21:9 LXX) to denote the elevation of the serpent.[22] The intended correspondence, therefore, is not between Moses and Jesus but between the effects of the two acts of "lifting up" and, implicitly, of seeing/believing the one who is elevated. It is also a connection that involves some degree of contrast: gazing at the serpent led to physical healing, but "seeing" Jesus with faith will lead to eternal life (3:15; cf. Wis 16:6–7).[23]

The role of ὑψόω within this comparison is complex and yet instructive. Its first occurrence (3:14a), to denote the raising up of the serpent (on a pole), inevitably prompts questions about the semantic force of its second appearance (3:14b): does it similarly refer to a literal "lifting up" of Jesus, thereby alluding to the manner of his death, or does it (in addition) connote the more widespread, figurative use of ὑψόω to denote exaltation? Semantic interaction between these two levels of meaning must be activated when the life-giving purpose (ἵνα) of the "lifting up" of the Son of Man is brought into view. And yet, the comparison appears to be phrased in a way that seeks to promote rather than settle possible ambiguities. While the analogy of two literal acts of "lifting up" would also work with other verbs (e.g., αἴρω), only ὑψόω has the capacity to point to other potential semantic associations. The elusive character of the comparison is also indicated by the passive form (ὑψωθῆναι), even if the element of necessity (δεῖ) suggests God as subject (cf. 10:16; 11:51; 12:34; cf. Mark 8:31), whereas the lack of concrete "hooks" (such as an explicit reference to the location of the Son of Man's elevation/exaltation) means that no steer is given as to the precise connotation of ὑψόω in the second part.

Even if the comparison with the serpent appears to presuppose the physical "lifting up" of Jesus by crucifixion, the second level of meaning associated with exaltation is left open at this point. The typological correspondence in 3:14–15 can certainly be interpreted in terms of Jesus' exaltation on the cross: in the same way as the Israelites must look at the image of the serpent set high on a pole in order to be healed (Num 21:8–9), it is

---

22. For a detailed examination of this passage, see Frey, "'Wie Mose,'" 153–205.

23. Although the second part of the comparison refers to "believing" rather than "seeing" Jesus, Frey ("'Wie Mose,'" 184) argues for their close alignment on the basis of the parallel structure and content of John 3:15 (πᾶς ὁ πιστεύων ἐν αὐτῷ ἔχῃ ζωὴν αἰώνιον) and Num 21:8 LXX (πᾶς ὁ δεδηγέμνος ἰδὼν αὐτὸν ζήσεται).

necessary to ("see" and) believe in the one who is lifted high and simultaneously exalted on the cross in order to receive eternal life (John 3:14b–15; cf. 19:36–37).[24] Salvific correspondence between these two acts is ascribed additional dimensions by Craig Koester,[25] who proposes that both the elevated serpent and the crucified Son of Man visibly exhibit the results of human sin and opposition to God, so that, through their "lifting up," they demonstrate God's ability to transform the results of sin (Num 21:4–7; cf. John 8:28) into a means of giving life.

Nevertheless, the elusive character of the "exaltation" of Jesus persists. John maintains the open-endedness of the image by referring to belief in (πᾶς ὁ πιστεύων), rather than seeing, the elevated Son of Man (3:15). Although verbs of sight are frequently used to denote belief (e.g., 6:40; 12:21, 45; 14:9), they may have been avoided here to ensure that "seeing" is not limited to the visually concrete "lifting up" of the crucified Jesus. Furthermore, the presence of the ascent-descent schema in the immediate context of this analogy cannot be overlooked. Notwithstanding the interpretative challenges posed by the initial reference to no one having "ascended" (ἀναβέβηκεν) to heaven except the Son of Man who descended ἐκ τοῦ οὐρανοῦ,[26] a link between this claim (3:13) and the subsequent scripturally based comparison (3:14–15) is suggested by their connecting καί and also by the use of the designation "Son of Man" in both statements. Some propose that the emphasis in 3:13 lies on Jesus' credentials as the exclusive revealer of the heavenly things (τά ἐπουράνια), with 3:14–15 then explaining how his death on the cross is the supreme moment of that revelation.[27] And although the two verbs in question (ἀναβαίνω and ὑψόω) are certainly not synonymous in John's Gospel,[28] their close proximity to each other and their shared vertical-spatial connotations make it difficult to isolate them from one another in this part of Jesus' discourse.[29] The question, then, is the extent to which the "lifting up" of Jesus on the cross belongs to the pattern of his ascent to heaven and return to the Father; in other words, does the first of the Johannine "lifting up"

---

24. The visual aspect implicit in this interpretation of the correspondence is highlighted by Knöppler, *Die theologia crucis*, 155–60. Cf. Moloney, *Johannine Son of Man*, 59–61; Frey, "Die 'theologia crucifixi,'" 228.

25. Koester, "Messiah," 178.

26. On the various possible interpretations of John 3:13, see now Pierce and Reynolds, "The Perfect Tense-Form," 149–53.

27. See, e.g., Moloney, *Johannine Son of Man*, 59.

28. Cf. Frey, "'Wie Mose,'" 182 n.40, for the different semantic context of both verbs in John's Gospel.

29. On ἀναβαίνω (3:13) as the guiding category for the meaning of ὑψόω (3:14), see Theobald, *Herrenworte im Johannesevangelium*, 204–6, 588.

sayings view the exaltation of Jesus as somehow "completed" in his death or must necessarily include his resurrection-ascension? No further clues are provided at this narrative juncture to enable one to give a decisive answer.

Some illumination is offered by the second saying, where the Jewish opponents of Jesus are ascribed the role of agents in his elevation: "When you have lifted up (ὑψώσητε) the Son of Man, then you will know that I am he (ἐγώ εἰμι)" (8:28). The primary reference is undoubtedly to the physical raising of Jesus on the cross, even though John's Gospel certainly has the capacity to present these words as an ironic anticipation of how "the Jews" will ultimately exalt Jesus to heaven by means of his death. That the use of ὑψόω in this pronouncement points to other levels of meaning is strongly suggested by the way in which it overtly attributes revelatory significance to the crucifixion: the consequence of the "lifting up" of Jesus is that it will bring about recognition of his true identity as the visible manifestation of God, as the bearer of his exclusive self-declaration (ἐγώ εἰμι).[30] In what is arguably John's most thoroughgoing attempt at explaining Jesus' appropriation of ἐγώ εἰμι, the claim is set within the context of his unique relationship with the Father: everything he does and says comes from God (8:28b; cf. 8:26), the one who sent Jesus and remained with him throughout his mission, even on the cross (8:29). As a result, the depth of their unity is revealed when Jesus submits fully to death by crucifixion, and this concrete-visible sign of his divine identity becomes the locus of κρίσις for salvation or condemnation.[31] That Jesus' elevation-exaltation on the cross involves his "lifting up" to the Father's presence is more overtly expressed in 8:28-29, although it is difficult to determine whether this also assumes his return (to heaven) after his resurrection and ascension. The different time periods of the predicted exaltation (8:28a: ὅταν) and anticipated knowledge (8:28b: τότε) indicate that recognition is not concurrent with the act of "lifting up," and yet once again, this declaration—despite its inevitable shaping by the Gospel's post-Easter perspective—yields no clear signals as to whether exaltation is deemed to be fully enclosed within, or extends beyond, Jesus' death by crucifixion.

The final "lifting up" saying of the Johannine Jesus occurs in a narrative section dominated by declarations about his imminent death and departure (12:20-36). The arrival of the eschatological "hour" amounts to judgment (νῦν) on this world and its ruler (12:31), which then leads (κἀγώ) Jesus to pronounce that when he is lifted up from the earth (ἐὰν ὑψωθῶ ἐκ τῆς γῆς)

---

30. See further Williams, *I am He*, 255-303.

31. Whoever accepts or refuses this revelation will come to life or death (cf. John 3:16-21; 3:31-36; 5:19-29; 12:46-50). See Williams, *I am He*, 269-70.

he will draw all (πάντας) to himself (12:32). With regard to the immediate context of this declaration—but also the cumulative effect of the three sayings—there is no doubt that the primary connotation of ὑψόω here is the physical elevation of Jesus on the cross. That it refers to the manner of his death is confirmed by John's inclusion of an explanatory aside (12:33: ποίῳ θανάτῳ; cf. 18:31-32), although it cannot be ruled out that a second-level connotation (elevation-as-exaltation) is also embedded in that explanation. Nevertheless, with an echo of Jesus' initial (3:14b), rather than final, words (12:32) about his "lifting up," the crowd's response indicates that they interpret Jesus' declaration in terms of his departure by death and fail to grasp any other possible level of meaning.

As with the other two "lifting up" sayings, the immediate—and in this case slightly wider—context provides some clarification about the intended meaning of ὑψόω (12:32a), particularly with a view to its anticipated consequences (12:32b). In this respect the drawing of people to Jesus as a result of his elevation is often interpreted in the light of the earlier statement about the necessity for a grain of wheat to die (12:24): it is by means of his death that Jesus brings fruit and draws "all" to himself, as proleptically implied by the request of the Greeks to see him (cf. 12:20-22).[32] Indeed, as was highlighted earlier in this essay with reference to texts other than John's Gospel, the description of Jesus being lifted up "from the earth" may deliberately play on the visual aspect of him being set up high on a cross *for all to see* (cf. 3:14), so that it is Jesus exalted to God on the cross who can offer salvation for those who "see" him. This need not imply that he literally draws believers to himself at the moment of crucifixion; it is rather the consequence of post-Easter "remembering" of the true significance of his death. Having said that, the inclusion of the phrase ἐκ τῆς γῆς (12:32b), otherwise not encountered in the "lifting up" sayings, opens up—or even confirms—the other semantic possibilities of ὑψόω: Jesus' exaltation involves his return from the world "below" to the heavenly sphere "above," in full circle following his descent to earth ἐκ τοῦ οὐρανοῦ (3:13).

What is striking, and rarely noted by scholars, is that John's gradual elucidation of the "lifting up" theme coincides with a progressively more explicit outworking of links between Jesus and the Isaianic servant. On the first occasion (3:14), the possible influence of Isaiah's portrayal of the servant is restricted to the verb ὑψόω itself (3:14). The connection between them is more apparent in the second saying (8:28), particularly due to the linking of two key Isaianic motifs (ὑψόω and ἐγώ εἰμι). Indeed, the reasoning behind

---

32. See in particular Frey, *Die johanneische Eschatologie III*, 279-80. Cf. also Knöppler, *Die theologia crucis*, 161-63.

drawing these two motifs together—as an expression of Jesus' oneness with God—becomes clearer when it is noted that the closest Deutero-Isaianic parallel to Jesus' words (τότε γνώσεσθε ὅτι ἐγώ εἰμι) occurs in Isa 43:10 LXX: God's role as witness is added to that of "the servant whom I have chosen," so that the ἐγώ εἰμι claim that follows can even be read as their joint proclamation. Nevertheless, the fullest and most intricately woven explication of Jesus' mission through an Isaianic lens (52:12–53:1) occurs in relation to his final "lifting up" saying: declarations about his future glorification (12:23) and exaltation (12:32, 34) come about as a result of the approach by the Greeks to "see" (ἰδεῖν) him, thus fulfilling Isaiah's prophecy that nations who had not previously been told about the servant will eventually see (52:15 LXX: ὄψονται).[33] This stands in stark contrast, "as the prophet Isaiah said," to the inability of "the Jews" to believe in Jesus because their eyes have been blinded (John 12:37–40; quoting Isa 53:1 and 6:9–10). Thus, the Isaianic testimony bubbling under the surface since the early stages of this narrative now comes to clear expression in John's reflections on seeing—and not seeing—Jesus' true identity and mission.

SEEING THE EXALTED ONE

It seems evident, after examining all three of the Johannine "lifting up" sayings, that semantic interaction between the literal and metaphorical use of ὑψόω is designed to underscore the opaque character of Jesus' words. That Jesus' death by crucifixion is central to John's "elevation-as-exaltation" framework is indicated by both the content and sequential effect of the sayings, particularly their emphasis on the necessity of the cross as a means to divine revelation and salvation for those with eyes to "see" (cf. 3:13–21; 12:27–36). What is less frequently observed is that these passages also exhibit another level of verbal dynamics, due to the multilayered significance of ὑψόω *within* its second (figurative) level of meaning. In other words, a degree of open-endedness characterizes the Johannine use of ὑψόω until the very end, because even the process of gradual elucidation from the first, through the second, to the third pronouncement does not conclude with a clear-cut scenario of exaltation. What kind of exaltation is envisaged? Is it Jesus' elevation in honor and glory on the cross, or does it (also) anticipate his exaltation in heaven following his return to the Father? Its description as a characteristically Johannine example of *double entendre* does not, as a

---

33. The influence of Isaiah 52–53 on John 12:20–43 has received considerable attention in recent decades. See especially Evans, "Obduracy," 232–36; Beutler, "Greeks," 341–46; Frey, "'Wie Mose,'" 188–89.

result, really capture the polyvalence of ὑψόω and the way that it operates within the narrative.

A post-Easter perspective inevitably shapes the way(s) in which John interprets Jesus' death, which is why so many scholars have claimed that his "lifting up" by crucifixion cannot be viewed in isolation from his return to the Father; it belongs to the "cross event" which must also incorporate Jesus' resurrection and ascension.[34] Raymond Brown, for this reason, draws the following conclusion:

> In John, "being lifted up" refers to one continuous action of ascent: Jesus begins his return to the Father as he approaches death (xiii 1) and completes it only with his ascension (xx 17). ... The first step in the ascent is when Jesus is lifted up on the cross; the second step is when he is raised up from death; the final step is when he is lifted up to heaven.[35]

Though describing Jesus' ascent as "continuous," it seems that Brown envisages a temporally orientated three-stage process, but one that plays down the *metaphorical* focus of the language of "elevation-as-exaltation" and, arguably, literalizes the second-level meaning of ὑψόω in order to (re)introduce the notion of ascent through physical "lifting up." This is not to deny the inextricable link between Jesus' death and resurrection in the Gospel of John, as indeed has been persuasively argued by Andrew Lincoln in a number of his studies on John's Gospel.[36] The heightened ambiguity of ὑψόω within the Gospel narrative in fact accentuates the inseparability of Jesus' death and resurrection insofar as the salvation of believers is concerned. Nevertheless, it does not follow that the interplay of the literal/figurative associations of ὑψόω is being used by John to convey the "beginning" of a temporal sequence of events. To argue in this way is to overlook the fact that John's Gospel is underpinned by two different axes—vertical and horizontal. There is no doubt that, with a view to the vertical-spatial perspective of John's "lifting up" imagery, Jesus' ascent "from the earth" (12:32) involves his elevation to, and oneness with, the Father. However, by virtue of the complex, sometimes "irrational,"[37] nature of metaphorical language, to speak, *within discourse,* about the vertical-spatial "lifting up" of Jesus cannot necessarily be dovetailed with the horizontal-temporal perspective

---

34. See, e.g., van der Watt, "The Cross/Resurrection Events," 123–41, who speaks of the "cross-resurrection events" as different facets of one integrated event, albeit without collapsing the different events into an undistinguishable whole (123 n.1).

35. Brown, *John*, I:146.

36. Lincoln, "'I Am the Resurrection and the Life,'" 122–44; Lincoln, *John*, 13.

37. Meeks, "Man from Heaven," 191.

that characterizes John's *narrative* of the death, resurrection (and ascension) of Jesus (cf. John 19–20). Thus, while the vertical and horizontal axes of John's Gospel may frequently intersect with each other, it does not always follow that they can be fully harmonized with one another.[38] Jesus' heavenly exaltation on/from the cross may well be viewed as a prefiguring of his post-resurrection exaltation, but this is not explored in the text because this is simply not where John's interest lies.

The enduring effect of ὑψόω within John's narrative is that it succeeds, through a single metaphorical image, to encapsulate two fundamentally different perspectives on the significance of Jesus' death by crucifixion. From an earthly perspective, this is no more than his physical "lifting up" on the cross, but, for those with eyes to "see," it signifies his exaltation to the Father's presence, whether on the cross or in heaven—it is a vision of divine reality that can only be seen "from above."

---

38. For another example of how the vertical and horizontal axes of John's narrative cannot be superimposed on each other, see Williams, "Abraham," 216–18.

6

John, Jesus, and "The Ruler of This World"
Demonic Politics in the Fourth Gospel?

N. T. WRIGHT, with J. P. DAVIES
University of St. Andrews

INTRODUCTION

ONE MIGHT THINK THAT of all the New Testament books the least likely to be caught up in debates about anti-imperial politics would be the Gospel of John. The old nineteenth-century prejudices about John linger on. John is a "spiritual" gospel, a "theological" gospel, not like the rough-and-tumble Synoptics, still less like that argumentative fellow Paul. John is about the incarnation of the Word, the love of God in sending the Son, and the glory revealed on the cross. At the heart of John we find the Farewell Discourses, seen by many as the deepest and richest focus and source of Christian spirituality. What can all this have to do with the messy business of politics, still less the dangerous suggestion of a counter-imperial agenda?

And yet, before we even glance at contemporary scholarship, we should pause. John is a deeply *Jewish* book: the older prejudice that screened out his

Jewishness in favor of non-Jewish Hellenistic settings is just that, a prejudice. From the first two chapters we ought already to know that this author is soaked in Genesis and Exodus, in Isaiah and the Psalms, and not least in a temple-theology from which both his christology and his Pneumatology gain their meanings. His closest cousins—different, but with family likenesses—are Ben-Sirach, the Wisdom of Solomon, and indeed the Scrolls, rather than the Stoics or the gnostics. The running battle in the Fourth Gospel between Jesus and the Judaeans (I call them that because "the Jews" is obviously misleading, and it is not clear to me that John's οἱ Ἰουδαῖοι always and only means "the Jewish leaders") is a family squabble, and should not be seen as a non-Jewish gospel breaking free of Judaism altogether. And from all we know about first-century Judaism we have to say that the political agenda was never far from the surface. To put it no more strongly, if we are telling a story about a would-be Jewish leader, whose followers considered him to be Messiah, who clashed repeatedly with the Jewish authorities and was finally put to death by the Romans, then this story is a lot more "political" than many older views would have allowed. And as for the Farewell Discourses—well, that is where Jesus warned his followers that the world would hate them, that they would be put out of the synagogues, and that (whatever this means) "the ruler of this world," ὁ ἄρχων τοῦ κόσμου τούτου, was coming to get him, but that Jesus had conquered the world, νενίκηκα τὸν κόσμον (15:18; 16:2; 14:30; 16:33). What does this mean, and how does it all fit together? Might there, after all, be some links, however submerged, to that other great Johannine book, the far more obviously political "Revelation of St. John the Divine"?

In offering this gift, in admiration, to a scholar whose company I have enjoyed in our shared pursuits over forty years or so, I should make it clear that I claim no long or deep acquaintance with contemporary Johannine scholarship. However, in some of my more popular speaking and writing I have frequently been drawn to the extraordinary scene in chapters 18 and 19 where Jesus and Pilate confront one another, representing the kingdom of God and the kingdom of Caesar, and I have ventured the suggestion that this is the heart of the New Testament's political theology.[1] So I want here to take a fresh look at that scene, drawing in some key strands from earlier in the Gospel, and make some tentative suggestions. I am bracketing out any discussion of history, whether the actual events concerning Jesus or the putative situation of the Johannine community. I want to focus on the text and what seems to me its own inner dynamic, rhetoric, and logic.

---

1. E.g. Wright, *How God Became King*, esp. 144–47; 229–32.

RECENT STUDY

Many recent studies of John have bypassed the theme of politics and empire altogether. Craig Keener's massive two-volume commentary says almost nothing on this subject. Richard Bauckham's collection of essays on John[2] does not address the subject, even in his quite substantial piece on Jewish Messianism in the Fourth Gospel (ch. 10, 207–38). The solid volume on *The Gospel of John and Christian Theology* which emerged from the St. Andrews conference of 2003[3] seems to ignore the theme altogether, though there are some interesting related reflections in the essay by Sigve Tonstad (193–210). At the popular level, commentaries and introductions proceed as though there were nothing there to discuss, an example being the work of Andreas Koestenberger.[4]

Some of those who have written on empire in the New Testament have actually suggested that John's whole presentation is running in the other direction from the counter-imperial material that many discern elsewhere. The articles of Kvalbein and Hengel[5] are fairly adamant on the subject. A much more nuanced statement is found in Stephen Moore's book *Empire and Apocalypse*.[6] His chapter on John argues for two quite different strands. In one sense, he says, John is the most political of the Gospels, recognizing the political dimensions and dangers inherent in Jesus' presence and mission. At another level, however, "John is also the *least* political of the canonical gospels . . . because the same passion narrative seems to place Jesus' kingship front and centre only in order to depoliticize it."[7] Moore at once applies a classic postcolonial hermeneutic of suspicion:

> If the Roman prefect's "I find no crime in him" (18:38) is to be construed—approvingly and unequivocally—as meaning that the Jewish Messiah's brand of kingship is not, in the end, a threat to the Roman Emperor's brand, then pro-Roman apologetics would here seem to be extending themselves to the limit and paving the royal road to the fourth century and an unproblematic fusion of Christianity and Rome.[8]

---

2. Bauckham, *The Testimony of the Beloved Disciple*.
3. Bauckham and Mosser, eds., *The Gospel of John and Christian Theology*.
4. Koestenberger, *Encountering John*.
5. Kvalbein, "The Kingdom of God and the Kingship of Christ," 227–28, following Hengel, "Reich Christi, Reich Gottes und Weltreich"; see the discussion in Moore, *Empire and Apocalypse*, 51.
6. Moore, *Empire and Apocalypse*.
7 Ibid., 50f.
8 Ibid., 52.

The irony then, says Moore, is that it is the chief priests who see Jesus as a political danger. However, though for Moore the Fourth Gospel thus appears to be the charter document of Constantinian Christianity—appearing to allow Rome the freedom to develop without the threat of the imminent judgment that is found in the apocalyptic tradition in the Synoptics and Revelation—it nevertheless contains embedded within it "the most trenchant critique of Roman imperialism of any of the canonical gospels," partly through its inclusion of Rome within the "world" that it denounces, partly through its structuring of the narrative of Jesus' trial and torture, and partly through "the searing critique of the fundamental machinations of the *imperium Romanum*" within that same narrative structure.[9] As will become apparent, my conclusion about Moore is the same as Moore's about John: absolutely right in some ways, massively wrong in others.[10]

There has recently been a flurry of detailed "John-and-empire" studies. There is a useful survey by Francis Moloney in the *Expository Times*,[11] pointing out some of the "back markers" in this discussion, and offering a brief and clear description of the three main recent works, those of Richey in 2007,[12] Carter in 2008,[13] and Thatcher in 2009.[14] Warren Carter steps aside from the usual idea of positing a church/synagogue split behind the Fourth Gospel, and suggests that the anti-synagogue material is a "hidden transcript" in which "the Jews" are actually to be subsumed under the larger entity of Roman imperial power. Carter locates the whole drama in Ephesus, where the privileged Jewish elite have been over-accommodating to the empire, while John is urging Christ-believers to distance themselves from any such position. Moloney, summarizing Carter's position, says that, if Carter is right, "everything written [about John] over the past 150 years will become marginal."[15] I see this as itself a hidden transcript for Moloney's own view, which is that Carter has considerably overstated his case, not least where Carter suggests that we should read Johannine christology in the light of Caligula's attempt in AD 40 to install in the Jerusalem temple a statue of himself as Zeus. That is a cat-among-the-pigeons proposal which is so sharp and surprising that it deserves more study, certainly in the light

---

9 Ibid., 74.

10. Ibid., 74–75.

11. Moloney, "Recent Johannine Studies," 424–26.

12. Richey, *Roman Imperial Ideology and the Gospel of John*.

13. Carter, *John and Empire: Initial Explorations*.

14. Thatcher, *Greater than Caesar*.

15. Moloney, *Recent Johannine Studies*, 424.

of the Fourth Gospel's temple focus. But at this point I am inclined to agree with Moloney that Carter has stretched the evidence further than it will go.

Lance Richey retains the usual view of a church/synagogue split, but he finds explicit anti-Roman polemic in several parts of the Gospel. In particular, he offers a counter-imperial reading of the Prologue that even I, straining my ears to catch such overtones, found hard to detect. He does, however, have an interesting discussion of the trial narrative, which as I have said I consider to be the heart of the matter.[16]

Tom Thatcher attempts to answer Stephen Moore. He, like Carter and Richey, focuses on Johannine christology, arguing that "imperial terms were foundational to John's Christology, and that his thinking about Christ was always informed by the premise that Jesus is greater than Caesar."[17] Like Carter, he sees the Jewish authorities in John as a puppet aristocracy doing its best to maintain the status quo and thus effectively being a sub-branch of empire. This turns on its head a more usual reading of the Gospel, in which the Jewish authorities are the real enemy throughout, with Pontius Pilate being wheeled on reluctantly at the end to do what the chief priests tell him. In particular, Thatcher goes against the grain in reading John 12:31, "now this world's ruler is going to be thrown out,"[18] as referring not to Satan but to Caesar.[19] That is important, and we must return to the point.

This is hardly a complete literature review on this topic.[20] But I hope it is sufficient to indicate that John belongs on the map of current studies of early Christianity and the Roman Empire, and to form something of a platform for the close readings of the text to which I now turn.

Before we move on, however, it is important to face one question in particular. Almost all commentators seem to take it for granted that the phrase ὁ ἄρχων τοῦ κόσμου refers naturally and only to the devil or "the

---

16. Richey, *Roman Imperial Ideology and the Gospel of John*, 153–84.

17. Thatcher, *Greater than Caesar*, 11.

18. All English translations of the NT are taken from my own translation, *The Kingdom New Testament* (in the UK, *The New Testament for Everyone*).

19. Ibid., 116–17.

20. In his work *Truth on Trial*, Andrew Lincoln suggests that the "ruler of the world" is Satan (106). But at several points in the book he firmly holds together the "cosmic" nature of the "trial" that is taking place with the "political" dimension; though I think he is sometimes using the word "cosmic" to indicate a universal, worldwide significance (as opposed to a merely local, Jewish one): e.g., 123–24.; 256; 321 (the opposition is "both supernatural and human," though the latter, the "unbelieving world," is represented by "the Jews"). At p. 258 Lincoln appears to distinguish between "the ruler of this world" and the Jewish and Roman authorities. I hope in this tribute to bring some further clarity to these and related matters.

Satan."[21] But is this really the best way to take ἄρχων? The entry in BDAG, when dealing with Luke and Paul, lists human officials, whether Jewish or pagan, as possible meanings; but when it comes to John, it classifies the word in reference to evil spirits, placing John 12:31, 14:30, and 16:11 alongside the ἄρχων τῶν δαιμονίων of the Synoptics (e.g., Matt 12:24).[22] But this seems simply to beg the question. Walter Wink, in his quite thorough survey, points out that in the Septuagint the word always denotes human authorities, and that this holds true for Josephus and Philo as well, despite them having plenty to say about evil spirits.[23] The more we read John within an assumed broadly Jewish setting, the more the language of world rulership ought to remind us of the apocalyptic literature in which "suprahuman" rulers are invoked in order to highlight the cosmological dimensions of earthly "political" life, not to separate the one from the other. From this background, it would be natural to assume that a phrase like ὁ ἄρχων τοῦ κόσμου in John could refer *both* to the devil/the Satan *and* to the political regime of Caesar. John, like Daniel, would be seeking to reveal to his readers the "spiritual" battles being fought behind the scenes of the "political" empires of the world. That is, more or less, the case I now want to present.

JOHN 12:20–36

As is well known, John's Gospel divides into two distinct parts, breaking at the end of chapter 12. After the Prologue, the first twelve chapters take Jesus to and fro between Galilee and Jerusalem. The narrative oscillates between the "signs," starting with the wedding at Cana, and the "discourses" which draw out their meaning. John's multiple themes are displayed from many angles: light, water, life, and so on. The advance summary statement in the

---

21. Though cf. Haenchen, *John*, 98, who reads the phrase politically in 12:31, mentioning war, torture, and the "powers of state, business, and political parties, of the mass media." Lindars, *John*, 433, says that ὁ ἄρχων τοῦ κόσμου τούτου is "obviously a reference to the Devil . . . though there is no precise parallel for it in Jewish literature." Rensberger, *Johannine Faith and Liberating Community*, tellingly, has no listing in the index for John 12:31, 14:30, or 16:11, despite the book being ostensibly about politics in the Fourth Gospel.

22. BDAG, 140.

23. See Wink, *Naming the Powers*, 151–52. The exceptions are that Philo can use *archon* for God himself; and that, in LXX Daniel, ἄρχων is used for "spiritual" authorities. In Daniel, of course, part of the point is that "spiritual" realities are shown up as standing behind scenes of earthly political domination: see Portier-Young *Apocalypse against Empire*. Wink reads the Johannine "ruler of the world" as Satan (*Naming the Powers*, 42 n.9; 61), but links this with the Jewish authorities (9) and elsewhere says that the Satan "could scarcely avoid being identified as the special patron of Rome" (33–34.).

Prologue that "he came to his own, and his own people did not receive him" is demonstrated in numerous confrontations, some very sharp, between Jesus and οἱ Ἰουδαῖοι, "the Judaeans," the inhabitants of Jerusalem and its immediate environs. Jesus is threatened with stoning for blasphemy, and his death is openly plotted, for nakedly political reasons, by Caiaphas and his colleagues at the end of chapter 11: "If we let him go on like this, everyone is going to believe in him! Then the Romans will come and take away our holy place and our nation!" (11:48). Caiaphas' answer is totally political and, for John, totally theological: "This is what's best for you: let one man die for the people, rather than the whole nation being wiped out" (11:50). John comments that this was an unintended prophecy, since Jesus would die not only for the nation, "but to gather into one the scattered children of God" (11:52). That is the background to chapter 12, and in particular to 12:20–36.

In 12:20 "some Greeks" at the festival ask Philip if they can see Jesus. This has been prepared for by the continuing irony earlier in chapter 12, where Jesus rides into Jerusalem in fulfillment of the Zechariah prophecy, with the crowds all around him, and the Pharisees conclude that they can do nothing because "the world has gone off after him" (12:19). The κόσμος is of course another major Johannine theme, straddling the line (as all creational monotheism must do) between "the world" as created by God, loved by him, and to be redeemed, and "the world" as the sphere of rebellion, corruption, and death. Here the Pharisees mean it contemptuously. But, as with Caiaphas' prophecy, John believes that they have said more than they knew. Hence the arrival of the Greeks. "The world" is the pagan world; who then is its present "ruler"?

When Philip and Andrew tell Jesus about the Greeks' request, Jesus does not say, "Very well; I will see them presently." He appears to go off into quite a different subject: "The time has come. This is the moment for the Son of Man to be glorified" (12:23). As often in John, however, within the apparent *non sequitur* we should discern a deeper theme. Jesus sees the arrival of the Greeks as the sign that the hour had come—"the hour" which was "not yet" from 2:4 up to this point. Does John intend his readers to understand that Jesus is invoking the scenario in Dan 7, where "one like a Son of Man" becomes lord and ruler of the whole world? As usual in John, we are not told. But clearly this glorification has to do with Jesus' death, with the grain of wheat that must fall into the earth and die in order to bear much fruit (12:24). Then comes the real "response" to the Greeks. Jesus prays that the Father would glorify his name, and the thunderous voice responds that this has been done and will be done. John's Jesus draws the conclusion, in other words, that *the arrival of the Greeks is the sign that he himself, through his death, is going to be the new ruler of the world, displacing the present one:*

"Now comes the judgment of this world! Now this world's ruler is going to be thrown out! And when I've been lifted up from the earth, I will draw all people to myself" (12:31–32).

With this we are suddenly introduced to a new theme. The "ruler of the world" has not been mentioned before in John. The parallels often adduced to this phrase are not exact. Second Corinthians 4:4 speaks of "the god of this αἰών," and Eph 2:2 of "the ruler of the power of the air"; we might compare Eph 6:12; Jas 4:4, Luke 4:6; and, back in the Johannine literature, 1 John 4:4 and 5:19, the last of these speaking of the whole world lying ἐν τῷ πονηρῷ, in the power of the evil one. Taken together, even though none is exactly parallel, all these seem to indicate the conclusion that almost all commentators have reached: that "the ruler of the world" here refers, unambiguously and only, to the Satan, the devil. This then points on to some kind of *Christus Victor* reading of Jesus' death: the cross will be the means of the Satan's overthrow.[24]

But ought we to accept this either/or so easily? Are we so sure that John, or any of the early Christians, would have pushed such a thick wedge between satanic power and political power? Granted the clearly political edge to the machinations of Caiaphas and his colleagues, and granted the clearly political hints earlier in the Gospel—such as Jesus perceiving that the crowd want to come and make him king—I have my doubts. And these are confirmed when we look into both the Farewell Discourses and the trial narrative itself.

THE FAREWELL DISCOURSES

The Farewell Discourses (chapters 13 to 17) are so well known that we often fail to note their extraordinary rhetorical effect within the book as a whole. From the tense moments in chapters 7, 8, and 9, the narrative has been gathering pace. The "Good Shepherd" discourse in chapter 10 is not, as it has been so often portrayed, a soft-focus pastoral scene. It is nakedly political: all who came before were thieves and brigands, κλέπται καὶ λῃσταί, but the sheep did not listen to them. Jesus, however, will lay down his life for the sheep. We are not surprised when things again turn ugly, and stoning is threatened. Jesus goes off to the Jordan, but then, despite the disciples' warnings, comes back to Judea to raise Lazarus. The reader knows how this will end, and Caiaphas' prophecy confirms it. Then comes the triumphal

---

24. See, e.g., Barrett, *John*, 426–27; Morris, *John*, 597–98. An interesting exception is Temple, *Readings in St. John's Gospel*, 198–99, assuming without argument that the reference is to Caiaphas and Pilate.

entry, and then the passage we have just seen: the grain of wheat falling into the earth, the world's ruler being thrown out, and Jesus himself being lifted up to draw all people to himself.

By this time—this is my point about rhetorical effect—the reader is on tiptoe with excitement. Each time Jesus has been to Jerusalem, up to now in the narrative, there has been some kind of confrontation, usually in connection with one of the great festivals (Passover, Tabernacles, Hanukah, now Passover again). Each time we hear overtones from the Prologue, where the Word became flesh and "tabernacled" in our midst; from chapter 2 onwards we have been informed that Jesus himself is the new temple, so that the long-awaited returning Shekinah is coming back to Zion at last. The prophecies, particularly of Isaiah, are now coming true. Now, therefore, the reader is agog: how is it going to play out? How will Jesus be "lifted up"? What will happen in his final showdown with the authorities?

John surely knows what he is doing, but in narratival terms it feels very strange. Instead of taking us straight into the final flurry of activity, he leads us into the upper room, and holds us there for five chapters, nearly a fifth of the whole Gospel. There is barely any activity, other than the initial footwashing, the departure of Judas, and the hint at the end of chapter 14 that the little party is leaving the upper room ("Get up. Let's be going"; 14:31). The discourse is helped on its way by a few short questions, but these chapters consist almost entirely of teaching. What is John saying?

For a start, he is at last taking us, not into the present temple in Jerusalem, but into what he has hinted all along is the true temple. This is where heaven and earth meet, because this is where Jesus bares his heart and soul to his friends. Here he explains that through the Spirit the temple is now to be extended into all the world. This picks up the strange little passage in 7:38, where Jesus says that "anyone who believes in me will have rivers of living water flowing out of their heart," in accordance with a scriptural prophecy that, though unnamed, must be Ezek 47:1–12, distantly echoing Gen 2:10–14. All this reaches its peak in the so-called high priestly prayer in chapter 17, where the long-promised revelation of the divine glory is to take place, not in the Jerusalem temple, but in Jesus and his followers and in their common life.

One might say that all this was already "political." The Jerusalem temple was after all the center, not of a "religion" in a modern sense, but of an embattled but proud community. It was the symbol of hope and, sometimes, of resistance. That was why Antiochus Epiphanes had paganized it two centuries earlier, and it was why Caligula wanted to do the same thing in the 40s. To say, as John's Jesus does, "but *this* is the true temple" is thus both to upstage the present temple—and its hierarchy, of course—and to reaffirm the central symbol of Jewish monotheism and culture against all pagan cult and culture, of which the most obvious new example was Rome. All this might be said, simply on the basis of a temple-understanding of the Farewell Discourses.

But at key points in the Discourses, not as their main theme, but as a persistent sub-plot, we hear a dark note that looks back to 12:31 and points forward to chapters 18 and 19. This is part of how the Discourses work. Before we get to the trial and death of Jesus, John wants us to know what these events will actually mean. In the Synoptics this is accomplished by (among other things) the Last Supper, through which Jesus says, in effect, "this is how you are to understand what is about to happen." John does something like this, only far more so: not only the footwashing, but the whole complex of the Discourses, explains from one angle after another how the reader is to grasp, and then to live by, the meaning of Jesus' death and resurrection.

The dark note in question is the express mention of the Satan. The dark powers feature less in John than in the Synoptics. There has been one mention earlier, at the end of chapter 6: one of the twelve "is a devil" (6:70); and in chapter 8 Jesus charges "the Judaeans" that they are true children of "their father the devil" (8:39–59). Now, in chapter 13, we are told in verse 2 that the devil (ὁ διαβόλος) had already put it into Judas' heart to betray Jesus; then, terrifyingly, at verse 27, Judas receives the bread from Jesus, and "the Satan entered into him," ὁ Σατανᾶς, rather than simply ὁ διαβόλος. This is the only explicit mention of "the Satan" in John, and it has its literal Hebrew force; it isn't just that Judas is demon-possessed, but rather that he becomes "the accuser," setting the prosecution of Jesus in train. So he went out, says John; ἦν δὲ νύξ, "and it was night" (13:30).

I wonder whether we should hear a larger echo at this point. If in these chapters John is constituting Jesus and his followers as the true temple, the place where God is dwelling with his people, then it is striking that in this company, as in the heavenly court in the Old Testament, we find a public prosecutor, namely, "the Satan." But he, for his own reasons, leaves the company. Is there an echo of the Satan being ejected from heaven, as in Rev 12:8-9 and indeed Luke 10:18, both echoing Isa 14:12? This is only a suggestion. But it might fit with other elements of the developing picture.

This scene, and the sense of excitement and joy that immediately follows Judas' departure, again indicates that, as with the arrival of the Greeks, John's Jesus is "reading" these events as signals which indicate where the divine plan now stands. "Now the Son of Man is glorified," he says, "and God is glorified in him" (13:31)—an explicit glance back to 12:23. In its context, Jesus is recognizing that the battle with the dark enemy is coming to a head. But how will that happen?

The end of chapter 14 provides at least part of the answer. "The ruler of this world is coming (ἔρχεται)," declares Jesus. "He has nothing to do with me"—that's how I translate the somewhat compressed ἐν ἐμοὶ οὐκ ἔχει οὐδέν—"but all this is happening so that the world may know that I love the Father, and that I'm doing what the Father has told me to do" (14:30-31). This passage, of course, likewise echoes 12:20-36. The theme introduced at that point is starting to expand and find its way into the interpretative grid through which John wants us to understand chapters 18 and 19.

In particular, it compels us to question whether "the ruler of this world" in these passages can simply be "the Satan" or "the devil." What would it mean, in chapter 14, to speak of the Satan as "coming"? When we finally reach chapter 18, the one who "comes" (ἔρχεται) is Judas himself (18:3), with an entire cohort of Roman troops (a σπεῖρα, under the authority of a χιλίαρχος (18:12), an officer above a centurion), as well as the police under the command of the chief priests and the Pharisees.[25] However we divide up this company, John seems to intend that we should see the arrest as fulfilling the prediction of 14:30; and, if that is so, we already find a further link with 12:20-36. "The ruler of the world" may, in one sense, be the Satan. But if we continue with that meaning we have to say that Judas, the one into whom the Satan had entered (13:2, 27), was leading a Roman force, with Jewish assistance as well, that was doing the Satan's work. As in chapter 12, the "ruler" is the one who currently has charge of the gentile nations, and when the Greeks come to see Jesus this is taken as a sign that Jesus, in being lifted up as the Son of Man, will cast out the world's ruler and draw all people to himself instead. I thus agree with, but go much further than, Craig Keener's suggestion that "one might think of a coalescence of imperial and antichrist images."[26] At this point I think we are looking at a phenomenon whose most obvious parallel would be in the book of Revelation, where the imperial power and the satanic force are somehow either combined or at least in close alliance, working hand in glove. One thinks of the dragon and the beast in Rev 13:2.

This impression is strongly confirmed, for me at least, by the difficult passage in 16:8-11. The coming Spirit, Jesus declares, will act not only as Advocate on behalf of the disciples, but also, through them, as prosecuting counsel—against "the world." The Spirit will "prove the world to be in the wrong on three counts: sin, justice and judgment." The tables will be turned. Instead of the world holding the church to account, through the Spirit the

---

25. See Moore, *Empire and Apocalypse*, 53

26. Keener, *The Gospel of John*, 879-80, points out that in pagan literature phrases like "ruler of the world" could be applied both to divinities and to the emperor.

church is to hold the world to account. And "the world" here cannot simply be the demonic power or powers that stand behind actual people and events. These are real humans, real human systems.

The critical charge, for our present purposes, is the third one. The first two matter as well, of course: the world is guilty of sin (of which disbelief in Jesus is the all-important symbol); the world is guilty in relation to justice (because God is vindicating Jesus, thereby proving that the world's judgment on him was wrong). But the third charge points to a further dimension: the world is guilty in relation to judgment itself, "because the ruler of this world is judged."

Once again, we have a clear echo of 12:31. Once again, therefore, we ask, who is "the ruler of this world"? Is it enough to say that this is the Satan, or more generally the diabolical force? I think not. When the Satan is thrown out of heaven, the human powers that have attained their status through their Faustian pacts with the Satan are overthrown as well. "The ruler of this world" is coming to get Jesus: that is, Judas is coming with the Roman cohort, and with the temple police to back them up. In the lurid imagery of Rev 13, the beast from the sea is accompanied by the beast from the land. "The world has gone after him," but now in a different sense (John 12:19).

But this is to be the moment, not of Jesus' defeat, but of his victory. The last word of teaching, before the prayer of chapter 17, is a shout of triumph: "Cheer up! I have defeated the world! (νενίκηκα τὸν κόσμον)" (16:33). This is again an unmistakable *Christus Victor* statement, comparable to Col 2:14–15 and to the hint in 1 Cor 2:8, where "the rulers of this world" put the Lord of glory to death because they did not understand the "hidden wisdom" of the gospel—a very Johannine passage. All this leads the eye up to the great scene with which John's Gospel reaches its climax. John's readers are to leave the exalted world of the Discourses, but they are to take with them, as they return to the messy and dangerous world of event, the rich and layered world of meaning which they have now been shown. The Word of chapters 13–17 becomes the flesh of chapters 18 and 19.

JOHN 18–19

There is a sense in which, for John, Gethsemane has already taken place in chapter 12, where Jesus' heart was troubled, wondering if he should pray for rescue but determining to pray for God to be glorified (12:27–28). We know, by now, that these events are to be the way in which God will indeed be glorified: this is how Jesus will accomplish that goal, how he will conquer and cast out the ruler of the world, and so draw all people to himself. The brief hearing before the high priest, interspersed with Peter's denial, leads the eye quickly to the main scene, which comprises 18:26—19:16. Here we find the three-cornered conversation between Pilate, Jesus, and the chief priests, with "the Judaeans" as the crowd in the background.

There are many points we could make here. Stephen Moore draws attention to the flogging and violent mocking coming in 19:1–3—right in the middle of the "trial." This is how Roman justice works, and John may well be making that point. There are many levels of irony, particularly in what the chief priests say. There are many ways of reading Pilate's character and of suggesting the levels of motivation, manipulation, and political machination that seem to be going on between him and the chief priests.[27]

But the themes that dominate this set piece are those of kingship, truth, and power. This is where the kingdom of God finally confronts the kingdoms of the world; putting it like that will rightly re-awaken echoes of Daniel, and once more of Revelation as well. This is a *political* scene that can only be understood through the lens of *apocalyptic* imagery. Just as, throughout his gospel, John has wanted his readers to think of the *logos* whenever they look at Jesus, so, more subtly perhaps, he wants his readers now to think of 12:31, 14:30–31, 16:33, and perhaps especially 16:8–11, as they overhear the conversation between Jesus and Pilate. They are, in other words, to listen to Pilate and recognize the voice of "the ruler of this world." They are to listen to Jesus and realize that this is what it sounds like to convict the world of sin, of justice, and of judgment. They are to watch the whole scene, ending with the crucifixion itself, and are to discern that this is what it looks like when the ruler of this world is defeated and cast out.

The main theme that arches across the whole discourse is kingship and kingdom. "Are you the king of the Jews?" asks Pilate (18:33), who has obviously got this information from somewhere else because the chief priests, in this narrative, are remarkably reticent on the point. The theme returns again and again: Pilate uses the phrase "king of the Jews" as a title when asking if he should release Jesus (18:39); the soldiers use it in mockery (19:3); Pilate, showing Jesus to the crowd, says "here is your king" (19:14), and then asks "shall I crucify your king?" (19:15). Then, of course, comes the greatest irony, when Pilate places the "title" on the cross, "Jesus of Nazareth, the King of the Jews" (19:19), deliberately offending the chief priests (19:21–22). Clearly, kingship—and the "king of the Jews" motif in particular—is what John regards as the underlying theme of the entire scene.

---

27. Moore, *Empire and Apocalypse*, 56–63.

That goes part of the way to explaining the sudden introduction of the charge that Jesus made himself "son of God" (19:7). This title is, of course, messianic, as in Ps 2 and elsewhere.[28] Jesus' messiahship, as well as his divine sonship, is as prominent a theme in John as in any part of the New Testament. But already by the time of Paul, and arguably for Jesus himself, the title had come to carry as well the idea of some kind of identity between Messiah and God himself.[29] That is part of the point of the Prologue, as in its final flourish: the Word who became flesh and tabernacled in our midst is the only-begotten Son of God who has uniquely made the Father known (1:18). But to assume that the messianic (and hence political) meaning has thereby been relativized or abandoned is to capitulate once more to an older ideological disjunction which historical scholarship has been teaching us to overcome.

We should not, then, assume that with the charge that "he made himself son of God" in 19:7 the Jewish leaders have shifted to the "spiritual" or "theological" plane and hence away from the political one. Pilate's nervousness in 19:8 ("when Pilate heard that, he was all the more afraid") is often explained as the result of religious superstition, but I suspect that John intends something else. "Son of God" or "son of the deified" was of course a regular Caesar-title.[30] If Pilate were to release someone who had claimed that title, Caesar might have something to say about it. This would fit exactly with the next move from the chief priests: "if you let this fellow go, you are no friend of Caesar! Everyone who sets himself up as a king is speaking against Caesar!" (19:12). If we start our analysis with that verse and look back, we might well conclude that "Son of God" in verse 7 is at least as much about a challenge to Caesar as it is about Trinitarian christology (and are we so sure that those two are on opposite sides of some great divide?). And the last line of the trialogue seems to confirm this. The chief priests come out with the crowning irony: "We have no king except Caesar!" (19:15). They have turned the Jewish revolutionary slogan upside down: "No king but God" has collapsed into total collusion with the imperial force. Ultimately, there are only two kingdoms, God's and Caesar's, and they have chosen the latter.

Already this suggests that, for John, Jesus' death is *in some sense or other* "political." That begs several questions, of course, but nobody with any knowledge of first-century Jewish messianism could miss the point. There

---

28. Ps 2:7; cf. 2 Sam 7:12-14. See my discussion of "Son of God" as a messianic title in *Paul and the Faithfulness of God [PFG]*, 690-701.

29. E.g., Rom 1:3-4, 8:3-4, on which see again ibid., 692-700; 818-19.

30. See further ibid., 327-28.

is no precedent for, as it were, a non-political "king of the Jews." If a "king of the Jews" were to emerge, then, according to Pss 2, 72, and 89, not to mention Isa 11, he would be king of the whole world. When the Romans led Simon bar-Giora at the back of Titus' triumphal procession and then had him killed, this was the ceremonial killing of "the king of the Jews."[31] We do not have an account of bar-Kochba's last stand, but there is every reason to suppose that it would have had the same overtone.

But in what sense "political"? And in what sense "king"? Clearly John wants his readers to believe that, despite Pilate's cynicism, the title on the cross was true. But Jesus has already redefined what this "kingdom" means in the much misunderstood verse 18:36. The Authorized (King James) version, as is well known, has Jesus say "My kingdom is not of this world." Those words have been quoted times without number in support of a supposedly "other-worldly," and hence non-political, kingdom. Faced with that regular misunderstanding I have translated that verse, "My kingdom isn't the sort that grows in this world." The Greek is Ἡ βασιλεία ἡ ἐμὴ οὐκ ἔστιν ἐκ τοῦ κόσμου τούτου: my kingdom is not *from* this world. It does not take its origin from the present world—if it did, Jesus' followers would be fighting. His kingdom has a radically different character from that of Caesar. But the whole point of John's Gospel, seeing Jesus and the Spirit as the new temple, is that Jesus' kingdom is *for* the world: for the world in the sense that the creator God is decisively launching his project of new creation from within the heart of the old. There is therefore bound to be a clash: a clash of Pilate and Jesus, of Caesar's kingdom and God's, of the kingdom that comes from the world and the kingdom that comes from somewhere else. Jesus is the new king, over a new kind of community, a new πόλις which will challenge, defeat, and displace all the other sorts.

There are two particular ways in which Jesus' kingdom is marked out. The first is striking: in Jesus' kingdom, his followers will not fight to defend him (18:36b). That shows how perilously close Peter came to ruining the whole project with his sword in the garden (18:10–11), but the point stands and is vital for the theology, not only of John, but of the New Testament as a whole. The victory which Jesus wins on the cross is, by definition, the victory of *love*. That is how the second half of the Gospel begins: having always loved his own, Jesus loved them right through to the end (13:1)—which is John's introduction to the footwashing scene, a tableau which serves as both metaphor and metonymy for the themes of incarnation and crucifixion. The

---

31. On the death of Simon bar-Giora, see Josephus *War* 7.153–57; for his "royal" aspirations, punished as such by the Romans, see my *The New Testament and the People of God*, 177–78.

note of love is often restated, as for instance in chapter 10, but it is far more often enacted, and never more so than in chapter 13.

The second qualification of Jesus' kingdom is found in another apparent *non sequitur*. Pilate pounces on Jesus' mention of a kingdom: "So you *are* a king, are you?" (18:37). Jesus turns the question in an unexpected direction: "You're the one who's calling me a king. I was born for this; I've come into the world for this: to give evidence about the truth. Everyone who belongs to the truth listens to my voice" (18:37). The most famous line here is of course Pilate's response: "Truth! What's that?" (18:38), and many appropriate comments can be made about the way in which, in Caesar's kingdom, there is no such thing as truth—only power. But did Jesus just change the subject? What has "truth" got to do with "kingdom"?

This fits into another of John's major themes, not only "truth" itself but, as in the title of Andrew Lincoln's book, "truth on trial."[32] The whole Gospel is framed as a courtroom drama: indeed, if we are looking for "forensic justification," John is a much richer place to start than Paul. And Jesus himself is, of course, the supreme witness to the truth. This goes to the heart, not only of John's soteriology, but of his cosmology, and that in turn provides the frame for the political point. Truth, for John, is neither simply "the facts on the ground," nor simply "the ideal" which one may infer behind them. John is neither an Aristotelian nor a Platonist. He believes that the world is God's world, *and that the world is being redeemed and remade in, through, and around Jesus himself.* Jesus himself *is* the truth, because he embodies God's new world; he is the new reality, the new creation. His death will be the means of breaking the grip of sin and death, the grip (in other words) of the Satan on the old world; his resurrection will launch the new creation whose radical truth will reshape all other truth. Bearing witness to the truth means telling, and enacting, God's judgment on the untruth of the present world, and enabling the launch of the new one.

Caesar's empire, in the person of Pilate, can make neither head nor tail of all this. Nor can the priests and the crowd, who choose the truth of the old world when they choose Barabbas, the brigand. And that is where the flogging and the mocking begin: legalized violence is Pilate's real answer to Jesus' strange words about his kingdom. That, John is saying, is paradoxically the way in which Jesus reveals the truth. "Look, here's the man!" (19:5) answers directly to the ὁ λόγος σὰρξ ἐγένετο in the Prologue: here is the Image of God, bruised and bleeding, in royal crown and robes. Here, on the sixth day of the week, is the Son of Man, now to be given glory and honor,

---

32. Cf. also the similarly titled work of Harvey, *Jesus on Trial.*

with all things in subjection under his feet, as he is lifted high upon the cross, drawing all people to himself.

There are many points one could make here. Anyone with half an ear for irony would, by now, have seen that John is denouncing the empire of Caesar as a hollow sham. It doesn't care about truth; it doesn't know about justice; it has never heard of love. It is a kingdom "from this world," full of the inevitable idolatry, self-aggrandizement, and brutal dehumanization that goes with that. It is wrong about sin, it is wrong about justice, it is wrong about judgment. Anyone reading John's Gospel would know that, if Jesus is indeed the truth, Caesar's world is based on a lie. Is that a "political" statement? Of course it is.

And so to the final point, with even greater paradox. "Don't you know," asks Pilate, "that I have authority to let you go, and authority to crucify you?" (19:10). We might imagine that Jesus would say, "Yes, but your authority comes from Caesar, who is a blaspheming tyrant!" Instead, Jesus says, astonishingly to our ears, "You couldn't have any authority at all over me, unless it was given to you from above. That's why the person who handed me over to you is guilty of a greater sin" (19:11). Here is the balance that the early Christians seem to have kept and which subsequent generations all too easily lose. Jewish-style creational monotheism insists that God wants his world to be run by obedient humans.[33] Even Caesar has his God-given place, like the Assyrian in Isaiah or the Kittim in Habakkuk.[34] But he will be held accountable for how he exercises that role. So too will those who collude with him. "The ruler of this world is judged." And, as Jesus has thus convicted Pilate of sin, justice, and judgment, the church—this is the point of 16:8–11—must now look at this model and learn to do the same. "As the Father sent me," says the risen Jesus, as he breathes the Spirit on his disciples, "so I send you" (20.21). That is why the Farewell Discourses are what they are.

These, I suggest, are the vital elements of a Johannine political theology. I think that, taken together, the passages at which we have glanced point strongly towards "the ruler of this world" meaning *both* the Satan *and* Caesar. Teasing out how that combination works has always been difficult, but I do not think we gain anything by screening out one of the two elements. This, I think, puts me within reach of writers like Thatcher, though without embracing his overall construction. It puts me in direct conflict with Hengel and Kvalbein and most commentators. It clarifies, I think, the combination of "cosmic" and "political" advocated here and there by

---

33. Rom 13:1–7; Col. 1:15–20; *Mart. Pol.*10:2.
34. Isa 10.5–6; Hab 1:5–6.

Andrew Lincoln. The danger here, as with Horsley and others in Pauline studies, is that one might fall into the trap of saying "politics, therefore *not* theology": if any book is theological through and through, it is John.[35] That, indeed, is one reason why I think it is also political, because for John theology is about the God who loves the world, who judges the present ruler of the world, and who in Jesus the Messiah wins the victory over the world and launches his new world from within the old one. We cannot, as Stephen Moore would like to do, collapse a full-orbed political theology into a mere postcolonial critique, but nor can we allow the great Johannine themes of the word becoming flesh, of his being lifted up to reveal the divine glory, of the love that sent the Son into the world to save the world, and of the Son's own love for his own, even to the uttermost, to float free of the world where real communities live under real empires and have to learn both how to navigate them wisely and how to hold them to account.

CONCLUSION

A test for any fresh reading of a book like John might include the question: how does this proposal contribute to a fuller or richer understanding of the other great themes in this narrative? How does it contribute to incarnation, atonement, the new temple, the new exodus, new creation itself? This would be a proper subject for a whole book, but let me say just two things in conclusion.

First, the large outer themes of John's Gospel and indeed of the Bible—creation and new creation, and the role of humans within that—can never ignore their necessary political dimensions. Precisely because the one God wants his world to be wisely ruled by humans, and precisely because, in the truly human Word made Flesh, God was establishing, and now has established, his own rule of love and judgment in the heart of the world, all other human systems are called to account. Because they idolize themselves, they become blasphemous parodies of the truly human rule, and they use violence to sustain themselves in their power. In the Second Temple Jewish world, deeply informed by Daniel in particular, this bestial anti-empire was believed to have raised itself to its full height, at which point the one God was to take his judgment seat and vindicate "one like a Son of Man." Reference to Daniel is elusive in John, but this scenario illuminates the very passages we have been studying. John, I think, can be claimed as another example of a Daniel-based apocalyptic and therefore political message, in

---

35. On the pitfalls of political readings of Paul see my *Paul and the Faithfulness of God*, ch. 12.

which Rome becomes the fourth Monster from the Sea who is judged as the Son of Man is vindicated. Jesus is now the true ruler of the world, and the church must figure out what that means in practice.

Second, by placing the *Christus Victor* motif at the heart of John's atonement theology, defeating the powers at every level in order to provide the new exodus and thereby the new creation, we have not eliminated, but have rather properly contextualized, the many other strands of atonement theology in the book. Indeed, John furnishes us with powerful reasons for thinking that atonement is not a theory but an acted narrative, a narrative that reached its climax on the cross, but that now continues in the form of a community.[36] The footwashing, itself a deeply subversive social action, was a pointer, not only to what Jesus was to do on the cross, but to what his followers were to do for one another. As many have discovered, communities that follow that model, whether literally or metaphorically, work quite differently from the ways in which empires normally work. And empires do not usually appreciate that.

John's Gospel is notoriously open-ended. "What is that to you?" asks Jesus to Peter. "Follow me" (21:22). Yes, says John, ending with a comment that, though typically cryptic, is nevertheless full of explosive political and theological charge. "If all the other things which Jesus did were written down one by one, I don't think the world itself would be able to contain the books that would be written" (21:25).

---

36. For this theme see McKnight, *A Community Called Atonement*.

7

Land, Idolatry, and Justice in Romans

———⊙◆⊙———

SYLVIA C. KEESMAAT
Trinity College

IN A WORLD WHERE the destruction of land and water is the single most threatening issue for human life, it is astounding that biblical scholars still fail to grapple with the depth of biblical concern—including that of Paul—with the destruction of arable land and flowing water. By focusing the discussion on such global issues as the melting of the polar ice caps, the warming of the atmosphere, and rising sea levels (which were, of course, not even remotely in the imagination of the biblical writers), it becomes easy to sidestep the biblical call to repent of our lives of mass destruction. However, limiting our focus to these larger, global environmental issues blinds us to the fact that all environmental degradation begins in a place, a local place, a place where greed and economic exploitation trumps the care and affection of service to the land.[1] When we cease to talk about the environmental crisis in macro terms and focus rather on the abuse of the land, specific land, in the service of imperial economics, we find that the biblical writers not only had an extensive knowledge of the issues, they also named the powers and economic forces that threatened abundance, undermined fertility, and denied a sustainable future for the covenantal community.[2] In the words of

---

1. Berry makes this point in many of his writings: see, e.g., "Money vs. Goods" and "The Total Economy" in *What Matters?* 3–30; 177–93.

2. E.g., 2 Kgs 11; Isa 13:19; 20:1–6; 23; 31:1–3; 47; Jer 2:18–19; 50–51; Ezek 20:7–8;

Ellen Davis, "the Hebrew Scriptures [have a] pervasive interest in land, not only as national territory, but also, and more fundamentally, [an] interest in land as fertile, and further, in the primary human vocation to maintain its fertility (Gen 2:15)."[3] This means that Torah is concerned with faithful life in a particular place, the land of Canaan, "shared with other creatures—trees (Deut 20:19) and birds and animals (Deut 22:4, 6–7; 25:4)—whose own lives are precious and valuable."[4]

This was true not only for the writers of the Torah and prophetic literature, as Davis has shown, but also for an urban writer like Paul. Just as Jeremiah, Hosea, and Isaiah have specific realities in sight when they described the mourning of the land and the reversal of creation brought about by Israel's lack of covenantal faithfulness,[5] so also we rob Paul's language of its prophetic power if we neglect to ask what he might have meant when he said that creation was "waiting with eager longing," "subjected to futility," and "groaning in travail" (Rom 8:19, 20, 22). Reading Paul on the level of theological abstraction and dogmatic discourse prevents us from asking what, precisely, he might have meant. It is clear that *human* suffering had a solid, rooted referent for Paul, why is it that we do not assume the same for his creational references? Was there a referent that would have made sense for his language, both for him and for the hearers of his letter? What was the narrative symbolic world within which his thought moved and might this provide some insight into possible meaning for his words?[6]

I will argue that in the letter to the Romans Paul was engaged in an act of prophetic imagination that brought to expression the pain of creation in the Roman Empire, and that also provided a vision of hope for creation

---

25–32; Amos 1; 4:1–4; 5:2, 26; Hab 1–3. Watts, "Babylonian Idolatry," 115–22, notes that idols represented particular social, economic, mytho-political, and religious views and value systems. E.g., Babylonian idols are symbols of human greed, arrogance, and pride. Bel (Marduk) and Nebo were symbols of imperial privilege, power, and wealth.

3. Davis, *Scripture*, 9.

4. Ibid., 82.

5. Ibid., 3, points out that "from the eighth century B.C.E. on . . . the economics of food production was a matter contested between the crown and its agents, on the one hand, and the bulk of the population, on the other." See Jer 4:23–28 (discussed on pp. 10–11 of ibid.); Hos 4:1–3; Isa 24:1–13.

6. Although Horrell et al., *Greening Paul*, 76, also root their reading of Romans 8 in a narrative hermeneutic, their approach seems to be limited to the narrative that can be discerned from the pericope at hand. For instance, the Adam narrative is precluded from providing a background to Rom 8:19–23, even though they admit that Paul refers to it in Rom 5:12. My narrative concern is much broader, drawing not only on the wider letter, but also the intertextual context of the Scriptures of Israel to which Paul refers.

in the face of such pain.⁷ On the one hand, Paul was doing this in a manner akin to the prophets of ancient Israel; on the other, he was explicitly addressing the environmental degradation wrought by the Roman Empire.

PROPHETIC CRITIQUE

Not only do Paul's echoes of imperial rhetoric in Rom 1:1-18 (gospel, faith, justice) function to challenge the ideology of the empire,⁸ Paul's quotation from Habakkuk—"The just shall live by faith[fulness]"⁹—sets the tone of the discussion around the faithfulness of God in the letter to the Romans as a whole.¹⁰ Throughout the Psalms and Prophets, the cry is for God to come and defeat with justice those idolatrous nations that appear to be triumphing. For the Christians in Rome, living within a story where Rome's military might and victory demonstrated the blessing of the gods, where is the justice and faithfulness of their God?

Paul's quotation of Hab 2:4 raises these issues. Habakkuk's affirmations of the faithfulness of God occur in a context of judgment against the Chaldeans for their arrogance, their greedy grasping of the property of others (2:6), their economic exploitation of the poor (2:6), their shedding of human blood, and their profanation of the earth, the cities, and all who live in them (2:8). Just in case the point had not been made emphatically enough the first time, it is repeated in Hab 2:17: *this judgment is because of human bloodshed and violence to the earth, to cities, and all who live in them.* Between these two identical verses in Habakkuk 2:8 and 2:17 there is a movement between greed (πλεονεξίαν κακὴν, Hab 2:9; cf. Rom 1:29), shame (αἰσχύνην, Hab 2:10; cf. Rom 1:16) and the profanation (ἀσεβείας, Hab 2:8, 17; cf. Rom 1:18) of not only the earth in general, but of a specific piece of land (Lebanon), and the destruction of the animals (Hab 2:8, 17). The verbal echoes with shame, greed, and profanity (usually translated ungodliness in Rom 1:18) in Rom 1 are striking.

Moreover, this abusive economics, with its violence toward both land and people, is linked with idolatry (Hab 2:18-19). Such violent economic idolatry causes creation to cry out with anguish (the very stones cry out

---

7. These are the categories of Brueggemann, *Prophetic Imagination*.

8. Keesmaat, "Reading Romans in the Capital of the Empire," 51-54.

9. I am translating δικαιοσύνη as "justice" rather than "righteousness" in this chapter. Δικαιοσύνη in the LXX translates both the Hebrew משפט (justice) and צדקה (righteousness).

10. Hays, *Echoes*, 39-41.

from the wall, and the beams from the woodwork, 2:11). In contrast, in God's presence, the earth is reverently silent (2:20).

Habakkuk's affirmation of life for the just, therefore, quoted by Paul, occurs in a context of bloody idolatrous economic exploitation, with deadly effects for humanity, animals, and, as is stated repeatedly, the earth.

It would be easy to dismiss these intertextual overtones if Paul's thoughts did not immediately move to these very themes in the next verses of Romans chapter 1. Just as the wrath of God in Habakkuk is against those who profane God's earth, so Paul describes God's wrath as against those who are profane (ἀσέβειαν, usually translated "ungodly") and unjust (ἀδικίαν). Paul then links that injustice with idolatry and with a description of sexual and economic violence (Rom 1:26-31).

At the heart of such idolatry is blindness to the face of creation. Those who practice injustice do not recognize that creation reveals God's nature to them (Rom 1:19-20). Their futility (ἐματαιώθησαν, v. 21) and foolishness (ἐμωράνθησαν, v. 22) mean that they misunderstand both creature and creator (1:25). It is widely acknowledged that in the midst of this description Paul alludes to three passages from his Scriptures that provide depth for his assertions: Ps 106:20 (105:20 LXX); Jer 2:11; and Hos 4:7. What is not so widely noted, however, is the link between idolatry and the land in these passages. In Ps 106, for instance, after describing the judgment for their idolatry with the golden calf, the narrative describes Israel's turning aside from the land that they had desired, due to lack of faith in God's word (Ps 106:24).

Strikingly, the echo from Jer 2:11 comes as the climax to a section in which the Israelites are described as those who went after worthless things and became worthless (ἐματαιώθησαν, Jer 2:5 LXX), the same word root that is usually translated "futile" in Rom 1:21.[11] In Jeremiah, this futility meant that the Israelites defiled the plentiful and fruitful land that they were brought into (v. 7) by their God. Idolatry destroys the land.

Even more striking is Paul's echo of Hos 4:7. This chapter begins with God's indictment against the people who have been abusing the land: there is no faithfulness or loyalty, no knowledge of God in the land; there is swearing, lying, murder (φόνος, Hos 4:2; cf. Rom 1:29), stealing, and adultery in the land, and bloodshed follows bloodshed. Therefore the land mourns, all who live in it languish, together with the wild animals of the fields, the reptiles of the earth, the birds of the heavens, and the fish of the sea are dying. (Hos 4:2-3 LXX; MT omits the reptiles of the earth, which Paul has

---

11. Beale, *We Become What We Worship*, 209, also notes the parallel between idolatry and futility in 2 Kgs 17:15.

included in Rom 1:23). Hosea then goes on to describe the greed, injustice (ἀδικίαις, Hos 4:8; cf. Rom 1:18), and worship of idols practiced by the people (vv. 7-19).

The imagery is heartbreaking: the land is mourning, keening over the violence it has been subjected to. Every creature is languishing, has grown feeble, lost vitality. Mourning, the sapping away of life, and death; this is where idolatry leads.

Attending to these inter-texts helps explicate Paul's allusion in Rom 1: idolatry leads to a defilement of the land, to greed and violence on the land, and to a futile impotence that results in the abuse rather than the fruitful care of creation.[12]

Paul's description of idolatry in Rom 1 parallels prophetic literature and the Psalms at every point. Idolatry prevents knowledge of the true creator,[13] it is rooted in falsehood,[14] and results in futility and foolishness.[15] There is in idolatry a loss of glory,[16] and a misunderstanding of creation.[17] Finally, idolatry engenders greedy patterns of consumption, both sexually and economically.[18] No wonder idolatry always manifests itself in the lives of ancient Israelites in abuse of the land. So Davis notes:

> beginning here [Gen 3] and continuing throughout the Old Testament, land degradation (e.g., Lev 26:18-20; Deut 28:15-18) is a sure sign that humans have turned away from God. Conversely, the flourishing of the land (e.g., Lev 26:3-6, 10; Deut 28:2-5, 11-12; Isa 35; Pss 65; 72) marks a return to God. In short, the Old Testament represents the condition of the land as the single best index of human responsiveness to God.[19]

Psalmic and prophetic texts on idolatry consistently contrast knowing God as the creator of heaven and earth and giver of good gifts to God's people, with those idolaters who do not know God, who practice deceit, are

---

12. Most commentators note the parallels with Wisdom of Solomon 12-16, where the link with idolatry and economic oppression is also evident.

13. Rom 1:20-21; Hos 4:6.

14. Rom 1:25; Jer 10:14//51:17; Hab 2:18.

15. Rom 1:21-22; 2 Kgs 17:15//Jer 2:5; Pss 97:7; 115:3-8; Isa 44:9; Jer 10:2, 15; 51:17-18; Hos 5:11.

16. Rom 1:23; Pss 106:20; 115:8; Isa 42:8; Jer 2:11; Hos 4:7.

17. Rom 1:25; Isa 44:10-20; Jer 10:3.

18. Rom 1:24-31; 1 Kgs 21; Isa 2:6-8; Jer 5:7-9; 22:9-17; Ezek 18:1-19; 22:1-16, 22; Hos 4; Amos 2:6-8; Mic 6:9-16; Hab 2:9-10. Beale, *We Become What We Worship*, 203.

19. Davis, "Learning our Place," 114.

greedy for dirty money, and whose unfaithfulness brings ruin to the land.[20] These contrasts are central to Rom 1. In a letter that has God's gift of grace at its heart, seeing God's power, and indeed God's very nature through the revelation of creation is crucial. Idolatry, however, is blind to the gift that the creator has offered, and attempts to seize the abundance and fertility of the gift on its own terms—terms that result in economic exploitation, control, and death. Idolatry always renders creation mute, silencing the praise of creation. And, Paul will argue, idolatry leads to a certain kind of violent consumption which results in an abusive sexuality and an economics of greed rooted in deceit and unfaithfulness. This is where an inability to see the earth as gift will lead.[21]

Neil Elliott has made much of the parallels between Paul's description of violent sexuality in Rom 1 and the imperial household.[22] Jeramy Townsley has convincingly argued that these verses reflect the idolatrous sexual practices of the goddess religions.[23] While not wishing to dispute those overtones, I suggest that Paul's hearers would have recognized the imperial household here only because the characteristics of the rulers of Rome would have shaped the whole of Roman society.[24] Similarly, insofar as liturgy shapes wider society, the exploitative practices of sexuality found in various religious contexts would have been reflected in the practices of the household. What kind of sexuality was practiced at all levels of Roman society? A violent and predatory sexuality of exploitation and consumption. The sexual exploitation of women, slaves (of either gender), and temple prostitutes is legitimated by the idolatrous narrative of the empire, where social division and exploitation is rooted in the divine cosmology. People can be used and treated as sexual commodities when they are merely slaves of the gods rather than the image of God.[25]

Paul's description then moves from an exploitative and predatory sexuality to an exploitative and predatory economics.[26] Of the twenty be-

---

20. E.g. Pss 97; 115; 135:1–7; 146; Isa 41:17–20; Isa 45:1–8; 18–19; Jer 8:10; 9:3–14; 10:14; Hos 4:6; Hab 2.

21. On idolatry and wealth see Marcus, "Idolatry in the New Testament," 152–64; Rosner, *Greed as Idolatry*, 103–129. Beale, *We Become What We Worship*, 203, refers to Ezek 22.1–16, where idolatry is described as the root of economic and sexual sin.

22. N. Elliott, *Arrogance*, 78–83.

23. Townsley, "Paul, the Goddess Religion, Queer Sects," 707–28.

24. See MacDonald, "Slavery, Sexuality and House Churches," 94–113.

25. On humanity as slaves of the gods found in Sumero-Akkadian and Babylonian creation accounts in contrast with humanity as image of God in Genesis 1 see Middleton, *Liberating Image*, 149–219.

26. The link between violent sexuality and violent economics has been noted not

haviors that manifest a "debased mind and improper conduct" (v. 28), the first nine are used to describe economic injustice in the LXX (injustice, wickedness, greed, evil, envy, murder, quarrelling, treachery, malice; v. 29),[27] three describe the deceit that the Psalms link to economic oppression (informers, slanderers, inventors of evil; vv. 28, 29),[28] three characterize those who inhabit superior socio-economic situations, a link between riches and pride also found in the LXX (conceited, arrogant, boastful; v. 30),[29] and the last three describe attitudes that shape an ethos of injustice (faithless, heartless, and without mercy; v. 31). When Paul described the debased mind and practices of the empire, he was doing so in a way that highlighted a context of injustice, greed, and heartless, merciless economic conceit and violence. It was a world where some were the victims of the malicious and faithless actions of those who could afford to boast about their wealth and social standing, a world where envy fed backroom dealings (inventors of evil), and where the covenant ideals of economic justice had no place. This was, in short, the predatory economy of the Roman Empire.[30] As Peter Oakes points out, it is quite likely that a slave would have recognized the behavior of her master in these verses, not just in terms of sexual abuse, but also in terms of economic and social practice.[31]

Further, it is important to note that throughout Paul's Scriptures, as well as in the Roman Empire (and indeed, throughout history), economic oppression is always linked to the land: who has access to land, who is able to foreclose on land, who can bribe the judge to strip someone of their land, and, tied in with that, who has access to food and resources from the land.[32] Consequently, as Paul goes on to describe injustice in Rom 3:10–18 by means of a complex unit of quotations from various psalms, land is never far from his sights. As he describes the unjust who have no understanding and do not seek God—those whose mouths are full of death-dealing and

---

only in a biblical context (Brueggemann, "Land: Fertility and Justice"), but also more generally. On the link between the violent abuse of women and the violent abuse of the earth throughout history, see Griffin, *Women and Nature*, and Jensen, *Endgame*.

27. See Deut 2:13–15; Jer 6:6, 9; Hos 4:1–3; Mic 6:9–16; 7:1–13; Hab 2:6–17.

28. E.g., Pss 5:9; 10:7; 36:3; 140:3. All of these are quoted in Rom 3:10–18.

29. I reference here only those that use the vocabulary of Rom 1:29: Prov 15:25; 16:19; Isa 2:7–11; 13:11; Hab 2:4–5. Πλεονεξία (Rom 1:29) occurs repeatedly in the LXX to denounce violent oppression and unjust gain: Ps 10:3; Jer 22:17; Ezek 22:27–29; Hab 2:9. A number of these texts also use ἀδικία and φόνος, both found in Rom 1:29.

30. Described in N. Elliott, "Disciplining the Hope of the Poor," 180.

31. Oakes, *Reading Romans*, 133.

32. E.g., 1 Kgs 21; Hos 4:1–3; Mic 7:1–3; Hab 2:6–17. This is, of course, true in every economy, including our own.

poisonous lies that create a curse and bitterness, whose way of walking only leads to death and who create ruin and misery for the innocent who get in their way, who have no knowledge at all of what makes for peace because they do not know or seek God—we hear echoes of classic texts that describe idolatry in Israel. When we realize that the verses that Paul quotes here are largely from psalms of lament, where the faithful cry out to God for justice in the face of economic oppression that results in loss of land, we see that the classic linking of idolatry with economic abuse is as present for Paul as it was for the prophets.[33] Just as the prophets were engaged in naming the sexual, economic, and creational abuse of their times, so Paul's evocative echoes carried a whispered judgment of the powers of his own day. Such a judgment does not remain a whisper, however, as the letter progresses.

The narrative arc of Romans as a whole draws on the story of Israel, in all of its complexities around land, land loss, and land promised. The story of Adam, Abraham, the exodus, the deuteronomic promises of blessing and curse with their effect on the land, as well as the prophetic promises of restoration are all explicitly referenced in Romans.[34] The narrative arc of Romans 8 also evokes, in a tightly allusive number of verses, the calling of human beings in relation to creation, the subjection of creation to futility, creation's bondage to decay, the groaning of creation, believers, and the Spirit, and the future expectation of the freedom of the glory of the children of God, which is somehow linked to the redemption of their bodies.

Let me highlight three of these points. First, in Rom 8:20, Paul uses the language of futility to describe the bondage that creation is suffering. Futility is the language of idolatry throughout the Scriptures,[35] and as we saw, such idolatry is overwhelmingly linked to an abuse of the land. By returning to the theme of futility at this point in his argument, Paul is bringing to completion the circle that he began in Rom 1:21: the idolatry that manifests itself in Roman society is merely one act in that larger narrative of creation, that stretches throughout Israel's Scriptures. Just as the prophets named the specific imperial realities of their day as manifestations of God's larger story

---

33. The psalms quoted by Paul with these themes are: Pss 71 (70 LXX); 14 (13 LXX); 10 (9 LXX); 140 (139 LXX). See also Jer 7:6, 9; Hos 4:1–13; Mic 7:1–13; Hab 2:6–17.

34. Adam: Rom 5:12–21; Abraham: Rom 4; exodus: Rom 6–8; deuteronomic promises: Rom 8:1–2; prophetic restoration: Hos 2:23 in Rom 9:25; Isa 10:22 in Rom 9:27; Isa 59:20–21 in Rom 11:26; Isa 11:10 in Rom 15:12.

35. Contra Horrell et al., *Greening Paul*, 77, who indicate that the word for futility (ματαιότης) only occurs in the LXX in the Psalms, Prov 22:8, and Ecclesiastes, noting especially 3:19. Words formed from the root of ματαιο-, however, occur throughout the historical books and the prophets in relation to idolatry, e.g., 2 Kgs 17:15/Jer 2:5; Isa 44:9; Jer 10:3, 15; Hos 5:11.

in the world, so does Paul: the suffering of creation under Rome is rooted in the idolatrous and violent practices of the empire.

Second, Paul's description of the groaning of creation in Rom 8 echoes those places in the Scriptures that describe Israel's cry to God under a situation of violent economic oppression, first in the exodus event, where Israel's bondage enabled Egyptian economic exploitation of the land (the building of storehouses; the work in the fields).[36] The groaning of creation has often been viewed as generic metaphorical language; a poetic way to describe the fact that creation also suffers as a result of human sin. However, just as such language pointed to specific economic and social practices in the Scriptures of Israel, I suggest it does here as well.

This is reinforced by my third point. When Paul describes the suffering of the Roman believers in Rom 8:35, he includes both poverty (oppression, distress, famine, and nakedness are all economically rooted in the LXX) and political persecution (persecution, peril, and the sword). Paul's language of the groaning of believers in v. 23, therefore, is not just a theological formulation of the suffering that precedes the inauguration of the new age, but has a specific face on the ground in this place, in this community. It looks like poverty and abuse.[37] I suggest, therefore, that Paul's language of the groaning of creation is, similarly, not just a suffering that creation is undergoing because it is "unable to achieve its purpose or emerge from the constant cycle of toil, suffering, and death,"[38] but that creation is groaning for the same reason that believers groan: because it is suffering under the exploitative economic practices and violent militarism of Roman imperial rule.

My argument thus far is that Paul's language evokes various themes from his Scriptures that highlight the abuse of creation in specific socio-economic contexts. Further, I am arguing that Paul intended to challenge the practices of the Roman Empire in this text. How plausible is this given what we know of the environmental practices of ancient Rome? What was the environmental impact of the empire? And how likely is it that anyone, especially Paul, would have been concerned with this issue in the first century?

Romans was written at the time of Nero. Like the mythology of a creational "golden age" that accompanied the rule of Augustus, it was claimed that under Nero nature had been restored "to its original state in the primeval Age of Saturn, when beasts of the field were so tame that they herded

---

36. I have drawn out the linguistic parallels at some length in Keesmaat, *Paul and His Story*, 107–10. See also Fretheim "The Reclamation of Creation," 354–56; and Fretheim, "The Plagues," 385–96.

37. See also Oakes, *Reading Romans*, 114–15.

38. Horrell et al., *Greening Paul*, 77.

themselves and when the earth brought forth its harvest without the use of the plow."[39]

The reality, however, was considerably different. In the face of official economic affluence, the *practices* of Rome revealed the land-destroying economic oppression that underpinned the empire. While Rome (like so many empires before her) *claimed* to be the source of creational renewal, descriptions of the creation-destroying character of empire were common. Not only did Roman victory often require the destruction of the infrastructure of the conquered, continued Roman control depended upon an ongoing exploitation of both people and land. The army alone needed enormous resources: wine, olive oil, pork, garum, pepper for food, horses, pack animals, and animals for sacrifice (all these animals needed food as well). Leather (which came from animals that needed to be fed) was needed for everything, as was metal.[40] Mining that metal consumed enormous amounts of wood for building mine shafts, smelting, and washing earth from the ore.[41]

Roman roads, along with ships, enabled produce to stream more quickly from the exploited provinces to Roman garrisons and Rome itself.[42] In addition, the increasing need for grain in Rome led to the systematic ruin of forests and pasture-land, not only in Italy, but also in Africa, contributing to its desertification.[43]

Many ancient authors mention the air quality in Rome itself, which had very high levels of pollution due to fires for cooking, heating baths and houses, cremations, and industrial activities.[44] Cities were also the locus for epidemics, such as tuberculosis and malaria.[45]

Underlying all environmental concerns was the loss of arable land by individual farmers. Inability to work due to illness, low yields, erosion, and conscription affected a farmer's ability to subsist on the land, making it possible for those with more socio-economic power to take it over. At the

39. Jewett, "The Corruption and Redemption of Creation," 31. On the importance of the imagery of fruitfulness in the empire, and the challenge to such imperial assertions throughout Israel's history, see Walsh and Keesmaat, *Colossians Remixed*, chapter 4.

40. Morley, "Distribution," 276. See also LoCascio, "State and Economy," on the increased burden that the army placed on the land, 632–38; and Jongman, "Consumption," 609–11, on the sheer amounts of marble quarried, metal mined, and wood burned in the empire.

41. Kehoe, "Production," 567.

42. Wengst, *Pax Romana*, 30; Girardet, "Rome and the Soil," 60.

43. Girardet, "Rome and the Soil," 59; Hawkin, "The Critique of Ideology," 169; Wengst, *Pax Romana*, 35.

44. Sallers, "Ecology," 22.

45. Ibid., 35–37.

heart of all of this consumption, therefore, is a carefully hidden reality of land-loss, a reality that the official poets and artisans did not depict when extolling Roman virtue and might. While the empire claimed to be at the apex of world renewal and abundance, life on the ground was dramatically different.

J. Donald Hughes carefully and convincingly argues not only that environmental destruction was widespread at Paul's time, but also that some ancient authors described and decried the devastation.[46] The question, of course, is whether Paul would have shared these concerns. His context suggests that he did, for two reasons. First, Paul had spent a considerable amount of time in Judea, where imperial economic policies wrought destruction both for the people and for the land itself. Hughes graphically describes the environmental impact of Roman military practices, agricultural technology, economic practices, and population relocation, all of which were widespread in Galilee and Judea.[47] Paul would have seen the effect on the land of decades of military occupation, the expansion of imperial estates with the loss of familial land, and the despair that accompanied such violence.[48]

Second, the cities in which Paul stayed and worked had varying relationships to the land surrounding them. In general, their inability to live sustainably within their immediate environment was evidenced by the eroded and desiccated landscapes that surrounded them.[49] Moreover, larger urban centers were filled with those who had been forced off their land for various reasons and who were now part of the urban poor.[50] Many of these urban residents not only had recent memories of their land, but also close ties to the agrarian contexts from which they came. The Roman Empire was still, by and large, an agrarian culture, and hence concerns regarding the land, its fertility, its abundance, and its economic exploitation were never far from the consciousness of those who lived there, including those with whom Paul lived and worked.[51]

---

46. Hughes, *Environmental Problems*, 1–16, 56–68; 88; 144–45.
47. Ibid., 70–76; 11–120; 124–26.
48. Horsley, *Galilee*, 207–21; S. Adams, *Social and Economic Life*, 89–90, 171–81.
49. Hughes, *Environmental Problems*, 2, 163–64, 183.
50. Oakes, *Reading Romans*, 95, refers to the large number of migrant workers and immigrants in Rome; Scheidel, "Demography," 49, indicates that rising population levels created competition for cultivable land at this time. He also notes that may of the slaves in Rome were transported from outlying rural areas in the empire.
51. According to Scheidel, "Demography," 65, even marginal land was in high demand by the early imperial period.

Given this context, Paul's description of idolatry at the outset of this letter, alongside his graphic description of the suffering of creation in Rom 8, could only have been heard as a trenchant prophetic critique of the dominant mythology of creational abundance and renewal that sugarcoated the violent land-destroying practices of the empire.

PROPHETIC HOPE

Prophetic texts about idolatry, however, were not only texts of critique. They also embodied a powerful vision of hope. The problem with idols is their impotence. They have neither knowledge or understanding, they cannot hear or speak, they cannot move, and, most importantly, they cannot save.[52] Idolatry can never deliver on its promises, can never live up to its ideological rhetoric, always disappoints, and therefore always breeds hopelessness. In contrast, the God of Israel is not only the creator of all, but also the one who saves the weak and the orphan and maintains the right of the oppressed and the poor.[53] The dynamic of judgment giving birth to hope is found throughout Romans. Space does not permit me to explore this fully here; I will focus only on how this theme is evident in Paul's language of resurrection and glory.

First, in those psalms where God is called upon to act in the face of the oppression of gentile nations, the language of resurrection is central. "Rise up (ἀνάστα) O God, and judge the earth!" says the psalmist.[54] Why should God rise up? Because of God's steadfast love towards Israel (Ps 44:26). Throughout Romans that call has been answered. How do we know that God is faithful? Because in Jesus God has acted against injustice (Rom 1:18), in Jesus God has ended the dominion of death (5:17), in Jesus God has ended the power of wickedness, in Jesus God has proved his love for us (5:8), because in Jesus we hope to share in the glory of God (5:2), in Jesus we are not only made just but also glorified (8:30), in Jesus we hope for the

---

52. Brueggemann, *Israel's Praise*, 94–95, 106–18.

53. The most classic articulation of this latter point is Psalm 82 (81 LXX), which uses the vocabulary of the oppressed (ταπεινός), also found in Rom 12:16; Brueggemann, "Reflections on Property," 278. On the contrast between the impotence of the gods and the creating and saving action of God see Deut 4:25–34; 10:12–22; 32:36–43; 33:23–29; 1 Kgs 18:20–38; Pss 115; 135; Jer 10:1–13, Hab 2:18–19; and consistently in every chapter of Isa 40–48.

54. Ps 82:8 (81:8 LXX); see also Pss 3:7 (3:8 LXX); 7:6 (7:7 LXX); 9:19 (9:20 LXX); 10:12 (9:33 LXX); 17:13 (16:13 LXX); 44:26 (43:27 LXX); 68:1 (67:2 LXX); 102:13 (101:14 LXX); 132:8 (131:8 LXX).

redemption of our bodies (8:23). All of this happens because Jesus rose from the dead (1:4).

This hope of resurrection is intimately tied to the restoration of creation that Paul describes in Rom 8:19-21. In these verses creation not only waits for the children of God to take up their task as image bearers (vv. 19, 29), but also waits for "the freedom of the glory of the children of God" (v. 21). The loss of glory that results from idolatry in Rom 1:23 is restored to those who are conformed to the image of the Son in Rom 8:30. In light of texts such as Ps 8:4-9 and Dan 7:14, as well as various texts from Qumran and the inter-testamental literature that link the glory of Adam with care of the land, Paul appears to be working in a symbolic world where the loss of "glory" and its restoration has very tangible effects on the land.[55]

There are two ways that Paul's emphasis on the glory of the children of God challenges the imperial story. In the first place, according to Rome, the emperor is the one who images the gods and engages in a glorious rule over the world.[56] Paul tells a different story: rather than Caesar being the one who brings restoration, abundance, and peace to creation, it is the restored people of God who bring such restoration as part of their creaturely calling. Paul applies the image of God language, usually reserved for the king, to those who are the sons of God, those conformed to the image of Jesus (Rom 8:29; cf. Col 3:10). In this way the special status of the emperor as image of God is challenged by this motley assortment of people who claim to be followers of a different Lord with a radically different calling.[57]

In the second place, the so-called abundance and fertility of the empire are rooted in the power and strength of Roman military might. Violence is the basis for *all* that the empire offers. As Rom 8 progresses, Paul makes it abundantly clear that the children of God who will exercise right rule over creation are those who bear the first fruits of the Spirit and hence groan in travail with creation itself (Rom 8:23).[58] That is to say, not violent rule over creation, but entering into the suffering of creation fits the children for the redemption of their bodies and entrance into glory. The false "glory" of

---

55. I treat these motifs at some length in Keesmaat, *Paul and His Story*, 84-101.

56. In fact, throughout the ancient Near East the king as the image of god or the gods was ubiquitous, along with the corollary: the rest of humankind exists to serve the gods by serving the king. Already in Gen 1, the description of humanity as the image of God was a challenge to these other stories. See Middleton, "The Liberating Image?" 8-25; Middleton, *The Liberating Image*, 185-219.

57. On the contrast between Jesus as Lord and Caesar as Lord see Keesmaat, "Crucified Lord or Conquering Saviour?" 69-93.

58. Of course, as the chapter continues, the Spirit also enters into this groaning (v. 26).

Rome that results in abuse of the land is replaced by the redemptive glory of healing service.

If we accept the claim of Paul that creation is groaning, and if we acknowledge not only that Scripture bears witness to this groaning, but that we ourselves live in a world that engages in idolatrous economic practices that violently abuse both people and land, what does this mean for our interpretation of Romans? It is clear that Paul's letter to the Romans called the community to very specific practices with regard to the shape of their local communities. These practices resulted in a life of community faithfulness that challenged imperial social structures and imperial economics. As we have seen, the biblical writers are clear that such embodied faithfulness can't help but impact the land as well. At the very least, as those who acknowledge the key claims of Paul to live our lives in such faithful community, we need to ask ourselves what such faithfulness looks like in our lives, in the places we find ourselves, in the place of creational fidelity that we ourselves are called to.

8

A New Translation of Philippians 2:5 and Its Significance for Paul's Theology and Spirituality

MICHAEL J. GORMAN
St. Mary's Seminary & University

Τοῦτο φρονεῖτε ἐν ὑμῖν ὃ καὶ ἐν Χριστῷ Ἰησοῦ...

PHILIPPIANS 2:5 REMAINS AN exegetical and translational conundrum, yet it is a "*crux interpretum.*"[1] The bridge between a key exhortation in the letter (Phil 1:27—2:4) and its poetic, theological foundation (Phil 2:6-11), Phil 2:5, needs to be interpreted well in order to understand the nature of the connection between exhortation and foundation. Furthermore, since the great significance of Phil 2:6-11—in multiple respects—is universally acknowledged, we will gain the highest degree of clarity about it only if we properly explicate 2:5.

---

1. O'Brien, *Philippians*, 203. His treatment of 2:5 is one of the most thorough in print (203-5, 253-62).

In this essay I make an extended case for an interpretation of 2:5 that I have previously presented briefly:[2]

> Cultivate this mindset—this way of thinking, acting, and feeling—in your community, which is in fact a community in the Messiah Jesus . . .

The key element of my proposal is not the language of cultivation or the three-part definition of "mindset."[3] Rather, it is the last half of the verse, "which is in fact . . . ." This relative clause is the link between the imperatival clause φρονεῖτε ἐν ὑμῖν and the following poem, and it is what has most thoroughly beguiled translators. I submit that this translation best captures the point Paul is making in Philippians and also has highly significant implications for understanding Paul's theology and spirituality as a whole.[4]

A SAMPLE OF TWO BASIC INTERPRETATIONS

The exegesis of Phil 2:5 affects the interpretation of the connection between poem and exhortation, between christology and spirituality. The basic question that has divided interpreters is this: Does Paul exhort the Philippians to adopt a "mindset" that Christ had, or does he tell them to maintain a mindset that they already have "in Christ" and under his lordship? Does he promote imitation of the suffering, dying Jesus, or does he promote obedience to Christ the Lord? Or, somehow, does he do both? Or, again—as we will argue here—does he do something different?

Two basic interpretive options have been proposed in modern scholarship:

1. something like "Have the attitude that was in Christ" or "Have the mindset that Christ had"; and

2. something like "Have the attitude which is yours in Christ."

The first interpretation is purely imperatival, urging imitation of Christ. The second includes an indicative statement about already possessing the attitude,

---

2. Gorman, "The Self, the Lord, and the Other," 694–98; *Cruciformity*, 39–44. This specific formulation, with one change (from "Christ" to "the Messiah"), derives from my *Becoming the Gospel*, 117–18.

3. For this understanding of "mindset," see Fowl, *Philippians*, 88–90; cf. 28–29.

4. I am delighted to make this small contribution to honor a colleague's vocation-long commitment to careful exegesis and theological reflection. Andrew Lincoln's writing has always demonstrated the kind of literary sensitivity and theological and spiritual concern that Phil 2 both requires and rewards.

or condition, that is the basis for the imperative. These two basic interpretations are sometimes referred to as (1) the "ethical" and (2) the "kerygmatic," "doctrinal," or "soteriological," respectively. For my part, I prefer the terms (1) "imitative" and (2) "locative" to characterize these two basic perspectives. The former stresses imitation *of* Christ, the latter being *in* Christ.

Bible translations largely represent one or the other of these two interpretations, with the imitative option being the more popular:[5]

Imitative Translations

- Adopt the attitude that was in Christ Jesus: (CEB; cf. NASB)
- and think the same way that Christ Jesus thought: (CEV)
- You should have the same attitude toward one another that Christ Jesus had, (NET; cf. NLT)
- In your relationships with one another, have the same mindset as Christ Jesus: (NIV)
- Make your own the mind of Christ Jesus: (NJB)
- Let the same mind be in you that was in Christ Jesus, (NRSV)

Locative Translations

- Have this mind among yourselves, which is yours in Christ Jesus, (ESV)
- Have among yourselves the same attitude that is also yours in Christ Jesus, (NAB)
- Have this mind among yourselves, which is yours in Christ Jesus, (RSV)
- This is how you should think among yourselves—with the mind that you have because you belong to the Messiah, Jesus: (*Kingdom New Testament* [N. T. Wright])[6]

Recent commentators who provide their own translations fall generally into one of these two interpretations, too. An example of each will suffice:

---

5. I have included any final punctuation in the verse used by each translation. Translation options in other languages are generally similar to those in English.

6. Though technically similar to other locative translations, Wright's rendering is quite close in spirit to the interpretation offered in this essay.

Let this be your pattern of thinking, acting, and feeling, which
was also displayed in Christ Jesus, (Stephen Fowl; imitative[7])

Think in this way among yourselves; it is the way you also think
"in Christ Jesus," (John Reumann; locative[8])

Although, as we will see, the exegetical issues are quite complex, there is one fundamental difference between the imitative and the locative interpretations. It is whether one understands the missing Greek verb in the relative clause—"which also [verb] in Christ Jesus" (ὅ καὶ [verb] ἐν Χριστῷ Ἰησοῦ)—as referring to Christ or to the Philippians. Most often, the verb supplied for the imitative reading is something like "was" (ἦν), or occasionally "you see/saw" (perhaps βλέπετε or εἴδετε[9]), with Jesus as the one who possessed the disposition: "have this attitude that was in Christ"; "think how Christ thought."[10] "In Christ Jesus" refers to the location of the disposition in Jesus. The verb supplied for the locative reading, on the other hand, is normally an indicative form of the explicit imperative "think" (φρονεῖτε), with the Philippians as the ones who possess the disposition: "have the mindset you have"; "think what you think." "In Christ Jesus" refers to the location of the Philippians in Christ.[11]

The kerygmatic or soteriological approach—what I am calling the locative interpretation—was championed especially by Ernst Käsemann and then Ralph Martin, each expressing concern about the pervasive ethical (imitative) interpretation.[12] They rightly emphasized that Paul was focused on the lordship of Christ and on the church's being in Christ and under his lordship. Christ and the hymn do not constitute the *model* of Christian ethics but the *foundation* of it. Nevertheless, their reaction was an over-reaction, a textbook example of throwing out the baby with the bath water. What looked to them like a necessary exegetical and theological choice between

---

7. Fowl, *Philippians*, 88.

8. Reumann, *Philippians*, 333.

9. This would be similar to Paul's descriptions of what could be seen in him (1:30; 4:9).

10. As already noted, and as we will see further below, the verb φρονεῖν means more than simply "think."

11. In the locative reading, the location of the disposition is ultimately also in Christ, such that believers have the disposition only by virtue of their being in Christ. But the emphasis in the translation is on the location of *believers* in Christ, not the location of the *disposition* in Christ.

12. Käsemann, "Critical Analysis," esp. 83–84; R. Martin, *A Hymn of Christ*, esp. xii–xix, 68–88.

two opposite readings of the text, one ethical and the other kerygmatic, is a false dichotomy, as Larry Hurtado ably showed in a 1983 essay.[13]

In a similar spirit, Markus Bockmuehl has proposed a third option for the translation of 2:5 that attempts to blend the two basic approaches, as follows:

> This is the attitude you should have among yourselves, which [attitude] is also in Christ Jesus.[14]

Bockmuehl is on to something important. He contends that Paul is clearly making an ethical point, as the "close parallels" between 2:1-4 and 2:6-11 reveal.[15] Furthermore, he agrees with many exegetes that an appeal to Jesus' example probably requires a form of the verb "to be." But rather than using the commonly supplied "was," Bockmuehl claims that

> the simplest reading is to supply the *present* tense of "to be" [i.e., ἐστίν]: "have this attitude amongst yourselves, which *is* also in Christ Jesus." While it leaves intact the moral analogy with the narrative that follows, this reading has the advantage that the indicated attitudes of the mind of Christ are seen to be not just a past fact of history but a *present reality*.[16]

Bockmuehl continues: "In some sense, therefore, the 'mind-set' of unselfish compassion which Paul encourages in the Philippians 'is present' in Christ Jesus both historically and eternally." Furthermore, "this translation may narrow the gap between the usual two options."[17] What is more, Bockmuehl briefly suggests that the continuity between the Jesus Christ of faith and of history implies *participation* more than mere remembrance.[18]

Bockmuehl advances the conversation by focusing on the likelihood of the implied verb being in the present tense, as well as the theological implications of that with respect to the present-ness of Jesus and his ongoing disposition of self-giving love. He does not, however, develop the insight about participation (though that theme figures in his commentary as a whole). His translation of 2:5 itself remains a variation on the imitative reading because

---

13. Hurtado, "Jesus as Lordly Example."
14. Bockmuehl, *Philippians*, 114. Cf. REB, "what you find in Christ Jesus," as Bockmuehl himself suggests (124). See also Meeks, "The Man from Heaven," 332, and the (French) Bible de Jérusalem: "Ayez entre vous les mêmes sentiments qui sont dans le Christ Jésus."
15. Bockmuehl, *Philippians*, 122-23.
16. Ibid., 123-24.
17. Ibid., 124.
18. Ibid.

it does not recognize "in Christ Jesus" as the location of the church; Christ is still the location of a disposition, even if the disposition "is" rather than "was" located in him.

Two observations might be helpful at this point. First, like Bockmuehl, most interpreters of Philippians today—even if chastened a bit by Käsemann and/or Martin—recognize that Paul is presenting Jesus as a model for Christian behavior in some sense. Precisely how Paul envisions the relationship between Jesus and the Philippian believers, or Christians more generally, is still debated and, in my view, sometimes articulated in less precise and less accurate language than should be the case.[19]

Second, since the phrases ἐν ὑμῖν and ἐν Χριστῷ Ἰησοῦ are syntactically parallel, they are almost certainly in some sense semantically parallel. Indeed, I would submit that the most critical exegetical question for the translation and interpretation of Phil 2:5 is the semantic significance of the parallelism between these two phrases. I would further submit that the key to understanding this parallelism lies in (1) assuming that the phrase ἐν Χριστῷ Ἰησοῦ here means what similar phrases most often mean in Paul, namely, "within the community of Christ the Lord," and (2) rethinking the sense of the phrase that connects the two parallel phrases, that is, ὃ καί.

In other words, it is time for a fresh exegesis of the text that might yield a true third option. To do this, we need to step back a bit in order to name and discuss the various exegetical issues. The solutions I will propose to a series of questions will lead to the translation noted at the beginning of the essay. I will refer to this option as the *participatory* interpretation, an alternative to the traditional imitative and locative interpretations.

SOME KEY EXEGETICAL QUESTIONS

The standard critical editions of the Greek New Testament provide the interpreter with this text of Phil 2:5[20]:

Τοῦτο φρονεῖτε ἐν ὑμῖν ὃ καὶ ἐν Χριστῷ Ἰησοῦ

---

19. A number of commentators in the imitative tradition have rightly suggested that "conformity" is a better description of Paul's ethics than "imitation" (e.g., Hooker, *From Adam to Christ*, 90–92; O'Brien, *Philippians*, 205). This suggestion approaches the language of participation. For Christ's participation in humanity enabling our participation in him, see Eastman, "Philippians 2:6–11," though she does not deal directly with 2:5.

20. We will not discuss the variants, none of which has found significant acceptance among textual critics or exegetes. We will, however, propose a possible variant rendering of the omicron that is assumed to be the relative pronoun ὅ.

This short text raises a host of exegetical issues, which can be summarized as five main questions.

1. Does the neuter demonstrative pronoun τοῦτο look backward, forward, or both? That is, is it retrospective, prospective, or both?
2. What is the sense of φρονεῖτε?
3. Does ἐν ὑμῖν mean "in [each of] you" or "among you"? That is, does the phrase refer (or refer primarily) to individuals or to the community?
4. What is the meaning of the phrase ὃ καί?
   a. Is the first word a neuter relative pronoun (ὅ), as generally assumed and therefore universally printed, or is it possibly a masculine, singular, nominative definite article (ὁ)?
   b. If it is the neuter relative pronoun ὅ, does it refer back to τοῦτο, or is there another option?
   c. If it is the definite article ὁ, what is its significance?
   d. What is the force of καί?
   e. What verb should be supplied, or is inferred, after the phrase ὃ καί or ὁ καί?
   f. In what sense, if any, are the phrases ἐν ὑμῖν and ἐν Χριστῷ Ἰησοῦ, which are linked by ὃ καί, parallel, both syntactically and semantically?
5. To what does ἐν Χριστῷ Ἰησοῦ refer—to something "in" Christ or to the community of believers as those who are "in" Christ? Is there any significance to the presence of Ἰησοῦ in a phrase that is normally in Pauline usage simply ἐν Χριστῷ?

Space does not permit a full response to each of these issues, so relatively brief replies will be necessary. We will consider them in sequence, except that there will be some unavoidable overlap and anticipation of subsequent questions.

1. Retrospective τοῦτο

There are two main reasons to think that τοῦτο is primarily retrospective. First, forms of the verb φρονεῖν, of which τοῦτο is the direct object, appear twice in the immediate context of 1:27—2:4, specifically in 2:2[21]:

---

21. The verb appears also in 1:7, to which we will return.

> πληρώσατέ μου τὴν χαρὰν ἵνα τὸ αὐτὸ φρονῆτε, τὴν αὐτὴν
> ἀγάπην ἔχοντες, σύμψυχοι, τὸ ἓν φρονοῦντες
>
> make my joy complete: be of the same mind, having the same love, being in full accord and of one mind (NRSV)

Paul uses the neuter pronoun τοῦτο in 2:5 to sum up the φρόνησις that he has described in 2:1–4, a φρόνησις that is characterized by unity, love, humility, and concern for others rather than self. This is clearly a community φρόνησις, one that originates in the shared reality identified in 2:1 as being ἐν Χριστῷ together and being co-participants in the Spirit (κοινωνία πνεύματος). The retrospective neuter pronoun τοῦτο does not refer to a grammatically neuter linguistic entity (such as a noun) in 2:1–4, but rather to the "idea" described in those verses.[22] It is therefore unnecessary to posit an allegedly suppressed word (as may be necessary later in the verse), such as [τὸ] φρόνημα.[23]

Second, in both the previous and the following chapters of Philippians (1:7; 3:15), Paul also combines the neuter singular pronoun with a form of φρονεῖν, and in each case the pronoun functions retrospectively. In 1:7, Paul tells the Philippians that it is appropriate for him to feel or think a certain way about them:

> Καθώς ἐστιν δίκαιον ἐμοὶ τοῦτο φρονεῖν ὑπὲρ πάντων ὑμῶν
>
> "It is right for me to think this way about all of you" (NRSV; NIV, NJB, RSV: "feel")

Paul has described this fitting mindset of thanksgiving, joy, and confidence in the previous verses (1:3–6). Philippians 3:15 is also a sentence in which τοῦτο is clearly retrospective, as indicated both by the preceding content to which it refers and by the presence of the conjunction οὖν:

> Ὅσοι οὖν τέλειοι, τοῦτο φρονῶμεν ...
>
> "So all of us who are spiritually mature should think this way" (CEB)

The φρόνησις to which Paul refers in 3:15 is contained in the paradigmatic autobiographical account found in 3:3–14.

Of course we cannot restrict Paul's use of τοῦτο to retrospective senses, as Philippians itself makes clear,[24] but it does seem to be the case that the

---

22. See BDAG s.v. οὗτος 1 b α; the neuter demonstrative pronoun can be used for what precedes it in a text.

23. As suggested by, e.g., O'Brien, *Philippians*, 205, following Moule, "Further Reflexions," 265.

24. Τοῦτο is retrospective in 1:7, 19, 22, 25, 28; 3:15, but prospective in 1:6, 9. In

combination of τοῦτο and φρονεῖν is routinely retrospective. Furthermore, it appears to be the norm in Paul that the sense of a demonstrative pronoun before an imperative, as in 2:5, is retrospective.

This *syntactical* conclusion does not, however, mean that there is no prospective *semantic* significance to 2:5 as a whole. The verse functions clearly as a bridge between what precedes and what follows, and there is an obvious material, or semantic, parallel between at least 2:2-4 and 2:6-8. However, if τοῦτο is syntactically retrospective, then the relative pronoun ὅ (if that is what it is) does not have to refer back to the demonstrative pronoun because the content of τοῦτο has already been identified. We will return to the implications of this conclusion below.

2. φρονεῖτε: "Cultivate this way of thinking, acting, and feeling"

It is quite obvious that φρόνησις is on Paul's mind in Philippians. Forms of φρονεῖν appear ten times in the letter, in 1:7; 2:2 (twice); 2:5; 3:15 (twice); 3:19; 4:2; and 4:10 (twice). The only other Pauline letter that remotely resembles Philippians in this regard is Romans, especially where concerns and exhortations similar to those of Paul in Philippians are expressed in Romans 12-15.[25]

Φρόνησις, a common word in ancient moral philosophy, may be defined as "practical reasoning."[26] It is more than just thinking; we might refer to it as an attitude with consequences. As noted above, Stephen Fowl has translated it as a "pattern of thinking, acting, and feeling" or, more simply, "a common pattern of thinking and acting."[27] It is a combination of a perspective and a set of corollary practices. "There is clearly an intellectual component to this activity. Equally important . . . is the assumption that such a common perspective will generate, direct, and sustain a particular course of action."[28]

This practical φρόνησις also has an emotional dimension. New Testament scholars have often neglected this aspect of early Christian spirituality.[29]

---

addition, the plural ταῦτα is retrospective in 3:7; 4:8, 9.

25. See the nine occurrences of forms of φρονεῖν in Rom 8:5; 11:20; 12:3 (twice); 12:16 (twice); 14:6 (twice); and 15:5. Cf. the occurrences of φρόνημα in Rom 8:6 (twice), 7, 27 and of φρόνιμοι in Rom 11:25 and 12:16.

26. Meeks, "The Man from Heaven."

27. See Fowl, *Philippians*, 77, 82-83 (without "feeling" in his discussion of 2:2) and 88-90 (with "feeling" in his exegesis of 2:5). Fowl does not explain why he adds "feeling," but its inclusion is appropriate, as we will see.

28. Fowl, *Philippians*, 82.

29. For an exception, see the work of Stephen Barton, such as "Spirituality and the

But in the immediate context of 2:5 we have references to the emotional as well as the practical dimensions of Christian φρόνησις: παράκλησις ... παραμύθιον ἀγάπης ... σπλάγχνα καὶ οἰκτιρμοί (encouragement, consolation deriving from love, deep affection, and compassion). Moreover, Paul expresses his profound, emotional (as well as practical) love for the Philippians by saying that he shares in the deep affection of Christ Jesus: ἐν σπλάγχνοις Χριστοῦ Ἰησοῦ (1:8). That is, Paul's practical-emotional affection for them has its source in the practical-emotional affection of Christ Jesus.

Paul's claim implies three things: that the story of Christ Jesus can be described as one of deep affection; that this deep affection persists into the present because Jesus is not dead but alive; and that others can participate in this deep affection by loving others in similar practical-emotional ways. This is in essence what it means to be "in Christ" (2:1) for both Paul and his communities. Already in Phil 1:7, then, Paul anticipates the main point of 2:1-4 and suggests that both his and the Philippians' practical-emotional affection have a common source in the story and the living reality of Jesus, narrated in 2:6-11.

So the φρόνησις of which Paul speaks involves thinking, feeling, and acting. I have translated the imperative [Τοῦτο] φρονεῖτε as "Cultivate this mindset" as a way of summarizing Paul's call to this three-dimensional φρόνησις, and followed that general imperative with an explanatory phrase that names these three elements. I have chosen the word "cultivate" to suggest that this is a process that has begun, but that also needs attention and, thereby, growth.[30]

3. ἐν ὑμῖν: "in your community"

The translation of the phrase ἐν ὑμῖν is probably the least difficult and controversial of the various parts of this verse. Both from the strong emphasis on community in Philippians and from Paul's overall understanding of ethics and spirituality as a communal experience and responsibility, we can be quite certain that the imperative is directed primarily to the community and refers to communal relations. As in 1:6 and 2:13, ἐν ὑμῖν means "among yourselves," "within your community," rather than "in you as individuals in your individual lives." In fact, the attitudes and corollary practices described in 2:1-4 only make sense as community attitudes and practices,

---

Emotions."

30. That the Philippians already experience some measure of unity and love in Christ (Paul's desire expressed in 2:1-4) is evident from their joint support of Paul (1:5, 7) and his wish that their love would increase (1:9).

that which should characterize life together "in Christ" and inspired by the Spirit. Moreover, as Silva suggests, Paul would probably have used the plural reflexive pronoun (ἐν ἑαυτοῖς) if he had meant to say "within yourselves."[31] The phrase ἐν ὑμῖν is similar, instead, to ἐν ἀλλήλοις in Rom 15:5, where Paul again issues a call to unity using the verb φρονεῖν: ὁ δὲ θεὸς . . . δῴη ὑμῖν τὸ αὐτὸ φρονεῖν ἐν ἀλλήλοις.

At the same time, however, there can be no community without individuals, and no community mindset without individuals displaying that mindset. This becomes especially clear and explicit in Phil 2:4 with its emphasis on the individual (ἕκαστος) in relation to others. Thus Paul is really making his plea to each and to all, to the individual and to the body, to cultivate certain appropriate ways of thinking, acting, and feeling toward one another.

4. ὃ/ὁ καί: "which is in fact" ("that is")

If the phrase ἐν ὑμῖν is the least difficult and controversial, we come now to the most challenging aspect of the verse. Its complexity has already been signaled by the six sub-questions listed above. Although the phrase is clearly functioning to link two parts of the verse, there is no verb after it to indicate what precisely is being linked to what, and what the significance of that link is. Hence we have the various translations, each nuancing one of the two basic options, the imitative or the locative.

I want to propose two alternatives to the standard interpretations of this phrase, either of which would provide a fresh reading of the text, a true third option beyond the imitative and locative options. Each of these alternatives yields a similar final result: that ὃ/ὁ καί means something like "that is," a kind of *id est* phrase.

Interpreters universally assume that the first word in this two-word phrase is the neuter singular relative pronoun ὅ, "which." We will shortly suggest that since the unmarked omicron could be either the neuter relative pronoun ὅ or the masculine article ὁ, this assumption needs to be challenged. But for now, let us assume that ὃ καί is the right transcription of the Greek text.

We argued earlier that τοῦτο was retrospective. If that is the case, then another unexamined assumption about the phrase ὃ καί does need to be challenged immediately: the supposition that ὅ refers back to τοῦτο. But ὅ only *needs* to refer to τοῦτο if τοῦτο is prospective, for then it must have something to define its content, to fill the semantic space called "this." Such

---

31. Silva, *Philippians*, 95-96.

content would be provided either by a vague implicit reference to that which the Philippians already "think" (so the locative interpretation) or by the poetic narrative in 2:6–11, or at least in 2:6–8 (so the imitative interpretation). If, however, the content of "this" (τοῦτο) has already been defined as the "mindset" depicted in 2:1–4, it is not necessary for the demonstrative pronoun to be linked, via the relative pronoun, to something later in the text. Although ὅ *might* still refer back to τοῦτο, it has been essentially liberated from its assumed *obligatory* syntactical and semantic role, resulting in the interpreter's freedom to explore other possible roles.

Like neuter demonstrative pronouns, neuter relative pronouns can also refer "generally to the idea or sense of the context"[32] and therefore to grammatical constructions or other generic, non-gendered linguistic or semantic entities. It is quite common for a neuter relative pronoun to refer back to a phrase, clause, or word that is then explained in the clause introduced by the relative pronoun.[33] The antecedent may be a prepositional phrase.[34] In such cases, there is "*ad sensum*" agreement between the neuter pronoun and the antecedent. For instance, the rather common phrase ὅ ἐστιν is often used as a formula of translation (e.g., Mark 7:11; Heb 7:2) or explanation (e.g., Mark 15:42), and is roughly equivalent to the Latin *id est*.[35]

Something like this, I suggest, is happening in Phil 2:5 if the omicron is in fact the relative pronoun ὅ. It is referring, not to τοῦτο, but to the nearest "neuter," or neutral, linguistic item, namely the phrase ἐν ὑμῖν. In conjunction with ὅ καί, the result is something approximating *id est*, an explanation formula, making the phrase ἐν Χριστῷ Ἰησοῦ an apposition to ἐν ὑμῖν:

ἐν ὑμῖν = in you

ὅ καὶ = "that is" (literally, "which also")

ἐν Χριστῷ Ἰησοῦ = in Christ

---

32. Boyer, "Relative Clauses," 244. According to Boyer (243, 244), more than 20 percent of the antecedents of relative pronouns in the NT need to be determined from the context.

33. BDAG s.v. ὅς 1 g α, β.

34. Boyer, "Relative Clauses," citing Acts 2:39; 2 Tim 1:5; and Heb 12:25–26 as examples.

35. See Boyer, "Relative Clauses," 246, 248. He does not distinguish between "translation" and "explanation" formulae, lumping all NT examples into the former category, but Mark 7:11, at least, is more explanatory than translational. On *ad sensum* agreement, see also BDAG s.v. ὅς 1 c β. On ὅ ἐστιν, see BDAG s.v. ὅς 1g β; BDF 132 (2); Robertson, *Grammar*, 713–14. The phrase is essentially genderless.

The missing verb, then, is the present tense of "to be," namely ἐστίν.³⁶ What we have here, it appears, is the suppression of the verb ἐστίν from the explanatory phrase ὅ ἐστιν—a common phenomenon, especially in impersonal constructions³⁷—and the addition of the particle καί, to which we will return momentarily. We might also translate the phrase as "which is also" or "which is to say"; it functions to link the two syntactically parallel prepositional phrases and thus to show their semantic parallelism, too. The point is not, however, that what is supposed to be "in you" is already in Christ, as Bockmuehl has suggested. It is rather that ἐν Χριστῷ Ἰησοῦ is another way of saying ἐν ὑμῖν. G. B. Caird interprets 2:5 similarly, calling ὃ καί the equivalent of *id est* and translating the text as "this is the disposition which must govern your common life, i.e., your life in Christ Jesus, because he . . . ."³⁸

The expression ἐν Χριστῷ Ἰησοῦ is not, however, just an *additional* way of describing ἐν ὑμῖν. It is a more theologically thick way of saying ἐν ὑμῖν. The reality that can be described as ἐν ὑμῖν is better and ultimately understood as ἐν Χριστῷ Ἰησοῦ. The particle καί functions adverbially, then, not merely to mean "also" but to mean "indeed" or "in fact." It is a strengthening, not merely an additive, particle in this instance.³⁹ The life of the corporate entity (in [= among] "you") is further defined as life in Christ. The result in our translation is, "Cultivate this mindset . . . in your community, which is in fact a community in the Messiah Jesus." This interpretation, substituting "in fact" for "also" as the translation of καί, means that Paul is not exhorting the Philippians to cultivate a mindset because *it* was also in Christ, but because *they* are in Christ.

We return now to the other potentially erroneous assumption about the phrase ὃ καί. It is possible that the phrase ὃ καί is really ὁ καί.⁴⁰ The phrase ὁ καί was used in inscriptions and elsewhere to equate two names as references to one person, to say that so-and-so was also called such-and-such. There is one definite example of this linguistic phenomenon in the New Testament, in Acts 13:9:

---

36. The imperfect ἦν was almost never omitted (BDF 128 [3]).

37. BDF 127.

38. Caird, *Paul's Letters from Prison*, 118–19.

39. See BDF 442 (10) and (11) for epexegetical ("i.e.") and ascensive ("even") uses of καί, in addition to adjunctive ("also"). The particle can give emphasis to what follows, and after a relative pronoun it often gives a sense of independence to the following clause (BDAG s.v. καί 2 b, f). In some instances the particle καί may be "colorless" (i.e., without semantic significance) when it follows the relative (so Cadbury, "The Relative Pronouns," 157), but in this case it seems to point emphatically to what (who) follows.

40. It is worth noting that there appears to have been some confusion among Greek speakers about the uses of ὃ and ὁ, resulting in some overlap in usage. See BDF 249.

Σαῦλος δέ, ὁ καὶ Παῦλος, πλησθεὶς πνεύματος ἁγίου ἀτενίσας εἰς αὐτὸν

"But Saul, also known as Paul, filled with the Holy Spirit, looked intently at him" (NRSV)

This kind of formulation was often used to identify a Roman citizen with respect to his various names (the *praenomen, nomen,* and *cognomen*), as well as to indicate someone's alternative name used among close friends—his nickname (Latin *signum* or *supernomen*). The Latin equivalent was normally *qui et*. The phrase ὁ καί was a kind of technical term for expressing the common phenomenon of "double names."[41]

It is highly likely that Paul would have been familiar with the use of ὁ καί to indicate double names, from inscriptions, literature, and/or daily conversation. It is therefore quite possible that in Phil 2:5 Paul has instinctively introduced a common expression for indicating someone's other name as he writes to the community of believers at Philippi about their double identity. He characterizes them, not merely as a community, but as an in-Christ community. "Have this mindset in you, since your true identity is in Christ Jesus."

We now have before us two ways of construing the phrase in question, whether read as ὃ καί or as ὁ καί, that point in the same direction: away from seeing it as having an antecedent in τοῦτο and toward seeing it as equating ἐν ὑμῖν and ἐν Χριστῷ Ἰησοῦ. In either case, the phrase does not indicate the existence of a disposition in both "you" (the Philippians) and Christ, but rather refines the description of the Philippian community as an in-Christ community. That is who they are in the most fundamental and significant sense. The parallelism in the text is only between ἐν ὑμῖν and ἐν Χριστῷ Ἰησοῦ, not between the initial clause Τοῦτο φρονεῖτε . . . and a hypothetical related clause consisting of [verb +] ἐν Χριστῷ Ἰησοῦ. The particle καί functions to indicate that the Philippian fellowship has another name, another identity. Its perspectives and practices do not merely exist in a human community but in a community constituted at the core of its being as participating in the sphere of Christ's lordship and in his identity-shaping narrative.

---

41. For an older but still significant discussion, see Harrer, "Saul who also is Called Paul." See also BDF 268 (1) and BDAG s.v. καί 2 h for the phenomenon and secondary literature.

5. ἐν Χριστῷ Ἰησοῦ: "a community in the Messiah Jesus"

Nearly every interpreter acknowledges some sort of parallelism between ἐν ὑμῖν and ἐν Χριστῷ Ἰησοῦ. As already noted at various points, the phrase ἐν Χριστῷ Ἰησοῦ is best read as an appositional prepositional phrase to ἐν ὑμῖν and thus a description of the church's true identity: participating "in" Christ. The phrase is not, then, a reference to something (e.g., an attitude) that existed and/or continues to exist in Christ. On this point, the locative (kerygmatic) interpreters are right. There are two main reasons for this position.

The first reason is the larger context of Paul's writings. Although the phrase ἐν Χριστῷ and variants in Paul have various senses, they normally refer to life in the community, life together in personal relation to Christ the Lord.[42] If 2:5 is referring to "something" in Christ, it would be a unique use of ἐν Χριστῷ in Paul.

The second reason is the context of Philippians itself. A similar phrase appears in the immediate context (2:1) that is clearly a reference to the community: Εἴ τις οὖν παράκλησις ἐν Χριστῷ, "Therefore, if [there is] encouragement in Christ." Paul is beginning a series of four conditional ("if") phrases that are actually assumptions, "since" phrases. Together they form the basis of the imperative πληρώσατε ("make [my joy] complete) in 2:2. The phrase ἐν Χριστῷ should be understood as associated with all four of these "since" phrases: since encouragement, consolation from love, participation in the Spirit, and deep affection and compassion do indeed exist in Christ (i.e., in the church), the Philippians should follow the exhortations in 2:3-4 and thereby make Paul's joy complete by the way in which they live in community, as those in Christ. The occurrences of ἐν Χριστῷ [Ἰησοῦ] at the beginning (2:1) and the end (2:5) of the preface to the Christ-poem function together as bookends, forming an inclusio that sets off the description of concrete practices. Another similar phrase occurs in Phil 4:2: Εὐοδίαν παρακαλῶ καὶ Συντύχην παρακαλῶ τὸ αὐτὸ φρονεῖν ἐν κυρίῳ, which clearly echoes both 2:5 and the general exhortation in 2:2: ἵνα τὸ αὐτὸ φρονῆτε. Paul wants these two women to be unified in their relationship within the community constituted by the Lord Jesus.

Thus ἐν Χριστῷ Ἰησοῦ in 2:5 is referring to the church, not to Christ. At the same time, however, the practices Paul calls for can and do exist in Christ (i.e., in the church) because they are analogous to what Christ himself did; those who participate in his life are shaped by him. Paul has already spoken of his participation in Christ's compassion (1:8), and he is about to narrate Christ's self-emptying and self-humbling (2:6-8) in ways

---

42. Campbell, *Paul and Union with Christ*, 73, though he interprets Phil 2:5 as a reference to Christ's interior disposition (105-6).

that echo the exhortations in 2:3–4. Thus, although it is wrong to interpret "in Christ" as an indication of Christ's inner attitude, it is nonetheless true that there is a correlation between Christ and those in Christ, as 2:6–8 will make especially clear.[43]

It is probably the vivid parallelism between the story of Jesus in 2:6–8, which stresses his death, and the community life Paul prescribes for the Philippians that explains why Paul has added "Jesus" to his typical expression "in Christ." As in 2 Cor 4, where the name "Jesus" appears nine times, in Phil 2 Paul is saying that the normal shape of Christian ministry and life is one that resembles the dying of Jesus. This is the kind of very human life, one of obedience to the point of death, that Jesus the Messiah and Lord lived. Paul's vision of cross-shaped participation in Christ is coherent with the Gospels' portrayal of Jesus' understanding of Messiahship and his call to radical, death-like discipleship as participation in his death. This tradition of Jesus as suffering Messiah likely stands behind Paul's own spirituality of cruciformity, and it is for this reason that it is better to refer to the community "in Christ Jesus" as the community "in the Messiah Jesus."[44] Paul is not describing an ethic of imitation, but a spirituality of participation.

THE SIGNIFICANCE OF PHIL 2:5 FOR PAUL'S THEOLOGY AND SPIRITUALITY

We have argued that Phil 2:5 is best translated as "Cultivate this mindset— this way of thinking, acting, and feeling—in your community, which is in fact a community in the Messiah Jesus." This interpretation means that what is "in" Christ is not a disposition that is to be adopted or imitated, but a community that is to be shaped by the person the community inhabits, the person whose story is narrated in 2:6–11. Thus, while 2:5 is not imitative, it is also not merely locative. The location is inseparable from the story; the Messiah is inhabited only as his story is continued in analogous ways in the

---

43. Some interpreters come to similar conclusions about the overall thrust of the passage by supplying a phrase like "as is fitting in Christ" or "as is necessary in Christ," suggesting that [ὃ] δεῖ φρονεῖν (cf. Rom 12:3), [ὃ] πρέπει φρονεῖν, or a similar phrase is implied. See, e.g., Silva, *Philippians*, 97: "Be so disposed toward one another as is proper for those who are united in Christ Jesus." This is closer to a participatory than to a purely imitative reading. Romans 15:5 makes it clear, in either case, that Christ is the norm for the church's unified disposition: τὸ αὐτὸ φρονεῖν ἐν ἀλλήλοις κατὰ Χριστὸν Ἰησοῦν.

44. On the correspondence between Jesus and Paul in this regard, see my *Death of the Messiah*, 78–94, 106–11, 114–27. The participatory language of Jesus is about sharing in his cup and baptism (e.g., Mark 10:38).

community. This is a theology and spirituality of participation, as Paul had already hinted in 1:8. Paul presumes a continuity between the self-emptying and self-humbling Messiah Jesus and the reigning Lord Jesus in whom the church exists.[45]

Thus, 2:5 is indeed a bridge between 2:1-4 and 2:6-11, but it does not connect potential imitators to the model. Rather, 2:5 grounds Paul's exhortation in 2:1-4 in the narrative of Christ in 2:6-11, on the assumption that this narrative defines the suffering Messiah, not merely as a historical figure, but as the present, living Lord. The Messiah Jesus who emptied and humbled himself is the Lord in whom the Philippians, and all Christians, live, and he in them (e.g., Gal 2:19-20). Because the Philippians' life together is life together in the Messiah Jesus, that common life must have the same basic pattern as did Christ's; *their* story must be shaped by *his* story, because his story identifies him and therefore them.

Paul's mode of exhortation, then, is not simply to present Christ as an example of the correct inner attitude nor even of correct actions. Rather, Paul emphasizes the "in-the-Messiah-Jesus" dimension of the church's existence, grounding his exhortation in that dimension: those who live in the Messiah are to be conformed to the pattern of his self-humbling and self-emptying, not merely as imitators of a model, but as persons whose fundamental identity is to participate in him and thus in his story. Paul may speak of "obedience" (Phil 2:12), but it is an obedience to the Obedient One (2:7) and enabled by participation in him.[46]

If, as I have argued elsewhere, Phil 2:6-11 can in some sense be called Paul's "master story,"[47] then the significance of Phil 2:5 and of how it is a bridge between Christ and the community is weighty indeed. Again and again in Paul's letters, what looks like imitation is really participation. Even calls to "be[come] imitators of me" (e.g., 1 Cor 4:16; 11:1) are really invitations to more thoroughgoing participation in Christ.

Furthermore, participation for Paul is a two-way street; it is not merely believers being in the Messiah, but also the Messiah being in believers, as Gal 2:19-20 and Rom 8:1, 9-10 make especially clear. Indeed, these two texts from outside Philippians remind us that the reciprocal residence of Christ and the community also exists between Christ and the individual

---

45. This is what Bockmuehl emphasizes in arguing that ἐστίν rather than ἦν is the missing verb in 2:5 and briefly raising the subject of "participation." I agree with Bockmuehl about the suppressed verb, but contend that what is in Christ is not a disposition but a community.

46. The obedience to which Paul calls the Philippians is not to himself (contra CEB, NRSV).

47. See my *Cruciformity*, 23, 88-94, 164-74, 366-67, 383-85, 400-401, et passim.

believer. Paul may be speaking representatively in Gal 2, but he is also speaking personally. So, too, he may be speaking about the community in Phil 2, but he also envisions a parallel personal relationship with the Messiah for all believers, as Phil 3 makes clear.

Finally, if Phil 2:5 is about participation in the person and story of the Messiah Jesus, it is also about the inseparability of that participation from participation in the Spirit and indeed in God the Father. We have already noted the important language about participation (κοινωνία; "sharing" in CEB, NIV, NRSV) in the Spirit in 2:1. Paul's theological ethic (if that is even the right name for it), or spirituality, is one in which the reality of a living Messiah and an active Spirit make the Christlike life possible. We must also note that Paul credits God (the Father) as well, in 2:13, as he says that "God ... is at work in you," or better, "in your community (ἐν ὑμῖν)," enabling you [all] both to will and to work for his good pleasure" (NRSV, alt.). Furthermore, if the case for translating ἐν μορφῇ θεοῦ ὑπάρχων in 2:6 as "because he was in the form of God" is found convincing, it will be necessary to conclude that Paul's participatory spirituality is about self-giving love as sharing in the very character of God.[48]

All of this is to say that Paul's theology and his notion of participation, his spirituality, is not merely cruciform or Christocentric; it is not merely charismatic, focusing on the Spirit; it is inclusive of Father, Son, and Spirit. Here in Phil 2, we see yet more evidence that Paul's theology and spirituality of participation were inherently Trinitarian, even if his language did not fully express what came to fruition later. And this implicit Trinitarian theology and spirituality is why it is appropriate to speak of Phil 2:5 not only as a *textual* bridge, but also as a *theological* one: a bridge from Paul to the doctrine of the Trinity and to the spirituality of theosis, or deification: transformative participation in the life of the triune God.

But Phil 2:5, in context, makes it quite clear that such theosis—or, more simply, transformation and life—does not come primarily through contemplation or private holiness, but through service to others and faithful, even sacrificial witness to the world (Phil 1:27—2:4; 2:12–16).[49] It is by such participation in the exalted crucified Jesus that fullness of life and of God, as Andrew Lincoln would say, is found.[50]

---

48. See my *Inhabiting the Cruciform God*, 9–39, and the literature cited there.

49. On missional theosis in Paul, see my *Becoming the Gospel*.

50. See, e.g., Lincoln, "Spirituality in a Secular Age"; "The Spiritual Wisdom of Colossians." I am grateful to my research assistant, Gary Staszak, for his help on this essay, and to Tom Wright for conversation about it.

9

Wine, Debauchery, and the Spirit (Ephesians 5:18–19)

LLOYD K. PIETERSEN
Newman University

INTRODUCTION

It is widely acknowledged that Paul's injunction against the drinking of wine to destructive excess in Ephesians 5:18 was not primarily aimed at addressing a particular problem of alcohol abuse in the Ephesian congregation.[1]

A SUMANG'S CONFIDENT ASSERTION ECHOES Andrew Lincoln's conclusion in his magisterial commentary on Ephesians, which remains a significant resource for commentators on this letter more than twenty years after its publication. Lincoln has a particularly fine discussion of the verse under consideration in this chapter, Eph 5:18. There he considers whether the prohibition against drunkenness concerns misconduct in the assembly as in 1 Cor 11 or the influence of pagan mystery cults, especially that of Dionysus. He is unconvinced by these proposals and instead argues that drunkenness is a prime characteristic of the darkness mentioned earlier

1. Asumang, "Filled," 22.

(Eph 5:8) and that the drunkenness/Spirit contrast here demonstrates the folly/wisdom contrast of the immediate context.[2] In this chapter I survey the discussion on this verse in the period since Lincoln's commentary, focusing particularly on the renewed emphasis on the Dionysian cult. While, like Lincoln, I remain unpersuaded by the specificity of the Dionysian hypothesis, I disagree with him concerning the reference to drunkenness and conclude that actual, or at least potential, drunkenness in the community was being addressed and that the contrast being drawn here is between worship in the Christian community and acceptable behavior in the context of Greco-Roman *symposia*.

DRUNKENNESS

Some commentators, in agreement with Lincoln, see no evidence for any specific issue of drunkenness and, noting the immediate context of wisdom and folly, suggest drunkenness here is used as an example of folly in contrast to being filled with the Spirit, which is the way of wisdom.[3] The vice lists of Ephesians in themselves contain no reference to drunkenness (Eph 4:31; 5:3–5). Although this is not exceptional, as a number of vice lists in the New Testament also do not include drunkenness amongst the vices listed (Mark 7:21–22; Rom 1:29–31; 2 Cor 12:20–21; Col 3:5–8; 1 Tim 1:9–10; 6:4–5; 2 Tim 3:2–4; Titus 3:3; 1 Pet 2:1; 4:15; Rev 9:21; 21:8; 22:15), it is strange that drunkenness is drawn attention to in 5:18 outside the context of such a list. Of course, drunkenness does feature as one of the vices elsewhere (Rom 13:13; 1 Cor 5:10–11; 6:9–10; Gal 5:19–21; 1 Pet 4:3). This combination of the lack of mention in the Ephesian vice lists and the specific mention at this point in the letter suggests that drunkenness is indeed a specific issue in the congregation(s) addressed. This is strengthened by the fact that some of the earliest commentators on this passage had no hesitation in assuming the reference was to actual drunkenness. Clement of Alexandria, for example, refers to drinking in the context of feasting and advocates moderation at such events. He graphically describes drunken behavior resulting from excess drinking at feasts and specifically quotes our text in this context.

> Wherefore most people say that you ought to relax over your cups, and postpone serious business till morning. I however think that then especially ought reason to be introduced to mix in the feast, to act the part of director (pedagogue) to

---

2. Lincoln, *Ephesians*, 343–5.

3. R. Martin, *Ephesians*, 64–65; Yoder-Neufeld, *Ephesians*, 238–40; O'Brien, *Ephesians*, 387–94; Schnackenburg, *Ephesians*, 236–37.

> wine-drinking, lest conviviality imperceptibly degenerate to drunkenness.... But the miserable wretches who expel temperance from conviviality, think excess in drinking to be the happiest life; and their life is nothing but revel, debauchery, baths, excess, urinals, idleness, drink. You may see some of them, half-drunk, staggering, with crowns round their necks like wine jars, vomiting drink on one another in the name of good fellowship; and others, full of the effects of their debauch, dirty, pale in the face, livid, and still above yesterday's bout pouring another bout to last till next morning.... With reason, therefore, the apostle enjoins, "Be not drunk with wine, in which there is much excess" (*Paed.* 2.2).

Augustine can assume in passing that some whom he is addressing are struggling with drunkenness and he quotes our text in this context (*Tract. Ev. Jo.* 49.14). Chrysostom, in his homily on this passage, clearly takes the reference to drunkenness literally. "Wine has been given us for cheerfulness, not for drunkenness.... For it is of all things right for even a private individual to keep himself far from drunkenness" (*Hom. Eph.* 19).

Caesarius of Arles (sixth century) gave a number of sermons against drunkenness, which was obviously a problem in the Christian community of his day. In Sermon 46 he specifically inveighs against drunkenness at banquets.

> Indeed, dearly beloved, although the vice of drunkenness is serious and exceedingly hateful to God, it has spread into the daily life of men throughout the world because of the example of many, with the result that men who refuse to acknowledge God's precepts no longer think or believe that it is a sin. The matter has reached a point where they ridicule at their banquets men who can drink less, and in their harmful friendship do not blush to encourage men to take more drink than they should. A person who forces another to saturate himself with excessive drink would cause less harm by wounding his body with a sword than if he kills his soul with drunkenness (*Serm.* 46.1).

Three main solutions have been proposed to the question as to why drunkenness is mentioned at this point in the letter. First, the situation is either similar to that of the Corinthians in 1 Cor 11:21 or drunkenness as a means of escape from the pressure of evil days (5:16) is affecting the congregation.[4] Second, the issue concerns cultic inebriation especially associ-

---

4. Dunn, *Jesus and the Spirit*, 238; Houlden, *Paul's Letters from Prison*, 328; Muddiman, *Ephesians*, 247-48. M. Barth is attracted to this possibility, *Ephesians*, 580-82.

ated with the worship of Dionysus.⁵ Third, the warning is directed against drinking practices associated with *symposia* or feasts connected with guilds and clubs.⁶

Similar to Corinth

Muddiman sees this as the clearest explanation as to why the contrast between drunkenness and being filled with the Spirit leads immediately on to a description of Christian worship in vv. 19–20. He thinks this must be a reference to drunken disorder at the Eucharist in a similar manner to 1 Cor 11:21.⁷ However, the lack of any specific reference to the Eucharist in our passage, unlike 1 Corinthians, makes this unlikely.⁸ Nevertheless, the reference to both the Spirit and to singing is significant and, when the broader context of 1 Cor 11–14 is taken into account, does suggest some parallels as I argue below.

Dionysus

The Dionysian hypothesis was argued by Cleon Rogers, who claimed that he pursued this following reading Marcus Barth's commentary on Ephesians.⁹ Rogers supported his claim with reference to both the widespread (in the sense of temporal, geographical, social, and cultural) character of the cult and the specific worship associated with it. The former means that the cult was undoubtedly to be found in Ephesus and the latter specifically included intoxication with wine, frenzied dancing, and musical accompaniment. Rogers suggests that "debauchery" (ἀσωτία) "is certainly a fitting and descriptive term to describe the behavior of Dionysian worshipers."¹⁰

Porter criticizes Rogers for not focusing specifically on the Ephesian context and relying too heavily on secondary sources.¹¹ Instead Porter draws on evidence from Euripides' *Bacchae*, lines 279–301, in which mortals are filled with wine and Dionysus is a god who is poured out, produces proph-

---

5. Evans, "Ephesians 5:18–19"; Hendriksen, *Exposition*, 238–41; Porter, "Ephesians 5:18–19"; Rogers, "Dionysian"; Witherington III, *Letters*, 311.
6. Best, *Ephesians*, 506–10; Gosnell, "Ephesians 5:18–20."
7. Muddiman, *Ephesians*, 247.
8. So, rightly, Lincoln, *Ephesians*, 343.
9. Rogers, "Dionysian," 249 n.1.
10. Ibid., 256.
11. Porter, "Ephesians 5:18–19," 71.

ecy, and enters fully into the body of a person. He notes the similarities between this and Eph 5:18-19. Porter continues by citing the evidence for the Dionysian cult at Ephesus at the time of the letter and arguing for the significance of singing as part of the ritual of the cult. He concludes, however, that these observations do not prove decisively that there is a Dionysian background to Eph 5:18-19, but rather that the question needs to be reopened in the light of these indicators.[12]

Evans takes up this challenge.[13] He thinks that the parallels with the *Bacchae*, suggested by Porter, are impressive, but goes on to find possible Dionysian echoes in Luke 1:15; John 2:1-10; 4:10-14; 6:54-58; 7:37-39; 15:1-5; Acts 2:13-15; 5:39; 16:26; 26:14, 24-25; 1 Cor 12:13; 14:23. His final section examines attitudes in late antiquity to religious intoxication, drawing on both Greek and Jewish sources. He concludes:

> It is probable, therefore, that Paul's warning in Eph 5:18, which deliberately echoes Prov 23:31 in the Old Greek, was directed against pagan religious intoxication, best known in the form of the cult of Dionysus. It is hard to imagine that Paul's readers would not have thought of this well known cult, which was especially well known in Asia Minor and in Ephesus particularly.[14]

Both Porter and Evans have provided sufficient examples to counter Lincoln's view that there is "no clear evidence that [the Dionysian cult] had a continuing negative influence on the churches of Asia Minor."[15] However, Porter and Evans fail to demonstrate conclusively that this is the issue being addressed in the text of Ephesians. However remarkable the parallels with Euripides are, and despite Evans' impressive evidence concerning religious intoxication from Jewish literature, neither of them are able to produce evidence from the text of Ephesians itself. The ritual similarities that Porter notes (hymn singing and parallels with Jewish hymnody and Dionysian practices) are intriguing but not decisive, particularly when these ritual components are compared to the far more prevalent phenomenon of the *symposium*.

---

12. Ibid., 79-80.
13. Evans, "Ephesians 5:18-19."
14. Ibid., 200.
15. Lincoln, *Ephesians*, 343.

Symposia

Every commentator wrestles with the sudden and unexpected command not to be drunk with wine. Few notice the specific "with wine" (οἴνῳ) in this text. Of course, many note that the first half of the verse is a direct quotation from the LXX of Prov 23:31 μὴ μεθύσκεσθε οἴνῳ but this does not solve the problem as to why this quotation? Μεθύσκομαι of itself simply means "to become intoxicated" without any indication of the alcoholic beverage involved and other texts that refer to drunkenness likewise do not specify the beverage (Matt 24:49; Luke 12:45; 21:34; Rom 13:13; 1 Cor 5:11; 6:10; Gal 5:21; 1 Thess 5:7). Beer was another contender for drunkenness in the ancient world. In ancient Mesopotamia beer was much more readily available than wine and was considerably cheaper.[16] Beer was also the drink of choice in ancient Egypt and the "strong drink" (שֵׁכָר) of the Hebrew Bible is almost certainly beer.[17] Pliny the Elder (*Natural History* 14.29.149) regarded France and Spain as essentially beer provinces. Strabo states that beer is a "common drink to many peoples, although the ways of preparing it are different" (*Geography* 17.2.5). Athenaeus has a very interesting passage on wine and beer that indicates that beer was the favored drink of those who could not afford wine:

> But Hellanicus says, that the vine was first discovered in Plinthina, a city of Egypt; on which account Dion, the academic philosopher, calls the Egyptians fond of wine and fond of drinking: and also, that as subsidiary to wine, in the case of those who, on account of their poverty, could not get wine, there was introduced a custom of drinking beer made of barley; and moreover, that those who drank this beer were so pleased with it that they sung and danced, and did everything like men drunk with wine. Now Aristotle says, that men who are drunk with wine show it in their faces; but that those who have drunk too much beer fall back and go to sleep; for wine is stimulating, but beer has a tendency to stupefy (*Deipn.* 1.61).

So we cannot automatically assume that drunkenness is a result of excess *wine* drinking in the ancient world without further contextual evidence.

A handful of "drunkenness" texts, besides Eph 5:18, do, however, mention wine: Matt 11:19; Luke 7:34 (οἰνοπότης); John 2:10 (πᾶς ἄνθρωπος πρῶτον τὸν καλὸν οἶνον τίθησιν καὶ ὅταν μεθυσθῶσιν τὸν ἐλάσσω); 1 Cor 11:21 (μεθύω but implying wine due to the context of the Lord's Supper); 1 Tim

---

16. Powell, "Wine," 106.
17. Homan, "Beer."

3:3; Titus 1:7 (πάροινος); 1 Pet 4:3 (οἰνοφλυγία). This last text is instructive in that it combines the notion of excess wine, drinking parties (κώμοις, πότοις), and debauchery (ἀσωτίας). The semantic field of κῶμος and πότος takes us into the realm of the *symposium*.

Plato, as always, is instructive in connection with drunkenness at *symposia*. Whilst in the *Republic* he clearly condemns drunkenness, his position is more nuanced at the time of writing the *Laws*. In the latter work carefully controlled drunkenness is advocated for those aged forty and over. Specifically, he argues that the function of wine is to enable the old, who would otherwise be ashamed, to join in *singing*.[18]

> How then shall we encourage them [older men] to take readily to singing? Shall we not pass a law that, in the first place, no children under eighteen may touch wine at all, teaching that it is wrong to pour fire upon fire either in body or in soul, before they set about tackling their real work, and thus guarding against the excitable disposition of the young? And next, we shall rule that the young man under thirty may take wine in moderation, but that he must entirely abstain from intoxication and heavy drinking. But when a man has reached the age of forty, he may join in the convivial gatherings and invoke Dionysus, above all other gods, inviting his presence at the rite (which is also the recreation) of the elders, which he bestowed on mankind as a medicine potent against the crabbedness of old age, that thereby we men may renew our youth, and that, through forgetfulness of care, the temper of our souls may lose its hardness and become softer and more ductile, even as iron when it has been forged in the fire. Will not this softer disposition, in the first place, render each one of them more ready and less ashamed to sing chants and "incantations" (as we have often called them), in the presence, not of a large company of strangers, but of a small number of intimate friends? (*Laws* 2.666a–c).

So Plato encourages older men to get drunk at banquets in order to enable them to sing without shame. Drunkenness, for Plato, enables singing. It is important to note that drunkenness, for Plato, means getting really intoxicated. "The text of the *Laws*, Plato's other dialogues and other sources all suggest that the Greeks got, if anything, even more drunk than do modern

---

18. See the excellent discussion in Belfiore, "Wine." She argues that σωφροσύνη for Plato is a constant combat against the anti-rational. However, older people suffer from excessive coldness and sobriety and thus need to become drunk with wine in order to restore the fiery disposition of the young and thereby enable them to once again engage in the combat that is essentially required for σωφροσύνη.

imbibers of distilled spirits."[19] This, it seems to me, provides the most appropriate background to our text. Rather than requiring becoming drunk with wine in order to sing, being filled with the Spirit enables gathered believers, as "a small number of intimate friends," to sing freely among themselves.

EARLY CHRISTIAN WORSHIP AS SYMPOSIA

Although, as stated above, the specific abuses at Corinth in connection with the Eucharist are unlikely to be in view here, nevertheless the wider context of 1 Cor 11–14 does provide some clues as to what is going on in our Ephesian text. Smith has provided a detailed case for viewing all meals in the Greco-Roman era (defined by him as peoples of the Mediterranean world from 300 BCE—300 CE) as derived from a common banquet tradition comprised of a broad set of banquet customs and ideology.[20] Smith includes mystery cult meals, *symposia*, funerary banquets, Jewish banquets, and Christian banquets in this common banquet tradition. Specifically, for the purpose of this chapter, he argues that "*[w]henever they met as a church*, early Christians regularly ate a meal together."[21] Although Smith overstates his case, particularly with respect to Jewish banquets, he does make some relevant observations concerning the Pauline churches. He argues that the early church's gathering followed the common banquet tradition in which they ate a meal (δεῖπνον) together and followed this with the *symposium* (συμπόσιον). Christian instruction, prayers, and singing were the ways in which the church adapted the Greco-Roman tradition of post-dinner entertainment. Smith argues persuasively that this makes the most sense of 1 Cor 11–14, where chapter 11 concerns issues around the δεῖπνον and chapters 12–14 issues around the συμπόσιον. In this context, the contrast between the drunkenness of 1 Cor 11:21 and the statement in 1 Cor 12:13 that "we were all made to drink of one Spirit" is instructive. Also instructive is the repetition of συνέρχομαι (1 Cor 11:17, 18, 20, 33, 34; 14:23, 26). The church comes together to eat, sing, and receive instruction. Noteworthy is the inclusion of ψαλμός in 1 Cor 14:26 as this is also found in Eph 5:19 and only elsewhere in the Pauline corpus at Col 3:16. Although Smith does not deal with Ephesians, if he is correct that early Christian gatherings consisted of eating together followed by worship then this should apply here. I suggest that this analysis does makes most sense of this letter. Given this common banquet tradition and that drinking wine took place during the *symposium*,

19. Ibid., 430.
20. Smith, *Symposium*.
21. Ibid., 1; his emphasis.

if Christian worship is seen as the equivalent of the *symposium* then the contrast between wine drinking to excess and drinking of/being filled by the Spirit follows naturally. The pattern in both 1 Cor 11–14 and Eph 5:18–19 is "do not get drunk with wine, but drink of/be filled with the Spirit."[22]

WINE AND THE GOOD LIFE

Although *symposia* might be criticized by the author of Ephesians for their excessive drinking, I think there is more going on here than just a condemnation of such drinking. In the Greco-Roman philosophical world εὐδαιμονία (well-being) was the goal of life. But how was such happiness to be achieved? *The* model for the happy life or of human well-being was Socrates. "To adopt Socrates as one's paradigm, as Plato and many others did, was already to concede wine a place in the good life."[23] Socrates, through the vehicle of the *Symposia* of both Plato and Xenophon, is at his most inspired in the context of drinking wine. Wine thus becomes a powerful symbol of the good life, human happiness, and well-being. An abundance of wine demonstrates that one is enjoying the good life. But this is precisely what our author seeks to counter. It is not wine, but the Spirit, that brings inspiration and produces human well-being.

Our author also has to contend with the Hebrew Scriptures where wine is also seen as a symbol of the good life. Melchizedek famously brings out bread and wine to Abram (Gen 14:18), and a sign of God's blessing is plenty of grain and wine (Gen 27:28); wine is offered as a drink offering to Yahweh (Exod 29:40), and is the source of joy (Ps 104:15). Abundance of wine is a mark of prosperity (Prov 3:10), and the planting of vineyards accompanied by the drinking of wine is a sign of the restoration of the land (Amos 9:14). Third Maccabees 6:30–36 provides a good example of the association of wine with celebration and thanksgiving:

> Then the king, when he had returned to the city, summoned the official in charge of the revenues and ordered him to provide to the Jews both wines and everything else needed for a festival of seven days, deciding that they should celebrate their rescue with all joyfulness in that same place in which they had expected to meet their destruction. Accordingly those disgracefully treated and near to death, or rather, who stood at its gates, arranged for a

---

22. This does not necessarily imply Pauline authorship of Ephesians nor that the author knew 1 Corinthians. I am simply suggesting that both letters reflect the fact that the early church met both to share a meal and worship.

23. Tarrant, "Wine," 22.

banquet of deliverance instead of a bitter and lamentable death, and full of joy they apportioned to celebrants the place that had been prepared for their destruction and burial. They stopped their chanting of dirges and took up the song of their ancestors, praising God, their Savior and worker of wonders. Putting an end to all mourning and wailing, they formed choruses as a sign of peaceful joy. Likewise also the king, after convening a great banquet to celebrate these events, gave thanks to heaven unceasingly and lavishly for the unexpected rescue that he had experienced. Those who had previously believed that the Jews would be destroyed and become food for birds, and had joyfully registered them, groaned as they themselves were overcome by disgrace, and their fire-breathing boldness was ignominiously quenched. The Jews, as we have said before, arranged the aforementioned choral group and passed the time in feasting to the accompaniment of joyous thanksgiving and psalms. And when they had ordained a public rite for these things in their whole community and for their descendants, they instituted the observance of the aforesaid days as a festival, not for drinking (ποτός) and gluttony, but because of the deliverance that had come to them through God.

This text, probably to be dated around 100 BCE, combines drinking of wine with singing and specifically includes psalms. But interestingly, the writer is careful to insist that this occasion for rejoicing with wine and singing should not be interpreted as a classic drinking party (ποτός). So, from a Jewish perspective, wine too is a symbol of the good life, but drinking it in the context of feasting, singing, and thanksgiving to God has to be carefully distinguished from the Greek *symposium*.

THE PROBLEM WITH WINE

Although, as we have seen, wine is a powerful symbol for rejoicing and the "good life" it is also problematic when imbibed in excess. Both classical authors and the Hebrew Bible note this dark side. Moderation or self-control (σωφροσύνη) was a key virtue and the Plato of the *Republic*, for example, advocates this with regards to eating and drinking:

> And for the multitude are not the main points of self-control (σωφροσύνη) these—to be obedient to their rulers and themselves to be rulers over the bodily appetites and pleasures of food, drink, and the rest? (Plato, *Republic* 389d-e)

Later, Plato is somewhat disparaging of those who are "lovers of wine": "'Again,' said I, 'do you not observe the same thing in the lovers of wine (φιλοίνους)? They welcome every wine on any pretext'" (Plato, *Republic* 475a). In the Hebrew Bible there are clear warnings about the effects of intoxication with wine: "Wine is a mocker, strong drink a brawler, and whoever is led astray by it is not wise" (Prov 20:1). Isaiah condemns those who pursue strong drink and wine without regard for the deeds of Yahweh (Isa 5:11–12); priests and prophets err in vision due to their intoxication with strong drink and wine (Isa 28:7). Temperance, rather than abstinence, is advocated, just as in the classical Greek writers. Sirach 31:25–31 is the clearest example of this attitude to wine:

> Do not try to prove your strength by wine-drinking,
>   for wine has destroyed many.
> As the furnace tests the work of the smith,
>   so wine tests hearts when the insolent quarrel.
> Wine is very life to human beings
>   if taken in moderation.
> What is life to one who is without wine?
>   It has been created to make people happy.
> Wine drunk at the proper time and in moderation
>   is rejoicing of heart and gladness of soul.
> Wine drunk to excess leads to bitterness of spirit,
>   to quarrels and stumbling.
> Drunkenness increases the anger of a fool to his own hurt,
>   reducing his strength and adding wounds.
> Do not reprove your neighbor at a banquet of wine (ἐν συμποσίῳ οἴνου),
>   and do not despise him in his merrymaking;
> speak no word of reproach to him,
>   and do not distress him by making demands of him.

The Sirach and 3 Maccabees texts provide differing perspectives. Eating and drinking in the context of praising God must specifically not be seen as the equivalent of a drinking party. On the other hand, *symposia* are not condemned as such. It is fine to engage in such drinking and feasting as part of human well-being as long as such drinking is done in moderation. On this, both Jewish and classical authors agree. Even in the *Laws*, Plato insists that for younger men drinking should be done in moderation and without intoxication; he only advocates inebriation for older men in order to counter their predisposition towards sobriety and to provide a context for the combat necessary for true σωφροσύνη as noted above.

EPHESIANS 5:18–19

Given the above background concerning wine as a powerful symbol of the good life and yet the clear expectation that drinking should be in moderation expressed in Greek moral philosophy, the Hebrew Scriptures, and intertestamental literature, we turn now to Ephesians itself.

As is widely acknowledged, Ephesians is in two halves, with the first half ending with the "Amen" at the end of chapter 3. The first half, in the form of an extended thanksgiving,[24] reminds readers of their calling in Christ whereas the second half exhorts them to "lead a life worthy of [that] calling" (Eph 4:1). The paraenesis of the second half holds out the writer's version of "the good life" as constituted in Christ. This life is characterized by humility, gentleness, patience, love (Eph 4:2), righteousness and holiness (Eph 4:24), truthfulness (Eph 4:25), kindness and forgiveness (Eph 4:32), and thanksgiving (Eph 5:3). Throughout this section the contrast is made between the old life as futility, licentiousness, darkness, and folly, and the new life in Christ as light and wisdom. Finally, before moving into the instruction as to how groups of believers should relate to each other (the so-called "household code"), the author makes a bold move. His readers, both Jew and gentile, would well know the symbolism of wine and its association with merriment, the good life, and especially wisdom, as exemplified on the one hand by Socrates in the context of the *symposium* and on the other hand by writings such as 3 Maccabees and Sirach. The classic literature of both Jew and gentile is replete, however, with warnings that excess drinking of wine leads to debauchery. The exception is Plato's instructions for older men in the *Laws*. For the author of Ephesians, therefore, wine, because of its inherent ambiguity, can now no longer function as a symbol of the good life in Christ. Instead *the* symbol of the good life is the Spirit with which believers are exhorted to be continually filled—there can be no excess here and the external manifestation of this filling with the spirit is singing, so characteristic of the wine-filled life! Rejoicing and merriment are still to characterize the lives of believers (the author is no kill-joy), but the source of this rejoicing is entirely different to that valued by both Jew and gentile outside of Christ. Furthermore, unlike the Plato of the *Laws*, inebriation is not necessary for older members of the Christian congregation to participate in community celebration. For it is the Spirit, rather than wine, that enables young and old to sing without shame.

This bold association of Spirit-filling with wine-drinking does resonate with Acts 2:13–15 as has been widely noted (with no suggestion of

---

24. Lincoln, *Ephesians*, xxxvi.

literary dependence either way). It also resonates with Philo's notion of "sober intoxication":

> For in the case of those who are under the influence of divine inspiration, not only is the soul accustomed to be excited, and as it were to become frenzied, but also the body is accustomed to become reddish and of a fiery complexion, the joy which is internally diffused and which is exulting, secretly spreading its affections even to the exterior parts, by which many foolish people are deceived, and have fancied that sober persons were intoxicated. And yet indeed those sober people are in a manner intoxicated, having drunk deep of all good things, and having received pledges from perfect virtue (Philo, *De ebriatate* 147-48).

CONCLUSION

Drunkenness is characteristic of the life of folly as argued by Lincoln. However, the fact that drunkenness is not mentioned in the Ephesian vice lists suggests that its specific mention at this point in the letter indicates that actual drunkenness is a problem being addressed by the author. Clearly subsequent interpreters of this passage used it to address issues of drunkenness affecting their congregations as seen above. It is unlikely, however, that the issue is abuse of the Eucharist as in 1 Cor 11, but commentators who take this view are on the right lines due to the subsequent reference to Christian worship in 1 Cor 12-14. Rather, the widespread practice of drinking wine to excess at banquets is in view. This is in the light of early Christian worship taking the form of a banquet and in the light of Plato's specific encouragement of older men to become intoxicated in the *Laws* and of wine being seen as a symbol of the good life in both Jewish and Greco-Roman literature. The good life for our author is manifested not in the "obscene, silly, and vulgar talk" (Eph 5:4) so characteristic of excess drinking,[25] but in thanksgiving (this frames Eph 5:4-20) expressed in song inspired by the Spirit.

Finally, the fact that the author has *symposia* in view does not completely negate the Dionysian hypothesis. For, of course, Dionysus was regularly invoked at banquets. "When the unmixed wine is poured during the dinner [δεῖπνον], the Greeks call upon the name of the 'Good Deity,' giving

---

25. In 5:4 μωρολογία is a hapax but the word occurs, for example, in Plutarch, *De garrulitate* 4: "but it is foolish talk (μωρολογία) which converts the influence of wine into drunkenness."

honor to the deity who discovered the wine; he was Dionysus."[26] But this invocation of Dionysus in the context of the banquet does not, of course, make every banquet an instance of the Dionysian cult. It is this wider context of the consumption of excess wine at banquets rather than the specific instance of the cult of Dionysus that is in view.[27]

---

26. Athenaeus, *Deipn.* 15.675b-c.

27. For a clear exploration of the banquet as a social institution in the ancient world, see D. E. Smith, *Symposium*.

10

The Metaphor of the Face in Paul[1]

STEPHEN C. BARTON
University of Durham

INTRODUCTION: THE PHENOMENOLOGY OF THE FACE

To ask after the meaning and significance of the human face is to engage with a subject of complexity and wonder.[2] For we are considering more than the front of the head and related matters of an anatomical kind. Rather, we are dealing with *the self* and *the self in relation*, that is, matters of a psychological and socio-cultural kind, and ultimately matters of morality and metaphysics. More than any other part of the body, the face is the place,

---

1. It is a privilege to contribute to a *Festschrift* in honor of Andrew Lincoln. Over many years, I have benefited greatly from Andrew's wide-ranging scholarly contributions to New Testament theology and spirituality, not least in Pauline and post-Pauline studies. For their comments on an earlier draft of this essay, I am grateful to Michael Lakey, George H. Van Kooten, and Walter Moberly, and to audiences at Ripon College Cuddesdon, and at the New Testament Research Seminar, Durham University.

2. See further, Ford, *Self and Salvation*, 17-29, in fruitful engagement with Emmanuel Levinas; also, Scruton, *The Face of God*, 73-111. From a neurophysiological perspective, discussing especially the experiences of people with facial *losses*, see Cole, *About Face*.

and facing is the action, where the self receives and expresses its identity, character, and values, especially in *relations of the face*, including relations which, as we say, are "face-to-face."

And, of course, what we say about the face has the potential for multiple elaborations and intensifications, not least by virtue of the face's special privilege and burden as the site of the senses. Furthermore, because the face is the site of the senses, and because also the face is at the "interface" between our inner and outer worlds, it is a *communicative* surface, both intense and complex. The face reveals, but it also conceals. It reaches out, but it also turns inward. It displays sincerity, but also hides in practices of dissimulation. It is active, but also passive, acted upon. It regards, but is also regarded, a matter both moral and aesthetic. It registers emotions, but what the emotions register is often fluid, gravitating between pleasure and pain, desire and disgust.

To speak of the face is also to speak of recognition, time, memory, and change. Knowledge of the other comes through the imprint that the face (the life, the character) of the other leaves on our memories; and such knowledge is sharpened by face-to-face encounter repeated over time. Just as important: knowledge of *oneself* comes through the recognition, acceptance, hospitality, love, and judgment one finds in face-to-face relations with the other. It is significant others who help us know who we are; and such knowledge comes in relations of the face, where people are turned towards each other, or where the face of the other is carried in the memory.

To speak of people who are turned toward each other in relations of the face is to speak of practices of human sociality; and, of course, in theological terms, one critical set of such practices is the church. Church is the place, time, people, and practice where people engage, week by week, in relations of the face—quite literally: for example, in the liturgical act where lips and cheeks touch in the kiss of peace. But those relations of the face are also memorial and eschatological, and are expressed in ritual and symbol, as in "Do this [i.e., eat this bread, drink this cup] in memory of me." Here, the self, both individual and communal, in the intimate act of ingestion, which is also an act of *communion*, is made open to transformation in the presence of the (invisible!) face of an Other who is transcendent, the face of Christ.

THE FACE IN THE BIBLICAL WORLD

Paul and the Self-in-Relation

Having offered some phenomenological observations regarding the face, hinting at the ways in which face-to-face relations have a revelatory, formative, and even transformative potential, I turn now to consider the metaphor of the face in Paul. Focusing on a quite limited sample, my aim is to discern how this metaphor plays in his letters. The examples I have in mind all come from the Corinthian correspondence: 1 Cor 13:12; 2 Cor 3:18; 2 Cor 4:6.

The rich complexity of the facial metaphors in these three texts is profound. Broadly speaking, these metaphors have their roots in Paul's Scriptures and Jewish heritage. They have to do with *the eschatological knowledge of God through personal encounter*, an encounter mediated by Christ and the Spirit. As a corollary, they have a corresponding notion of the transformation of both the self and the community.

Before proceeding to analyze the metaphor of the face, however, it is worth observing that Paul is a master in the use of metaphor generally to communicate what he wants to say. Many of these metaphors, like the facial metaphor, have to do with *salvation and the Christian life*, with transformed identity in Christ and with how to live that out. These include metaphors from the world of politics, the law, economics, athletics, and warfare; as well as metaphors from the world of the cult. They also include metaphors from Paul's Scriptures: and, as we shall see, the metaphor of "the face" is a metaphor with strong scriptural overtones. In general, it is safe to say that one primary focus of Paul's use of metaphor is *the self-in-relation*—the self in relation to God, to oneself, to the community, to the wider world, and to the cosmos. Such metaphors of self-in-relation are integral to the narrative dynamics of Paul's thought and practice as a whole.

The Face in Scripture

I referred just now to the scriptural roots of Paul's thought, so our next step must be to inquire briefly into facial imagery in the Old Testament and early Judaism. In the Old Testament, the Hebrew word for "face" is the plural פנים (*pānîm*) which, in its various forms, occurs over 2,100 times. As well as the literal usage, where פנים refers to the front part of the head, a number of more metaphorical uses may be identified.[3]

---

3. See further, Drinkwater Jr., "Face," 743–44; Lohse, "πρόσωπον κτλ.," 768–80; Simian-Yofre, "*pānîm*," 589–615.

(1) Commonly, it is the word used to denote proximity and presence, as in being in the presence of a superior or a king or God. A classic case is Jacob's wrestle with the mysterious "man," following which he names the place of encounter "Peniel" (i.e., "face of God"), a pun on פנים which is made clear in the explanation Jacob offers: "For I have seen God *face-to-face*, and yet my life is preserved" (Gen 32:30).

(2) Conversely, to "hide" one's face expresses withdrawal, absence, hiddenness, or distance, as when Adam and Eve hide from "the face" of the Lord God when he comes walking in the garden (Gen 3:8), or when Moses reminds the Israelites, in Deut 32:20, of God's promise to "hide" his face from them in consequence of their idolatry, or when the psalmist cries, "Do not hide your face from me. Do not turn your servant away in anger, you who have been my help" (Ps 27:9a; cf. 102:2; 143:7).[4]

(3) "Face" also stands for the person as a whole, as in Yahweh's promise, "My presence [lit. "my face"] will go with you" (Exod 33:14), meaning simply that Yahweh himself will go.

(4) Unsurprisingly, facial terminology is used for expressions of the emotions, both positive and negative: a "fallen" face expresses anger at rejection; a "shining" face expresses joy, commonly at the giving or receiving of a blessing or favor. Thus, in the famous words given to Moses in Num 6:24–26, the blessing of God is spoken of in terms of God making his face to "shine" upon the people, and of God "lifting up" his face upon them (cf. Ps 31:16; 67:1).

(5) Actions involving the face are also an indicator of social relations of subordination and superordination: to "fall on one's face" indicates homage to a superior (e.g., Gen 17:3); to have one's face "lifted up" indicates acceptance and approval, including reception of a blessing (e.g., Ps 27:6a).

(6) In relation to Yahweh, the aniconic tradition of Israel makes "seeing Yahweh's face" a sensitive and complex matter. The classic text here is Exod 33:20, where Yahweh tells Moses, "you cannot see my face and live; for no one shall see me and live"—this, in spite of the fact that, earlier in the same theophany narrative, the narrator informs us that "the Lord used to speak to Moses face-to-face, as one speaks to a friend" (Exod 33:11a). The echoes of this Moses tradition in Paul will be considered later. Here, what is important is the assumption that,

---

4. On the phrase "hide the face" in the OT, see further, Balentine, *The Hidden God*, 45–79.

while certain privileged people may see the face of God in certain circumstances, in general the individual has to be shielded from God's unmediated presence (e.g., by smoke and cloud or by God's protective "hand"), or that God's presence is granted in representative form only (e.g., in the form of an angel or of the divine כבוד, *kābôd* ["glory"]), or that God's presence is manifested in the cult, where "to see God's face" is to go up to the temple (e.g., Ps 42:2; 95:2).

(7) In a number of texts, the emphasis is not on seeing *per se*: rather, to speak of "seeing God" is to speak of being confident of God's grace and blessing. Thus, Ps 105:4 says, "Seek the Lord and his strength; seek his presence [lit. "face"] continually." Similar is Ps 27:8: "'Come,' my heart says, 'seek his face!' 'Your face, Lord, do I seek.'" What is important in such texts is the priority of keeping up an ongoing relation with God (not least through participation in temple worship), and understanding one's selfhood as *fulfilled in relation*—relation to God in particular.

The Face in Early Judaism

Broadly speaking, the same range of meanings is found in early Jewish writings, though with some interesting developments. For present purposes, I will cite evidence from Philo, Qumran, and 2 Enoch.

Philo of Alexandria.

Philo puts the face to the service of his Platonizing body-soul dualism.[5] First, on the question of whether language regarding the face of God is to be taken literally—itself part of a larger philosophical debate in which he is engaged, to do with how to understand anthropomorphic representations of God—Philo is vehement in his denial, concerned as he is sharply to distinguish his ontology from that of certain others.[6] Commenting on Gen 4:16 ("Then Cain went away from the presence [lit. "face"] of the Lord"), Philo says:

> For if the Existent Being has a face, and he that wishes to quit its sight can with perfect ease remove elsewhere, what ground have we for rejecting the impious doctrines of Epicurus, or the atheism of the Egyptians, or the mythical plots of play and poem of which the world is full? (*Post.* 2).

---

5. See further Lohse, πρόσωπον κτλ., 774.
6. See further, Van Kooten, "Man as God's Spiritual or Physical Image?" 128.

The same Platonizing dualism is evident in Philo's anthropology. For example, and following the lead of the Septuagint, Philo has God, at creation, breathe into the man's *face*, not his nostrils (cf. Gen 2:7). He thereby makes it clear that the face is, by divine design, the most important part of the body—because the face is most closely associated with the mind and the soul, and therefore with divine reason. As he says in *Legum Allegoriae*:

> The breathing "into the face" is to be understood both physically and ethically: physically, because it is in the face that He set the senses; for this part of the body is beyond other parts endowed with soul; but ethically, on this wise. As the face is the dominant element in the body, so is the mind the dominant element of the soul: into this only does God breathe, whereas He does not see fit to do so with the other parts, whether senses or organs of utterance and of reproduction; for these are secondary in capacity (*Leg. All.* I.39; cf. *Spec. Leg.* IV.123)

But particularly pertinent to our consideration of Paul are a number of texts where Philo elaborates on *transformed faces*—in particular, those of Abraham and Moses.[7] Speaking of Abraham, he says:

> Thus whenever he [Abraham] was possessed, everything in him changed to something better, eyes, complexion, stature, carriage, movements, voice. For the divine spirit which was breathed upon him from on high made its lodging in his soul, and invested his body with singular beauty, his voice with persuasiveness, and his hearers with understanding. (*de Virt.* 217)

Speaking of Moses, he says:

> For we read that by God's command he [Moses] ascended an inaccessible and pathless mountain.... Then after ... forty days ... he descended with a face far more beautiful than the one he had when he ascended, so that those who saw him were filled with awe and amazement; nor even could their eyes continue to stand the dazzling brightness that flashed from him like the rays of the sun. (*de Vita Mos.* ii.70)

What Philo's accounts of Abraham and Moses show is how readily facial idioms from Scripture offered rich resources for a theological anthropology, including ways of expressing the personal transformation arising from a graced relation to God. What his accounts show also is how the face functions as an outward expression of a person's inner life. Interestingly, Philo,

---

7. These two texts are cited in Martyn, "Epistemology," 104.

like some among his pagan philosophical contemporaries, posits outward bodily (and especially facial) beauty as a positive corollary of the inner beauty achieved through the transformation of mind and soul. Not so Paul, as we shall see.

Qumran.

Significant also among early Jewish sources are some texts from Qumran to which Joseph Fitzmyer drew attention.[8] Here are two:

> I will praise you, Lord, for you have *illuminated my face with your covenant* and from [. . . .] I will seek you; like the true dawn of the morning, you have appeared to me for enlightenment. (1 QH 4:5–6)

> Through me you have *illumined the faces of many* and you have shown yourself immeasurably strong. For you have given knowledge through your wondrous mysteries, and through your wondrous secret you have manifested your might with(in) me; you have done wonders before many *for the sake of your glory* and to make known your mighty acts to all the living. (1 QH 4:27–29)[9]

Interesting in relation to what we find in Paul is the image of God illuminating the face of the Teacher of Righteousness, and he in turn illuminating the faces of "the many" (i.e., the members of the community). Significant also is the role of the covenant (i.e., the Torah) as the medium of illumination imparting saving knowledge, all in the context of the revelation of God's glory. All told, it is as if the biblical narrative of the shining face of Moses (of Exod 34), along with his role in mediating the covenant to the people, provide a template for, on the one hand, the Teacher of Righteousness and his role in illuminating the community, and, on the other, for Paul in his transformative encounter with the Risen Christ, and in his role in mediating Christ (the "face" of God) to the eschatological community of Christ-followers.

---

8. Fitzmyer, "Glory Reflected," 630–44.
9. Ibid., 640.

2 Enoch.

That the metaphor of the face may also have a strong *moral aspect* (related, of course, to its theological and anthropological aspects) is well illustrated in a passage from *2 Enoch*:

> The Lord with his own two hands created mankind; in a facsimile of his own face, both small and great, the Lord created them. And whoever insults a person's face, insults the face of a king, and treats the face of the Lord with repugnance. He who treats with contempt the face of any person treats the face of the Lord with contempt. He who expresses anger to any person without provocation will reap anger in the great judgment. He who spits on any person's face, insultingly, will reap the same at the Lord's great judgment. (2 *En*. 44:1–3)

Remarkable here is the way in which the fundamental idea (from Gen 1:27) of humankind as made by God in the image of God is depicted in specifically facial terms—the human face is nothing less than "a facsimile" of God's own face—all this in order to constrain violence against the face and, by implication, to warrant an ethic of respect in face-to-face relations.[10]

The Face in the Roman World of Paul

What of the face in the wider world of Paul, the Roman world, in particular? Here, and to epitomize a vast subject, the face, along with other physiological features, plays a crucial role as a barometer of selfhood, identity, individual character, social relations, and moral and aesthetic values—particularly in connection with the ubiquitous quest for honor and the cultivation of shame. To take one example, there is the remarkable attention given to the phenomenon of *blushing* as a facial marker of the individual's sense of shame. Thus, Caitlin Barton argues that the blush, more precisely the *involuntary* (and therefore "natural") blush, expresses the Roman individual's competence as one thoroughly socialized in the norms of society. In other words, the involuntary blush expresses on the surface of the face the internalization of social norms in matters of appropriate self-control which makes one a proper member of society. Barton puts it well:

> To have a "sense of honor" in ancient Rome was to have a "sense of shame," of *pudor*. Latin *pudor* embraced a set of finely calibrated and counterpoised emotions ranged along a balance bar

---

10. See further, Van Kooten, "Man as God's Spiritual or Physical Image?" 102.

pivoting on the fulcrum of the blush. Every man or woman of honor in ancient Rome walked a high wire simultaneously supported and aggravated by the great ballast weight of shame. To move, to live, while balancing this burden required energy, grace, and skills finely honed in the course of a lifetime. The blush was the totter, the tremor, the disequilibrium at the center. Roman shame was felt first at the core of one's social being: the face, the *imago animi*. Even more particularly, shame was felt on the skin, the delicate and penetrable barrier through which the ancient Romans contacted one another and the world.[11]

A fine example, revealing of the coercive power of social norms and public *mores* over even the most senior of public performers, comes from Seneca:

> Certain even very constant men, when in the public eye, break out in a sweat, just as if they were fatigued and overheated. The knees of others, when they are about to speak, begin to tremble; I know of those whose teeth chatter, whose tongues falter, whose lips quiver. Training and experience can never eradicate this propensity; nature exerts her power and by this weakness makes herself felt by even the strongest man. I know that the blush, too, is like this, spreading suddenly over the faces of even the most dignified men. While the young are most likely to blush, nevertheless, the blush touches even the veteran and the old.[12]

Now, there is no evidence of blushing in the letters of Paul, either on the part of Paul himself or of his implied addressees or of implied third parties. But one can imagine it occurring, not least because Paul and his contemporaries participated in a society whose values were calibrated according to degrees of honor and shame. Did Peter blush when confronted by Paul, "*to his face* [κατὰ πρόσωπον]" in Antioch, over his withdrawal from table-fellowship with gentiles? Did "the strong" in Corinth blush when Paul urged them by letter to accommodate to "the weak" in accordance with his own practice modelled on Christ? Did the women prophets blush when Paul instructed them to cover their heads? Whether or not they did, it is an intriguing question opened up by what we know of the face and its performance in Roman society at large.

---

11. Barton, "The Roman Blush," 212.
12. Seneca, *Epistles*, 11:2, cited in Barton, "Roman Blush," 214–15.

THE METAPHOR OF THE FACE IN PAUL

Against this rich scriptural and socio-cultural backdrop of the multiple meanings of the face and facing, especially in the realms of the formation and transformation of the self and of selves in relation, we are now in a good position to offer an account of the face in Paul—that is, of how the face functions in Paul's reflections on God, Christ, the self, the community, the world, and the cosmos. The texts I will deal with are the three from Paul's Corinthian correspondence cited at the outset: 1 Cor 13:12; 2 Cor 3:18; and 2 Cor 4:6.

The Face as a Relational-Epistemological Metaphor

I begin with 1 Cor 13:12. This text comes at the climax of Paul's famous "hymn to love," which is located strategically in the center of an extended paraenesis on the understanding and practice of "spiritual things" (τὰ πνευματικά) in the Christian assembly (1 Cor 12–14). The situation appears to be that at least some people in the churches have developed what has been termed an "over-realized eschatology"—the conviction that, having received the Spirit, the new age has arrived, and believers are participating *already* in the life of heaven, as manifested in various kinds of gifts of knowledge and discernment, ecstatic speech, wonder-working, gifts of healing, and so on.

Problematic for Paul, however, is that these people—probably the ones who call themselves "the strong," and whom J. Louis Martyn labels the "Enthusiasts"[13]—are exercising their new-found spiritual powers in ways that threaten what is supremely important for any leader in the ancient world, namely, the leader's own authority and the peace and unity of the people as a whole. What Paul does in response is to make love (ἡ ἀγάπη) the measure of everything else. Paul's point is that whereas love is the full and final eschatological reality, the gifts of the Spirit are partial and transitory. Contrary to the Corinthians' understanding of the gifts and the power they bestow, the value of the gifts is relative and temporary. The *charismata* make possible what would not be possible otherwise in the time prior to the coming of the kingdom of God: anticipatory, partial sharing in the life of heaven. But when the kingdom of God comes (cf. 1 Cor 15:24–28), the mediation of revelation through "prophecies" and "knowledge" will not be necessary, since revelation will be direct and unmediated: God will be "all in all" (1 Cor 15:28). The gift of "tongues" likewise will be unnecessary because

---

13. Martyn, "Epistemology," 101.

communication will be total and transparent. All that will be left, all that will be necessary, will be the completeness (τὸ τέλειον, v. 10) of relation, human and divine, which is love.

At the climax of his paraenesis, and to drive home the point that the Corinthian "strong" have not yet "arrived," Paul introduces the metaphor of the mirror along with an interpretative elaboration: "For now we see in a mirror, dimly, but then we will see face-to-face. Now I know only in part; then I will know fully, even as I have been fully known [βλέπομεν γὰρ ἄρτι δι᾽ ἐσόπτρου ἐν αἰνίγματι, τότε δὲ πρόσωπον πρὸς πρόσωπον· ἄρτι γινώσκω ἐκ μέρους, τότε δὲ ἐπιγνώσομαι καθὼς καὶ ἐπεγνώσθην]" (1 Cor 13:12).

Note, first, the repeated distinction between "now" and "then" in the two, carefully balanced parts of the statement: Paul is making an eschatological distinction—introducing a note of eschatological *reservation*—uncongenial to the Corinthian "strong." They do not yet participate fully in the life of heaven; and they must moderate their self-understanding and behavior accordingly.

Then, second, there is the implied contrast between seeing "in a mirror, dimly [or, "in a riddle": ἐν αἰνίγματι]" and seeing "face-to-face." For the latter expression, there is an undoubted allusion to the "face-to-face" traditions in Scripture mentioned already, such as Jacob at Peniel (Gen 32:30), and Moses in Exod 33:11, which says that, in the tent of meeting, "the Lord used to speak with Moses face-to-face, as one speaks to a friend." Against this scriptural background, the implication of the "face-to-face" metaphor is one of enormous privilege—limited in the past to a select few—the privilege of having unmediated access to the divine presence, and being transformed accordingly.

The connotations of the metaphor of seeing "in a mirror ἐν αἰνίγματι" are debated.[14] Most likely, there is an allusion to Num 12:6–8, where God tells Aaron and Miriam that, whereas to prophets he makes himself known in visions and dreams, to Moses he speaks "face-to-face [lit. "mouth to mouth"!]—clearly, not in riddles [ἐν εἴδει καὶ οὐ δι᾽ αἰνιγμάτων, LXX]" (v. 8). Given the allusion, what is remarkable is Paul's sense that, in the eschaton, the privilege accorded by God to Moses will be accorded to all (and certainly not just to "the strong"). But what is clear also is that Paul is making a distinction between sight (and with it, relationship) that is indirect or mediated and sight (and therefore relationship) that is direct and unmediated, "face-to-face."

Third, as the language of "knowing" and "being known" in the parallel second part of the saying shows, the issue Paul is dealing with here is the

---

14. See most recently, Litwa, "Transformation through a Mirror."

claim to *knowledge* (γνῶσις) of a certain kind, what Paul refers to earlier as "all mysteries and all knowledge" (1 Cor 13:2). This is knowledge that *matters*. Most likely, it has to do with the nature and fate of the cosmos, human salvation, and how to live (cf. 1 Cor 8:1–3). Such knowledge is a valuable commodity. It offers a certain self-understanding and it confers status. It also provides a warrant for behaving in certain ways. Given that the churches in Corinth are prone to factionalism and that the factionalism is fuelled by rivalry, the claim to possess esoteric knowledge on the basis of experiences of the Spirit bestows a considerable advantage in the honor stakes.

Therefore, as with seeing, so with knowing: Paul offers a corrective by *re-describing reality*. As "seeing" in the present age is indirect, so "knowing" in the present age is partial only (cf. also v. 9). What is more, the knowledge of which Paul speaks is of a quite particular kind: not a matter of the acquisition of esoteric information, but knowledge that is *relational and interpersonal*, embedded in an implied narrative of human fulfillment predicated on, and enabled by, divine grace—hence, the final clause, "even as I have been fully known [καθὼς καὶ ἐπεγνώσθην]," the aorist passive implying the sovereign, saving initiative of God (cf. 1 Cor 8:3; also Gal 4:9). In the end, for Paul, knowledge is trumped by love. It is love, not knowledge, that "abides" (13:13); and it is that love which is implicit in the anticipation of seeing "face-to-face."

The Face as a Metaphor of Revelatory Encounter, Liberation, and Eschatological Transformation

I turn now to the passage from 2 Corinthians that runs from 2:14 to 4:6, in order to give special attention to the following two texts:

> And all of us, *with unveiled faces, seeing the glory of the Lord as though reflected in a mirror*, are being transformed into the same image from one degree of glory to another; for this comes from the Lord, the Spirit [ἡμεῖς δὲ πάντες ἀνακεκαλυμμένῳ προσώπῳ τὴν δόξαν κυρίου κατοπτριζόμενοι τὴν αὐτὴν εἰκόνα μεταμορφούμεθα ἀπὸ δόξης εἰς δόξαν καθάπερ ἀπὸ κυρίου πνεύματος]. (2 Cor 3:18)

> For it is the God who said, "Let light shine out of darkness," who has shone in our hearts to give the light of the knowledge of the glory of God *in the face of Jesus Christ* [ὅτι ὁ θεὸς ὁ εἰπών· ἐκ σκότους φῶς λάμψει, ὃς ἔλαμψεν ἐν ταῖς καρδίαις ἡμῶν πρὸς

φωτισμὸν τῆς γνώσεως τῆς δόξης τοῦ θεοῦ ἐν προσώπῳ ['Ιησοῦ] Χριστοῦ]. (2 Cor 4:6)

A major concern of 2 Corinthians is Paul's defence of the legitimacy of his apostleship. Reading between the lines, it is clear that his relations with the churches in Corinth are in jeopardy, in a way not at all evident in 1 Corinthians. Apparently, rival Christian preachers have appeared on the scene following his departure from Corinth, and his reputation has been disparaged. Paul, they were saying, is not a true apostle: he does not display the signs of an apostle, and the gospel he preaches is defective. The rivals are not identified—Paul refers to them disparagingly elsewhere as "pseudo-apostles [ψευδαπόστολοι]" (11:13)—but from what Paul says, they boasted in their Jewish heritage (cf. 11:22).

If we pick up the story at 2 Cor 2:14ff., it seems that one of the slurs against Paul made by these Jewish-Christian rivals is that Paul is a fraud, insincere, a huckster, just in it for the money (cf. 2:17). What is their evidence? For a start, so the accusation will have gone, Paul carried with him no authenticating letters of recommendation (presumably from Jerusalem) when he came to them (3:1–3). But the mention of *letters*, of things *written*, provides Paul with an opportunity to counter-attack in defense of the legitimacy of his apostolic ministry. Paul does not need a letter of recommendation like his rivals: the *Corinthians themselves* are his letter, written on the hearts of Paul and his co-workers, authored by none other than Christ, carried by Paul, and written, "not with ink but with the Spirit of the living God, not on tablets of stone but on tablets of human hearts" (3:3).

As Richard Hays has shown, this is not just "witty troping of the 'recommendation letter' motif,"[15] but language echoing against a very weighty scriptural background: "written on our hearts" echoes Jeremiah's "new covenant" written on the heart (cf. Jer 31:33); written "with the Spirit of the living God" echoes the picture in Exodus of God as covenant writer (Exod 31:8; cf. Deut 9:10–11); "not on tablets of stone but on tablets of human [lit. "fleshy"] hearts" echoes Ezek 36:26 ("And I will give you a new heart, and a new spirit I will give among you, and I will take away the stoney heart out of your flesh, and I will give you a fleshy heart"). What Paul is doing—probably with his Jewish-Christian rivals in mind (cf. 11:22)—is preparing the ground for a full-blown scriptural defence of the legitimacy of his apostleship and of himself as a true minister of the new eschatological covenant. This becomes explicit at v. 6: "[God] has made us competent to be ministers of a new covenant [καινῆς διαθήκης], not in a written code but in the Spirit; for the written code kills but the Spirit gives life."

15. Hays, *Echoes*, 127.

Paul's scriptural defense of himself as a true minister of the new eschatological covenant now proceeds by means of a comparison and contrast between his ministry and that of Moses. He does so against the backdrop of Exod 34, especially vv. 29–35. It is this Exodus tradition that supplies the motif of the face veiled and unveiled. It tells of Moses' descent from Mount Sinai carrying the two stone tablets of the covenant, of the skin of Moses' face shining with the divine glory "because he had been talking with God" (v. 29), and of his veiling his face before the people of Israel and unveiling it when speaking alone with God. The basic thrust of Paul's defense in vv. 7–11 is to argue from the lesser to the greater, from the temporary glory of the Mosaic covenant and of Moses himself (both described with enormous equivocation) to the far greater and permanent glory of the new covenant and the ministry of the eschatological Spirit in which Paul is engaged.

In 3:12–18, where the figure of Moses is treated dialectically, sometimes negatively, sometimes positively (since Moses did, after all, meet God face-to-face!), particular attention is given to the motif of "the veil" (κάλυμμα), and the veiling and unveiling of the face. Significantly, the passage begins and ends with a fundamental contrast: between the veiled face of Moses (v. 13) and the unveiled face of believers (v. 18). This provides the framework for other contrasts: between Paul's boldness and openness (cf. v. 12, πολλῇ παρρησίᾳ χρώμεθα) as a minister of the gospel and Moses' apparent reticence in veiling his face (v. 13); between the old covenant of the written law which is veiled (v. 14) and the new covenant of the Lord who is the Spirit (v. 17); and between a people whose minds are veiled (v. 15), so that they cannot read Scripture with regard to its true (christological) goal, and a people from whom the veil has been lifted and who have been brought to freedom and glory (vv. 17–18).

The crucial fulcrum of the passage is the reference in the middle to a "*turning*," in v. 16: "but when he [i.e., Moses, now interpreted for positive ends!] turns [ἐπιστρέψῃ] to the Lord, the veil is removed." As Hays puts it:

> Moses' act of entering God's presence and removing the veil becomes paradigmatic for the experience of Christian believers ("we all") who "with unveiled face, looking upon the reflected glory of the Lord, are being transformed into the same image, from glory to glory." . . . Moses prefigures Christian experience, but he is not a Christian. He is both the paradigm for the Christian's direct experience of the Spirit and the symbol for the old covenant to which that experience is set in antithesis.[16]

---

16. Ibid., 143.

As Hays also goes on to point out, there are two differences between the old and new covenants implied here. First, whereas Moses' unveiled turnings to the Lord were intermittent, those who now turn to the Lord through the agency of Christ live in a *continuous* experience of the divine presence, since the veil has been removed permanently. Second, whereas unmediated entry into God's presence was limited to Moses alone (cf. vv. 7, 13), now, under the new covenant, the experience of "seeing the glory of the Lord" is the privilege of "*all of us*" (v. 18).[17]

Seeing the glory of the Lord is *transformative*. In 3:18, the term μεταμορφόω, rare in Paul, is used in the passive to convey the radical idea that the person who turns to the Lord and gazes upon his glory is changed progressively by coming to share that same glory. What that means—and in particular its christological inflection—is developed in the crucial elucidation in 4:3–6:

> And even if our gospel is veiled, it is veiled to those who are perishing. In their case the god of this world has blinded the minds of the unbelievers, to keep them from seeing the light of the gospel of the glory of Christ, who is the image of God. For we do not proclaim ourselves; we proclaim Jesus Christ as Lord and ourselves as your slaves for Jesus' sake. For it is the God who said, "Let light shine out of darkness," who has shone in our hearts to give the light of the knowledge of the glory of God *in the face of Jesus Christ*.

With the juxtaposition of "light" and "darkness," there is an unmistakable allusion to Gen 1:3a, "Let there be light." But in the Greek, the verb for "shine" is in the future tense, so that the translation should read, "For it is the God who said, 'Light *will shine* out of darkness,' [ἐκ σκότους φῶς λάμψει] . . .'"; and this points us to another biblical allusion, Isa 9:2 (LXX, 9:1), where the prophet writes, "O people who walk in darkness, behold a great light. You who dwell in a land and shadow of death, light *will shine* upon you." Importantly, this double scriptural allusion is both creational and eschatological. Its significance is well brought out by Hays:

> The creator-redeemer God is said to shine light "in our hearts," because the new creation is manifest, according to Paul, precisely in the community of faith. This illumination yields knowledge "of the glory of God in the face of Jesus Christ." With that phrase, Paul catches up his foregoing discussion of glory and completes the unveiling of which he spoke in 2 Cor. 3:16–18. Moses covered his face to veil the glory, but his unveiled turning

17. Ibid.

to the Lord is recapitulated in the church, where all "with unveiled face" now gaze upon the glory of the Lord. The imagery of 3:18 paints a picture of the community of faith being transformed as they contemplate a vision of glory, but does not yet show the reader what they are gazing at. The source and character of the radiance remain, as it were, offstage. *The progression reaches its consummation in 4:6, as Paul, speaking openly as he had promised to do, declares that it is "the face of Jesus Christ" that manifests the glory.* Christ is the glory-bearing *eikōn* into which the community is being transformed, the paradigm for the prosopography of the new covenant.[18]

In Paul's religio-cultural context, his claim regarding the face of *Christ* as the reflecting mirror of the divine glory that transforms the faces of God's people is of utmost significance.[19] The comparison with the Qumran texts cited earlier is instructive. As Fitzmyer puts it: "For Paul the crucial factor in the development is *Christ as the image or mirror of the glory of the creator-God*. In the Qumran literature the crucial factor is the Mosaic law, for that is what illumines the face of the Teacher of Righteousness or of the priests and which is the means by which he or they illumine the faces of the Many."[20] Paul's claim regarding Christ corresponds with his claim that he is the minister of a *new* covenant and that, as he says subsequently, "if anyone is in Christ, there is a new creation: everything old has passed away; see, everything has become new!" (2 Cor 5:17).

It is worth adding that, for Paul, the transformation that comes from beholding the glory of God in the face of Christ is, in the present age at least, primarily *an inner, spiritual and moral, transformation*. There is a polemical context here, a clash of cultures and worldviews (cf. 2 Cor 4:4!). Probably influenced by physiognomic notions of an aesthetic kind, his Corinthian opponents appear to have held that divine wisdom manifests itself in physical beauty, not least in the lineaments of the face and in rhetorical prowess. They therefore impugned Paul's teaching and apostolic status on the basis of his physical and rhetorical weakness (cf. 2 Cor 10:10). But Paul sees things otherwise; and on the basis of a very different, cruciform, theological aesthetic, denies such a correlation altogether.[21] Indeed, he parodies it by boasting of his "weakness" and humiliations (e.g., 2 Cor 11:23–29), and

---

18. Ibid., 153; my emphasis. Cf. Fitzmyer, "Glory Reflected," 639.

19. Notably, only here does Paul speak of "the face of Christ" in this way—an observation I owe to John Barclay.

20. Fitzmyer, "Glory Reflected," 643.

21. Especially illuminating is Van Kooten, *Paul's Anthropology*, 326–28. On ancient physiognomics, see Swain, ed., *Seeing the Face*.

by drawing attention, not to his bodily perfection, but to his unremedied "thorn in the flesh" (2 Cor 12:7–9). For Paul, it is not outward appearance but inner transformation that is crucial. Thus, in Rom 12:2, the only other place where Paul uses μεταμορφόω, he speaks of being transformed "by the renewal of your *mind* [τοῦ νοὸς]." And in 2 Cor 4:16, he states pointedly, "Even though our outer nature is wasting away, *our inner nature* [ὁ ἔσω ἡμῶν] is being renewed day by day."

CONCLUSION

The face and the metaphor of the face in Scripture, in early Jewish and Greco-Roman antiquity, and in Paul, is of more than academic interest. At least as much as any time in human history, Western modernity has a fixation with the face, itself part of a wider fixation with sex and the body.[22] If Mary Douglas helped us to see that the body is cultural as well as natural, and that purity rules and rituals related to the surface of the body express in an emotionally powerful way the values of a society,[23] this is true in an especially concentrated way of the face. Thus, the "face-lift," both in mythology and as a form of cosmetic surgery expresses the desire for eternal youth and an anxiety about personal dissolution in death.[24] Advertisements for facial cosmetics communicate aesthetic norms about the construction and maintenance of beauty, and therefore of desirability: and such communication is effected through the faces of cultural icons we call "celebrities." Facial piercings and tattoos make the face an art-form, a space for self-expression, and a badge of group identity. Veiling the face as a practice among women offers empowerment (in certain contexts) and conveys identity through the separation effected by concealment. Such examples could be multiplied. In general, the face is the surface on, behind, and in front of which individual and group negotiations take place regarding matters of the self and the self-in-relation, whether identity, power, self-expression, or moral integrity. Furthermore, such negotiations are continuous and ubiquitous, aided now, not least, by the tellingly named internet social medium "*Face*book"!

In this context, Pauline anthropology speaks with salvific weight. With its focus on the eschatological transformation of the "face" of humankind (individual and communal) through the face (the person) of Christ as the image of God, creation and redemption come together in *new creation*, in faces—however frail or disfigured or in pain—that radiate divine glory.

22. Cf. Turner, *The Body*; also, Fraser and Greco, eds., *The Body*.
23. Douglas, *Natural Symbols*.
24. Cf. Doniger, "Face-lift."

Such a conclusion merits elaboration and development. In *spirituality*, it points to the transformation of self and society mediated by paying attention in love to the face of Christ displayed iconographically, and to the lives of the saints and martyrs. In *liturgy*, it invites sensual practices of sight, taste, touch, smell, and hearing that draw the face towards its eschatological destiny, towards true beauty. In *moral formation and social life*, it represents a turning *from* practices that render the face (of oneself and the other) alienated, even obliterated, and a turning *to* practices that hold the face (of oneself and the other) in regard.

This kind of elaboration has begun already. A very good example is David Ford's study, *Self and Salvation*, where he makes the image of the face and facing a key to Christian soteriology and a Christian understanding of both the self and the self-in-relation. In a profound development of the image of facing, Ford offers a characterization of the self under headings like "oneself as another," "the hospitable self," the "self without idols," the "worshipping self," the "singing self," and the "eucharistic self."

Particularly noteworthy, for present purposes, is that he takes as his seminal biblical texts the two from 2 Cor 3 and 4 discussed above. I conclude with his comment on "communities of the face" in the context of Christian faith and practice:

> Christianity is characterised by the simplicity and complexity of facing: being faced by God, embodied in the face of Christ; turning to face Jesus Christ in faith; being members of a community of the face; seeing the face of God reflected in creation and especially in each human face, with all the faces in our heart related to the presence of the face of Christ; having an ethic of gentleness (*praütes*) towards each face; disclaiming any overview of others and being content with massive agnosticism about how God is dealing with them; and having a vision of transformation before the face of Christ "from glory to glory" that is cosmic in scope, with endless surprises for both Christians and others.[25]

---

25. Ford, *Self and Salvation*, 24–25.

Part II

Theological Interpretation

11

Born of a Virgin?
The Conversation Continues

DAVID R. CATCHPOLE
University of Exeter

Andrew Lincoln's fine book *Born of a Virgin?* represents not only a much-needed evaluation of the diverse evidence in the Gospels concerning Jesus' origins but also a piece of scholarship that conveys how finely balanced some of the decisions are that that evidence permits or requires. The sensitive and restrained tone of the whole discussion makes it easy to continue the conversation, and that is what I would like to do.

The starting point is that the Gospels provide support for at least two of three different reconstructions of Jesus' parentage: (A) that he had no human father at all, but resulted from some sort of divine liaison with Mary; (B) that he had a normal human father, Joseph; and (C) that his normal human father was a person unknown. Andrew Lincoln has surely established beyond a peradventure that more than one of these three schemes is conveyed by the Gospel writers. He opts—just!—for an A + B situation and—just!—against C, but it is a close run thing and C is recognized as having a lot going for it, even if in the end not quite enough. In what follows, I would like tentatively to offer some pro-C reinforcement.

I

A preliminary question concerns the standing of a child born to an engaged/married woman when the father is not the husband. The not exactly enlightened observations of Jesus ben Sirach concerning women do at least have the usefulness of highlighting sleep-disturbing, parental anxieties about the risk that daughters may get themselves into trouble. It can hardly have been abstract, prejudiced theorizing that includes the fear that "while a virgin" (ἐν παρθενίᾳ), she may be seduced and become pregnant in her father's house (42:9–11, esp. v. 10; cf. 26:10–12).

> A daughter is a secret anxiety to her father, and worry over her robs him of sleep: when she is young, for fear she may not marry, or if married, for fear she may be disliked; while a virgin, for fear she may be seduced and become pregnant in her father's house; or having a husband, for fear she may go astray, or, though married, for fear she may be barren. Keep strict watch over a headstrong daughter....

But what if she did become pregnant, during the period of betrothal and before the marriage was finalized and consummated, that is to say, when she has a legally bound man in her life? Perhaps Jesus ben Sirach again throws some light with a passage (23:22–24) that assumes that the husband (and our impression is that the term husband may cover both the betrothed and the finally married male partner) will make the most drastic form of response.

> So it [public exposure and punishment] is with a woman who leaves her husband and presents him with an heir by another man. For first of all, she has disobeyed the law of the Most High; second, she has committed an offence against her husband; and third, through her fornication she has committed adultery and brought forth children by another man. She herself will be brought before the assembly, and her punishment will extend to her children.

Human nature being what it is, this situation doubtless arose from time to time. But what if the husband, at whatever stage of the contracting of marriage, chose not to go the way of public exposure? Then, according to Sirach 23:22, he found himself with a child whom he did not father but who is his heir. In other words, since one of the purposes of a linear genealogy is the establishing of rights of inheritance,[1] if the father is X the child is "son of X"

---

1. Cf. Fulton, "Genealogies," 662.

and will figure in the genealogy. This situation, we may reasonably suppose, must also have been not unknown. And if for X we read Joseph, or even on that basis David, then Jesus may still have been both "son of Joseph" and thereby, if Joseph was indeed a Davidic family member, "son of David," while still having resulted from a liaison between Mary, herself until that moment in time a virgin (cf. Sir 42:10), and some male person unknown. In other words, the aggregate of references to Joseph as the parent or father of Jesus, and the aggregate of definitions of the status of Jesus as "son of David," would in no way undermine proposal C. Actually, they do not undermine proposal A either. That option, however, suffers from serious drawbacks and indeed fatal flaws, as Andrew Lincoln has compellingly demonstrated.

It is worth observing that the situation described is one in which terms like "legal adoption" or "naming as a sign of legal paternity" probably skew the discussion.[2] That adoption was unknown in Jewish law at that time, though well known in Roman law, has been established,[3] but the situation of Jesus in relation to two adults, themselves married prior to his birth, places him inside a family unit rather than outside it. He was "in": he did not need to "get in."

2

The Marcan tradition of Jesus' visit to Nazareth is subjected by Andrew Lincoln to thorough and extremely cautious appraisal. Does it suggest at least a lingering memory of illegitimacy in Jesus' case? The conclusion: almost certainly not, it seems. But the argumentation is interesting in two respects.

First, there is a hint of the antithesis between the scribe and the artisan in Sir 38:24—39:15: "here in Mark 6 Jesus' status as carpenter is seen by the crowd as incompatible with the claim to impart wisdom and the study that was necessary for such a role . . . ."[4] Having once favored this possibility myself,[5] I now question whether it represents a sufficiently sharp criticism to count as lack of honor and to express being "scandalized." After all, the artisan may not have the prestige of the scribe, but he is convincingly accorded appreciation and honor by Sirach.

Second, there is a merger of the questions in Mark 6:2-3 into a single whole: "The series of questions raised by the inhabitants of Nazareth in 6:2-3 are meant to undermine Jesus as a teacher and miracle worker by pointing

2. Soares Prabhu, *Formula Quotations*, 237; similarly R. Brown, *Birth*, 139.
3. Levin, "Jesus," 415–42.
4. Lincoln, *Born*, 35.
5. Catchpole, *Jesus People*, 90.

to his less than exalted artisan status and family of origin."[6] The problem here is the implicit merger between the two reactions to Jesus (ἐξεπλήσσοντο and ἐσκανδαλίζοντο). But as I shall try to argue, these are quite different: the first relates to the questions in v. 2, and the second to the questions in v. 3.

Having established that the original Marcan text did read, "Is not this the carpenter, the son of Mary . . . ?," and after setting aside the mistaken attempt to find behind that text the thought of a virgin conception, Lincoln builds on the groundwork provided by Tal Ilan[7] concerning metronyms.[8] In the end, he concludes that "none of the various explanations offered for the unusual occurrence of the metronyme in Mark 6:3 is very convincing."[9] That reads like stalemate. If so, perhaps there may be a way forward by (i) revisiting the tradition in and of itself, setting it in a redaction- and narrative-critical context; and (ii) bringing insights from cultural anthropology to bear on the earliest version of the tradition.

(i) The reference to dishonor in the context of family and home (v. 4) contributes to Mark's narrative strategy, developed already in the two "sandwich structures" in Mark 3:20–35 and 4:3–20. There the birth family, those "outside," are critically contrasted with the fictive family of those who are "around him," listening to his teaching and receiving "the mystery of the kingdom of God." The redactional introduction of the family members opposed to Jesus makes Mark's view of the relationship between them and Jesus clear enough, though it means that in effect the residents of Nazareth, when scandalized by him, are effectively aligning themselves with those family members. That is perhaps an unintended consequence, and the earlier pre-Marcan stage in the history of the tradition, i.e., before the Marcan addition of "among his own family, and in his own home," and the setting of the story in the developing Marcan narrative, will not have been so negative about the family. At that stage, dishonor from the πατρίς alone, the scandalized community, was probably in mind.

But the scandalized community had started in a different frame of mind. The verb ἐκπλήσσομαι is recurrently a verb of appreciative amazement, at home in any setting where human persons confront evidence of a divine intervention and/or are forced to ask questions about a phenomenon that is beyond their ken. There is not the slightest whiff of critical distance, let alone of being scandalized. Mark 1:22, amplified in 1:27, and subsequently adopted for the indubitably appreciative response to the sermon on

---

6. Lincoln, *Born*, 38.
7. Ilan, "Man born of Woman," 23–45.
8. Lincoln, *Born*, 33–38.
9. Ibid., 38.

the mount (Matt 7:28), sets a trend in Marcan storytelling, with an exorcism exemplifying and effecting the authority of the teaching which provokes appreciative astonishment. The teaching in question is aptly characterized as "resplendent with divine power,"[10] though less aptly as a matter of "being overcome with shocked numbness," for the persons who are astonished are not so numb as to fail to turn their astonishment into questions. The same reaction is put into words in Mark 7:37, where Jesus has looked to God (*sic*) for miracle working power (7:34) and, after exercising it, caused extreme astonishment and the acclamation that "he has done all things well." Luke follows the same train of thought: Jesus' healing of the epileptic has the effect that ἐξεπλήσσοντο δὲ πάντες ἐπὶ τῇ μεγαλειότητι τοῦ θεοῦ (9:43). Supporting examples abound from elsewhere—Wis 13:4–5; Mark 11:18; Acts 13:12—to name but three.

If this reaction of "being astounded" is appreciative and at the same time such as to provoke questions, the questions of the Nazareth residents are telling. "Where did this man get all these things?" is clarified and expanded by "What is this wisdom that has been given to him? What deeds of power are being done through his hands?" They go some way towards answering their own question with the use of the divine passive "has been given." Their combining teaching, which is the primary focus, with miracle working points especially towards healings ("done by his hands," cf. 1:41; 5:41), and healings have precisely provoked the reactions appropriate to a divine epiphany (see "fear and trembling," 5:33; "overcome with amazement," 5.42).

(ii) As far as the end of Mark 6:2 everything that is said has to do with being impressed, aware that God is somehow actively involved in the speech and action of "this person." But if that is the case, the change to a diametrically opposite and disparagingly negative reaction in Mark 6:3 represents not more of the same, but a complete *volte face*. How can this be understood? In Jesus' view, the issue boils down to a matter of honor. Cultural anthropology now comes to our aid, with its distinction between ascribed honor and acquired honor. All that Jesus has done and is doing as summarized in Mark 6:2 falls into the category of acquired honor, honor actively sought and achieved through a person's own efforts and the social recognition that excellence of achievement brings about.[11] Over against that, the category of ascribed honor covers what is obtained by kinship or personal endowment, not in any way resulting from effort or activity. Once the question has got past the term "artisan," which would belong to the category

10. Dwyer, *Motif*, 122.
11. Malina, *New Testament World*, 32–36.

of activity and therefore of acquired honor, but which could not possibly generate ἐσκανδαλίζοντο, the aggressive question detailing Jesus' family introduces the thought of ascribed honor or rather the lack of it.

If the family members detailed in the question of the Nazareth residents do damage to Jesus' identity and represent some kind of social dishonor, even stigma, then one has to ask how this could be. This can hardly be a case of a man's being called after his mother because of her superior lineage. If being called after one's forefathers or "foremothers" is normally and most importantly a matter of pedigree,[12] then for Jesus something works in the opposite direction. Therefore, unless some better explanation of the dishonor suffered by Jesus is forthcoming, it may be necessary to reconsider Mark 6:3 as reminiscent of and support for possibility C above.

It is true that Ilan's important survey of metronyms brings to light just one single parallel case of illegitimacy, and that is a weakness, but if Jesus' being "son of Mary" by itself gives rise to the reaction ἐσκανδαλίζοντο, what else could be implied?

3

Of the two Gospel witnesses to early Christian reflection on the birth of Jesus, Luke has arguably been the more influential theologically and Matthew the more revealing historically. Not that the final version or even any hypothetical precursor of Matthew's account in 1:18–25 is historical, but the question is whether it gives access in some way to retrievable historical data.

The study of Matthew's account of the birth of Jesus is jeopardized by several debated issues: its presuppositions, its purpose, its tradition history, its familiarity with and/or dependence on Greco-Roman schemes involving sexual partnership between a god and a woman to produce a son of God. The vital question that presses itself upon us is whether any given perspective on these issues is *demanded* by this tradition, and how we may resist its being assimilated to a world of thought which is not its own. How may we inch forward in trying to address these issues?

First, the widely accepted mutual independence of the final versions of the Matthean and Lucan stories suggests the possible existence of earlier tradition in respect of at least some of the shared data: the engagement of Mary to Joseph; Joseph's having Davidic ancestry; Mary's being a virgin, at least until her conception of Jesus; the involvement of the Holy Spirit; the giving of the name Jesus; the destiny of the child to bring benefit to Israel. Any or all of those details may be congenial to the minds of Matthew and

---

12. Ilan, "Man born of Woman," 43.

Luke, but they are not *thereby* attributable to either or both of the Gospel writers. Their presence in both accounts could be a coincidence, but it does not have to be.

Second, the women inserted by Matthew into his genealogy show that he accepts the assumption of a deviation from sexual norms in the case of Mary. Had Matthew wanted to invoke the Abrahamic promise to the gentiles, even as a subordinate thought,[13] he could have done so convincingly by introducing Sarah (cf. Gen 17:1–16), but he did not. The gentile hypothesis vis-à-vis Tamar, Rahab, Ruth, and Bathsheba is indeed no longer viable.[14] So sexual irregularity in their cases sets the scene for sexual irregularity in the case of Mary, for which the careful, even if cumbersome, formulation about "Joseph the husband of Mary, of whom Jesus was born" (1:16) provides confirmation. There would be no point in preparing the ground for the birth story with this kind of editing of the genealogy if Matthew wanted to say, "To those who suggest there was a problem, this is a foul slander"; he was gratuitously providing ammunition when he inserted Tamar, Rahab, Ruth, and Bathsheba. The tacit assumption behind the four insertions is, of course, that Judah, Salmon, Boaz, and David had their own contribution to make. In other words, Matthew prepares us to begin reading 1:18–25 on one and only one basis, that is to say, with a biological father and sexual irregularity in mind.

Third whether the citation of Isa 7:14 LXX, with its use of the word παρθένος, is pre-Matthean (unlikely) or the result of Matthean redaction (likely), Matthew must have agreed with its relevance to the situation he is describing. He could of course have opted for a version of the text that did not use the word παρθένος, but on any showing a narrative-critical reading of the tradition means taking seriously the movement from v. 18 through to v. 22. That means that παρθένος stands for a woman who has no previous sexual experience—until, that is, the encounter with some male person other than Joseph who has made her pregnant. In that sexual encounter, she who had been up to that moment a παρθένος lost her παρθενία. That is entirely consonant with the standard situation in which a young woman, still living in the home of her family, is expected to be protected from any adverse sexual experience by that family (cf. Gen 24:15–61; Deut 22:13–21; Judg 11:34–38; Sir 42:10). The terminology chosen suggests not that Mary retained her virginity when becoming pregnant, but that she had been a virgin *until* she became pregnant. Just as the loss of virginity was said by the phrase "from the Holy Spirit" (vv. 18, 20) to be woven into the tapestry of

---

13. Cf. Brown, *Birth*, 72–74.
14. Lincoln, *Born*, 80–81.

God's paradoxical and providential dealings with Israel, so too the loss of her virginity was said by the introduction of Isa 7:14 to be woven into God's providential purpose for the Christian community. Thus, "they (sic) shall name him Emmanuel," which encapsulates precisely the experience envisaged in Matt 18:20; 28:20. Taken in its straightforward sense, then, Matt 1:22–23 envisages a normal sexual experience for someone who had been a virgin before conceiving a child, but who was rather obviously no longer a virgin when she gave birth to that child.

Fourth, that a cautious-cum-conservative policy[15] is called for in establishing what may have been the content of a pre-Matthean tradition underlying 1:18–25 must be wise. In principle, aporias are our best resource in distinguishing the pre-Matthean from the Matthean, though it is also possible in principle that details that cause no aporia may have been skillfully woven into the tapestry of the text. But, leaving aside the introduction (v. 18a), which is not controversial, there are three aporias that command widespread consent: (i) the initial "from the Holy Spirit" (v. 18b), which agrees with, but unhelpfully anticipates, the angelic declaration (v. 20); (ii) the detailing of Joseph's considerate strategy (v. 19), which weakens a little the force of the intention to divorce Mary; and (iii) the quotation of Isa 7:14, which interrupts the flow of the story between v. 21 and v. 24.

Two other possibilities remain to be assessed: (iv) the address, "Joseph, son of David" (v. 20), and (v) "he had no marital relations with her until she had borne a son" (v. 25a). The former does indeed build a bridge to the preceding genealogy, and has no counterpart in the other dream units in Matt 1–2,[16] but it is a Matthew/Luke agreement, and could just as easily be traditional as redactional.[17] The latter is more uncertain, but should probably be given the benefit of the doubt. First, its intention is unlikely to be to underline that the child was not Joseph's, for that is a given for the whole story (cf. vv. 18b–19) and scarcely in need of repetition. Second, to note Joseph's honorable conduct as a man who is now married (vv. 20, 24), respecting the Jewish norm that marital sex should not take place during pregnancy or for any reason other than the procreation of children (thus Josephus, *Against Apion* 2.199–202; Philo, *Special Laws* 3.9, 113), is a natural even if not strictly necessary continuation of the earlier reference to no sexual relations having taken place between Joseph and Mary (v. 18b). Third, without v. 25a there is no reference to the actual birth, and continuity and closure in the unit of tradition requires that there should be such a reference. All in all,

---

15. Cf. Lincoln, *Born*, 77–78.
16. Soares Prabhu, *Formula Quotations*, 237.
17. Brown, *Birth*, 159.

one may say that v. 25a does not interrupt the straightforward account of his obedience to the angelic command,[18] but rather details how that obedience was effected.

On the basis of these considerations, the following pre-Matthean tradition emerges:

> 18b When [Jesus'] mother Mary had been engaged to Joseph, but before they lived together, she was found to be with child. 19 Her husband Joseph, being a righteous man, planned to divorce her. 20 But just when he had resolved to do this, an angel of the Lord appeared to him in a dream and said, "Joseph, son of David, do not be afraid to take Mary as your wife, for the child conceived in her is from the Holy Spirit. 21 She will bear a son, and you are to name him Jesus, for he will save his people from their sins." 24 When Joseph awoke from sleep, he did as the angel of the Lord commanded him; he took her as his wife, 25a but had no marital relations with her until she had borne a son; 25b and he named him Jesus.

Fifth, the intellectual milieu in which this story is set is crucial. Andrew Lincoln draws into the discussion the widespread Greco-Roman myths according to which illustrious persons, past or present, are regarded as the progeny of a god and a human mother.[19] He believes that a passage in Philo, *De Cherubim* 40–52, has been unduly neglected in the discussion of Matthew's tradition. He concludes that Philo's interpretation presumes his knowledge of the Greco-Roman myths and therefore attests the penetration of the world of Matthew by those myths. This, so runs the argument, is the thought world within which Matthew's story is told and heard/read. He notes, as important corroboration, the correspondence between Joseph, whose abstinence from sexual activity during the period of Mary's pregnancy ends the story, and Plato's father Ariston, to whom Apollo, who had intercourse with Plato's mother Perictione, appeared and ordered him not to have sex with Perictione for ten months until after the birth.

Several points may be made in response, but before offering those points one thing may be said. That is that it would be very surprising if Philo and indeed Matthew were unaware of the Greco-Roman myths, but whether Philo's putative use of them has any bearing on Matthew is a different matter, and similarly whether the pre-Matthean tradition on its own terms encourages any thought of those myths is also a different matter. *Prima facie* Matthew's way of thinking seems a million miles from the agile

18. *Contra* Lincoln, *Born*, 78.
19. Lincoln, *Born*, 91–93.

but eccentric theorizing of Philo. What has Antioch to do with Alexandria, one might ask? But of course this needs to be tested in respect of the text of *De Cherubim* itself.

(i) Philo makes clear that he distinguishes between a virgin and the state of virginity: thus, it is possible, in terms of the exegesis of scriptural texts, to see a woman returning to a state of virginity! The implicit order of existence, if one can call it that, therefore belongs to a quite different world. It is a world of "divine mystery for the initiated ... the holiest secret ... sacred revelation" (§§42, 48). (ii) In the real world, Philo is careful to note, "man and woman, male and female of the human race, in the course of nature (φύσις) come together to hold intercourse for the procreation of children" (§43), and again, "the union of human beings that is made for the procreation of children, turns virgins into women" (§50). This would seem to rule out rather emphatically any recourse to the Greco-Roman myths involving gods and real-life women. (iii) The scheme does not involve real women, the embodiment of sense-perception, but only women who *on the narrative level* stand for named virtues. Those virtues become the possession of the real-life heroes—from Abraham to Moses—as a result of the union of God and the virtue *within the parameters of the text*. (iv) The purpose of the union of God and the non-real-life and de-physicalized "woman" is the gift of the offspring of the union to the real-life husband. God does not need it or indeed anything else, so the purpose must be the benefit of the man.

The outcome seems to be that Philo envisages God as having non-physical union with a non-real woman, i.e., a virtue, the outcome of which is a virtue, which can then be "given" as a benefit to this and that real man (Abraham, Isaac, and so on), someone who "needs to receive" (§44). He does not believe in virgin conceptions in the real world, but lives in an intellectual world of his own, owing nothing at this point to the Greco-Roman myths. He does not stand as an exemplar of how those myths might affect a Jewish writer like Matthew. So my suggestion would be that Philo can be relegated from the debate, and the question that then arises is whether the world of Matthew, although in a broad sense the Hellenized world, is not primarily the world of the biblical tradition.

Here it becomes important to note two features of the Gospel story as it stands, both of which open a gap between pre-Matthew and the Greco-Roman myths.

(i) Nothing is said in Matthew's text about Jesus' being "son of God." This is so recurrent a feature of the myths that its absence here is striking indeed. The status of Jesus, conveyed by the circumstances of his birth, remains extremely vague and derives from whatever may be found in the angelic declaration that "he will save his people from their sins." His religious task is, as it were, the religious counterpart of the politico-military task of a Gideon (Judg 6:14–15) or a Samson (Judg 13:5). If Joseph's being of Davidic descent were accepted as pre-Matthean and then introduced to give more muscle to the role of the savior of Israel, the tradition would not take us outside the complex of ideas associated with the Davidic Messiah in *Pss. Sol.* 17, 18, and any idea of divine sonship other than that accruing to the appointed king is far from that text.

(ii) That the conception of Jesus is ἐκ πνεύματος ἁγίου also seems rather distant from the conceptions of the heroes in the Greco-Roman myths. With a considerable stretch the unusual observation by Plutarch might be brought alongside: wise Egyptians allow that "a woman can be approached by a divine spirit and made pregnant."[20] By "a divine spirit" he presumably means Mars, Poseidon, or Apollo in the cases of Romulus and Remus or Theseus or Alexander respectively, as specified in his other biographical texts. But whether "holy spirit" in a Jewish text can be used in such a personalizing way to implicate Israel's God in a sexual union with a woman seems extremely problematic and unlikely, especially when biblical tradition, as Lincoln rightly observes,[21] offers as an alternative a series of precedents for a bio-theological involvement of God in a normal male-female act of procreation.

4

If the main support for option C (human father, identity unknown) is supplied by pre-Matthew, Luke appears to be the main support for a simultaneous combination of options A (divine liaison with Mary) and B (human father, Joseph). Andrew Lincoln has dealt with this persuasively. We have also seen that a combination of options B and C is perfectly possible, assuming that the completion of the marriage transaction between Joseph and an already pregnant Mary has taken place before the birth of the child. But, with the Lucan narrative in mind, can more be said about its intention and its tradition history? Given the arguments in favor of taking option C seriously, maybe there is space to inject a little insecurity into the case that relies so heavily on Luke's annunciation story (1:26–38). Here is a possible line of approach.

First, a narrative-critical examination of Luke's story must take account of order, and in so doing presume that any uncertainties in the meaning of earlier material will be removed by later material. That means that the data

20. Cf. Lincoln, *Born*, 91.
21. Ibid., 73.

in Luke 3–4 can legitimately be checked to see what it is in Luke 1–2 that they may be intended to confirm.

The two words that seem like small pebbles thrown disturbingly, even if ambiguously, into the stillness of the Lucan millpond are ὡς ἐνομίζετο (3:23). Given that νομίζω means "to think," across a spectrum of nuances between the correct and the incorrect, and given that the imperfect passive ἐνομίζετο points to what was a settled and, as it turned out, respectful view of Jesus' contemporaries that he was "son of Joseph" (cf. 4:22), it is vital to decide where Luke stands. Lucan redaction must be responsible for (i) the insertion of the genealogy immediately after the divine declaration of sonship after the baptism; (ii) the addition of τοῦ θεοῦ (cf. 9:20 diff Mark 8:29), which boldly implicates God in the family tree via Adam; and (iii) the reordering of the following Q temptation tradition so that it is framed by a successful defense of that divine sonship which the devil questions. But being the son of Joseph also entails being descended from Adam: once the evil in the world is laid at the door of Eve, "from [whom] sin had its beginning, and because of [whom] we all die" (Sir 25:24), Adam can be given all possible honor: "Shem, Seth and Enosh were honored, but above every other created being was Adam" (Sir 49:15–16). So says Jesus ben Sirach (25:24; 49:15–16), and Jesus' genealogical connection to Joseph, and then to Adam and God can only be a matter of ascribed honor.

The two words ὡς ἐνομίζετο are boxed in by these data, and if they meant anything less than an unqualified "yes" the first link in the genealogical chain would be broken and the Lucan strategy left in tatters. So for Luke, contemporary thinking is entirely correct: Jesus is "son of Joseph." Moreover, the divine announcement of sonship (3:22), couched in terms reminiscent of Ps 2:7, causes the whole complex 3:21—4:30 to interpret sonship in traditional, Israelite, royal terms.

Perhaps we should weigh the fact that Lucan redaction of Mark 6:1–6 in his 4:16–30 involved the deliberate substitution of "son of Joseph" for "son of Mary." If the latter were entirely innocent, it might be taken as a neat allusion for the reader to the annunciation and birth stories, but Luke thinks otherwise. His intervention is at least in line with the scattered references in Luke 2 to Joseph's parenthood of the child Jesus. That being so, there remains however his very strange statement that Joseph "went to be registered with Mary, *to whom he was engaged*, and who was expecting a child" (2:5).

Luke 2:1–7, beset by fatal flaws in respect of historicity, and expressive of evident Lucan interests, very probably owes its existence to Lucan creativity. If the *lectio difficilior* principle is followed, Luke 2:7 will (contrary to Matthean evidence) have described Mary as betrothed to Joseph at the time of giving birth. At the very least, there is an implied breach of normal convention whereby a betrothed woman was still in the care not of her fiancé, but of her father. Either option A and C could easily be harmonized with that, but option B would be in a certain amount of trouble. Option A would have the minor problem that the finalizing of Joseph's marriage to Mary has to be set sometime in the forty-day period between Luke 2:7 and 2:22, the day of the (mistaken) purification of Joseph along with Mary. A bit hectic, one might say! Option B would involve an implied breach of the convention that sexual activity did not occur during the period of betrothal. A bit shocking, one might say! Option C would come into play via a hypothetical awareness on Luke's part of the implications of the pre-Matthean data, but in view of Luke's probable dependence on the tradition known to Matthew, that would be no surprise.

Second, and here the difficult issue of sources resurfaces, the question of Lucan dependence on pre-Lucan material in 1:26–38 needs to be addressed, and with it the question of whether the Jesus story was always connected to the John story. Both stories, be it noted, use the standard five-point scheme of an annunciation story, which precisely because it is standard does not in itself prove dependence either way between the annunciation stories of John and Jesus. Concerning the John story, despite the arguments of Raymond Brown that Luke is its creator, imitating an earlier Jesus story, the likelihood of an earlier tradition, retained in the ongoing circle of disciples of John and articulating how John was defined in that circle, has a lot going for it. (i) The intensely Jewish parameters within which the story unfolds may suit Luke's purpose but they can hardly stem from a writer who, when he tried to set Jesus within such parameters in 2:22–24, betrayed his ignorance. (ii) The complete absence of Christian concerns, and focus on John as the one preparing for the coming of God rather than Jesus, is not only in accord with what may be reconstructed concerning the mission of the historical John but out of accord with the persistent Lucan tendency, shared widely within early Christianity, to stress the inferiority of John to Jesus and to make the one the preparer for the other.

Third, if the common use of the standard annunciation pattern is evident in both 1:5–25 and 1:26–38, the latter is just as free to be pre-Lucan as the former. Of course, Lucan redaction may be evidenced from time to time. Since 1:36–37 serves a Lucan purpose and interrupts the smooth flow of the tradition, its presence is easily explained as just such a redactional adaptation. One might add that within 1:26–38 the reference to Elizabeth's pregnancy, modelled on that of Sarah, is singularly inapposite as any kind of confirmation of Mary's own prospective pregnancy. That God can achieve the "impossible" and bring parenthood to an elderly couple on the basis of their normal, marital sexual activity simply does not impinge on or provide confirmation of the prospective pregnancy of a young woman, whether or not her current fiancé is involved. Consequently, the removal of 1:36–37 from 1:26–38 enables the Jesus story to be interpreted on its own terms and not on the basis of the much-invoked "step parallelism." When Raymond Brown[22] urges that the Lucan story does, despite arguments to the contrary, envisage a virgin conception, his arguments are based entirely on the "step parallelism," notwithstanding his allowing that there is pre-Lucan tradition here. Pre-Lucan tradition, if it is indeed here, antedates the construction of a composite narrative. No composite narrative, no "step parallelism."

The Jesus story can therefore be lifted, as it were, from its present context and treated as a unified and coherent tradition in its own right. In particular this enables the two parts of the angelic announcement to be understood rather more straightforwardly than is often the case.

> The angel said to her, "Do not be afraid, Mary, for you have found favor with God. And now, you will conceive in your womb and bear a son, and you will name him Jesus. He will be great, and will be called the Son of the Most High, and the Lord God will give to him the throne of his ancestor David. He will reign over the house of Jacob for ever, and of his kingdom there will be no end." Mary said to the angel, "How can this be, since I do not know a man?" The angel said to her, "The Holy Spirit will come upon you, and the power of the Most High will overshadow you; therefore the child to be born will be holy; he will be called Son of God" (Luke 1:30–35).

Fourth, there is no need to add to the perennial, and quite correct, complaint against this narrative that "since I do not know a man" is fundamentally discordant with "a virgin engaged to a man named Joseph from the house of David." Respect for the narrative integrity of the whole story must surely mean that as soon as David is mentioned in v. 32, Joseph would come to the mind of the implied reader. But even more significant is the word τοῦτο in the question πῶς ἔσται τοῦτο, ἐπεὶ ἄνδρα οὐ γινώσκω; "This" has just been defined as pregnancy, which will result in the birth of the Son of the Most High, i.e., the Davidic ruler appointed by God and destined for everlasting kingship. How is *this* going to happen? Answer: by the "coming upon" and "overshadowing of" Mary—both verbs being agreed even by advocates of a virgin conception as non-sexual in nuance[23]—by the Holy Spirit. The Holy Spirit brings about a birth, and the child to be born is destined (so it is said, not once, but twice) to be "Son of God." The continuity of terms,

---

22. Brown, *Birth*, 301–3.
23. E.g. ibid., 290.

reinforced by the logic of the essential connection τοῦτο, establishes that there is no distinction between what is said about the child in vv. 31–33 and what is said in v. 35. What is said in v. 35 adds only one further detail to what was said in vv. 31–33: how the birth of the Son of God is going to happen. So the narrative, with its integrity intact, speaks *consistently* about the birth of the royal, Davidic, and messianic Son of God. Mary's question, on the surface not a very intelligent question, but one that enables the angel to provide some Spirit-focused amplification of what has already been said, is ultimately answered through a classic Jewish "three in the bed" act of procreation: Mary, Joseph, and the Holy Spirit.

The continuity between vv. 31–33 and v. 35 is understood otherwise by Andrew Lincoln.[24] He argues convincingly for the coexistence in the Lucan mind and total narrative of two contrasting positions on the birth of Jesus, and he takes seriously the continuity between "he will be great, and will be called the Son of the Most High" and "he will be called Son of God" (vv. 32a, 35b), but he separates off "the Lord God will give him the throne of his ancestor David" (v. 32b). Rightly or wrongly, I would question this separation of v. 32a and v. 32b and the inference that they envisage two different sorts of origin. They read—is this not right?—as a tightly integrated whole, concerning which Raymond Brown comments convincingly: "Gabriel's words in 1:32-33 constitute a free interpretation of 2 Samuel 7:18-26."[25]

Fifth, and in reinforcement of the fourth point, it remains, however, to challenge Raymond Brown when he goes on to invoke the early Christian credal formulation in Rom 1:3-4 as a parallel—"a passage that threw light on Matthean thought [but] throws even more light on Lucan phraseology."[26] This, one has to say with all due respect, simply does not work in this way. Romans 1:3-4 envisages two antithetical modes of personal existence, the second required to read in this way because the first has to be (κατὰ σάρκα versus κατὰ πνεῦμα ἁγιωσύνης), and distinguishes them timewise (ὁρισθέντος . . . ἐξ ἀναστάσεως νεκρῶν) by means of a verb (ὁρίζω) that defines boundaries and an event that constitutes the boundary (ἀνάστασις νεκρῶν). The terms πνεῦμα and ἁγιωσύνη, both in principle covering a wide spectrum of meanings, seem in this context to relate appositionally to heavenly existence. The net effect is that Jesus as a Davidide during his κατὰ σάρκα period is qualified, but not yet installed as Messianic Son of God; his consequent status as Son of God is exclusively post-resurrection. If Rom

---

24. Lincoln, *Born*, 123.
25. Brown, *Birth*, 310.
26. Ibid., 312-13.

1:3–4 does indeed throw light on Luke 1:32–35 it eliminates Luke 1:35 as a witness to a virgin conception.

The overall conclusion would be that, if Luke has adopted and adapted a pre-Lucan tradition, the meaning conveyed by Luke 1:26–35, 38 in its own right and in its own terms is one thing. The meaning imposed upon it by its incorporation in the extended sequence of Luke's Gospel is not necessarily the same.

5

The door is well and truly open to an assimilation of the life of Jesus to the biographies of the honored heroes of the Greco-Roman myths, and Luke very probably exploits the potential offered by such an assimilation. The Gospel stories do not demand such assimilation, but they could survive it.

There is much support within the Gospel traditions—implications here and there, and also a vivid narrative—for the view that Jesus was the son of Joseph. But if a study of tradition history alerts us not only to Luke's capacity for thinking two contrasting things at the same time, but also to the diversity within the traditions employed by all the Synoptic Gospels, perhaps we can then with relief turn back to Matthew, and with especial respect to pre-Matthew. The *lectio difficilior* principle swings into action again. If the two competing readings of the paternity of Jesus involved Joseph and A N Other, a movement from A N Other to Joseph is conceivable (pardon the pun), but would anyone have moved from Joseph to A N Other?

To pre-Matthew, therefore, we owe our best evidence of how it all began and what is not disclosed. The identity of Jesus' father: who knows?

12

Historical Criticism, Theological Interpretation, and the Ends of the Christian Life

※※※

STEPHEN FOWL
Loyola University

It is an enormous honor for me to be asked to contribute to a *Festschrift* for Andrew Lincoln. I had been working on my PhD thesis for a couple of years when Andrew Lincoln became my supervisor. I doubt very much that he remembers our first meetings to discuss my work; they are, however, vividly stamped in my memory. Andrew's questions were always clear and non-polemical, but also deeply probing. The more he probed, the more it became clear that my thesis lacked a thesis. It was more like a set of disconnected observations. Andrew's clear-eyed reading of my work helped me shape it into something far better than it would have otherwise been. More importantly, he shaped me as a scholar so that I aspired then and now to bring the same generous, yet rigorous acuity I had seen in him to whatever scholarly task I took up. Anyone who engages the astonishing breadth of Andrew's scholarship finds this regardless of the topic. This essay is one attempt to display publicly my gratitude for his guidance and friendship over the past thirty years.

Whatever success I have had in being able to bring a set of theological concerns to bear on Scripture, rests in great measure on the intellectual habits that Andrew began to help form in me when I was a graduate student. As I move through this essay I will return to the importance of formation when it comes to interpreting Scripture theologically. First, however, I want to reflect on a set of issues surrounding forms of theological interpretation and those loosely connected scholarly practices that often go under the name "historical criticism."

Although I would not have recognized this when I finished my PhD, the rich tradition of Christian theology from the patristic period down to the present is soaked in Scripture, even if it is sometimes hard to recognize. In fact, for the great majority of the church's history, you could not really be counted as a theologian if you were not a master of the sacred page, if you did not have a deep knowledge and sharp facility with Scripture and its interpretation. Indeed, I would go so far as to say that at its best, throughout its history, theology has always been a mode of scriptural exegesis.

You don't have to be an expert to see that biblical interpretation during the patristic, medieval, or early modern periods looks very different from the biblical interpretation I was trained to do in graduate school. One way of accounting for this difference, the way I was at least implicitly taught by virtually all of my professors, was that pre-modern biblical interpretation was simply a form of error. Just as physics has moved on from debates about phlogiston in the seventeenth century, we biblical scholars have left those failed interpretive remains behind.

I understand how this argument works in physics. Theories about phlogiston were replaced by theories about oxygen. Those superior theories accounted both for the data that had been observed and allowed scientists reliably to anticipate future data. Theories about oxygen did the same job, answered the same questions, that theories about phlogiston did and did so better and with fewer residual difficulties and anomalies. It is harder to make this case with scriptural interpretation over time. That is, it is harder to claim that modern biblical criticism is a clear advance over pre-modern biblical criticism.[1]

One way of making this claim is to say that modern biblical criticism leads readers to the meaning of biblical texts better than pre-modern biblical criticism did. By mastering a number of ancient languages and some modern scholarly languages; by studying the histories, cultures, and societies within which the biblical texts are set and within which the biblical texts were written; most importantly by developing a facility with a number

---

1. This point is made most forcefully by Steinmetz, "Superiority."

of critical skills that are often lumped together under the name "historical criticism"; one will be able to uncover the meaning of biblical texts in ways that pre-modern biblical interpreters did not, and could not, do. Although I cannot recall anyone ever saying it quite as sharply as this, this was certainly the widely assumed view when I was beginning my graduate training in the early 1980s.

In the intervening time, a number of things have rendered this account implausible to many scholars, including me. First, many of the practices of "historical criticism" were shown to be badly flawed in their assumptions and in their methods. The best example is Gospel form criticism.[2] The assumptions about the transition of discrete stories about Jesus from oral to written exposition and about the ways language functions in different contexts that made Gospel form criticism work have been demonstrated to be misguided, and badly so. This change in itself is not surprising. Gospel form criticism was the methodical working out of a set of theories. In the course of investigating those theories, they proved to be inadequate. This is how knowledge is tested and developed in any field. The failure of Gospel form criticism is not in and of itself a problem if it is replaced by a new theories and methods that can do the same things better, just as theories about oxygen replaced theories about phlogiston. It is not clear to me, however, that such a theory has emerged or can emerge.[3]

There could be a number of reasons for this. It may simply be that with more time and new data we will come up with a better account of how various pericopae functioned both in their original oral contexts and how they were ultimately taken up the evangelists who shaped them with their own interests in mind to produce something like the canonical production of those Gospels. I am not confident this will happen. Rather, there is a growing recognition that we do not really have a clear and reliable picture of how the Gospels were produced. Although each of the canonical Gospels became associated with specific churches, there seems little chance of discerning whether and how these specific communities played any role in the production of those gospels. Moreover, it is less clear that the evangelists wrote with the interests of particular communities in mind.[4] Further, al-

---

2. See Güttgemanns, *Offene Fragen*. This volume was translated as *Candid Questions*. Both the German and the English translation make for difficult reading. This may in large measure account for the limited influence of Güttgemanns' criticisms. When coupled with insights from speech-act theory and anthropological work on the transition between oral and written cultures, however, very few if any of the fundamental assumptions of Gospel form criticism survive.

3. See Berger, "Rhetorical Criticism," 390–96.

4. This is the point argued by Bauckham, in *Gospels*. See also the collection of essays

though Marcan priority still seems secure, the Q hypothesis has come under increasingly sharp and sophisticated criticism.[5] In this light, our newly won ignorance in these areas opens up the prospect for rethinking this aspect of study in ways that would completely obviate form criticism. We obviously will need to wait for further developments here. For my purposes it is enough to note this example of a practice of historical criticism that is being eclipsed. As a result of these and other tensions internal to the practice of historical criticism, its claims to deliver the meaning of a biblical text are less plausible now than they ever have been.

Further, it became clear that the other various practices that went under the name historical criticism did not actually work together to produce a single result called meaning. The more proficient we became at these various practices, the clearer it became that their results were rarely compatible with each other. That is not to say that the results of each of these practices were false. Rather, it meant that these results could rarely if ever be combined into some summative result called the meaning of a biblical text. When you add to that the advent of new critical practices that were entering biblical studies from such fields as classics, history, literature, and sociology, the beginning graduate student's hope of finding the meaning of the biblical text became even more remote.

Finally, and most importantly, those working in fields such as philosophical hermeneutics began to show us that the notion of the meaning of a text was a lot more complex than we once thought.[6] Initially, there was great resistance to addressing these philosophical claims. If the practices of historical criticism had been as internally cohesive and coherent as was once thought, these more philosophical arguments about meaning might have been kept at arm's length. In the absence of such cohesion, in the presence of newer critical practices, the questions about the nature of textual meaning were too pervasive, too compelling, and too important to simply ignore. Arguments among biblical scholars about the meaning of a text became very intense. That intensity remains and often grows whenever someone has a stake in claiming that the meaning of a biblical text is simply one thing and all other interpretations are either error or something subsidiary or derivative.

The large institutions that support biblical scholarship have, for the most part, not directly confronted these intense arguments. Instead they

---

edited by Klink, *Audience*.

5. See Goodacre's *Case*.

6. No single scholar put these philosophical issues on the agenda of biblical scholars more profoundly than Andrew Lincoln's predecessor in Sheffield, Anthony Thiselton. See in particular, *Two Horizons* and *New Horizons*.

simply allow a variety of interpretive interests and approaches to have their own space. This does not resolve any serious theoretical issues, but it allows us all to operate in the absence of any coherent way of resolving the various challenges to "historical criticism" noted above. This is not to say that the intensity of arguments over "historical criticism" and its alternatives have completely dissipated. Rather, it simply means that these arguments are now generally carried on by discrete groups arguing with themselves.

I take it that despite its own inner tensions, arguments over historical criticism and the subsequent fragmentation of biblical scholarship into numerous discrete interests are at their root very specific examples of the larger fate of arguments about textual meaning that one finds in other disciplines. One can still pursue a grand unified theory of textual meaning and methods for attaining or displaying it, but I am not optimistic of success here. Although some might consider this a crisis, for those who are interested, as I am, in reinvigorating forms of biblical interpretation that are genuinely theological, this fragmented state of affairs is more an opportunity.

Although Christians have always read Scripture theologically, within the guild of professional biblical scholars these practices had largely fallen out of favor with the rise of "historical criticism" beginning in the late eighteenth century.[7] By the time of the methodological ascendance of "historical criticism" its practices were often seen as the only viable scholarly option and they largely worked to keep theological considerations at arm's length. Whereas in pre-modern times one could not be counted a theologian unless one was a master of the sacred page, by the time of "historical criticism's" ascendancy one could either be a theologian OR a biblical scholar, but *not both*. That disjunction persists down to today and is rigidly enforced in the structure of most graduate school curricula.[8]

As I already mentioned, however, the fragmentation of biblical scholarship has provided an opportunity to reinvigorate practices of theological interpretation. Here is what I mean: since no one set of interpretive considerations can guarantee access to textual meaning, it becomes difficult to deny a place to most thoughtful ways of interpreting Scripture. Theological considerations can no longer be ruled out of court simply for being theological. The past twenty years have witnessed a significant growth in scholarship directed towards what might be called the theological interpretation of Scripture.[9] Within the profession of biblical studies there has been some op-

---

7. See Legaspi, *Death of Scripture*.

8. The conceptual roots of this can be traced at least to Wrede, "Tasks," 68–116. See also the discussion in Fowl, *Engaging Scripture*, 13–21.

9. The *Journal of Theological Interpretation* is now in its twentieth year. There are several major commentary series devoted to theological interpretation that have

position to these developments. This opposition, however, seems primarily directed at and driven by poorly done examples of theological interpretation or inept arguments about the place of theological interpretation as a scholarly practice. To the extent that this is true, theological interpreters should be as opposed to poor practice and inept argument as anyone else. These are not, however, principled objections.[10] There cannot be substantial methodological objections to theological interpretation done well apart from prior agreements about method in biblical studies that would rule out theological considerations. Such agreement is lacking and is not likely anytime soon.

In the same breath, it would be foolish to say that theological interpretation of Scripture is now the dominant mode of biblical interpretation in the academy. It is not. I do think it is safe to say that theological interpretation has sufficient support among scholars and the institutions that support them that it seems set to continue as a distinct scholarly activity for some time to come. Given this reality, I would like to set out three separate issues facing theological interpreters of Scripture as they move into the future. The first of these issues concerns debates around the nature and practice of theological interpretation. These debates are largely matters of self-definition. There may be less to say here than one might first think.

The second concerns the relationships between theological interpretation and the other practices of biblical scholarship, particularly those that still go under the name "historical criticism." When theological interpretation of Scripture was trying to get a foothold in the academy there was a good deal of overheated rhetoric from both theological interpreters and historical critics about either the necessity of or the bankrupt nature of historical criticism. I think the time is right to reflect on these relationships in less fevered tones.[11]

Finally, in the light of these other two discussions, I would like to propose some considerations and concerns for those interested in the growth and formation of theological interpreters of Scripture. In this regard, I believe there are some reasons for concern and some opportunities for further thought.

---

already published numerous volumes. There are at least two SBL groups that work primarily in this field and their sessions are usually very well attended.

10. See the initial essay by Hendel, "Farewell," 70–74, and the subsequent discussions in such places as http://www.brookelester.net/blog/2012/4/12/farewell-to-sbl-revisited-biblical-studies-religious-faith-a.html.

11. Green's essay, "'History,'" 159–74, reflects a similar concern. I am less certain that the various sets of interests he ascribes to his three types of historical criticism can be retained as clearly as he seems to.

Many new academic ventures are marked by extraordinary methodological self-consciousness and great fussiness over self-definition and boundary marking. Theological interpretation of Scripture was not different in this respect. Although theological interpretation of Scripture was new to the modern university, it was not a new practice. To the extent that I have participated in these arguments, I have tried to point out that rather than starting something new, scholars should speak in terms of reviving something older, a practice or sets of practices that used to be considered normal but had largely been eclipsed. Clearly, one should not repristinate or fantasize about the past and then seek to repeat slavishly something that never was.

Although such attention need not define theological interpretation, it seems wise to me that the aims of contemporary scholars interested in theological interpretation should be directed to discerning and reflecting on the habits and practices of those pre-modern interpreters who saw scriptural interpretation as one of the central tasks of theology, not as a separate discipline distinct from theology. Those habits and practices would need to be made serviceable for our modern contexts and related to other interpretive habits and contexts, but this did not and does not require an overly narrow definition of theological interpretation or a distinct interpretive method for it.

In this regard, it is striking to note that unlike our own time, pre-modern interpreters produced very few works on interpretive method. Origen's *On First Principles* contains some methodological material and, of course, Augustine's *On Christian Doctrine* comes immediately to mind. In addition, in the medieval period Nicholas of Lyra and Thomas Aquinas write what might be called methodological reflections, though Aquinas' reflections are part of a much larger theological endeavor. One can also learn much from the debates between Erasmus and Luther. There are, no doubt, others besides these that come to mind. Nevertheless, in comparison with the modern period there are very few works dedicated to what might be called interpretive method. Moreover, despite the various differences between Origen, Augustine, Aquinas, and Luther, they all share an approach that does not treat scriptural interpretation as an end in itself. Instead, what they all seem to share is the view that Scripture is to be interpreted in the light of the larger ends of the Christian life. They use different idioms to describe this end. Some invoke the vocabulary of salvation; others speak of ever deeper love of God and neighbor, or ever deeper union with the triune God or deeper friendship with God. These differing vocabularies can lead one to think that there are many different views about the end of the Christian life, but that would be a mistake. There is enormous agreement on this matter; no one of these idioms rules out the others. Moreover, given the fact that there is an in-built element of mystery about the precise nature humanity's ultimate end in God, it is not surprising to find a variety of ways of describing this.

Nevertheless, by focusing on the end or purpose of the Christian life one can see that scriptural interpretation is never an end in itself for believers. Scripture becomes one, perhaps the primary, gift of God for drawing believers toward their ultimate end. Scripture has a role to play in the divine drama of salvation. To use Augustine's image it becomes the vehicle on which one rides towards one's true home along the road laid down by Christ.[12] Reading Scripture theologically, then, involves those habits and practices that will enable believers to interpret Scripture in ways that will enhance rather than frustrate their progress toward their ultimate end in God.

I recognize that this is a very open-ended account of theological interpretation. That it is so is not simply a factor of the space constraints on this chapter. There is little to gain and much to be lost by trying to offer too narrow a definition of theological interpretation.[13] In fact, I would be very happy for all to adopt the view that theological interpretation is that interpretation that keeps theological concerns primary. Keeping theological concerns primary means that Scripture and/or scriptural interpretation does not become a source, tool, or means to attain some other goal or project that is not theological, that is not serving the ends of ever more faithful faith and practice so that Christians might be drawn into ever deeper love of God and neighbor.

Although a definition such as this one is capable of bringing rigorous scholarly forms of interpretation as well as homilies and congregational Bible studies all under the umbrella of theological interpretation, I am primarily interested here with scholarly forms of interpretation. In this respect, I would also at least propose for discussion the view that one need not personally share the doctrinal and theological convictions of Christians in order to reflect on and even display the ways those convictions may influence and be influenced by scriptural interpretation. Jews, Muslims, those with no religious faith at all, could, in principle, interpret Scripture theologically. Indeed, one can only think that believing Christians would benefit from such intellectual generosity by those who do not share their theological

---

12. See *On Christian Doctrine*, 1.39.

13. Porter is simply one of the most recent scholars to press this issue. See "Theological Interpretation," 234–67. For a list of others who press this question see Green, "'History,'" 163 n.4.

convictions yet are still willing to engage in the practice in helping display how such convictions shape and are shaped by scriptural interpretation.

When it comes to the life and practice of specific Christian communities there may well be aspects of this scholarly work, whether done by believers or non-believers, that they will not want to or be able to engage. There may be additional forms of interpretive expression that are crucial to the lives of these communities that are not part of the standard scholarly discourse. Further, within such communities there may be different standards and procedures for authorizing interpreters and specific interpretations from those of the academy. These realities should not obscure the prospect of non-Christians or non-believers engaging in the scholarly practice of theological interpretation of Scripture. At the same time, I realize that there are not likely to be many such scholars. Nevertheless, engaging in debate over a suggestion such as this one could be extremely useful for clarifying the nature and scope of the practice of theological interpretation of Scripture, at least at a scholarly level. Moreover, I think that whether it is this issue or others, engagement in discussion and debate over focused and specific questions regarding the practice of theological interpretation will be the most fruitful way to clarify the "definition" or "definitions" of theological interpretation.

My second area of concern is to chart some of the relationships between theological interpretation of Scripture and some of the other types of biblical interpretation common in the academy. In my narration of the rise of contemporary interest in theological interpretation I hinted that when theological interests were trying to assert themselves into the scholarly mainstream, advocates for theological interpretation often made overheated claims about the bankruptcy of historical criticism. At the same time there has also been an outpouring of articles by scholars arguing that allowing theological concerns a hearing within such institutions as the Society of Biblical Literature will have a deleterious effect on biblical scholarship. These, too, tend to rely on overheated claims about such things as scholarly objectivity, historical integrity, and so forth. Often each side points to poorly executed or poorly defended examples of whatever it is they are arguing against. This seems to be not so much an argument in favor of one sort of interpretation over another as an argument in favor of doing whatever work one does better. As long as each side continues to make overheated claims about the logical necessity of their approach relative to all others, we can expect a lot of rhetorical heat, but little hermeneutical light.

For those of us who are both interested in theological interpretation and recognize the legitimacy of other interpretive interests and practices, the question remains, "how should theological interpreters engage other forms of biblical criticism?" The short answer is: theological interpreters can and should make use of historical, literary, social scientific, and all other types of biblical interpretation as long as they understand that such work needs to be subsidiary to the task of keeping theological concerns primary. Scholars can and will interpret biblical texts from a variety of interpretive interests, employing diverse interpretive practices. They can and will offer these interpretations as ends in themselves or contributions towards larger historical, literary, or social scientific projects. This is all to the good. Theological interpreters should read, engage, and learn from such works. This is because theological interpreters can and should make use of them when and as they can help in the tasks of theological interpretation. The practice of engaging and making use of the best work of those who don't share one's theological convictions has a long history in the church. Origen, for example, argued for a deep and thoughtful engagement with pagan philosophy to the extent that it helped Christians think about Christianity better. He used the trope of the Israelites plundering the Egyptians in Exodus to justify this practice.[14] Many have followed in his footsteps.

If theological interpretation of Scripture is marked by a sustained interpretive commitment to keep theological concerns primary in one's interpretation, it seems plausible both that one can and should make ad hoc use of other interpretive habits, practices, and results. This raises questions about how to make such ad hoc use of other interpretive habits, practices, and results without sacrificing the primacy of theological concerns. There is no method or procedure that will guarantee success here. Just because there is not a method, however, does not mean that we cannot think methodically about these questions and come up with some insights. Rather than pursuing a method to keep all of the various interpretive interests of biblical scholars in some sort of proper order, theological interpreters would be better served by working to cultivate a set of interpretive virtues which will help them make wise judgments about how to keep theological concerns primary in their interpretive work. I would also like to suggest that the formation of any virtue, interpretive or otherwise, requires institutional contexts that will nurture such virtue in scholars. Recognition of this latter point will lead to my final consideration.

First, although I am certain that theological interpreters of Scripture should cultivate numerous virtues, both moral and intellectual, two in particular come to the forefront. These are charity and prudence or practical reason. At their best, these two virtues work together to help theological

---

14. See Origen's letter to the as yet unbaptized Gregory Thaumaturgos. "*Letter To Gregory,*" paras. 1 and 2 in PG 11.88–89. See also the discussion in Fowl, *Engaging Scripture*, 181–83.

interpreters engage the wide variety of biblical interpretation while working to maintain the primacy of theological concerns. Further, although I will discuss each of these virtues as if they were discrete things, they ultimately must be manifested along with other virtues in a more or less unified human life.

Charity in interpretation is always directed towards maximizing agreement between interpreters. The point of this is not to reduce disagreement because disagreements are bad and upsetting. Rather charity assumes that if interpreters read each other's works in ways that maximize their agreements, then both the nature and the scope of their disagreements will be clearer and more capable of resolution. Such charity is particularly important when dealing with interpreters and interpretations that come from times, places, and cultures far different from our own. When we seek to maximize the agreements between ourselves and such interpreters we diminish the temptation simply to reduce those interpreters to inferior versions of ourselves who can be easily dismissed. In this respect, when historical critics emphasize the temporal and cultural "strangeness" of the Bible, they are emphasizing a necessary, but not sufficient, aspect of interpretive charity. They see the importance of understanding interpreters and interpretations on their own terms.

This is a necessary, but not sufficient aspect of interpretive charity because the charitable interpreter will not simply desire to display the strangeness of alternative interpretations. In addition, the charitable interpreter will want to present alternative interpreters and interpretations in the most positive light possible. This might require going above and beyond the work done by those who hold these alternative views; this may involve doing more for one's argumentative opponents than they did for themselves. Nevertheless, if one is to produce a better interpretive alternative, then one must build upon and extend the strengths of alternative views without replicating their weaknesses. Doing this requires one to address the strongest possible version of any alternative. It should be clear from this discussion that charity is not about artificial forms of humility. It does not require one to support weak or erroneous interpretations in favor of keeping interpretive peace. There is no reason for charitable interpreters to shy away from disagreement or argument. Indeed, this side of the eschaton, Christians can expect that disagreement and debate will mark all their engagements with Scripture. In such a situation, charity is that virtue that will give us the best chance of resolving our disputes well.

The second virtue to examine is practical reason or prudence. If you pick up a journal in the field of biblical studies or attend a professional conference of biblical scholars, two things would strike you. First, the material under discussion is both exceedingly diverse and complex. Secondly, those who are fully participating in the discussions and debates are able to address the diversity and complexity relatively well. They are able to figure out where the critical issues lie; they can make judgments about the weight and relevance of particular claims; they can come to a conclusion which they can defend, revise, or abandon in the light of new evidence or superior arguments. What this shows in part is that these scholars have been more or less well-formed to be particular types of readers.

It is simply the case that one cannot successfully and proficiently enter into these professional discussions and debates without prior formation. In part this is because there is a great deal of technical information to master. This is not the whole story, however. This technical information is not self-interpreting. It does not organize itself; it cannot identify its own problems, tensions, and underlying patterns. Professional proficiency presumes technical mastery. Such proficiency is distinguished from technical mastery, however, by the professionals' abilities to engage in interpretive debates and discussions and to re-formulate the issues as needed; to marshal evidence both arguing for its relevance to a particular issue and showing how that evidence should lead to specific conclusions; to defend, refine, and reformulate views in the light of counter-claims and in all of this advance a particular interpretive debate or discussion.

The virtue that enables one to move beyond technical mastery to professional proficiency is what Aristotle would call *phronēsis*, or practical reasoning, or prudence. Although it is rarely specified this way, the graduate formation of biblical scholars is primarily an exercise in cultivating the virtue of practical reasoning. The aim of this is so that scholars can deploy their technical knowledge and skills in ways that are appropriate to specific problems, contexts, and audiences. The prudent or practically wise scholar perceives the relevant similarities between complex problems and already agreed standards, and then moves by analogy to use already proven standards to elucidate the unknown or the contested.

Given that theological interpretation of Scripture is marked by debates, discussions, and arguments about how to interpret and embody Scripture so as to enhance Christians' prospects of worshipping and living faithfully before God, cultivating the virtue of practical reasoning or prudence will be as important as cultivating interpretive charity. This is so that the technical skills and knowledge of the scholar can fruitfully be displayed, deployed, and directed toward the larger ends of the Christian life. Without practical reasoning, it is too easy to displace theological concerns from their primacy in theological interpretation.

How are such virtues formed and cultivated in people? The academy has relatively clear ways of doing this for professional biblical scholars and does so pretty well. Theological interpreters of Scripture can and should benefit from such formation. In my view, however, the academy is weakest in developing both the technical skills and knowledge attendant to theological interpretation and the precise ways in which one needs to be formed to be a charitable and prudent theological interpreter. In large part, this is because the skills and knowledge distinctively related to theological interpretation will cross the disciplinary and departmental boundaries that shape most institutions. There is much work to be done here with regard to the curricula and aims of graduate education that will develop theological interpreters of Scripture. Historical and systematic theologians will need to work with biblical scholars and others in ways that graduate training does not equip them to do well

One might well ask if the academy does such a poor job of forming theological interpreters, how would I account for the presence of current theological interpreters? Apart from any detailed surveys, I would suggest that contemporary theological interpreters have benefitted from sets of contingent circumstances and contexts that have formed them. Without denigrating such circumstances and contexts, this is not a systematic and intentional pattern of formation. I believe it is now time to focus on just such a systematic and intentional set of processes.

In this light, we must not forget that the aims of theological interpretation will always have an eye on the church, on that primary context where Christians argue, debate, and discuss Scripture with the aim of deepening their love of God and neighbor. Having said that, I think I can assert without much argument that in regard to both of these virtues that are crucial to theological interpretation, the academy does a much better job than the church in cultivating charitable and prudent interpreters.

In some respects this is not all that surprising. The academy and the church have different missions. The academy seeks to form a relatively select group of readers; the church seeks to form all members of Christ's body. In the academy, failure in formation means that you simply are excluded from the academy—hardly a fate worse than death. At least in theory, the church does not exclude those who do not measure up, because Christians understand that they, too, often fail to measure up.

Perhaps more significantly, when it comes to forming scholars of any stripe who might serve the ends of the church in any one of a number of contexts, the church has handed over a significant portion of that formative work to the academy. There are, doubtless, numerous reasons for this and I have no expertise in displaying them. Apart from such expertise, however, it appears to me that this situation raises some significant concerns for the future practice of theological interpretation of Scripture.

Although the practices of theological interpretation of Scripture have always operated in some form within ecclesial contexts, it now appears that the practices of theological interpretation have established some space within the modern academy. The various institutions of the modern academy do a relatively good job of forming many of the requisite skills, habits, and dispositions biblical scholars need. For the most part, these institutions are neither interested in nor well placed to form the specific skills, habits, and dispositions required to form theological interpreters of Scripture. Further, although churches benefit from the presence and work of contemporary theological interpreters of Scripture, and although one might argue that such scholars are essential to the long-term health of the church, churches have not generally invested in the formation and sustenance of such scholars. Given the current questions surrounding the state and future of higher education and related concerns and questions about seminary education, there is, perhaps now more than ever, a need for institutions within which theological interpreters of Scripture can be formed in ways that both impart the requisite technical mastery of languages, history, philosophy, and doctrine, and such interpretive virtues as charity and prudence. The primary question is, who will invest in such formation? The output of contemporary theological interpreters will no doubt continue apace. Will there be sufficient younger scholars who will be formed and supported to carry this practice on into the future? I would submit that questions such as these, rather than further debates about the nature and definition of theological interpretation of Scripture and its relationships to historical criticism should be far more pressing on all interested parties.

13

What Makes New Testament Theology "Theology"?

ROBERT MORGAN
University of Oxford

THE QUESTION PRESUPPOSES WHAT the phrase itself implies: that "New Testament theology" is or should be in some sense "theology." What that contention might mean depends not only on the contested phrase "New Testament theology," but, prior to that, on how "theology" itself is understood, whether (to condense the range of non-disparaging dictionary meanings) in the strong sense of articulating and perhaps advocating a religious stance by expressing its belief and practice in a rational way, or in the secondary sense of philosophical, historical, and related scholarship describing and analyzing the commitments of others. Both senses imply an adjective indicating which religion or group is intended because theological discourse is normally internal to some specific religious community, tradition, or practice.

These two senses of "theology" overlap with, but are distinct from, the two meanings of "biblical theology": the seventeenth-century pietist "theology *in accord with* the Bible," a meaning that reflected the intentions of the Reformers who also had wanted a contemporary theology in accord with

Scripture, and the later "theology or theologies *contained in* the Bible."[1] The latter originated in Protestant orthodoxy's proof-texting. When that was superseded by the new historical scholarship the second, descriptive sense of "biblical theology" remained uppermost in the new historical discipline, "biblical theology of the New Testament." However, both the theological motivation of the old proof-texting and the pietist loyalty to the intentions of the Reformers remained latent in the new discipline and gave a strong existential dimension to this critical biblical scholarship. Its origins in those older, strongly theological forms of "biblical theology" are visible in its standard nineteenth-century label.[2] The attempted revival of this phrase again reflects the theological dimensions of the discipline, including a theological interest in overcoming the historically driven separation of Old and New Testament interpretation.

The effect of the pietist meaning of "biblical theology" on New Testament theology has been obscured by unclarity about "theology" itself. Its two senses are usually related and sometimes confused because participation in and observation and analysis of a religious tradition or practice are far from mutually exclusive. Constructive theology necessarily involves some historical scholarship, which must inform it, and may also spark theological criticism. Conversely, the historical study of Christianity can be stimulated by constructive theology. In biblical study the walls between the historical study of Christian origins and theological reflection on the New Testament texts are sufficiently porous to have allowed the Reformers' and pietists' religiously motivated "biblical theology" to have affected some rigorous and some less than rigorous historical study of the New Testament, particularly in New Testament theology.

The strong meaning of "theology" is the primary meaning, but the secondary sense is most apparent in the phrase "New Testament theology" because this discipline has been a sub-division of New Testament scholarship, rather than of systematic theology. The pietist "biblical theology" that preceded it wanted to replace Protestant orthodox dogmatics. The echoes of this ambition in more recent "biblical theology" did not endear it to systematic theologians. Some New Testament scholars have also been hostile to New Testament theology for this and other reasons (below nn.5, 17).

---

1. Cf. Ebeling, "The Meaning of 'Biblical Theology.'" A shorter version had appeared in *JTS* 6 (1955) 15–25.

2. "Biblical Theology of the New Testament" is the title of handbooks by G. L. Bauer (below, n.6), Lossius (1825), Cölln (vol. 2, 1836), Schmid (1853), Weiss (1868), Hofmann (Part xi, 1886), Weidner (1891), Weinel (1911, oddly), Hübner (1990–1905), Childs, (1992, Part 4), Stuhlmacher (1992-99). Cf. Beale, *A New Testament Biblical Theology*.

The two senses of "theology" and the uneasy combination of history and theology in New Testament theology multiplies the ambiguities, but our question is how or how much (if any) of the primary meaning of "theology" can be found in the discipline called New Testament theology. It involves the relationship between modern critical biblical scholarship and constructive theology which Gabler discussed and so triggered the modern discipline.[3] Gabler's two-step solution in which historical description of the biblical material was to be followed by a critical theological sifting that removed what was out-dated or time-conditioned had many successors among liberal theologians and non-theologians, but few among biblical theologians. These latter restricted themselves to Gabler's first step and implied something of their own theological interests through that.[4] Other two-step solutions[5] have followed Gabler in preventing too much theological weight being accorded to the historical descriptions provided by New Testament theology, a natural tendency where Scripture is valued as highly as in classical Protestantism. That hegemonic "biblical theology" was surely debilitating to theology as was the converse subordination of biblical interpretation to dogmatics, though neither perhaps so damaging as these disciplines drifting apart. New Testament theology since Gabler and Bauer[6] was developed to overcome that hiatus and allow Scripture as read in modern biblical scholarship to inform and nourish systematic theology, and where necessary to challenge it.

The absence of an indefinite article in our title draws attention to a further ambiguity in "New Testament theology." The phrase usually refers to presentations of the theological content of the New Testament in articles and monographs on particular passages and themes, in theological dictionaries, in commentaries on individual writings and in discussions of individual writers, as well as in handbooks that sum up a scholar's relevant conclusions across the whole New Testament. These handbooks or lecture courses are themselves often called this or something similar, making that genre itself a further meaning. An indefinite article in the title of this essay would have

---

3. Gabler, "On the Proper Distinction between Biblical and Dogmatic Theology and the Correct Delimitation of their Boundaries." 1787. See R. Morgan, "Gabler's Bicentenary."

4. Surprising echoes of Gabler's two steps may be found in Barrett, "What is New Testament Theology? Some Reflections." See Morgan, "C. K. Barrett and New Testament Theology," 432–57..

5. Notably Stendahl, "Biblical Theology: Contemporary."

6. G. L. Bauer, *Biblische Theologie des Neuen Testaments*. The "*biblische*" in Bauer's title relates his work to Gabler's, and both to the older, less historically conscious "biblical theology." All saw their biblical theology as a theological discipline using whatever rational methods were available and appropriate.

suggested those handbooks. In what follows the whole discipline is intended, but a different implication of the missing article has some relevance to our argument: that there are potentially as many New Testament theologies as there are scholars who engage in this discipline, or Christians who think seriously about their faith and its relationship to its scriptural foundations The New Testament texts themselves set limits to the range of interpretations that are historically plausible, and therefore perhaps to what developments of the Christian tradition can now claim to be true to Scripture (*Schriftgemäss*), but that range is wider than what churches have accepted in defining their identity. Doctrinal decisions narrow the range of accepted interpretations. New Testament theology is more open-ended. Competent interpreters exercise their judgment freely in accord with the textual evidence of the New Testament authors. The intentions of the latter, however, usually keep their historically educated theological interpreters within the framework of the rule of faith that the doctrinal tradition aims to clarify and articulate under new social and intellectual conditions. The intentions of most churches, and the consent of most Christians to be true to the witness of Scripture while developing the tradition to meet new needs and new understandings of reality are reflected in the sometimes unadmitted influence of modern theological interests in most New Testament theology.

How far (if at all) anyone's New Testament theology reflects or should reflect their own theology has been contested ever since William Wrede appeared (to himself and to some others) to redefine the historical discipline in a way that excluded the interpreters' own theological interests.[7] He had good reasons for defending the integrity of historical scholarship in this way, even if modern historiography is more accepting of scholars' own perspectives and interests. In biblical studies apologetic interests are always likely to threaten the historian's impartiality. Wrede himself was a professor of theology and a preacher who had personal religious and theological interests in some of the biblical texts and assumed his scholarship was relevant to theology and church, but like most of his believing and unbelieving successors he saw the professional task of the biblical scholar as understanding the New Testament dispassionately with the rational instruments of his speciality, i.e., skills in language, literature, and above all history. Historians ought not twist the evidence to support their own theological presuppositions or religious preferences.

---

7. Wrede, *Über Aufgabe und Methode der sogenannten neutestamentlichen Theologie*, ET in Morgan, *The Nature of New Testament Theology*. My sceptical formulation ("appeared") anticipates the argument to follow that Wrede's history and New Testament theology are two different orientations of biblical scholarship, both legitimate.

In retrospect Wrede can be said to have drawn attention to the gap that in German universities around 1890 could already be discerned between a modern biblical scholarship whose methods and tasks bore no necessary relationship to the religious community, and the aims of most Christian biblical scholarship, even in the modern period, to guide and reinforce Christian belief and practice. One possible conclusion for him to have drawn had already been trailed by Overbeck[8] who had called for a "profane" church history. It would have been reasonable to distinguish between a biblical scholarship using all available and relevant methods but oriented to the interests of religious institutions and individuals, and the same scholarship set free in principle from such interests and guided by whatever research directions (usually historical, but also literary, social-scientific, and culture-critical) the scholars (or their market, or their employers) choose. Wrede did not consider such a distinction because in his day most of the best New Testament scholarship, including his own, was carried out in contexts governed by Christian religious interests. He was himself a theologian but was negative about inherited theological baggage corrupting the purely historical discipline, and unlike Schleiermacher did not say whether or how his historical "task and method" related to theologians' religious aims to clarify the identity of their religion. The new historical methods and results needed developing and defending, not qualifying (below n.13) or their scope restricting. The theological character of biblical studies was accordingly less well discussed around 1900 than it had been in earlier generations.[9] Wrede's emphasis upon the historical at the expense of the theological aims of biblical scholarship led him to dismiss any properly theological discussion from New Testament theology.[10] For him the religious and theological dimensions of the historical discipline were restricted to the human subject-matter of the texts, without reference to their transcendent claims. He did not deny the interpreters' possible interest in those claims, but considered that the business of systematic theology, not biblical scholarship.[11]

---

8. Overbeck (1837–1905) became professor in Basel in 1870. His *How Christian is Our Present-day Theology?* (1873) is still relevant. See ET 16 and 207.

9. E.g. Stäudlin, "Über die blos historische Auslegung des Neuen Testaments" (1814), excerpted by Kümmel, *The New Testament*, 113–16. The revival of hermeneutics in 1920s German theology was indicative of the persistence of theology in New Testament studies and a recognition of its problems.

10. He was caustic about the remarks of B. Weiss and W. Beyschlag about revelation (which are admittedly as unsatisfactory as his own apparent lack of understanding for what they were getting at). See ET 183.

11. Wrede in Strecker, *Das Problem*, 83; ET in Morgan, *New Testament Theology*, 69.

German universities offered courses on "critical introduction" and "biblical theology." Those on the religious ideas of both Testaments were here called "theology," not on account of their subject-matter or how it was studied—the human subject-matter of this historical study was ancient religion or religious ideas—but on account of how students and teachers understood this human historical material to refer (more or less) to the God whom they too worshipped. It was the institutional context, the interpreters' interests, and so the way the ideas were understood to correspond to those of contemporary Christianity and refer to God whom the interpreters also acknowledged that made biblical theology of the New Testament, and even Old Testament theology, "theology," rather than simply "history of religion."[12] Schleiermacher had been clear about what made historical study of Christianity into "historical theology," or the "historical knowledge of Christianity" into "a theological discipline": the aim "toward the further cultivation of Christianity," and a religious sense of the subject-matter, the "essence" of Christianity.[13]

By concentrating on its historical "aim and method" to the exclusion of the interpreters' pre-understandings, aims, and context, Wrede by contrast insisted that this sub-division of New Testament scholarship was exclusively history, not theology, and not both. He wanted the religious ideas to be described and explained historically without reference to, or influence from, the historian's own beliefs or interests. Many biblical scholars agree, but some only half agree. New Testament theologians and other Christian historians agree that their own religious standpoint cannot be allowed to distort their perception of the evidence, but add that it affects what they think it's all about. It should not affect their linguistic judgments or reconstructions of the history, but their view of the invisible subject-matter may affect how they interpret the visible evidence and assess the history. Human

---

12. Bauer's earlier title, *Theologie des alten Testaments oder Abriß der religiösen Begriffe der alten Hebräer* (Leipzig, 1796), contains both alternatives.

13. Schleiermacher, *Brief Outline on the Study of Theology*, §69: "what a different turn the study of the same mass of 'facts' would take, and even the manner of handling them, when these facts are assigned to historical theology, as compared with placing them within the general study of history. This is true even though the basic principles of historical research do not cease to be the same for both areas of study" (41). §21: "... a merely empirical method of interpreting Christianity ... cannot achieve a genuine knowledge of it ...." One needs "to understand the essence of Christianity" (24). Schleiermacher of course presupposed the institutional context in which this study of real theology took place: strongly confessional faculties of theology in a modern university. His commitment to "the basic principles of historical research" makes his proposals for theological study applicable outside confessional faculties. Theologians' grasp of the "essence," equivalent to Bultmann's *Sache*, need not distort their historical judgment, *pace* Wrede.

historical causation can be thought to reflect divine providence, but this personal belief is kept off the scholarly page.[14]

Wrede the theologian was able to tread his historicist path because his own understanding of Christianity depended not on its continuity with the witness (and so the theologies) of Paul and John and the other New Testament and some later ecclesiastical writers like Augustine and Luther, but more on what historians could discover of a Jesus free of dogma, and on what modern German culture from the days of Lessing and Kant had made of the Christian tradition, assimilating some of it in new forms of Protestantism. The loss and gain here can be differently assessed, but Troeltsch and his neo-Protestant contemporaries were as clear as their orthodox opponents about the novelty of their version of Christianity in relation to classical Protestantism and the beliefs of most other denominations. Many of their valid insights were subsequently incorporated into the more traditional versions of Christianity, which could claim a much stronger continuity with the New Testament witness even as they too were changing in the light of new knowledge and experience, but a neo-Protestant theology that has no need of Paul's or John's theology is very different from theologies aiming to re-state rather than re-invent Christianity.

The point here is that the late nineteenth-century argument was not simply (as Wrede implied) about the integrity of historical scholarship, but about how to read the New Testament in the churches and in a culture shaped by modernity. The battle in those German theological faculties between two opposing views of Christianity remains instructive. Disputes about syllabus and methods have again recently reflected theological disagreements as well as social change, in English universities as elsewhere. However, as the radically historical character of biblical studies was more widely accepted in England from the 1960s on, it began to feed less into the dispute between liberal and conservative theologies (which even the tamest biblical criticism had ignited) than into an alternative between fundamentally Christian and thoroughly secular approaches to the Bible.

Wrede's argument had serious consequences for religious faith and practice. The more church-related theological faculties of Germany and Switzerland could fight back with more sophisticated forms of theological interpretation than Niebergall's "practical interpretation" and Frick's "pneumatic

---

14. Cf. Butterfield, *Writings on Christianity and History*, xlix–li, 133–93.

understanding of the Bible."[15] Barth, alerted in part by Overbeck,[16] saw the danger and made his Christian perspective as explicit in his exegesis as in his dogmatics. But in secular universities the overarching category has to be the non-confessional New Testament *scholarship* that Wrede had advocated. New Testament *theology* is then likely to be seen as no more than a sub-division of that. When German theological faculties had anticipated that usage they had seen it as a pedagogical convenience within theological study of Scripture, not as historical description of religious ideas in sharp contrast to theology proper. Where all New Testament teaching was oriented to Christianity, the secondary meaning of "theology" was shadowed by the primary meaning. New Testament theologies informed and supported a revised dogmatics and taught future clergy to relate their modern critical readings of Scripture to their own faith and preaching. Paul retained his Reformation flavor, now refined by historical exegesis, and the humanity and divinity of Jesus were elucidated through the Synoptic Gospels' witness to the historical figure, and John's deeper reflection on the mystery of the incarnation. New Testament theology was the climax of a moderately critical biblical study in a properly theological faculty that existed (in Schleiermacher's phrase) for "the further cultivation of Christianity."

By contrast, Wrede's understanding of "New Testament theology" as "the history of early Christian religion and theology" led him to erase the phrase.[17] This suited a liberal Protestant theology that drew history rather than doctrine or preaching from the biblical texts. In a more secular context, however, Wrede's academic and theological adjustment could easily become a secularist move away from contemporary religious interests in the Bible. Despite the secondary meaning of "theology" in New Testament theology many biblical scholars still consider themselves theologians in the strong sense, not merely historians of religion or "theological scholars" in the sec-

15. Karl Barth's contempt for the two-step implications of F. Niebergall's *Praktische Auslegung* (1909) in Hans Lietzmann's series *Handbuch zum Neuen Testament*, is clear in *Romans*, 9. Bultmann called "spiritual exegesis" a "detestable expression," in "The Significance of 'Dialectical Theology,'" 158 (original 1928).

16. Barth, *Theology and Church*, 55–73 (the Overbeck article quoted appeared first in 1920).

17. Wrede in Strecker, *Das Problem*, 153: ET in Morgan, *Nature of New Testament Theology*, 116. Wayne Meeks' "provocation" that "we should start by erasing from our vocabulary the terms 'biblical theology' and, even more urgently, 'New Testament theology'" ("Why Study the New Testament?" 167), was similarly driven by concern for the integrity of historical research and (more contentiously) resistance to doing modern theology in and through scriptural interpretation. By contrast, Barth's "sole aim" to interpret Scripture (*Romans*, ix) is applied to a collection of historical-critical essays in New Testament theology in the title of Conzelmann, *Theologie als Schriftauslegung* (1974).

ondary sense. They see their historical exegesis as a theological responsibility. Wrede was also a theologian, although of a modernist stripe that did not need Pauline or Johannine theology, but in more secular contexts his proposal tended to extinguish the primary meaning of "theology" which had guided most Christian study of Scripture, both ancient and modern.

One recently reactivated solution is to abandon historical critical biblical scholarship in favor of an explicitly theological interpretation of Scripture. Cutting the connection with secular rationality could signal either an excess or a loss of intellectual confidence, and either would be more serious for some Christians than others. In practice all explicit theological interpreters continue to draw eclectically on any insights that their secular colleagues achieve, and some remain within the parameters of historical critical scholarship and so are writing New Testament theology, which is of course itself a form of theological interpretation,[18] however implicit. Since other theological interpreters break with historical interpretation in the interest of figural interpretation it is prudent to mark the distinction by retaining the phrase "New Testament theology" for theological interpretation carried out as normal biblical scholarship where the interpreter's own standpoint need not be paraded, but remains implicit. The religious importance of such a theologically oriented historical criticism in theological education will be discussed shortly.

The rational response of churches to the threat posed by some secularist proposals[19] is to clarify the different aims of biblical scholarship at work throughout the history of biblical interpretation, and to recognize that the phrase "New Testament theology" generally identifies historical critical scholarship that is guided by religious aims and motivations, even when it labels a sub-division of biblical scholarship. These different interests present in the same biblical scholarship affect choices of research topics and can stimulate the conversations essential to academic work. Different perspectives on the same data are often illuminating. A religious interest is usually the strongest motivation to biblical study, but biblical scholarship in universities, like all historical theology (n.13), has long been non-confessional, unlike most dogmatics. Students and teachers are given freedom to believe and think and research what they like by curricula open to both theological and non-theological interests.

---

18. The new *Journal of Theological Interpretation* represents this variety. Some essays are straightforwardly New Testament theology, such as those by Gaventa, Gorman, and Hays on Romans in *JTI* 5:1 (2011).

19. They are a threat when they try to suppress theological interests, e.g., by syllabus changes. The legitimacy of these other interests is not in question.

Understanding New Testament theology primarily in terms of the interpreters' religious interests, and the implications that follow from these, has parallels with the turn to the reader in literary theory and throughout the humanities and social sciences. It can avoid the suspicion of special pleading by the quality of its impartial historical scholarship. Examples of both good and bad critical practice are plentiful. Finding the meaning of the phrase in the spirit and often unspoken thoughts of modern interpreters makes explicit what has usually been implicit in the letter of their historical scholarship. The phrase referred to a sub-division of New Testament scholarship in a context where the old sub-divisions could all have been placed under the broad umbrella of a New Testament theology mostly done by Christians for religious (including theological) purposes. When that was presupposed it made some sense to reserve the "theology" label for the scholarly analysis of the theological concepts in the texts. The prominence of the secondary improper meaning of "theology" in the phrase "New Testament theology" is residue from that context where the religious aim of biblical scholarship, and so the primary meaning of theology, were taken for granted. In a more pluralist scholarship Christian assumptions about the subject-matter of Scripture need to be made explicit. They can be acknowledged by the phrase New Testament theology provided that the primary sense of "theology," usually unobtrusively present in the discipline alongside the secondary sense, is underlined.

Doing *theology* by interpreting texts normally implies a self-involving understanding of their subject-matter, however weak, residual, indirect, or non-existent the relationship of some theologians to their parent faith-community. Without interpreters' existential stance even Paul's or Augustine's theology looks like a dead carcass of ancient religious ideas for philosophers and historians to feed on. Their scholarship can be welcomed by Christian theologians more tightly bound to and dependent on the public religious tradition, but if New Testament theology is *theology* done through the interpretation of these texts, its historical and other scholarship are not self-serving, but directed to religious and theological ends. When the primary meaning of "theology" is reclaimed in order to distinguish religious from secular scholarly aims, confusion can be avoided by calling the sub-division of all biblical scholarship "New Testament ideas" or concepts, or vocabulary, or history of early Christian thought. Gabler's biblical theology and much of what followed differed from that in pointing towards dogmatics or contemporary expressions of Christian faith. Our "turn to the interpreter" is thus not an arbitrary change of meaning, but draws out what has been presupposed in most New Testament theology.

A possible objection is that emphasizing interpreters' aims and interests renders the phrase New Testament theology superfluous since these are often unstated and invisible. To avoid confusion the phrase should indeed disappear from among the subdivisions of biblical scholarship, as Wrede and Meeks recommended, but it remains desirable for New Testament scholars and their readers to know what they are doing. New Testament theology is critical biblical scholarship that is also theological interpretation, i.e., where interpreters think that like the biblical authors, they are talking about God whom (at least hypothetically[20]) they worship. Most interpreters know what they think the texts are about, and so whether they are writing New Testament theology or merely engaging in historical scholarship. Their "purely historical" scholarship might or might not imply a living relationship to their own theology, i.e., whether they themselves think the subject-matter[21] of the texts is what (they think) the biblical authors thought. It does not depend on their agreeing with everything the biblical authors thought about it, much less with how they expressed it. Modern interpreters are bound to express the theological subject-matter differently if they want to be true to it in a different culture because signaling the divine subject of Scripture involves speaking of the world and human existence, which are understood differently today. However, a shared sense that this talk of worldly reality is at the same time (implicit) talk about God is what makes some interpretation "theological interpretation," or New Testament theology "theology."

Defining New Testament theology by reference to the standpoint, aims, and interests of the implicit theological interpreters, rather than by the religious ideas contained in the texts, overcomes the main obstacle to making the content of the texts key to the definition of the discipline, but introduces the difficulty just mentioned. The obstacle was that Christians and non-Christians understand this content differently, but the difficulty about emphasizing that is that the Christian "content" (or subject) is invisible. All agree that these are religious texts. The hospitality of the concept "religion" opens a door to conversation about them with non-Christians. But this conversation is unlikely to resolve or even broach the all-important question of truth. Theologians must say that the texts are about God whom they worship, and that could end the conversation. To communicate with those who do not share their beliefs they need to justify the religious dimensions

---

20. This qualification resists making religious commitment a prerequisite for doing theology. Faith is elusive, and interpreting the texts from a Christian perspective in order to analyze, develop, or criticize the tradition is an option open to all. Where believers claim religious truth, theological interpreters need only write "as if" it were true.

21. Some now translate Barth and Bultmann's *Sache* "subject" rather than "subject-matter" to avoid the impression of objectifying God.

of their New Testament *theology* by pointing to aspects of their own writing that correspond to the religious character and aims of the biblical texts. Theology is public discourse, however much it owes to private prayer and reflection. New Testament theologians' thinking about God must therefore leave traces in what they write.

Gerd Theissen's five criteria (drawn from Luther) of what makes exegesis theology provide what is needed.[22] He argues (1) that a theological statement about a New Testament text needs to be sensitive to its aesthetic dimensions, since God is spoken of here in pictures. Others will agree with that warning against bad theological exegesis, and his other criteria distinguish theological from non-theological exegesis. Theological exegesis has (2) a transcendent reference or kerygmatic dimension, and (3) an existential reference, and (4) an ecclesial or canonical dimension, and (5) a critical function. The Bible itself is theological on this account because it transmits pictorial statements about God and humanity, makes possible dialogue with God, communicates salvation, has canonical authority. Interpretations that reflect that are, at least in principle, rationally defensible and likely to be theological. Not all theology has such a sharp critical function as Paul's or Luther's, but Theissen's indicators prevent New Testament theology from becoming a purely private matter.

Librarians do not need to know which of their authors understand the Bible to be about the God whom they worship and which read these ancient religious texts without reference to contemporary religious truth. They classify their books according to the sub-divisions of biblical scholarship and can include what some have called "New Testament theology" as "New Testament ideas" or whatever. Neither do the scholars' readers need to know which modern authors thought they were engaged in theological *and* historical (including literary), and which in only historical (and literary) interpretation. They can themselves choose to read a piece of scholarship either as New Testament theology or purely as history of early Christian thought. Believers are likely to assume that the subject-matter is "God whom we worship," non-believers that it is religious ideas that may or may not have truth or value. For example, some will read the key chapters 7–13 of John Ashton's magisterial *Understanding the Fourth Gospel* (2nd ed., 2007) or C. H. Dodd's *The Interpretation of the Fourth Gospel* (1953) as New Testament theology (as well as history of religion) because they as readers associate themselves with the religious stance of the evangelist. Others do not. In neither case are the beliefs of the scholarly authors relevant to how their books are read.

---

22. Theissen, *Polyphones Verstehen*, 139-49.

A more challenging example is Adele Reinhartz *Befriending the Beloved Disciple: A Jewish Reading of the Gospel of John* (2001). One may read this as New Testament theology, rich in *Sachkritik*, or as textual analysis that yields information and suggestions about some first-century religion and throws light on some twenty-first-century Judaism and Christianity. If anyone's understanding of God whom Jews and Christians worship is enlarged by reading this book they will call it theology in the strong sense, whatever the author intended. That confirms that it can sometimes be how the New Testament scholarship is read that makes it New Testament theology. Biblical scholars may or may not choose to tell their readers where they personally stand. Reinhartz does so, up to a point, as Ashton and Dodd for different reasons do not. The theological dialogue into which she draws (some of) her readers requires her to say more about her standpoint than most New Testament theologians do, but all three scholars would wish to be judged by what they have written, not by how they themselves understood their subject-matter. They give their readers the freedom to read it as history or literary criticism—or (if the readers align themselves with the witness of a biblical writer) as theology. That final option implies agreement with the male biblical writer about what his subject-matter is, but not necessarily with all he says about God, much less with the ancient worldview in terms of which he articulated that. If the interpreters' aims are definitive of New Testament theology the discipline rests on a pre-understanding of the subject-matter of the New Testament which can be expressed in terms of both ancient and modern worldviews, and which raises the question of the truth of Christianity that no genuine theology can defer indefinitely.

That, however, re-opens the question whether only believers can engage in New Testament theology (and any "theology" in the strong sense). If the answer were yes, neither would have any place in the secular university where students and teachers are free to believe what they like (within reason). A negative answer can be given by distinguishing faith from standpoint. Faith is too elusive to be made a pre-requisite of any academic discipline, but the interpreter's standpoint is not. A standpoint internal to the tradition, aligning the interpreter with the texts, may be adopted out of conviction. Unlike faith, however, it may be adopted hypothetically, in an attempt to understand a religion or read a religious text from a believer's perspective. Much theology has an "as if" quality. Theologians interpret and develop their tradition in ways that make room for a rational faith to exist by removing obstacles from bygone worldviews and offering formulations that seem to do justice also to believers' experience. They do not create faith or vouch for the truth of their tradition, let alone demonstrate that. They show it is coherent and credible, and that it may be true, but confessing its truth is a further religious step perhaps facilitated by the formulae tested by theologians and used by preachers and resonating with experience.

Another objection, that emphasis upon the interpreters opens a wide door to subjectivity, will be answered by insisting on the textual restraints laid on theological interpretation of the New Testament when carried out under the aegis of modern biblical scholarship. But first, the history of the discipline can be appealed to in support of our "turn to the interpreter," intended to identify or recover the theology in New Testament theology and find a place for this discipline in a pluralistic secular academy where much of the best biblical scholarship is not theology.

Most nineteenth-century New Testament theology had preserved within its new and historically better-informed exegesis the relationship always assumed to exist between the theological content of these texts and contemporary Christian belief, most professionally articulated in dogmatics. Much of this was by later standards insufficiently critical, but even the radical pioneer F. C. Baur had brought what he had learned from Schleiermacher, Schelling, and Hegel to his critical-historical readings of the New Testament and subsequent history of dogma, and developed theological interpretations of these texts, including his New Testament theologies,[23] that preserved (in what were soon seen as historically insupportable and theologically problematic new ways) the ideational content of the New Testament and dogmatic tradition.

German idealist syntheses of traditional Christian doctrine and modernity had a short shelf life. By the late nineteenth century not only enlightened free-thinkers and other "cultured despisers" but also the more radical liberal theologians had largely abandoned the dogmatic tradition and defined their Christianity in other ways, some especially by their historical constructions of the historical figure of Jesus and his religious and moral teaching. Their histories of Israelite, early Jewish, and Christian religion had limited relevance to their own modern Protestantism. Where Schleiermacher and Baur had developed modern theologies on the basis of philosophical and historical interrogation of Christian origins and the whole development, their more specialized successors weakened or abandoned the ambitious syntheses of the first half of the century in favor of more conservative ecclesial, or more positivist "scientific" agendas. The

---

23. His rather Kantian post-humous *Vorlesungen über neutestamentliche Theologie* (1864, repr. 1973, ET forthcoming) differ from the more Hegelian New Testament theology contained in his *Paul* (1845, ET 1875), *Die kanonischen Evangelien* (1847) and the first part of his *Church History* (1853, ET 1878-79).

gap between systematic and historical theology that Schleiermacher, Baur, Ritschl, and later Troeltsch had hoped to bridge now seemed unbridgeable.[24]

This split between the historical (scientific) and normative ecclesial disciplines in German academic theology[25] was addressed in new ways after the First World War by Barth and Bultmann, among others. The extent of their difference was in the 1920s initially masked by their common front against the older liberal Protestantism and their shared recourse to Paul and the Reformers, but by 1933 they had taken different theological turns within that shared Reformation heritage while united in their opposition to National Socialism. After forty years of political and military hostility, language barriers, and divergent philosophical and theological traditions, English language theology learned from both. Barth's importance for "theological interpretation of Scripture," and Bultmann's for New Testament theology is generally acknowledged, but the relationship between Barth's explicit and Bultmann's implicit theological interpretation has been made more adversarial than churches, which need both, can afford. Barth was more liberal[26] and Bultmann more a church theologian than most of their international admirers. The rival theological camps have generally failed to co-operate on an endeavor they shared, and since the 1970s neither Barth nor Bultmann has been much studied by biblical scholars who do not share their theological commitments.[27]

This argument that theologians who share their churches' recognition of the centrality of Scripture for Christian identity and vitality need both the critical theological biblical scholarship represented by Bultmann and the more explicit theological interpretation advanced by Barth can find support in some recent publications.[28] The most creative English contributions to New Testament theology have drawn fresh philosophical resources,

---

24. Bernoulli, *Die wissenschaftliche und die kirchliche Methode*. (Freiburg 1897), was accepted by Troeltsch in *GGA* 1898, 424–35, as a fair statement of the problem.

25. Zachhuber, *Theology as Science in Nineteenth-Century Germany*, shows how the idealist synthesis of theology, philosophy, and history was constructed, and (at 267–68) its weakness identified by Kaftan, *Das Wesen der christlichen Religion*. Kaftan's separation of "scientific" (historical) and confessional theology anticipates some twentieth-century critiques of New Testament theology.

26. From his conservative home background and liberal theological education Barth brought a more dialectical attitude to historical criticism than his conservative evangelical successors, as his Preface to the second (1922) edition of *Romans*, 2–15 makes clear.

27. The great exception in England was Anthony Thiselton, whose early study of Bultmann and Heidegger opened many evangelical eyes; Thiselton, *Two Horizons*.

28. E.g., Longenecker and Parsons, eds., *Beyond Bultmann*, where fair criticism is based on solid knowledge and appreciation for his project.

including speech-act theory, Gadamer, and Ricoeur, into their critical biblical scholarship. Among these, Andrew Lincoln and his former colleague Anthony Thiselton offer a welcome contrast to a new trend in evangelical "theological interpretation" which defines itself largely by its hostility to historical criticism. In celebrating the achievement of an outstanding New Testament theologian this essay aims to clarify the character of that discipline as *implicit* theological interpretation of New Testament. It is "thought of God" or theological reflection which in its historical scholarship cannot speak God's name. Its Godward orientation remains implicit because, as a form of modern biblical scholarship, it interprets these texts within the constraints and the conventions of a modern historical study which does not speak of God whom believers worship, except historically in describing the New Testament authors' beliefs.

The suggestion that New Testament theology has generally been (and should be) *implicit theological interpretation* of these texts implies, as does the phrase "New Testament" itself, that the discipline is primarily literary rather than historical. That does not mean "the death of the author," and does not license textual indeterminacy. Its use of literary theory is eclectic. Paul is alive and well-known to biblical scholars, even if most Christians see him more through Luke's narrative. The theological use of the New Testament as a norm leads to the historical quest for the authors' intentions.

Scripture can function as a *source* of Christian faith when understood quite differently from the human authors' intentions, as happens frequently in Christian reading of the Old Testament and in allegorical and much popular biblical interpretation. Even the New Testament can, in some religious as in some secular contexts, be treated as a free-floating literary classic open to multiple valid readings, but for it to function as a *norm*, textual meaning or authorial intention (which usually coincide) is essential.[29] This provides not only some degree of consensus about Christianity, but also (as in Barth's remark—and most Protestant theology) the basis of any claim that Scripture is the indispensable foundational witness to God in Christ, and that subsequent witness depends on this as a source and is guided by it as a norm. It is sometimes not possible to be sure what the various authors intended and there is always scope for disagreement. The multiplicity of interpretations is restricted, not eliminated, by insistence on authorial intention, but the

---

29. It seems the Old Testament functions as a scriptural norm only as taken up or received in the New where it provides the foundational identification of God and much more. Old Testament theology has its own integrity and value in mediating those Scriptures as a *source* of Christian faith alongside others, but the Old Testament functions as a *norm* of Christianity only within the Christian frameworks supplied by New Testament theologies.

on-going conversations between competent exegetes who agree on using rational methods is a necessary element in a modern theology wanting to be in tune with Scripture.

This emphasis upon the importance of historical study in a theological interpretation of Scripture that aims to clarify the identity of Christianity does not alter the general agreement that (as the phrase indicates) New Testament theology consists in the interpretation of texts and therefore implies a literary rather than a historical frame of reference. As Bultmann explained, New Testament interpretation

> may be guided by either one of two interests, that of reconstruction or that of interpretation—that is, reconstruction of past history or interpretation of the New Testament writings. Neither exists, of course, without the other .... But the question is: which of the two stands in the service of the other? Either the writings of the New Testament can be interrogated as the "sources" which the historian interprets in order to reconstruct a picture of primitive Christianity as a phenomenon of the historical past, or the reconstruction stands in the service of the interpretation of the New Testament writings under the presupposition that they have something to say to the present.[30]

Bultmann's interpretations of Paul's authentic epistles and the Fourth Gospel together with 1 John indicate what he thought they have "to say to the present."[31] His New Testament theology took the second, literary option whereas Wrede's "history of early Christian religion and theology" had proposed the first. But like other New Testament theologians he continued to make suggestions about the real anonymous New Testament writers in coming to historically informed understandings of all their texts. Andrew Lincoln and others have demonstrated the fruitfulness of narrative criticism of the Gospels in New Testament theology, but the literary framework proposed here does not require much literary theory. It is "literary" only in the broad sense of being more concerned with the meaning of the texts than with using the texts to reconstruct their historical contexts and content, necessary though that auxiliary role is in understanding their original meanings. The modern apparatus of implied author and implied reader is arguably more helpful in interpreting texts where the historical context is unknown, such as most of the Old Testament.

---

30. Bultmann, *Theology of the New Testament*, vol. 2, 251.

31. Hahn, *Theologie des Neuen Testaments*, refers to the *Gegenwartsbezug* of New Testament theology.

Wrede's contemporaries set New Testament theology in a historical frame of reference, and the mainly historical character of New Testament scholarship led most of his successors in similar directions. That was in part the residual legacy of idealist metaphysics having permitted critically reconstructed history to speak of Spirit, i.e., God. Without that metaphysics (or the supernaturalist alternative of a special *Heilsgeschichte*[32]) history is theologically silent, as Baur and Bultmann knew, and positivistic historiography has confirmed. Wrede rightly declined to call his project New Testament theology. The then-prevailing understanding of much New Testament historical scholarship as itself New Testament theology stemmed from Baur's critical history, interpreted in metaphysical terms, carrying within it a theological interpretation of the whole history and making his critical historical interpretation of the sources theology in the strong sense.[33] This synthesis was rejected when the correction of Baur's historical construction undermined the theological interpretation based on Hegelian metaphysics. Church history could then no longer be presented by New Testament theology as simultaneously theology and secular history. Since attempts to present it as "sacred history" are open to other objections, the discipline has reverted to theological interpretation of the texts done within the constraints of historical scholarship. Barth provided the decisive impulse without himself interpreting the New Testament as a historical critic. Bultmann's theological interpretation of Paul and John, like Baur's of the whole development, included more philosophical resources than most. Other New Testament theologians have been content with more conventional historical research. Their belief that they are talking of what Paul and the other New Testament writers were talking about has been sustained by their accepting more of the doctrinal tradition than those two radicals.

Barth's insistence on authorial intention vindicates New Testament theology as historical scholarship and therefore as only *implicit* theological interpretation, even though his own theological interpretation of Scripture was explicit, as befits a church dogmatician. Confronted with Paul's text, he wrote:

> I embark on its interpretation on the provisional assumption that he is confronted with the same unmistakable and unmeasurable

---

32. None of the translations is satisfactory, but the nineteenth-century "holy history" has the merit of warning historical theologians off it.

33. Paul's epistles were given a (historically mistaken) theological interpretation that aligned them with Baur's own view of spirit. When critically and historically analyzed the rest of the New Testament became part of his account of Christianity by contributing to a theologically interpreted history of Christian thought.

significance of that relation (between such a God and such a man) as I myself am confronted with.[34]

New Testament theologians who think the same would not say so directly in their historical-critical scholarship. They can, however, allow their scholarship to serve a literary and theological interpretation of the texts. That needs help also from the doctrinal tradition and/or from philosophy if they are to hear and understand a religious text as talk of God. Both speech-act and reader-response theory offer possible support and points of contact with Luther's (and Paul's) kerygmatic theology.

This limited literary turn can be expected to assist both explicit and implicit theological interpretation because, whereas history distances its human object, literature can draw readers into something that transcends the ordinary, and an appropriate literary criticism (one that preserves original meanings) can help mediate that. This commitment to authorial and textual intention requires historical scholarship in looking for original meanings. The *sensus plenior* or new meanings created in the history of interpretation may have theological validity in enabling Scripture to be a source of faith and theology, but they do not enable it to function as a norm. New Testament theology, unlike other theological interpretations, claims to be based on authorial or textual intention and provides some checks against arbitrary expansions of meaning. The thousand flowers that bloom in the church's use of Scripture need some roots in the literal meanings. That need not quench the Spirit. The original meanings have no privileged place when the churches search their Scriptures for guidance in Christian living and thinking, but their indispensable contribution requires historical scholarship in theological education, as Schleiermacher insisted (n.13).

Most Christians want to know what these texts and their authors wished to communicate, because like Barth they think that "Paul knows of God what most of us do not know; and his epistles enable us to know what he knew."[35] Christopher Rowland thinks (surely rightly) that "how people have interpreted, and been influenced by a sacred text like the Bible is often as interesting and historically important as what it originally meant,"[36] and that "biblical texts do not simply have one set, closed meaning, but are full of possibilities."[37] But even he, and theologians like him, see reception history as an expansion rather than a replacement of traditional biblical scholarship, unlike those who oppose historical criticism, sometimes under

---

34. Barth, *Romans*, 10 (corrected).
35. Ibid., 11.
36. Series editors' preface to Kovacs and Rowland, *Revelation*, xi.
37. U. Luz, quoted by Kovacs and Rowland, *Revelation*, xiii.

the banner of "theological interpretation." Barth's insistence on authorial intention in his defense of his own explicit theological exegesis, suggests that this is dependent on, and perhaps should be subject to, a measure of control by historical exegesis. In much the same way, St. Thomas insisted on the priority of the literal sense in doctrinal argument.[38]

Theologians and non-theologians alike are generally more interested in what these respected texts and authors intended than in how other modern readers can find meanings in them which were not intended.[39] Ancient readers were perhaps more often mistaken about the original meanings than modern scholars, but even Origen was usually trying to understand what the human authors of the New Testament intended. His search for spiritual senses "worthy of God" was triggered by what he considered unworthy literal meanings, mostly in the Old Testament. The Reformers placed much greater emphasis on the literal sense (close to our "textual intention") on account of their increased dependence on Scripture (having repudiated the Catholic magisterium) in theological argument about the identity of Christianity. When eighteenth-century writers and their successors turned to the human authors of Scripture rather than to its supposed Divine Author, they found a rational basis for agreement about what Scripture meant and so how Christianity should be understood and practiced. The New Testament theology that followed included some Christian understanding of the Old because it is all about the God of Israel. It today still provides an arena for arguments about the identity of Christianity.

Baur's synthesis, like Bultmann's, was theology, but its dependence on his flawed historical *reconstruction* made it vulnerable to subsequent historical research. However, Bultmann saw in it a model for his own anthropologically oriented theological interpretation which would prove less obviously vulnerable to historical falsification and a change of philosophical climate.[40] This also has proved defective, but may yet help stimulate further creative New Testament theology (n.28). Both these classics of theological interpretation bordered on being explicit because they understood Godtalk wholly in terms of human existence *and vice versa*, but as historical scholarship their theology remained implicit.

The suggestion that New Testament theology has generally been "implicit theological interpretation" of these texts implies that what makes New Testament theology "theology" (in the strong sense of the word) goes on privately in the interpreter's head and heart, and/or in the head and heart

---

38. *Summa Theologica*, 1.1.9.

39. Cf. Barth, *Romans*, ix.

40. See his discussion of Baur in "Zur Geschichte der Paulus-Forschung," 30–33.

of someone reading a piece of New Testament scholarship. Interpreters can think a text that speaks of God is about the God whom they too worship, even as they describe it in public historical terms as "religion." That existential reference to "worship," considered broadly, is part of what the Christians and many other religious people mean by "God."[41] When they speak as historians, however, they will say only that these are *religious* texts that they are interpreting, or sources for a history of *religion*. Those two accounts of the subject or subject-matter of the same texts (God and religion) reflect the different perspectives or standpoints (or "points of view") of insiders (theologians) and outsiders (historians and social scientists) with respect to the religious tradition they are all studying and interpreting. As a historical critic *and* Christian theologian, the New Testament theologian is at home in both camps, and some now make clear their own religious standpoints or theological commitments without any relaxation of their historical-critical rigor.[42] They disclaim neutrality, total objectivity, or lack of interests, but their scholarly exegesis and historical interpretations require no direct mention of or appeal to God. In this sense they are implicitly theological, unlike those that go beyond the bounds of a historical presentation in order to make their theological interpretations explicit. Traces or indications of theological interest and commitment were discussed above (n.22).

The shift of emphasis from the biblical authors' to the theological interpreters' intentions is not great in New Testament theology since the two broadly coincide. Both the New Testament writers and their Christian theological interpreters want to articulate and communicate the Christian gospel and what it entails. The shift owes a little to the turn to the reader in literary theory, and to the interests of the historians in historiography, and more widely in the humanities and social sciences and beyond, but it is only making explicit what has always been happening in New Testament theology. Secular methods that do not speak of God are used to help understand these culturally distant texts, but many of those using them think they are thinking about God, whom they worship. That has been so obvious in religious institutions and contexts as not to merit discussion. When that general religious presupposition is no longer present it is necessary for believers to distinguish between New Testament scholarship generally (the overarching category), and New Testament *theology*, i.e., that scholarship done from a perspective internal to the tradition by interpreters with often unspoken assumptions about the transcendent subject-matter of the texts.

---

41. See D. Evans, *The Logic of Self-Involvement*; Macquarrie; *Godtalk*; Smart, *The Concept of Worship*; Bultmann *passim*.

42. E.g., Lincoln, *Truth on Trial*, 1–4.

This "turn to the reader" does not excuse New Testament theology from its scholarly "tasks and methods" describing and explaining the religious ideas of the texts. That historical spadework uncovers the context and the institutions behind the texts, studies the manuscript evidence, and extends to the language and all other relevant data. Most of the work done by New Testament theologians is thus done also by other biblical scholars. That suggested restricting the label to a subdivision of scholarship and the secondary meaning of "theology" as theological scholarship. But what made sense when the scholars were nearly all Christians who saw their work as serving the church is problematic when that is no longer the case. The phrase "New Testament theology" is then (now) better reserved for a scholarship that wants to engage in (Christian) theology in the primary sense of expressing something of a Christianity that is credible today and true to the biblical witness. That requires historical scholarship but also literary critical and philosophical resources, and sufficient hermeneutical skills to make this use of scholarship for religious purposes appear as natural as for believers it is.

The improper usage of the phrase conflated "theology" and theological scholarship. That usage survived for some time in English universities even when these had become less confessional than theological faculties in Germany and Switzerland, or even Scotland. What were in reality departments of Christian studies staffed largely by clergy were called "theology" even when constructive theology was no part of their curriculum. That was corrected where the study of Christianity became a (large) part of "religious studies." Elsewhere systematic theology was introduced, despite the tensions caused by the normally confessional character of that enterprise. As in New Testament studies, it is possible to study the Christian tradition and contemporary theologians descriptively and analytically, evaluating their arguments, but remaining silent about whether we think they are talking about God whom we too worship. Modern religious thought, like the first-century religious thought reflected in the New Testament, can be studied with sympathetic detachment by those who do not share their authors' convictions, as well as with existential commitment by those who agree with the biblical authors on essentials while acknowledging the cultural differences. German university faculties have preserved their right to the confessional or ecclesial word "theology." Many English theologians are content to teach theology indirectly or implicitly by teaching history and exegesis, or in some universities by putting their Christian theologizing under the appropriate pluralistic umbrella of "religious studies." The tension that historical theologians who share their texts' convictions may feel in teaching, without preaching at, those who do not, is resolved by the way their discipline makes space for both standpoints. This enables it to thrive in secular universities, including "cathedral universities."[43] Instead of trading on the ambiguity of the word "theology" or reducing their contribution to the churches' intellectual tasks to a merely auxiliary "theological scholarship" they can affirm the genuinely theological character of their work while doing it in academic contexts that allow others to see it as no more than a scholarly exercise. No university takes a view about what its employees believe in their hearts, so long as they do not confess it with their lips in ways that would require their students to do likewise. Those who want to follow their tutors into the college chapel or even into the Christian ministry will do so anyway.

The projected application of these reflections to Andrew Lincoln's *oeuvre* would require a further essay, but these prolegomena were written out of a long-held belief that he is the most accomplished English representative of a discipline we both learned in part from being students and friends of Charlie Moule, whose admiration for C. K. Barrett and friendship with many German New Testament theologians extended our horizons.

---

43. The phrase refers to a group of English universities that have (mostly Anglican) Christian foundations.

14

Who and What is Theological Interpretation For?

ANGUS PADDISON
University of Winchester

INTRODUCTION

IN RECENT YEARS "THEOLOGICAL interpretation" has consolidated itself as a key contributor to the series of conversations that make up contemporary theology.[1] As a movement it has spawned commentary and book series, dedicated journals, countless monographs, and edited volumes. Amidst this flurry of activity is the particular contribution made by the edited volume that Andrew and I produced whilst we worked together at the University of Gloucestershire, *Christology and Scripture: Interdisciplinary Perspectives*. The volume arose out of an intensive and memorable weekend spent in a diocesan retreat house in the company of systematic theologians, church historians, and biblical scholars. At the heart of our discussions, and subsequently the book, was the question, "What is the relationship between the biblical texts and the way that Christian doctrine and tradition has cap-

---

1. In writing this essay it is a pleasure to record my debt of gratitude to Andrew, as mentor and friend.

tured the significance of Jesus?" The diversity of the group of scholars the volume gathered together points to one of the key features of theological interpretation, namely its desire to break down the disciplinary boundaries academic theology has erected as part of fixing itself within the modern university, boundaries that inhibit a full exploration of the meaning potential of Scripture. Nearly ten years after the publication of this volume it is worth reflecting that the inter-disciplinarity we aimed to foster had its limits, or perhaps better, blind spots. There were two (related) groups of theologians that the symposium and volume did not embrace to the full, namely practical theologians and public theologians. It is worth asking how the book's contribution to theological interpretation might have been deepened had these disciplines and their concerns been incorporated more intentionally. Provoked by this reflection on Andrew's and my practice, I want, in this short essay, to ask two related questions.

1. How might we "pick out" theological interpretation as a distinctive movement within theology?
2. What difference might it make to the future directions of this movement if it more intentionally attends to the insights and impulses of both practical and public theology?

The essay is therefore an exercise in testing the methodological foundations and initiating principles of theological interpretation. There will, of course, be those who say it is more important to *do* theological interpretation ahead of clarifying *how* it is to be done. Does theological interpretation need to do any more throat clearing? It is certainly true that we should do all we can to encourage more theological interpretation being evidenced in practice. Yet, the justification for returning to methodological questions must be because "all major methodological decisions have implications for the whole of the theological edifice."[2] The pursuit of theological interpretation's ends—what we think it is *for*—depends on how it is practiced and with whom. Quite simply, questions surrounding how theological interpretation is carried out are of signal importance and need to be returned to periodically so that the doing of theological interpretation might be refreshed. When Stephen Fowl says that *"if there is to be a revival of theological interpretation of Scripture among scholars and students, theological concerns must be given priority over other concerns,"* it only begs the question of the nature, articulation, and ownership of these theological concerns.[3] Just what is it

---

2. Volf, "Theology, Meaning, and Power," 99.

3. Fowl, "Theological and Ideological Strategies of Biblical Interpretation," 169 (emphasis original).

that makes theological interpretation theological? Who gets to define what counts as "theological"?

Before exploring these questions however we first need to explore what has distinguished theological interpretation in recent years. How might we pick out theological interpretation?

WHAT IS THEOLOGICAL INTERPRETATION?

Theological interpretation is not a monolithic movement and it is characterized by a notable diversity of approaches. One can see this by observing the different ways in which different contributors to the Brazos Theological Commentary series have tackled their brief as articulated by the series editor, R. R. Reno, namely to demonstrate that "doctrine provides structure and cogency to scriptural interpretation."[4] Stanley Hauerwas' theopolitical reading of Matthew is very different in style and tone from Jaroslav Pelikan's historically focused treatment of Acts. Not all see such diversity of approaches as evidence of a movement in healthy and quite proper contest about how it is best practiced. Stanley Porter, in a gloomy assessment, characterizes theological interpretation as little more than "an under-defined and varying set of tendencies or interests, with some overlap between proponents."[5] D. A. Carson labels theological interpretation "a disorganized array of methodological commitments" and argues that the disparate nature of the movement is a significant weakness.[6] It is possible, I would argue, to capture theological interpretation a little more positively—as a series of related moves and debates centered around ensuring that theological thinking and biblical reading are mutually informing activities, rather than understood (implicitly or explicitly) to be estranged from one another. Theological interpretation is a project of recovery,[7] in that proponents re-articulate in and for our time the implications of integrating the reading of Scripture with a host of convictions about the living God and the life of discipleship. What is now a self-conscious agenda was of course, at one time, the dominant, if not the only, mode of reading Scripture available. If there was once no

---

4. Reno, "Series Preface," 14.

5. Porter, "What Exactly Is Theological Interpretation of Scripture?," 247.

6. Carson, "Theological Interpretation of Scripture," 187. The charge of Porter and Carson is very odd. To give just one example, studies of the historical Jesus take on a huge variety of forms and embody great differences, yet no-one sees this diversity as a weakness, or a sign that one could not pick out a historical Jesus scholar.

7. Only when it is misconceived is theological interpretation a project of repristination. All theological interpretation necessarily involves some kind of negotiation with our context now.

such thing as theological interpretation as a distinguishable activity this was purely because in pre-modernity there was assumed to be little distinction between thinking theologically, liturgical action, scriptural reading, and a life lived in response to the grace of God. The reading of Scripture, for a pre-modern reader like Maximus the Confessor, was bound up with an integrative vision of life and liturgy.[8] Theological interpretation is the attempt to render a little less problematic what modernity slowly unpicked—the relationship between theology, the church, Christian living, and the Bible.

If we do wish to retain a sense that theological interpretation is a distinguishable movement then leverage in pinning it down can be gained by attending to a helpful insight provided by Nicholas M. Healy. We can, Healy argues, distinguish between a theologian's (and by extension, a theological school's) "agenda" and "argument," the two being necessary to advance a theological "project."

A theological agenda "is constituted by a set of desired changes in the life and thought of Christians and the church." This agenda is necessarily advanced by the arguments the theologian draws upon, the rationale that persuades "others of the reasonableness and benefits of the desired changes." It follows, Healy points out, that theologians can agree on a common agenda, but differ in the arguments they judge to be appropriate in supporting the agenda. Equally, it may well be that theologians can agree on an agenda and articulate a series of broadly similar arguments.[9] Applying Healy's reflections to theological interpretation one can represent the movement as being united around an agenda to rejuvenate (in the academy and, by extension, those parts of the church conversant with academic theology) attention to Scripture as a revelatory text that has pulsated and continues to pulsate through the life of the church and its members.[10] United behind this agenda there is considerable diversity in the arguments constructed to advance the agenda. There are those whose arguments are tilted more towards theocentric approaches.[11] There are those who place more emphasis on Scripture in the life of the church as reading community than they do on God's action in relation to the text and its readers.[12] Some take on a highly rhetorical, almost caustic, tone in their assessment both of historical criticism and

8. Blowers, "Theology as Integrative, Visionary, Pastoral."

9. Healy, *Hauerwas*, 4–5.

10. If we were to follow this definition then Andrew Lincoln's recent work on the virgin birth would clearly fall within the category of theological interpretation. See Lincoln, *Born of a Virgin?*

11. John Webster is an exemplar of this type of argument. See Webster, *Domain of the Word*.

12. See Hauerwas, *Matthew*.

modes of reading developed outside the life of faith,[13] whilst others adopt a more emollient tone and attempt to enlist historical criticism with theological ends in mind.[14] In many contributions to advancing the agenda there is a pronounced attempt to bring together the dynamic connection between the biblical text and the church's doctrinal tradition.[15] What unites all these different and often overlapping arguments is a shared agenda, what John Webster characterizes as a common desire to:

> treat the Bible as Scripture, that is, as more than a set of clues to the history of antique religious culture, and so as a text which may legitimately direct theological reason because in some manner it affords access to God's self-communication.[16]

This essay presumes that there is a united project we can term "theological interpretation of Scripture," in that there is a school of approaches and arguments with a broadly shared agenda. As an active contributor to this agenda it will not be surprising to learn that it is an agenda I keenly support and wish to advance.[17] Precisely with this advancement in mind I am aware that it is necessary to push at some shortcomings of the way the agenda has been supported by dominant arguments. As hinted at above, we can characterize these dominant arguments as the "theocentric" approach and the "ecclesiocentric" approach. The shortcomings of each are closely related and invite a new set of challenges to be posed for theological interpretation. Both the shortcomings and challenges will be brought out by appealing to the insights of public and practical theology. However, before we get to that stage in the argument I need to outline some of the features of ecclesiocentric and theocentric approaches to theological interpretation.

Stanley Hauerwas can be taken as representative of an ecclesiocentric approach to theological interpretation. For Hauerwas, disciples enjoy an interpretative privilege when it comes to reading the Bible. Practices and reading are mutually informing and necessarily sustain one another. With his customary flair for the provocative statement Hauerwas claims that only those who are pacifists can interpret the Sermon on the Mount correctly.

---

13. Much of Robert W. Jenson's writings lead the reader to the conclusion that the biblical world is an all-encompassing description of reality, the implication being that interpretative approaches not starting from this shared premise are likely to mislead. See, for example, Jenson, "The Strange New World of the Bible."

14. Billings, *Word of God for the People of God*, 54–61.

15. Jenson, "Identity, Jesus, and Exegesis."

16. Webster, "Theologies of Retrieval," 591. Cited in Sarisky, *Scriptural Interpretation*, 135.

17. See Paddison, *Theological Hermeneutics*, and *Scripture*.

Divorced from the non-violent community that Matthew presupposes the text has no meaning.[18] For Hauerwas therefore, a theological reading prioritizes the church and its performance of the gospel, an ecclesial emphasis entirely in line with the rest of his theology.[19] The following gives an indicative sense of how Hauerwas reads Scripture (in this case Matthew) theologically:

> A theological reading of Matthew, therefore, reaffirms that the church be an alternative politics to the politics of the world. The reading I try to provide of Matthew's gospel is not for "anyone," although I hope many "anyones" will be attracted to Matthew through the reading offered. Rather, this commentary is guided by the presumption that the church is the politics that determines how Matthew is to be read.[20]

In this ecclesiocentric approach to theological interpretation church and Scripture are mutually dependent. The way to Scripture is through the life—and witness—of the church. Theological interpretation is dependent on and determined by ecclesial performance. Healy understands Hauerwas' approach to be the displacement of a *sola Scriptura* stance in favor of a "*sola ecclesia* hermeneutic."[21] What is also noticeable in Hauerwas' account of Scripture is the slender role given to God and God's prevenient action. The emphasis is firmly on the church as reading community. The following statement typifies this stance:

> The authority of Scripture is mediated through the lives of the saints identified by our community as most nearly representing what we are about. Put more strongly, to know what Scripture means, finally, we must look to those who have most nearly learned to exemplify its demands through their lives.[22]

Although not always with the same striking intensity, one can see traces of an ecclesiocentric focus at work elsewhere in theological interpretation. A more nuanced account (what we might term theological interpretation expressed in an ecclesial mood) than Hauerwas' can be found in Matthew Levering's pathology of modern exegesis. For Levering, the church's liturgical performance is a means of conveying the participatory sense of history Scripture invites and makes possible, the church's history participating in God's history. It is this participative sense of history that modernity has lost

---

18. Hauerwas, *Unleashing the Scripture*, 64.
19. See Healy, *Hauerwas*, 17–38.
20. Hauerwas, *Matthew*, 29–30.
21. Healy, *Hauerwas*, 60.
22. Hauerwas, *Peaceable Kingdom*, 70.

a grip on and, if it is to be recovered, church and Scripture are to be plotted along the same figural movement.[23] Contemporary figural readings of the biblical text have been offered by Ephraim Radner: history as the church is to know and witness to it is as narrated by Scripture.[24] In this appeal to enveloping the church in figural and typological reading it is possible to hear echoes of a key turn in postliberal theology, George Lindbeck's call for an intra-textual theology in which "the text, so to speak ... absorbs the world, rather than the world the text."[25] Indicatively, Fowl asserts that if theological interpretation is about granting theological concerns priority over other concerns then this will "involve a return to the practice of using Scripture as a way of ordering and comprehending the world, rather than using the world as a way of comprehending Scripture."[26] We will explore later how attention to the insights of practical theology render this slogan more complex and unstable, serving to remind us of the ways in which church, Scripture, and the church's context are mutually influencing. What unites the different arguments highlighted here is an ecclesial emphasis to the point of ecclesiocentric, a stance that often leads to the conclusion that Scripture is an all-embracing text embodied in the self-contained culture of the church.[27] Notions of the text absorbing the world are bound together with robust notions of the church as culture.

We need to say something about theological interpretation carried out in a "theocentric" vein. The work of John Webster is influential on a cluster of related arguments.[28] Although, of course, Webster emphasizes the role

23. Levering, *Participatory Biblical Exegesis*.
24. Radner, *Hope among the Fragments*.
25. Lindbeck, *Nature of Doctrine*, 118.
26. Fowl, "Theological and Ideological Strategies of Biblical Interpretation," 169.

27. This last sentence needs to be glossed in two ways. First, it is necessary to remind ourselves that theological interpretation is systematic in that it is webbed within a wider set of theological assumptions. It relies upon theological notions of God's work and the life of the church. One simply cannot understand Hauerwas' or Jenson's mode of theological interpretation unless one is alert to their ecclesiology. Precisely because this is so, it is necessary always to query some of the foundations of theological interpretation from time to time. To query Hauerwas' theological interpretation one needs to destabilize the ecclesial foundations on which it is based. Second, to defend myself against the charge of polemical characterization of the church/world distinction the following pronouncement from Jenson could be appealed to: "The church must always know and show forth that she is one thing and the world another, which includes that she is one thing and any civilization is another." See Jenson, "Christian Civilization," 158.

28. Webster's influence is considerable on theological interpretation. If one reads the earlier work of Stephen Fowl or Kevin Vanhoozer and then some of their later work, for example Fowl, *Theological Interpretation*, or Vanhoozer, *Drama of Doctrine*,

of the church, it does not lie at the center of his theological approach. The ordering evident in the following sentence is not incidental in this regard. "[W]e will remain unclear," Webster advances, "about Scripture as long as we are unclear about God, providence and church."[29] For Webster, decisions about the nature of Scripture, its role in the divine economy, and our role as readers are all issues that can be resourced by attending to *God's* action. Webster's account of Scripture can be typified as "God in relation to this text and its readers," in contrast to Hauerwas' "the church in relation to the biblical text." God's relationship to the text is active and direct, whilst the reader's and the church's action is responsive. God "initiates and directs," he calls and commissions the biblical authors, through the Spirit he illuminates the text, he elects to be communicatively present within a people—the church—and the resultant disposition of the scriptural reader is passive, for they should expect "a disappointment of interpretation, a *being formed*, receiving rather than bestowing meaning."[30] Church and Scripture are bound together, but not as co-constitutive partners—rather, the church *hears* and *receives* the text. God, for Webster's account of Scripture, is always "antecedently present and active."[31] A theological account of Scripture is orderly insofar as it attends first to God, disorderly at the point it is diverted first to talk of the church and its practices.

What do these theocentric and ecclesiocentric approaches to theological interpretation share? Both prefer to work with accounts of Scripture abstracted from the life of the tangible, concrete church. Both have a tendency to work with "ideal" types of readers. Both presume that the church needs to take a clear (counter-)cultural stance. For Webster, one can choose poetics *or* obedient reception of the Word.[32] (It seems fair to assume that he has in his sights the fractious debates within the Anglican Communion on homosexuality.) For Hauerwas, the first priority for the church as a reading community is to recover "what it means for the church to be an alternative politics in the world in which we find ourselves."[33] Both stances are not immediately amenable to the articulation of public theology offered by Duncan Forrester, as that "theology which seeks the welfare of the city before

---

Webster's fingerprints on their thinking is evident. Webster's influence on emerging scholars like Sarisky (see *Scriptural Interpretation*) is also plain.

29. Webster, *Domain of the Word*, 3.

30. Ibid., 10, 24 (emphasis original).

31. Ibid., 26.

32. Ibid., 130–32.

33. Hauerwas, *Approaching the End*, 92. Hauerwas is not speaking directly of theological interpretation here, but the wording is portable.

protecting the interests of the Church."³⁴ Exploring some of the dissonances between the impulses of recent theological interpretation and public theology marks the next step of the essay, in which we will both critique and challenge these two dominant moods in theological interpretation.

THEOLOGICAL INTERPRETATION, PRACTICAL THEOLOGY, AND PUBLIC THEOLOGY

We now need to turn intentionally to the second question we set ourselves at the outset:

> What difference might it make to the future directions of this movement if it more intentionally attends to the insights and impulses of both practical and public theology?

In this part of the essay we will be considering practical and public theology as closely related enterprises. Practical theology is the enterprise that reflects theologically on how the Word is received and embodied contextually, in the lives of congregations and individual Christians. Its focus is on "Christian life and practice within the Church *and* in relation to wider society."³⁵ As theology it is "dedicated to enabling the faithful performance of the gospel and to exploring and taking seriously the complex dynamics of the human encounter with God."³⁶ Part of this complex dynamic is each individual Christian's and every congregation's involvement in the world, a world that is the proper object of Christian concern. Practical theology, as public theology, looks to "the world as the place of the coming reign of God."³⁷ If theological interpretation is, according to Fowl's quote we highlighted earlier, in the business of prioritizing theological concerns ahead of other concerns, then what might be the result of prioritizing practical and public theological concerns? How might the impulses of public and practical theology reshape theological interpretation? Here are three thesis statements in response.

> *Thesis one:* Theological interpretation needs to be less about ensuring the text absorbs the world and more about encouraging intensive forms of living, both with the text and in the world.

---

34. Forrester, "Scope of Public Theology," 6.
35. Ballard and Pritchard, *Practical Theology in Action*, 1 (emphasis added).
36. Swinton and Mowat, *Practical Theology*, 4.
37. Volf, "Theology, Meaning, and Power," 112.

An orientation of theological interpretation towards the impulses of practical theology is likely to make how we imagine the relationship between the text and the world more nuanced. Lindbeck evoked a competitive imaginary when he spoke of the need to ensure the biblical text "absorb[ed]" the world, "rather than the world the text."[38] This is an imaginary that has captured the attention of theological interpreters like Stephen Fowl and Robert W. Jenson, the latter being especially aware that an omnivorous text relies upon a robust notion of the church as a distinct culture. There is a sharp dissonance here with the impulses of practical and public theology for whom the relationship between the biblical text and the world in which readers are located is bound always to be framed as a negotiation and overlap of different authorities—the authority of the text, of reason, and above all of experience. Seeing the text and the world in relationship with one another is a constantly shifting, dynamic process of inhabitation, both of the text and of the world. In this sense it is more helpful to articulate the relationship between the biblical texts, culture, and context not as one of the text absorbing the world, but as reciprocal and fluid. Miroslav Volf points to the limitations of Lindbeck-inspired models, which imagine a text absorbing the world, models that he sees as distortive of how the church inhabits and shapes its cultural context:

> We can look at our culture through the lenses of religious texts only *as we look at these texts through the lenses of our culture.* The notion of inhabiting the biblical story is hermeneutically naïve because it presupposes that those who are faced with the biblical story can be completely "dis-lodged" from their extra-textual dwelling places and "re-settled" into intratextual homes. Neither dis-lodging nor resettling can ever quite succeed; we continue to inhabit our cultures even after the encounter with the biblical story[;] . . . *there is no pure space on which to stand even for the community of faith.*[39]

There is a need, in other words, to resist talk of biblical imagination being associated only with the proposal that the text is to *absorb* our world. Theological resources are needed to destabilize this competitive zero-sum game, in which it is imagined that the text absorbs the world, or finds itself absorbed by the world.

Practical theology has little time for what Heather Walton calls "canonical narrative theologies," where the presumption is that we must insert our story within the larger biblical story. Walton terms theological reflection a

---

38. Lindbeck, *Nature of Doctrine*, 118.
39. Volf, "Theology, Meaning, and Power," 103 (emphasis original).

form of weaving, "in which elements of experience and aspects of Scripture and tradition are woven together into innovative forms."[40] This represents a way of preserving the integrity and significance of our stories, and the stories of the world, alongside the scriptural narratives. We cannot presume that there will not be times when it is necessary for the church to interrupt and disrupt the stories of the world (one thinks of Apartheid South Africa or 1930s Germany) but it is not helpful for theological interpretation to presume that the biblical text exists automatically in a competitive relationship to the world. An imaginary alternative to that of a text absorbing the world will seek to understand theological interpretation as open and attentive to the contexts around us. Theological interpretation responsive to the world, and to our contexts, is not any the less theological. Indeed, it is *more* theological than the imaginary of a text absorbing the world. "Belonging completely to Christ, one stands at the same time completely in the world."[41] Theological interpretation formed by *this* imagination will want to say that living with the biblical text requires intensive engagement with the world. Being ready to think theologically about the resonances between the biblical text and the world is an alternative way to capture what counts as a "biblical imagination."[42]

> *Thesis Two: Theological interpretation needs to be alert to the risks of ecclesiocentric approaches.*

As we saw, theological interpretation has placed heavy emphasis on the distinctiveness of the church as reading community. Yet, in the light of the first thesis above, there is a need to be alert to two risks that this ecclesiocentric emphasis bears. First, there is a risk that theological interpretation will be inhibited from listening to insights that can properly correct the church. It is hard to see how theological interpretation could hope to make a public contribution without a healthy alertness to issues raised by ideological readings,[43] or to issues raised by those who have been publicly wounded by the text and now position themselves outside the church. Theological interpretation needs to guard that it does not deafen itself to such voices. Quite simply, the church is a necessary but not a sufficient resource. Again, we must resist a competitive imaginary between attention to the church and to

---

40. Walton, *Writing Methods*, 95.

41. Bonhoeffer, *Ethics*, 62.

42. If one had to highlight an exemplar of paying attention to the text and to the world as a text one could very well point to the work of Ellen Davis. See Davis, "Surprised by Wisdom: Preaching Proverbs." For the imagery of "resonances" see Bennett and Rowland, "'Action is the Life of All.'"

43. Moberly, "What Is Theological Interpretation of Scripture?" 168.

the world here. Craig Hovey writes, "[t]he church's learning so to recognize Christ in and as the church *entirely depends* on its success in discovering him outside the church."[44] So too, theological interpretation needs to equip itself for the task of discovering the Bible outside the church. A worldly attentiveness will help ensure that the church has the capacity to read the text against itself, a theological imperative rooted in the Gospels. The second risk that ecclesiocentric arguments bear is that such emphases make it hard to prioritize regard for the world ahead of the church's self-interest. It is not of course true that those who have promoted ecclesiocentric accounts of theological interpretation have no regard for the world.[45] It would be more accurate to say that a robust emphasis on the church can obscure the emphasis that is proper (as we saw above) to place on the world. The more piercing the attention on the church the greater the risk that theological attention to the world is eclipsed. There has been too much focus on the Bible in the church, too little focus on the biblical reader's prosaic yet intensive engagement with the world.

> *Thesis Three: Practical theology would shift attention from "the church" in the abstract to the actual church.*

"The church reads Scripture and tries to speak what it hears and orders its life accordingly."[46] This normative claim betrays the tendency of both theocentric and the ecclesiocentric approaches to talk of "the church" in abstraction from theological reflection on the actual church that variously wrestles and engages with the biblical text. If it is a truism that biblical readers always learn "discipleship in specific contexts and relations" then talk of the Bible and its reading that persistently avoids engaging with the vulnerability of this particularity is bound to be theologically deficient in some form.[47] There is an emerging literature in practical theology on the question of how "ordinary" readers—that is, those who are not in positions of leadership and/or have not had formal theological training—engage with the text.[48] How the church in its diversity wrestles and engages with the text urgently needs theological attention. The word "attention" is not used lazily.[49] To attend to the reader in front of me, perhaps the reader with whom I

---

44. Hovey, *Unexpected Jesus*, 46 (emphasis original).

45. Hauerwas, *Matthew*, 87, "[t]he difference between church and world is not that of realms or levels, but of response."

46. Webster, "'In the Society of God,'" 219.

47. R. Williams, "Making Moral Decisions," 8.

48. See Village, "The Bible and Ordinary Readers."

49. The influence of R. Williams, "Making Moral Decisions," is recognized in the reflections that follow.

share communion, is to take the reader seriously in their non-negotiable concreteness. Sometimes one's fellow reader will be a source of refreshment, as they open new vistas onto a biblical text that are far from ordinary. At other times one's fellow reader will be a source of exasperation and despair. Attention to the ordinary reader consistently offers theological interpretation an inbuilt resistance to talk glibly of "the church."

To pay attention to how individuals within churches read Scripture is constutuent to realizing that how the church learns to be a people formed in relation to *this* text in *this* place and in *this* time is part of the irreducible particularity of the Christian revelation. John Webster's warning to avoid the presumption "that context is fate" is helpful to the extent that it reminds us that descriptions of how the church engages with Scripture are not by themselves sufficient theologically.[50] Key here is that ethnography or empirical description should not by itself count as the completion of the theological task. Such descriptions need rather to be incorporated into the theological task.[51] Yet the warning that context isn't fate is unhelpful to the extent that its rhetoric suggests a nervousness about the historical, vulnerable conditions in which the gospel is always received *precisely as gospel*. In practice, if one delves into Webster's theological account of Scripture and its readers one will find scant reflection on how actual *churches* receive and read Scripture. This reveals a shortcoming in theological interpretation more broadly. Theological interpretation, as it has been dominantly carried out, employs the language of the church, yet ironically it is in effect a conversation largely carried out only with other theological interpreters primarily located in the academy. This carries the risk that theological interpretation will impact the academy ahead of the church.[52] Theological interpretation can be reminded by practical theology that it is first a practice, embodied in complex ways by a hugely diverse array of people bound together in the same body. Theological interpretation needs to work out, as a matter of priority, how the Bible's countless ordinary readers are already advocates of its agenda.

CONCLUSION

In this essay we have attempted to argue that far from being a disparate movement theological interpretation has a distinct agenda, and the arguments used to advance it have tended to cluster around theocentric and ecclesiocentric approaches. Neither of these dominant approaches have

---

50. Webster, "The Human Person," 220.
51. See Healy, *Hauerwas*, 98–99, for a related discussion.
52. See Miller-McLemore, "Five Misunderstandings about Practical Theology," 14

prioritized impulses that are central to public and practical theology. In the latter half of the essay I have turned to practical and public theology as a source of correction and challenge to theological interpretation. Theological interpretation is correct in its instinct that hearing the Word as "living and active" (Heb 4:12), and connecting this Word to our world, is a spiritually demanding task. There can be no short circuiting this difficulty, for example by merely repeating what theology has said in the past. Incorporating the impulses of practical and public theology within theological interpretation will highlight the concreteness of the way the Word is living and active in the lives of biblical readers, and the worlds of which they are part. Above all, public and practical theology offers to an academy at risk of talking only to itself the opportunity to fix as a permanent part of our landscape the question, "Who and what is theological interpretation for?"

15

The Use of the Old Testament in the Work and Preaching of F. W. Robertson of Brighton

JOHN W. ROGERSON
University of Sheffield[1]

Frederick William Robertson—F. W. Robertson of Brighton—died on 15 August 1853 at the age of thirty-seven. He did not live to witness, or take part in, the controversies that were provoked by the publication of *Essays and Reviews* in 1860 and the first volume of J. W. Colenso's *The Pentateuch and Joshua* in the following year. Two "broad" churchmen, F. D. Maurice and Charles Kingsley, whose names are often linked with that of Robertson, were distressed by these publications. Kingsley responded by publishing, in 1863, a small volume entitled *The Gospel of the Pentateuch*, in the preface to which he allowed that "every Cambridge man" (Colenso was one such) had the right to exercise "a reverent and rational liberty in criticism (within the limits of orthodoxy)."[2] However, Colenso's book (Kingsley did not name it specifically) was "like most other modern books on Biblical criticism ... altogether negative ... possessed so often by that fanati-

---

1. It is a great pleasure to contribute to this volume in honor of Andrew Lincoln, a valued colleague in the Sheffield Department of Biblical Studies, during its golden era.

2. Kingsley, *Gospel of the Pentateuch*, 1863, vi.

cism of disbelief, which is just as dangerous as the fanaticism of belief," and possessed of a spirit "utterly different from the spirit which the Scripture asserts that it possesses."[3]

What would Robertson's reaction have been? His biographer, Stopford Brooke, wrote as follows about the lectures on Genesis that Robertson delivered between February 1850 and May 1851:

> The lectures, when published, will show with what mingled wisdom and freedom he met the difficulties of the earlier chapters; how fairly he stated the claims of scientific and historical truth, even when they were in conflict with the narrative of the sacred text; and while declaring that the Mosaic cosmogony could not be reconciled with geological facts, still succeeded in showing its inner harmony, in principle, with the principles of scientific geology. Neither did he shrink from putting his congregation in possession of the results of German criticism upon Genesis. He made them acquainted with the discussion on the Jehovah and Elohim documents, but he did not deny the Mosaic composition of these documents. He discussed fully the question of the universality of the Flood.[4]

This summary will be checked later in this essay against the published version of the lectures.[5] For the moment, something will be said about Robertson's knowledge of the German language, German philosophy, and biblical criticism. Brooke does not tell us when Robertson began to study German, and only hints can be picked up from the biography. In the summer of 1841, Robertson travelled on foot through the Rhine region to Geneva and became acquainted with German neologism, a kind of rationalism tolerably within the bounds of orthodoxy.[6] Five years later he spent some time in Heidelberg, where he plunged deeply into German metaphysics and theology.[7] On 24 October 1846 he wrote about what he was attempting in spite of his "rudimentary acquaintance with the language."[8] Soon after his arrival in Brighton, on 18 August 1847, he stated some of his priorities including "I will not now give up German."[9] His progress was such that

3. Kingsley, *Gospel of the Pentateuch*, viii.
4. Brooke, *Life and Letters*, 126.
5. Brooke's biography first appeared first in 1872; the lectures were published in 1877.
6. Brooke, *Life and Letters*, 37.
7. Ibid., 56.
8. Ibid., 59.
9. Ibid., 77.

he completed an English translation of G. E. Lessing's *The Education of the Human Race*, which was published in 1870; and early in 1850 he mentioned, in connection with his work on Genesis, that he was reading "two of the best Germans, who in all matters of research are immeasurably before the English."[10]

One would dearly love to know the names of these Germans, and whether or not Robertson read them in German. The likelihood is that he did read them in German, because no recent German commentary on Genesis had been translated into English by 1850. This year was also too early for Robertson to have had access to the commentary by Franz Delitzsch, which appeared first in 1852.[11] Possible candidates for what Robertson consulted were the commentaries by Friedrich Tuch (1838) and Michael Baumgarten (1844–45), although he may not have necessarily been referring to *commentaries* on Genesis. He might have consulted works by E. W. Hengstenberg.[12]

The fact that Robertson translated Lessing's *The Education of the Human Race* cannot be without significance, for there is much in this work of 100 paragraphs that touches upon the Old Testament, as well as upon the relationship between reason and revelation. It is not difficult to admire what Robertson achieved in his translation.[13] Lessing's piece was written in 1776 and published anonymously in its full version in 1780.[14] It likens the education of the human race to that of a child growing into adulthood, and regards the Old Testament as the Primer designed for the stage of childhood. However, this does not make it redundant or obsolete. Fundamental to his argument is Lessing's account of the relationship between revelation and reason. These are complementary: what is disclosed by revelation can be adduced by reason, but revelation, which is vouchsafed to only exceptional individuals, enabled a people (ancient Israel) to proceed along the path of reason more quickly than would otherwise have been the case. Nisbett sums up this relationship neatly as follows: "revelation is the historical vehicle of reason, and reason is the necessary content of revelation."[15] One of the implications of this, according to Nisbett, is that the "ugly ditch" between the

---

10. Brooke, *Life and Letters*, 172.

11. Delitzsch, *Die Genesis Ausgelegt*.

12. On Tuch, Baumgarten, and Hengstenberg see J. W. Rogerson, *Old Testament Criticism*, 133, n.17; 117, n.48; and 85–90.

13. F. W. Robertson, *Education of the Human Race*. Reference is here made to the 1882 reprint in F. W. Robertson, *Lectures*, 283–312.

14. See Nisbett, *Lessing. Eine Biographie*, 746–47.

15. Nisbett, *Lessing*, 750: "Die Offenbarung ist das historische Vehikel der Vernunft, und die Vernunft ist der notwendige Inhalt der Offenbarung."

necessary truths of reason and the contingent truths revealed in the course of history is rendered unnecessary.[16]

Part of the way in which the Primer, the Old Testament, worked was by clothing abstract truths "in allegories and instructive single circumstances, which were narrated as actual occurrences."[17] Important examples are given.

> Of this character are the creation under the image of the growing day; the origin of Evil in the story of the Forbidden Tree; the source of the variety of languages in the history of the Tower of Babel.[18]

The reference to creation under the image of the growing day is evidently an allusion to J. G. Herder's *Aelteste Urkunde des Menschengeschlechts*, in which Herder had argued that the six days of creation in Genesis were successive days on which God revealed his creative work to primal man on the analogy of the light dawning at the beginning of day.[19]

Lessing's *Education* provided Robertson with a way of reading the Old Testament which could take account of its symbolic elements without this leading to a denial of its value as revelation. It also enabled him to allow the validity of the scientific discoveries of his day, and to see in them no threat to Christian belief or the interpretation of the Bible. How this affected his understanding of the book of Genesis can be indicated.

Robertson gave four lectures on Gen 1–3 from 17 February to 31 March, 1850, and the theme of progress was never far from the argument. The creation was not something enacted once and for all at the beginning; it was a work in progress and affected the moral and spiritual development of the human race in particular.

> It is a marvellous thing to look at human life, to mark the number of years spent in a mere animal existence, and then to see that mind appears just for a few years in later life. But slow as the progress is, it is progress.[20]

One of the implications of revelation as an educative process was that God, the educator, was personal, and that his laws were the basis for ordered human life.

---

16. Nisbett, *Lessing*, 756

17. Lessing, *Education*, para 48, Robertson's translation. For the German see Güpfest, ed., *Gotthold Ephraim Lessing Werke*, vol. 8, 500, in "Allegorien und lehrreichen einzelnen Fällen, die als wirklich geschehen erzählet werden."

18. Lessing, *Education*, para 48.

19. See Suphan, ed., *Herder Sämmtliche Werke* VI, 193–511.

20. F. W. Robertson, *Notes on Genesis*, 5.

Robertson did not shrink from confronting the results of biblical criticism and scientific discoveries. He allowed that there were two accounts of creation: the first, in Gen 1:1—2:3, used the divine name Elohim and the second, from chapter 2:4 used the name Jehovah (YHWH). They were different in character, yet included together by Moses to supplement each other. In the first account, God was creator; in the second he was the moral governor of the universe. With regard to science, Robertson noted that the discoveries of geology (he no doubt had in mind the writings of Charles Lyell) did not cohere with the account of Moses. The issue was that, according to the biblical chronology worked out by James Ussher, the world was created in 4004 B.C., whereas Lyell's discoveries implied that it must be at least 30,000 years old. Robertson sharply criticized those who either simply rejected the findings of science, or who tried to reconcile science and the Bible in either of two ways. The first was to interpret the days of Genesis as long periods of time; the other was to allow a time gap between the first two verses of Gen 1 and to say that the geological discoveries pertained to that time gap before a renewed creation was executed in six days as described in the Bible. Robertson would have none of this. There were two revelations. One was written on the page of creation and was understood by means of scientific investigation. The other was written on the page of Scripture, and it needed to be understood in accordance with the knowledge available at the time of its composition. It used the language of the day.[21] However, this factor did not invalidate its teaching about God as the creator, "who does all by degrees."

Another point at issue was whether the human race had developed from a single pair of human beings or from a number of different pairs. Discoveries of voyages to many parts of the world had disclosed the existence of many different types of human being, differentiated by color of skin and cultural conditions. The denial of the unity of the human race based upon these discoveries was no doubt convenient to those who carried on the slave trade. For Robertson, the essential spiritual unity of the human race under God was a fundamental part of his Christian faith. He noted a tendency for science now "to pronounce that the human race must have had a single origin."[22] Yet, and typically, Robertson did not dogmatically insist that the human race must be descended from a single pair if science were to prove that several pairs, not one, were originally created.[23]

21. Ibid., 7.
22. Ibid., 21.
23. Ibid., 20.

The fourth lecture was on the subject of the Fall in Gen 3 and has to be regarded as a sublime exposition of the nature of sin and its consequences. Especially admirable was the way in which Robertson avoided the issue of the historicity of the narrative in Gen 3. True, he spoke of Adam and Eve, but gave no clue as to whether he regarded them as historical persons, or as characters in a narrative. One thinks here of Lessing's observations of biblical narratives as clothing abstract truths in allegory or in instructive single circumstances narrated as actual occurrences.

Robertson drew the following lessons from the narrative of Gen 3. First, sinfulness was distinguished from criminality and understood as a want of a harmony of mind; not necessarily a state in which man was committing actual offences, but one in which the heart was no longer in harmony with the universe. It was an extinction of original nobility. The moral result of sinfulness was that it corrupted human relationships with things that were otherwise good in themselves:

> The worst misery a man can bring upon himself by sin is that those things which to pure minds bring nothing but enjoyment are turned for him into fuel for evil lusts and passions, and light the flames of hell within his soul.[24]

Secondly, a consequence of sinfulness was separation from God. Robertson did not elaborate this point, but it is reasonable to assume that he meant by this not a rejection by God of humanity, but an inability on the part of humanity to approach God. Third, sin led to selfishness. "The culprits [Adam and Eve] are occupied entirely with their own hearts; each denies the guilt which belonged to each; each throws the blame upon the other."[25]

In describing the penal consequences of sin, Robertson made two remarkable assertions. These stemmed from his essentially psychological view of sinfulness, and enabled him to bypass two problems raised by taking the narrative historically. First, he rejected the idea that there had been a time when what he called the law of labor did not exist and that the Fall had brought about its imposition. Thorns and weeds had always existed. What changed was that Adam's attitude to his work became one of drudgery and toil. Secondly, the Fall did not introduce death to the human race, only the fear of it. Death before the advent of sin "would have been simply a transition to a higher stage of being." Sin changed this. "Take away sin and you take away with it death's terrors; death becomes then as gentle as a sleep."[26]

---

24. Ibid., 25.
25. Ibid., 27.
26. Ibid., 29.

The last part of the lecture discussed the sentence passed upon the woman and is remarkable for its originality. Robertson was disturbed by what he evidently regarded as an injustice, that the tempted woman should suffer a harsher penalty than the tempting serpent. The woman would suffer the pain of childbirth; the serpent would merely move over the ground, without pain. Robertson used the contrast to describe the two types of person with regard to temptation, those frail (i.e., the woman), and those apparently strong (the tempter), and he expressed his revulsion at the kind of society in which the frail were especially singled out for punishment.

> When we turn to the life of Christ we find the voice of the Redeemer against it. He stands by the side of the weak and not of the strong. He shows no sympathy with those who have tempted frailty; he says, "Better that a millstone should be hanged about his neck, and that he should be cast into the sea, than that he should offend one of these little ones."[27]

Robertson distinguished between the voice of the Redeemer representing the voice of God, on the side of frailty, and the voice of nature also the voice of God, against the frail. The contradiction was to be resolved by seeing in the punishment of Eve "the remedial chastisement of love." Further, the suffering that love imposed had itself a redemptive element. "The penalty of suffering for others, which is the very triumph of the cross, know we not its blessing?"[28] With regard to the strong who tempted the frail and appeared to suffer no consequences, Robertson wrote that they suffered degradation in what they had done, made worse by the inability to know that they had degraded themselves.

In the light of Robertson's remarks on the temptation of the woman, in which anticipations can be found of an option for the poor and oppressed, as well as for a kind of feminism, one wonders what Robertson would have made of the most important part of Darwin's theory of evolution, that it was caused by the survival of the fittest and strongest. Would he have seen in this the voice of nature to be contrasted with the voice of the Redeemer, a voice that stood on the side of those less adapted to survive and whose sufferings were part of a redemptive process?

Robertson lectured on Gen 3 on 31 March 1850. His next lecture, on 2 June did not, as we might expect, deal with Gen 4–11, but with Gen 12. He did not, apparently, address the matter of the flood, and in this regard the statement of his biographer that Robertson discussed whether or not the

---

27. Ibid., 30.
28. Ibid., 31.

flood was universal is incorrect as far as the published lectures on Genesis go.

The remainder of the notes on the lectures vary considerably in length. Sometimes they are only three pages long, at other times they run from eleven to twelve pages. Evidently the short chapters are basic notes which Robertson expanded in an extempore fashion. Of interest from the point of view of critical scholarship are the discussions of Sodom and Gomorrah and the "sacrifice" of Isaac.

Lecture VII, on Sodom and Gomorrah, squarely faced up to the question of the miraculous. Robertson noted that there were some for whom the whole question of the truth of Scripture depended upon being able to prove that a miraculous destruction of Sodom and Gomorrah had taken place.[29] Others sought to get rid of God altogether by supposing that a natural occurrence such as a volcanic eruption have destroyed the cities. Robertson denied that there was a contradiction.

> We agree with the supernaturalist in saying that God did it; we agree with the rationalist in saying that it was done by natural means. The natural is the work of God.[30]

This might be seen as a sleight of hand, to have one's cake and eat it too; but Robertson meant to turn it to more radical thoughts, for his day. Noting that the destruction of Sodom and Gomorrah functions in the Bible as a symbol for the destruction of wickedness, he stressed that this symbol needed to be understood correctly in relation to the mention in the book of Revelation of eternal punishment, in the form of the lake which burned with fire and brimstone. This could not be taken literally.

> Our education has gradually got rid of belief in the literalness of these words. Everyone knows that they are symbolical, but with this it has unfortunately gotten rid of the deeper truth which lies beneath these images. There is no lake which burneth with fire and brimstone; but there *is* the hell of doing wrong, the infamous maddening of remorse. When we remember what we *might* have been, and what we never can become, then we crave for a drop of water to cool our tongue, and there is no water to be found. *That* is the world of fire, *that* is the lake which burneth for ever.[31]

---

29. Ibid., 44.
30. Ibid.
31. Ibid., 45.

This was said three years before F. D. Maurice was dismissed from his chair at King's College, London, for suggesting that the fires of hell were eternal and not everlasting![32]

Lecture IX, on Gen 22, tackled a subject that had caused many headaches to interpreters. Did God command Abraham to do something wrong, namely, to sacrifice his son? Did the fact that God had commanded it make it right? How could someone sincerely believe that a command to kill another human being could come from God? Robertson tackled these matters skillfully. One had to read the whole narrative, from which it was clear that God never intended Abraham to sacrifice his son. The initial command to do so was countermanded by the words in Gen 22:12 "lay not thy hand upon the lad." Secondly, because Abraham lived at a time and in a society in which child sacrifice was not uncommon, the command did not seem to him to be wrong. Abraham's moral conscience was not outraged by the command.

Having thus disposed of the two greatest difficulties in the narrative, Robertson was able to draw out a number of moral and spiritual lessons from the narrative. One important theme was that Christian sacrifice was the surrender of the will, something exemplified in the atoning death of Christ. Another was that for there to be a true sacrifice there must be love. God says "thy son whom thou lovest." Thirdly, there was no need to search for sacrifices.

> We often say, what shall I do for God? Be not anxious; you need make no wild, romantic efforts to find occasions. Plenty will occur by God's appointment. . . . This is what Abraham meant when he said, "my son, God will provide himself a lamb for a burnt offering."

Robertson preached mostly on the New Testament, according to the statistics of his published sermons; but twelve Old Testament sermons are helpfully gathered together in the Everyman edition of his sermons.[33] They are mostly centered upon particular Old Testament characters such as Jacob, Isaac, Joseph, Moses, Balaam, Eli, and Solomon. The most striking is the sermon on Jacob's wrestling at the river Jabbok, prior to his reconciliation with Esau, in Gen 32:22–32. This was given on Sunday 10 June 1849, and

---

32. In his *Theological Essays* of 1853, Maurice had argued that *aiōnios* does not mean everlasting and indeed has no temporal overtones. It refers to God himself and only by extension to creation. This stance was perceived to threaten the doctrine of everlasting punishment and cost Maurice his job.

33. Robertson, *Sermons on Bible Subjects*, 9–124.

is described as a confirmation lecture in the first series of his published sermons.[34] From the content, it appears to have been delivered in the afternoon to a group that had received Holy Communion for the first time that morning.

The incident of Jacob's wrestling had long presented commentators with a number of difficulties.[35] These included the question why Jacob's assailant had to depart before the dawn. Robertson did not try to justify such details. "Much of the story is evidently mythical," he declared at the beginning, and he continued, "It is clear at once, that it belongs to that earlier period of literature when traditions were preserved in a poetical shape, adapted to the rude conceptions of the day."[36] Robertson also rationalized the narrative in a psychological manner.

> To the uneducated mind that which is real, [i.e., in doubts and uncertainties] seems to be necessarily material too. What wonder if to the unscientific mind of Jacob, this conflict, [i.e., the anguish of meeting Esau again] so real and attended in his person with such tangible results, seemed all human and material—a conflict with a terrible antagonist? What wonder if tradition preserved it in such a form?[37]

Having said this, he drew profound lessons from the narrative for his hearers. They, unlike Jacob, were at the beginning of their religious journey, but they, like him, would have to learn that there is an awesome side of God, an awesome side that would play its part in deepening faith—in moving a believer from praying "save my soul" to "tell me thy name." This was the "struggle of all for earnest life."[38] Robertson mused upon the significance of names and issued this challenge to the hearers:

> [W]hat is the name of your God? What do you adore in your heart of hearts? What is the name oftenist (sic) on your lips in your unfettered, spontaneous moments?[39]

The evening into which his hearers were departing would, as night fell, reveal the awesome infinity of God's creation. Robertson prayed that the morning should not come without God leaving upon his hearers, "the blessing of

---

34. F. W. Robertson, *Sermons Preached at Brighton*, x.
35. See Rogerson, "Wrestling with the Angel."
36. Robertson, *Sermons on Bible Subjects*, 9; *Sermons Preached at Brighton*, 37.
37. Robertson, *Sermons on Bible Subjects*, 11; *Sermons Preached at Brighton*, 38.
38. Robertson, *Sermons on Bible Subjects*, 17; *Sermons Preached at Brighton*, 46.
39. Robertson, *Sermons on Bible Subjects*, 22; *Sermons Preached at Brighton*, 51–2.

a strength which shall be yours through the garish day, and through dry, scorching life, even to the close of your days."[40]

Robertson's ability to draw such profound thoughts from Old Testament narratives, and in this case one he describes as containing mythical elements, gave the lie to Kingsley's verdict that modern books on biblical criticism were altogether negative. No doubt some were, if readers were looking only for spiritual edification. Robertson showed that a knowledge of biblical criticism did not produce altogether negative results. But Robertson was also years ahead of his time in his ready acceptance of criticism. As late as 1882 Thomas Whitelaw in the *Pulpit Commentary* was still taking the six days of creation to be indefinitely long epochs so as to make the Genesis creation narrative agree with the findings of geology. At the same time, Whitelaw was reluctant to prefer the conclusions of geology as to the age of the earth to the date implied in the biblical narrative.[41]

If one compares Robertson's sermon on Jacob's wrestling with the treatment of the episode in S. R. Driver's commentary on Genesis of 1904 it again becomes clear how advanced his thinking was. Driver, who devotes much space to identifying the locations of Jabbok and Peniel, simply recounts the episode in a matter of fact way. Thus, on v. 25:

> So strong was Jacob, and so bravely did he wrestle, that his antagonist could not overcome him by the means which a wrestler would ordinarily employ; so, in order to escape before daylight, and at the same time to show that he was superior to Jacob, he sprained Jacob's thigh.[42]

Driver does not ask why the assailant needed to escape before daylight and, indeed, never seems to raise the question whether, and if so, in what way, the incident actually took place. At least Robertson's psychological interpretation, described above, dealt with this question. The only redeeming thing about Driver's exposition was that he recommended readers to consult Robertson's sermon!

Robertson's appropriation of biblical criticism and his positive use of the Old Testament no doubt owed much to his remarkable and unique gifts. But he had also worked hard to learn German and had taken to heart Lessing's observation about "the clothing of abstract truths in allegories and instructive single circumstances which were narrated as actual occurrences." Would he have been able to play a part in the bitter controversies

---

40. Robertson, *Sermons on Bible Subjects*, 19; *Sermons Preached at Brighton*, 47.
41. See Rogerson, "What Difference Did Darwin Make?" esp. 84–85.
42. Driver, *The Book of Genesis*, 294–95.

about biblical criticism that raged a decade after his untimely death? We do not know; but we can be grateful for what he achieved, and from which we can still learn much.

16

ὑπὸ πνεύματος ἁγίου φερόμενοι ἐλάλησαν ἀπὸ θεοῦ ἄνθρωποι

On the Inspiration of Holy Scripture

JOHN WEBSTER
University of St. Andrews

INTRODUCTION

CHRISTIAN THEOLOGICAL TEACHING ABOUT the inspiration of the Bible is one element in a comprehensive account of the nature and ends of Holy Scripture. A fully articulated theology of Scripture will treat five topics.

The first and principal topic, from which all the others derive and by which they are governed, is the place of Holy Scripture in the economy of revelation, reconciliation, and regeneration in which God loves creatures by communicating to them a share in his knowledge in the domain of the church, in order that they may know, love, and serve him above all things and so move to the fulfillment of their created nature. Second, the causes or authorship of Holy Scripture are to be treated, and, in particular, the ways in which the Holy Spirit acts as the mover of the human movements of writing. It is at this point that, after some attention to the election, calling, and formation of the prophets and apostles, the inspiration of Scripture is afforded direct treatment. Following from this is, third, a presentation of the properties of Holy Scripture, that is, the attributes that it has by virtue of its place in the work of divine instruction and its origin in divine inspiration. These properties include veracity, sufficiency, perspicuity, efficacy, canonicity, and authority. Having thus treated the location, origin, and nature of Scripture, a theological account then moves to consider the ends or purposes of Scripture, which may summarily be described as the restoration and maintenance of rational fellowship between God and his human creatures in the common life of the community of the baptized, teaching, reproving, correcting, and training in righteousness, so that the people of God may be perfected and enabled to enact their regenerate nature. From this account of the ends of Scripture flows, fifth, a presentation of the uses of Scripture, that is, the attitudes, habits, skills, and practices that characterize active reception of Scripture in the life of the church, and that enable the communication of the goods of divine instruction. This final element examines the range of settings in which Scripture is used (such as private contemplation, public reading and exposition, and the theological school), the nature and ends of exegesis, and the skills—spiritual as well as intellectual—required if the exegete is to read the scriptural text in ways that are fitting in view of its place, origin, nature, and ends.

In addition to the material requirement of attention to its proper *res*— a requirement that can only be met by strenuous application of intellectual powers allied to well-formed spiritual appetite and judgment and a measure of vigilance—a theology of Holy Scripture needs to observe a number of formal requirements if it is to prove well-ordered and instructive. It should have an eye to the whole, because only when the matter is envisaged comprehensively can the various components and their relations be understood. Neglect or omission of some element of the whole often lies behind the internal disarray of theological teaching about Scripture, and often leaves it exposed to critique. Further, in treating all its elements, a theology of Holy Scripture needs to follow the correct material sequence, in which the *principium* of the doctrine—God and his communicative works—precedes the *principiata*—the human causes of Scripture, and its human recipients. Even when for good pedagogical reasons the order of exposition adopts a different sequence, beginning, perhaps, with questions that arise in study of one of the later elements in the sequence, it will nevertheless need to bear in mind and to display that element's place in relation to what precedes it and what follows. If it should fail to do this, its account of the material risks misplacement and consequent distortion. And so, for example, an account of interpretive practices rests on prior material on the nature, properties, and ends of Scripture; these in turn derive from what has been determined about its causes, and that, finally, has its ground in a theology of God and God's revelatory will and work. A final formal requirement follows from this: the proportions of each part of the doctrine are to accord with its material rank and placement, so that each part has the correct extension and is not allowed to become too expansive or too restricted. Once again, disarray may result from hypertrophy or atrophy of one or other of the parts. The theology of inspiration, in particular, sometimes suffers from the effects of disproportion, whether by retraction (as in historical naturalist accounts of the biblical writings) or by over-inflation (so that inspiration comes to be expected to accomplish virtually all the work that is properly undertaken by a theology of divine revelation).

What follows is a sketch of inspiration as one of the parts of the second topic in bibliology, the causes or authorship of Scripture. Inspiration is the Spirit's work of illuminating the prophetic and apostolic writers, and providing both the impulse to write and the matter and verbal form of their writings. The adequacy of a theology of inspiration, it is suggested, depends on, *inter alia*, deployment of principles about the non-competitive relation of divine and human causality, informed by theological teaching about creation and the Spirit. In order to make an approach to the theology of inspiration, however, it is necessary first to pause over some prior material in the second topic—the election, calling, and sanctification of the prophets and apostles; but before proceeding to that, consideration needs to be given to the fountainhead from which all bibliological teaching flows, the doctrine of God the loving teacher who conducts ignorant creatures to knowledge of himself, and so to happiness.

SCRIPTURE IN THE ECONOMY OF REVELATION, RECONCILIATION, AND REGENERATION

A Christian theology of Holy Scripture begins far back, in the doctrine of God. The immediately presenting aspect of the doctrine of God to which bibliology gives attention is that of God's outer works of communication, the economy of divine instruction.[1] In God's work of revelation, the Fa-

---

1. A number of recent accounts of the theology of Scripture have drawn attention to its setting in the divine economy, often through retrieval of earlier patterns of theological thoughts; see, representatively, Yeago, "The Bible, the Church and the Scriptures," 49–93; Work, *Living and Active*; Martin, "*Sacra Doctrina*," 1–19; Levering, *Participatory Biblical Exegesis*; Paddison, *Scripture*; Swain, *Trinity, Revelation and Reading*; Fulford, *Divine Eloquence*; Crawford, *Cyril of Alexandria's Trinitarian Theology of Scripture*.

ther's purpose of renewed fellowship with fallen creatures is brought to effect by the missions of the Son and the Spirit, in which divine truth is manifest, and the church is established as the social domain in which that truth is received, preserved, and communicated. At every point, however, economy refers to and takes its character and movement from theology proper. Consequently, exposition of God's revelatory outer acts is preceded by contemplation of God in himself, his nature and properties. The ordered sequence of the economy of revelation may be schematized as follows.

God's Knowledge

"The Lord is a God of knowledge" (1 Sam 2:3). God's knowledge is infinite and perfect. Unlike creaturely knowledge, it is not acquired; there is no discursive process of learning, and God has need of no teacher:

> Who has directed the Spirit of the Lord,
>   or as his counsellor has instructed him?
> Whom did he consult for his enlightenment,
>   and who taught him the path of justice,
>   and taught him knowledge,
>   and showed him the way of understanding? (Isa 40:13-14; cf. 1 Cor 2:16; Rom 11:34, RSV[2]).

God knows himself and all things in a single, simple act of intuition; the depth of the riches of his wisdom and knowledge is beyond measure (Rom 11:32). As this one, God is the first and principal knower, and so the one from whom all other knowing derives.

God's Goodness

Such is God's superabundant goodness that he wills and brings into being the world of creatures. His act of creation is purely benevolent: God is in himself wholly realized, and the existence of creatures does not in any way augment, extend, or complete his being. The divine work of creation is sheer generosity. It is also wholly original: having no material cause, it is *ex nihilo*, not formation, but bringing into being. Among those things that divine generosity creates is the human creature, endowed with a particular nature (rational, deliberate, moral) and directed to a particular end (intelligent fellowship with the creator). This creaturely nature is, however, not achieved apart from its enactment over time; it is not so much a completed condition

---

2. Biblical quotations are from the RSV, unless otherwise indicated.

as a set of capacities whose exercise under God leads the creature to perfection. But because the creature is indeed a *creature*, having life and activity only in relation to God as the source of life and movement, the creature's realization of its nature is wholly dependent upon the creator's continuing works of ordering, maintaining, and perfecting creaturely being—that is, upon God's providence. These providential works, moreover, are not simply opaquely causal; they are at the same time acts of communication, intelligible acts, and by them the creature is led to knowledge of the ways of God and of its own nature, and is edged towards the completion of rational fellowship with the one from whom all things derive.

God's Acts

God's creative and providential acts—his work of nature—establish and superintend a realm of benevolent divine instruction and creaturely acquisition of knowledge, in which the creature's intelligence, affections, and will are engaged by the one whose communicative presence is essential to the right use of creaturely powers: "Teach me, O Lord, the way of thy statutes" (Ps 119:33); "Thy hands have made and fashioned me; give me understanding, that I may learn thy commandments" (Ps 119:73). Sin abandons this realm of divine instruction, and exposes the creature to futility, senselessness, darkness of mind, and folly (Rom 1:21–22). Sin involves an absurd bid for cognitive self-sufficiency; yet because sin is not the realization of our nature but its repudiation, it can only issue in the ignorance which accompanies alienation from the life of God (Eph 4:18; Col 1:21).

Sin and Created Nature

Sin's spurning of the creature's nature and finality is fruitless, and does not put an end to the workings of God's communicative goodness. On the contrary, sin intensifies these divine operations as they take the social form of reconciling instruction. This instruction begins with the election and summoning of the people of God, and includes the provision of law and prophecy as means through which knowledge of God is preserved and its application extended. At its center are to be found the reconciling and sanctifying works of the Word and the Spirit. The Word assumes flesh, and in so doing becomes the final teacher of creatures, one whose "word" is unsurpassable, having the critical power and capacity to bestow life, which derive from its (and his) derivation from the mandate of the Father: "the Father who sent me has himself given me commandment what to say and what to speak" (John 12:49); "The word that I say to you I do not speak on my own authority; but the Father who dwells in me does his works" (John 14:10). Further, the Son's definitive instruction is reiterated after his glorification by "the Holy Spirit, whom the Father will send in my name" and who "will teach you all things" (John 14:26). In this triune work of revelation, creaturely ignorance is overcome, and knowledge of God restored in the assembly gathered by Christ and the Spirit. In that assembly there is to be found a singular mystery: "You have been anointed by the Holy One, and you all know" (1 John 2:20).

Regeneration of Created Nature

Precisely because this mystery includes the regeneration of created nature, it has creaturely form and extension. The instruction that issues from and accompanies reconciliation does not set aside creatureliness, but points it to perfection. God's anointing generates knowledge. Further, in generating knowledge, it also brings into being a social order, provided with instruments through which knowledge of God can be shared and conserved. These instruments are various: liturgical, sacramental, official, and scriptural. Through public worship, the celebration of the dominical ordinances, the oversight of an ordered ministry, and the prophetic and apostolic writings, creatures are framed for intelligent fellowship with their creator and reconciler and prepared for their end, which is "to see him as he is" (1 John 3:2).

All this is the barest of outlines of the economy of revelation and its origin in the perfect life of God. It is only in relation to this setting or field of divine truth that Christian use of the term "Holy Scripture" makes sense. "Holy Scripture" does not refer simply to an instance of the more general phenomenon of sacred texts, the reverential reading that they command, and their authority to form the beliefs, imagination, and practices of a religious community. That to which the term refers is not a textual entity *tout court* but a text that possesses certain properties and that invites certain uses by virtue of the role it plays in the triune God's outer work in which he loves creatures by instructing them. Understanding how it comes about that Holy Scripture performs this role leads to consideration of its causes.

THE CAUSES OR AUTHORSHIP OF SCRIPTURE

God's providential and saving protection of the people of God includes provision of scriptural means for their governance and edification. By virtue of what agencies does this means arise? By what acts of authorship?

At this point, a theological account of Scripture's nature and ends, especially one that does not avert its eyes from the long history of anti-supernaturalism in study of the Bible, is drawn to consider the relation between divine and creaturely causality in the production of Scripture. If pre-modern theology could be relaxed and often quite minimal in treating this matter, the almost unrestricted authority of immanent historical causality in modern bibliology and hermeneutics invites greater explicitness in determining Scripture's authorship. The scriptural provision arises by virtue of the reconciling will and activity of God the teacher; and it also arises within the communicative life and activities of Israel and the church, taking the form of human authorship and its products. What is the force of that "also"?

Setting out this matter requires concurrent material and formal work. The material task is theological portrayal of two outer works of God: the calling and preparation of the prophets and apostles, and their authorial acts. The first may be set under the rubric of vocation and sanctification; the second is the concern of the theology of inspiration. As external operations of God which have creatures as their term, they are the works of the undivided Trinity. They may, however, be eminently (though not exclusively) appropriated to the Holy Spirit, so that much of what is said about the causes of Scripture will consist of application of rules about the nature of the Spirit's operations in the world.

Accompanying and serving this material work, the formal task is that of judicious deployment of concept and arguments to clarify the relation of divine and human causality in the case of Scripture. This formal work is auxiliary, governed and limited by the *res* into which theology inquires. But it is necessary, not the least because unease about or dismissal of the theology of the inspiration of Scripture is often driven by (metaphysical) assumptions about causality that require critical illumination.

The matter in its entirety may be seen as a consideration of a *locus classicus* of the inspiration of Scripture: ὑπὸ πνεύματος ἁγίου φερόμενοι ἐλάλησαν ἀπὸ θεοῦ ἄνθρωποι (2 Pet 1:21).

God as Primary Cause of Scripture

God is Scripture's primary cause or author. His first causal work in this regard is the calling and sanctification of the prophets and apostles, so that by divine appointment and superintendence they become fitting instruments of divine teaching. The deep origin of this calling is the election of grace, the fruit of the inner divine counsel which antecedes "the foundation of the world" (Eph 1:4). Thus, for Paul to be "an apostle of Christ Jesus" is for him to be an object of "the will of God" (1 Cor 1:1; 2 Cor 1:1; Eph 1:1; Col 1:1; 2 Tim 1:1). Apostolic office and activity are "not from men nor through man" (Gal 1:1); they cannot be assumed or conferred, they precede human appointment; indeed, they precede the apostle's existence. To be an apostle is to find oneself in a state of life that issues from another's will, to be a "chosen instrument of mine" (Acts 9:15). From election flow calling and separation for apostolic existence and work. Paul, again, is "called to be an apostle, set apart for the gospel of God" (Rom 1:1); having been thus "set . . . apart before I was born," Paul is "called . . . through his grace" (Gal 1:15).

Election and vocation may take historical-biographical form as an invasive divine summons, arresting the course of life and reorienting it, as in the conversion and call narrative of Acts 9. Yet apostolic existence may not be reduced simply to its disturbing inception. It is also formed by a range of other divine acts, through which there occurs an extended shaping and strengthening of the apostle's will, heart, and powers of mind, such as memory, conceptual and argumentative skills, or linguistic and literary abilities. These divine acts shape the apostle's particular nature and course of life and occupancy of a specific historical and social-cultural setting. This temporally extended formation is part of the apostle's sanctification. Baptized into Christ, the apostle is given a renewed nature and a set of powers so as to become by divine grace a capable agent in the fulfillment of the ministry for which he was chosen and to which he was called.

In this sanctification, God is the principal agent: formed by God, the apostle is recipient of "the gift of God's grace" (Eph 3:7). But this gift does not as it were hover above the apostle in such a way that the apostle is not changed and renewed. Divine grace animates creatures and bequeaths powers. Grace is that active divine goodness that enables lively action. As in the first creation *ex nihilo*, so in regeneration and sanctification: the term of God's "making" is not the production of an inert reality characterized chiefly by pure contingency, but the institution of a reality that—precisely because it lives and moves *in him*—really does live and move. Apostolic existence is thus an exemplary fulfillment of the confession: "You he made alive" (Eph 2:1). Like all believers, the apostle is God's "workmanship"; but to be God's workmanship is not to be an artefact but an agent to whom tasks are assigned, to be "created in Christ for good works, which God prepared beforehand, that we should walk in them" (Eph 2:10).

Prophets, Apostles, and Divine Teaching

The good works to which prophets and apostles are called include that of the communication of divine teaching. As servant of God and apostle of Jesus Christ, Paul is appointed "to further the faith of God's elect and their knowledge of the truth which accords with godliness, in hope of eternal life which God, who never lies, promised ages ago and at the proper time manifested in his word through the preaching with which I have been entrusted by command of God our Savior" (Titus 1:1–3). Prophetic and apostolic authorship is an extension of this sharing or distribution of knowledge of the truth. In this authorship, the prophet or apostle is an instrumental or secondary author in the service of God the principal author; the divine action which moves this prophetic and apostolic work is inspiration.

Two preliminaries should be observed before engaging more fully the concept of inspiration. First, it is important not to allow inspiration to become the principal element in the doctrine of Scripture. Polemic against reductive naturalism may encourage disproportionate attention to what is properly a derivative of more primary teaching about the economy of divine instruction and the grounds of that economy in God's immanent life.[3] Second, a satisfactory theology of inspiration rests on a well-developed theology of the eternal personhood of the Holy Spirit and of the character of the Spirit's work in the world. In his work of inspiration, the Spirit acts as one who is Lord and giver of life. Because the Spirit is Lord, he remains the principal mover in inspiration, his sovereignty and all-sufficiency uncompromised by his relation to creaturely textual embassies. Because the Spirit is life-giver, he is the perfecting cause of the creatures by whom he is served, so that by him their causal authorial powers are realized, brought to life and activity.

What, then, may be said of the inspiration of Holy Scripture? Inspiration is that work of God the Spirit by which the prophets and apostles, as God's chosen instruments, called, sanctified, and equipped with necessary gifts by divine grace, are caused to write, so that their acts of authorship and their products come to serve God's work of instructing the people of God. To put this more fully, inspiration is not ecstatic rapture, possession by the Spirit in which the biblical writers are alienated from their natural life and its powers. "Possession" is not the Spirit's ordinary mode of operation,

---

3. The common claim that such disproportionate attention to inspiration may be found in the post-Reformation divines can scarcely be maintained: see Preus, *The Inspiration of Scripture*, and Muller, *Post-Reformation Reformed Dogmatics 2*, both of whom demonstrate in some detail that teaching about inspiration is only one element in teaching about the nature of Scripture.

which is to quicken and direct creatures and to provide them with power to act. Pure inspirational extrinsicism is not only anthropologically but also pneumatologically deficient. Over against this, inspiration may be arranged into three acts that, though distinct, are nevertheless co-inherent and may often be concurrent.

First, there is the work of illumination of the biblical author. The Holy Spirit grants to the writer that measure of understanding (practical or theoretical) of God and all things in relation to God that is necessary for literary representation. This vivification of intelligence, countering the lingering cognitive damage caused by sin, is essential if the prophet or apostle is to communicate divine truth in writing. In the opening scene of the Apocalypse, the writer is "in the Spirit," and there is a divinely effected "seeing" that is the indispensable prelude to following the command: "Write what you see in a book and send it to the seven churches" (Rev 1:11). A similar pattern of illumination of the understanding as preparatory for a gift of words so that the apostle can serve as teacher in the church is found in 1 Cor 2. Apostolic activity is a communication of an otherwise arcane wisdom: "we impart a secret and hidden wisdom of God" (v. 7). This impartation has its source in God: in the divine counsel, for God "decreed [this wisdom] before the ages for our glorification" (v. 7), and also in the divine self-knowledge: "the Spirit searches everything, even the depths of God. For what person knows a man's thoughts except the spirit of the man which is in him? So also no one comprehends the thoughts of God except the Spirit of God" (vv. 10–11). From this same divine agent issues revelation: "'What no eye has seen, nor ear heard, nor the heart of man conceived, what God has prepared for those who love him,' God has revealed to us through the Spirit" (vv. 9–10). Revelation moves towards its creaturely term as the Spirit gives understanding: "we have received not the spirit of the world, but the Spirit which is from God, that we might understand the gifts bestowed on us by God" (v. 12). And, because this understanding is preparatory to a human work of apostolic teaching, the Spirit also supplies words: "we impart this in words not taught by human wisdom but taught by the Spirit" (v. 13).

Second, there is a Spirit-given impulse to write. Like the other works of the Spirit, this *mandatum scribendi* is complex. Somewhat narrowly understood, it may appear as a simple peremptory imperative: "Write what you see" (Rev 1:11, 19). More spaciously conceived, the impulse is to be grasped in terms of its proper finality, the goal of bringing about human authorship and a prophetic or apostolic communication of goods of knowledge. This involves the authorization of the biblical writer, in the sense of the writer's appointment (by one competent to make such an appointment) to an office in God's economy of instruction, along with permission and approval to undertake certain acts with validity and due recognition. Further, although the command and authorization come to the biblical writers *ab extra*, from the infinitely distant region of God's self-knowledge and eternal decree, they effect the inner formation of the prophet or apostle. The divine *mandatum* is appropriated, so that it becomes an inner impulse, and the text-acts to which it gives rise are in the fullest sense acts that also arise from the writer's own will and understanding. The Spirit's mandate also operates intrinsically, as an augmentation of creaturely powers, and not merely as an extrinsic efficient cause.

Third, the Spirit supplies both the *res* of the biblical writings and the *verba* by which that matter is expressed. This does not mean that the biblical writers are wholly passive; they are authors, not conduits: conscious, intelligent, deliberate. They speak and write. But this speech and writing of theirs is not wholly original to them: it is ἀπὸ θεοῦ.

Lecturing on dogmatics for the first time, Barth worried that verbal inspiration effects "a false stabilisation of the Word of God,"[4] which changed the mystery of God's act of revelation into "direct revelation,"[5] forgetting "the *indirect* identity of the Bible with revelation,"[6] and making Scripture into a deposit of revealedness. The worry is, however, misplaced: verbal inspiration does not eliminate what Barth later called "God's action in the Bible,"[7] but simply indicates one kind of action that God performs in relation to Scripture. Verbal inspiration is an extension of (not a replacement for) the theology of divine instruction.

An opposing worry is that verbal inspiration minimizes the human activity of literary composition, especially when set out through the idiom of "dictation." But dictation (along with associated concepts of the biblical authors as "secretaries" or "amanuenses") is best understood as a—possibly clumsy—term for the divine prompting and oversight of prophetic and apostolic writing, not as the elimination of subordinate human authorship.[8] More importantly, verbal inspiration is an instance of inner motion rather than mechanical efficient causality, and so accords with the principles of

---

4. Barth, *The Göttingen Dogmatics*, 218: his worry was probably prompted by study of Heppe's textbook of Reformed dogmatics, which gave voice to a similar disquiet: see Heppe, *Reformed Dogmatics*, 16–21.

5. Barth, *The Göttingen Dogmatics*, 217.

6. Ibid., 218.

7. Barth, *Church Dogmatics* I/1, 110.

8. Preus points out that *dictatio* is only one of a range of terms in post-Reformation divinity for the Spirit's relation to the scriptural *verba*; other, more intrinsic, terms include *influxus, afflatus, suggestio,* and *instinctus*; Preus, *The Inspiration of Scripture*, 53.

Christian teaching about the creative and recreative works of the Spirit as the giving of life.[9]

THE PROPERTIES OF HOLY SCRIPTURE

If the theology of biblical inspiration rarely persuades beyond a relatively narrow circle, it is most often because it appears to fall victim to a malign supernaturalism—"malign" because it is apparently lacking in attention to the human properties of the biblical writings, and so likely to mischaracterize both the scriptural media of divine instruction and the ways in which they are to be received by creaturely intelligence. If we ask why it should seem self-evident that a theology of inspiration is bought at cost to the properly human character of the biblical texts, no single answer may be returned. Inspiration's decline into implausibility is bound up with a number of common characteristics of the history of Christian divinity after the exhaustion of post-Reformation thought. Two such characteristics, to which allusion has already been made, may serve as examples.

Natural Properties

The theology of biblical inspiration has sometimes found itself overwhelmed in trying to articulate itself in the face of what, for want of a better term, may be called textual naturalism; that is, the magnification of the natural properties of the biblical texts and the processes of production and reception in which they are set. Textual naturalism is not simply a literary strategy, but a metaphysic, one that suggests that the explanatory setting for the biblical writings is not divine revelation and its creaturely instruments but a set of principles about cultural production, including the production of religious texts. Chief among these principles is a conviction of the unavailability for consideration of non-natural causes or referents of the biblical writings, and a corresponding restriction of explanatory inquiry to human authors and historical settings. If this set of convictions has authority, it is in part because it encourages the reader's intelligence to linger over the linguistic and literary properties of the texts, as well as to direct itself to historical referents in ways that seem to be inhibited by teaching about the Bible as Holy Scripture. This may be reinforced by other factors: a deep assumption that the real is the historical, and that the historical is patient of no reduction to a

---

9. In this connection, the notion of "organic inspiration," set out at length by Bavinck, *Reformed Dogmatics* 1, 387–448, and more briefly by Berkouwer, *Holy Scripture*, 139–79, deserves attention.

non-historical cause; fear of the deleterious effects of the political authority exercised by sacred texts and their interpreters; and valorization of a certain conception of rational freedom, and of the cognitive superiority of the academy over ecclesial society.

In considering these movements, however, Christian theology will not isolate them from the spiritual history of which the giving and reception of Scripture is part. Proposals about the nature of the Bible and about attendant practices of reading are, in theological judgment, not only elements in intellectual history, but also episodes in the progress of revelation and reconciliation. Holy Scripture is a set of texts that bears to us the divine Word in all its acuteness and power to penetrate and lay bare; as such, it evokes resistance. Among the ways in which we may shield ourselves from the Word in Scripture is evasion of the ambassadorial or ministerial status of its humanity—of the fact that its writers are truly the prophets and apostles of God—by not allowing that Scripture's human properties serve the announcement of divine judgment and consolation, and instead treating them as the term of inquiry. The most self-effacing and scrupulous reluctance to allow intelligence to pass through the *historia Scripturae* is also a spiritual stance, one whose innocence and profitability are not self-evident: "Hear and hear, but do not understand" (Isa 6:9)?

First and Final Causes

One of the principal motivations of the restriction of biblical study to its natural historical properties is loss of confidence in the explanatory power of appeal to first and final causes. To speak of literary-cultural products as also occupying a place in a causal order other than that of self-enclosed human communicative practice risks neglect of their human attributes: this, because to speak of a human activity as caused, excited, vivified, or brought into operation by another agent is to violate that activity's human integrity. If the Bible is to be thought to be human, it must be as *only* human.

Sed contra ... God is not one of an array of causes, but the cause of causes, the cause by virtue of which there is created causality. As cause of causes, God is not in competition with the causes that he creates. God wills creaturely causes, bringing them into being by limitlessly abundant goodness. Because God is in every way replete, he loses nothing by their existence or action. Created movements—precisely because they are brought into and preserved in being and motion by the one who is antecedently and infinitely full—present no obstacle or inhibition to God, and his causing of them does not oppose their operation or dignity.

Accordingly, a biblical author is "a true human author whose authorship remains whole and inviolate at the same time as it is permeated and embraced by that of God."[10] To say that God elects, calls, sanctifies, and illuminates the prophets and apostles and supplies both content and word, is not to espouse an account of the authorship of Scripture that opposes its integral human authorship. It is, rather, to say what *kind* of human authorship is exercised by the prophets and apostles, by tracing how it came to be and what is its end. Divine authorship is not partial or contributory; biblical inspiration is not joint authorship. Such conceptions once again envisage God as one of a string of causes, not as incommensurable first cause. But God the Spirit causes ("authors") prophetic and apostolic authorship. Grace intensifies creaturely movement, including the movement of literary intelligence.[11]

Once again, if this is no longer easy and natural, it may be because thought about divine action in relation to human action is doubly inhibited. On the one hand, we may instinctively restrict causality to efficient causality, the exertion of force on an external object, and so find ourselves defeated by a concept of intrinsic motion. On the other hand, we may assume less than adequate doctrines of God and creation, which treat uncreated and created being as occupants of the same territory, vying for supremacy. But God the creator is no such force. He is one whose wisdom and goodness maintain created integrity. To say that those moved by the Spirit spoke from God is to say that Scripture arises from no violation of the literary integrity of its writers, but the opposite: ἀπὸ θεοῦ indicates both the sovereign origin and moving power of their authorship, and its genuinely human phenomenality.

THE USE OF SCRIPTURE.

The church is that society that comes into existence and endures by virtue of the gifts of divine love. Among those gifts, Holy Scripture is the inspired embassy and instrument of the divine teacher. To be assembled before that teacher is at one and the same time a joyful and arduous matter. Joyful,

---

10. Rahner, "Inspiration in the Bible," 15. Along similar lines, James Burtchaell's witty and informative history of Roman Catholic theologies of inspiration from the early nineteenth century concludes with the suggestion that what is required above all is a sophisticated understanding of the relation of divine and human causality: Burtchaell, *Catholic Theories*, 279–305.

11. Preus' deployment of the term "monergism" to speak of the divine omnicausality that causes human authorship is imprudent, because it suggests sole causality, something that he clearly seeks to avoid in the theology of inspiration: *The Inspiration of Scripture*, 54–55.

because God has not left creatures in the misery of ignorance, but has sent out the light of his truth; arduous, because faithful hearers of divine instruction are to show virtues of expectancy, docility, and studiousness that even our regenerate nature finds hard to summon. But reading of Scripture is an extension of baptism, and when accompanied by prayer is an activity in the sphere of God's promise. And so: "Blessed Lord, who hast caused all holy Scriptures to be written for our learning; grant that we may in such wise hear them, read, mark, learn, and inwardly digest them, that by patience, and comfort of the holy Word, we may embrace, and ever hold fast the blessed hope of everlasting life, which though hast given us in our Saviour Jesus Christ. Amen."

PART III

Theology and Embodiment

17

Good Sex, Bad Sex

Reflections on Sexuality and the Bible

LOVEDAY ALEXANDER
University of Sheffield

Many years ago, in conversation with a German biblical scholar, I happened to mention that Andrew Lincoln was one of my colleagues in the Department of Biblical Studies in Sheffield. "Ah!" said my interlocutor: "Paradise Lincoln!" Andrew's *Paradise Now and Not Yet* was already making a favorable impression on the exacting world of German *neutestamentlicher Wissenschaft*. It is a pleasure to contribute to this collegial appreciation of Andrew's academic achievements, recalling those heady days back in 1986, when we had just joined the Sheffield Department (Andrew six months ahead of me), and enjoyed together the excitement of testing out new approaches to exegesis in the lecture-room, with the constant challenge of asking: what have these texts to do with the moral and political questions we wrestle with today?

The present paper offers a personal approach to this perennial challenge, from the critical and historical perspective of a biblical scholarship seeking to engage with theological issues in today's world. It owes its immediate genesis to the Church of England's current debates over sexuality.

The *Pilling Report*, published in 2013,[1] recommended that individual clergy who so wished should be permitted to offer a ceremony of blessing to same-sex couples seeking to affirm their commitment to a stable and faithful relationship. But *Pilling* also includes a dissenting report from one member explaining why he felt unable to accept the majority recommendation—and thus embodies the continuing disagreement within the churches. *Pilling* was closely followed (more quickly than anyone had imagined possible) with the UK government's decision to legalize same-sex marriage, a decision that came into effect on 29 March 2014. I am grateful to all who have helped me engage with this material (both those who agree and those who disagree)— right back to the Sheffield students who helped me reflect on Paul's teaching on "good sex" and "bad sex."[2]

HOMOPHOBIA AND THE SHIFTING MORAL LANDSCAPE

At the heart of the *Pilling Report* is a strong call to the church to resist homophobia and to offer a welcoming and inclusive space for people of homosexual orientation. Despite their disagreements, both sides agree that the Church of England needs to take a firm stance against homophobia and to offer a warm welcome to "gay and lesbian people" (pp. 22, 149). This welcome stance represents a major advance on previous church statements. It recognizes the existence of lesbian, gay, bisexual, transgender, and intersex persons ("LGBTI") as a small but constant percentage of the population for whom same-sex attraction is not a free choice but a "given," part of their sexual identity. People who fall into this category, like other minorities in human society, have experienced fear and loathing, mockery and discrimination throughout human history. It is good that the church is ready to recognize this and to repent of her own part in it.

But I don't think the implications of this stance have been fully grasped. The church doesn't speak of repenting of negative attitudes towards murder

---

1. The *Pilling Report: Report of the House of Bishops Working Group on human sexuality* (London: Church House Publishing, 2013). Also available online at www.churchofengland.org/pilling.

2. A shorter form of this paper appears as one of a series of "Writings to resource conversation" in *Grace and Disagreement: Shared Conversations on Scripture, Mission and Human Sexuality*, (London: Church House Publishing, 2014), Vol. 2, 24–51. I am grateful to the Editor, Dr. Malcolm Brown, for permission to use this material. In an earlier and longer form, this was the substance of my final Cathedral Lecture as Canon-Theologian at Chester Cathedral on 1st February 2014 ("Men and Women and the Bible").

(say) or financial fraud. (We will, of course, want to stress that the church is there for sinners—but we don't thereby condone the sin.) The language of "inclusion" is the language we use, not of moral categories, but of social or anthropological categories (race, gender, disability). In other words, simply by talking about "homophobia," the Report represents a significant shift from the biblical viewpoint, which has no concept of homosexual identity or "orientation" (a concept that did not emerge until the nineteenth century).[3]

This report thus represents—for both sides—a significant shift in what we might call the anthropology of desire: that is, the way we understand sexual preference and desire as part of our sexual identity. This shift is based not on the Bible, which works (as we will see) with a very different anthropology of desire. It is based on *reason*—that is, on a social perception widely shared across Western European culture. The jury is out (as *Pilling* recognizes) on just how far our sexual identity depends on genetic or on environmental factors, or on a mixture of the two. But the underlying perception that our sexual identity is not about moral choice but about "orientation" is now the consensus position in Western European society, and especially among the younger generation, who don't even remember how recently homosexual activity was decriminalized in this country. I don't think we should underestimate the huge (and surprisingly rapid) cultural shift that is involved here. Yet I am convinced that this is not simply a cultural fad but a genuine shift in moral perception, based not only on the solid evidence of psychiatry and medical science, but on the day-to-day experience of countless gay youngsters and their heterosexual parents and grandparents. It is a shift as momentous in its way as the shift in the nineteenth-century perception of the ethics of slavery—and as troubling in its challenge to centuries of biblical interpretation.

But if the moral landscape has shifted, where does that leave the Bible? If the world of the Bible and the world we live in have moved apart, like tectonic plates, where does that leave the Christian believer: with a foot on both sides, trying to straddle the cognitive gap? That, in essence, is the question at the heart of the debates that we have been wrestling with over the past decade. They raise acutely the question of the relationship between an authoritative religious text from the past and a society whose understanding of sexuality and gender roles is rapidly changing, along with its understanding of human psychology and physiology—all of which has to be factored into the ethical debate.

---

3. On the emergence and definition of the concept, see Nissinen, *Homoeroticism*, 5–10.

For some people, it's our culture that is wrong, not the Bible: the church needs to affirm biblical teaching and stand out against the prevailing culture. For many others (both inside and outside the church), the Bible's negative statements about women and gays belong with those "texts of terror" that have been used over the centuries "to authorize appalling abuse, even murder, of women, Jews, slaves, colonized peoples, homosexuals"—texts that come from "a culture whose ethical presuppositions and dispositions were inferior to the best of our own, a culture that was xenophobic, patriarchal, classist, and bloodthirsty."[4] The pace of criticism seems if anything to have accelerated during the debate over gay marriage over the pat couple of years, with many young people (under forty-five, that is) simply walking away from a church that they regard as "evil" and a Bible that speaks with the voices of prejudice and oppression.[5]

But "walking away" from the Bible simply isn't an option for me, or for the church. We can't just abandon this text, which has nourished the life of faith for two millennia. I can't turn my back on a text that has sustained and informed my own faith for as long as I can remember. We have to stay with the Bible—but we have to find a way of making sense of it in a world that is very different from the world (or rather worlds) in which it was written. This is (I believe) one of the key theological tasks facing today's faith communities; and in this paper I want to share some of the principles and strategies I would adopt, as a biblical scholar, to tackle it. I should stress that this is very much my own personal approach: but I hope it may help to open up some of the moves we might make to resolve the dilemmas we face in seeking to make sense of the Bible in today's church—and today's world.

SCRIPTURE, TRADITION, AND REASON

So the first set of questions raised by this report are questions about hermeneutical method. In an Anglican context, this often takes the form of a

---

4. Davis and Hays, eds., *Art*, 165.

5. This point is strikingly confirmed in research by Linda Woodhead and Rob Warner quoted in the *Church Times* on 31 January 2014 (reprinted in Doney, *Health Check*). Woodhead (Doney, *Health Check*, 17) notes a "striking disconnect between wider social values and the Church's official teaching." "There has been a values revolution since the 1980s in Britain over the status and treatment of women, gay people, and children," with the result that young people today "now state a strong moral objection [to the church]" and see the church as prejudiced because "it discriminates against women and gay people." Warner (Doney, *Health Check*, 25) notes that the church is increasingly coming under judgment from the "new moral consensus," which has "shifted irrevocably—not just among non-Christians but among Christians, too."

question about the relationship between Scripture, tradition, and reason. What happens when reason seems to lead in a direction that is (on the face of it) at odds with the united witness of Scripture and tradition? This is not, of course, a new problem: it is one the church has had to face over the gender issues, and one that most believers have to face (though the church has not attempted a public statement on this) over scientific issues such as evolution and creation. But we need to note that both sides represented in *Pilling* face the same problem here. It is a problem that is faced by any faith, culture, or discipline that invests authority in a canonic text. The text says one thing, the facts (science, perception, experience) say another: the task of *theological* interpretation (as opposed to historical interpretation, which doesn't have this problem) is to bridge the credibility gap. If we can't, then something has to give: either reason, or the authority of the text. And it is a measure of the seriousness with which we invest the authority of the text that we would even attempt to find a way of "making sense" of both. The task of creative hermeneutics is only for those who take Scripture seriously.[6]

We often speak as if Scripture, tradition, and reason are autonomous and isolated streams of revelation: but in fact they are inextricably intertwined.[7] Already in Scripture (as F. F. Bruce pointed out years ago) "we can recognise the threefold cord: Scripture; interpretative tradition (incipient, but already necessary); reason (apart from which neither text nor interpretation could have been understood)."[8] The scriptural writers themselves are embedded in the rational processes of their own culture, as are the continuous processes of translation, interpretation, and contemporization that preserve the Scriptures in the life of the church.[9] "Reason" in this debate stands not simply for an abstract process of logical deduction: we could also describe it as a way of paying attention to a changing world.[10] And it is a purely arbitrary assumption that everything that happens in the world is automatically contrary to the will of God. Not all moral shifts are godless: some of them (slavery is a case in point) may actually owe something to the effects of centuries of Christian thinking within society. Listening to the voice of reason and experience is consistent with the prophetic hermeneutic to which Scripture itself bears witness, a hermeneutic that starts by paying attention to what God is doing in the world before trying to make sense of

6. Alexander, "Canon," 115–53.
7. See the excellent series of studies in Bauckham and Drewery, *Scripture*.
8. Bruce, "Scripture," 35–64.
9. See for example Young, *Biblical Exegesis*.
10. It is an "error to think that the only law which God hath appointed unto men . . . is the sacred scripture:" Hooker I xiv.4, cited by Henry Chadwick in Bauckham and Drewery, *Scripture*, 294.

it within a scriptural framework. "Tradition" too should not be conceived in a static fashion. As Richard Bauckham points out, "The Christian tradition is by no means inevitably traditionalist. Its eschatological hope and its missionary orientation press it towards constantly changing contextualizations of the Gospel, in which the resources of the past are brought into critical relationship with the present context with a view to the future."[11]

I have suggested elsewhere that "if we are looking for biblical approaches to scriptural authority we have to look at the Bible's own treatment of Scripture: and that, I submit, is a model that treats the Bible not as a text frozen in time, but as the word of the Living God."[12] I have illustrated this approach from the narrative of the Apostolic Council in Acts 15, which shows Paul and the Jerusalem apostles wrestling with a paradigm shift every bit as traumatic—for them—as the debates over gender and sexuality we wrestle with today.[13] The debate over the admission of gentiles to the church challenged inherited taboos and traditional readings of Scripture just as acutely as those debates challenge ours. Luke presents a church that reads Scripture as a revelation whose meaning is not exhausted by its original context. Scripture has to be read in dialogue with what God is doing in the present: in other words, God's revelatory activity is not confined to Scripture. As Barnabas Lindars puts it,

> Early Christian exegesis starts with the church's present experience—of forgiveness, acceptance with God, of the power of the Spirit, the joy of table-fellowship with the living Lord. . . . Such experience is the truth about the messianic age. It is true that the theory that the eschatological age has dawned, resulting from faith in the risen Lord, controls the interpretation of these facts. But the facts themselves master the theory and transform it.[14]

This fundamental principle is perfectly expressed in the key verse of Peter's Pentecost sermon (Acts 2:16): "This is that which was spoken by the prophet." Starting with the present ("this"), Peter goes back into Scripture to find a correspondence ("that"). Once identified, the Scripture provides a revelatory framework for reaching a better understanding of what is happening now, and then provides the framework for interpreting where God is leading in the future ("What then shall we do?"). This process of reading Scripture requires guidance: reading is a process, a journey that requires "communal debate and discernment over time within an ecclesial

---

11. Ibid., 137. Cf. Davis, "Critical Traditioning," 163–80.
12. Alexander, "This is That," 71.
13. Ibid., 55–72. Johnson, *Scripture*.
14. Lindars, *Apologetic*, 283.

community."[15] It is inherently dialogical: the interpretation of Scripture is not a closed, predetermined system, but a process of exploration, in which we discover for ourselves, slowly and sometimes painfully, what God is revealing. This process of discovery then sparks a process of "remembering" or re-reading earlier events in the light of the progressive awakening of inspired understanding.[16]

This approach to Scripture is firmly embedded in the cultural praxis of its day, using exegetical techniques that embody the process of "contemporization," in which "older writings are brought into the present by the exposition and application of the later canonical writers."[17] The whole point of exegesis is to "make [the text] relevant through the application of certain exegetical principles."[18] The ancient exegetes developed a selective but highly flexible approach to their canonic texts, an approach that positively invites expansion and creative interpretation. But this creativity was governed by a profound fidelity to the "mind" of the sage, the true canon which was the key to unlocking all the rest.[19] And for Christians, the fundamental *canon*, the *regula* or carpenter's rule against which all scriptural interpretation is judged, is the story of Jesus, with its disconcerting habit of subverting all our moral certainties. In other words, exegetical dilemmas are not solved simply by collecting proof-texts or voting by simple majority. The church has always operated with a hierarchy of interpretation, a "canon within the canon," prioritizing New Testament over Hebrew Scriptures, Gospels over Epistles.

SAME-SEX RELATIONS IN THE BIBLE

The Bible actually says nothing about "homosexuality" as it is understood today—that is, about sexual orientation as a "given." The few biblical writers who mention same-sex relations share with other ancient writers the cultural assumption that same-sex attraction is not an "orientation" but a moral disorder, a voluntary choice made by heterosexual people, and thus an expression of uncontrolled and often aggressive sexual desire.

This is clear from the story of the destruction of Sodom in Gen 19, which includes an unfulfilled threat of (male) homosexual rape.[20] What is

15. Fowl, *Engaging*, 114.
16. On "remembering," cf. Fowl, *Engaging*, 100.
17. Ellis, *Old Testament*, 66. See further Davis, "Critical Traditioning."
18. G. Brooke, *Exegesis*, 353.
19. On this see further Alexander, "Canon."
20. This is the story that lies behind the popular identification of homosexual

really shocking about this story is Lot's readiness to sacrifice his daughters to gang rape in an attempt to salvage the honor of his (apparently) male guests. Like the equally horrific story in Judg 19, this story reflects a value-system in which it is acceptable for women to be treated as objects of predatory male lust, but not for men. In this cultural world, homosexual desire is a symptom, not of latent same-sex orientation, but of violent and unassuaged heterosexual desire.[21]

The ethics of same-sex desire in the biblical writers reflect this ancient anthropology of desire. Male homosexual activity is treated as an "abomination" in Lev 18:22; 20:13 (female homosexual activity is not mentioned at all). These passages are part of the "Holiness Code," which seeks to establish clear lines of demarcation between Israel's moral code and those of the pagan nations around. The "mixing" of gender roles in same-sex relations ("lying with a man as with a woman") is prohibited as part of a wider code prohibiting various kinds of "mixing" (mixed crops in a field, mixed fibers in clothing).[22]

This pattern is repeated in Rom 1:26–27. In Paul's anthropology of desire, same-sex encounters are "contrary to nature": that is, they represent a distortion of the default sexual identity, which Paul assumes to be heterosexual.[23] Like other post-biblical Jewish writers, Paul sees same-sex activity as a manifestation of the pagan world's underlying sin of idolatry (1:18–23): "worshipping and serving the creature rather than the Creator" leads to all manner of sexual impurity (vv. 24–25). As a result, Paul says, God "gave them up" to "all manner of wickedness, evil, covetousness, malice. Full of envy, murder, strife, deceit, malignity, they are gossips, slanderers, haters of God, insolent, haughty, boastful, inventors of evil, disobedient to parents, foolish, faithless, heartless, ruthless" (1:28–31, RSV). This passage forms part of a more general theological description of a fallen world in which

---

activity with "sodomy" (cf. Jude 7)—though many biblical writers (including Jesus) identify Sodom's sin as pride and the abuse of hospitality, specifically the failure to recognize angelic visitors (cf. Matt 11.23–24). Nissinen, *Homoeroticism*, 46–47.

21. Other stories in the Hebrew Bible offer more positive images of the close ties of affection and loyalty that can arise between men (David and Jonathan) and between women (Ruth and Naomi), recognizing perhaps that such "homosocial" relationships offered a kind of companionship that was often lacking in marriage in traditional societies (cf. Nissinen, *Homoeroticism*, 17). Nevertheless, both stories of friendship presuppose a background of (heterosexual) marriage as the default sexual relationship.

22. Ibid., 42–44.

23. Besides ibid., 103–13, see also the excellent discussion of this passage by M. Davies, "New Testament Ethics," 315–31; Martin, "Heterosexism," 332–55; Moore, "Que(e)rying Paul," 250–74. For more recent discussions see also Via and Gagnon, *Two Views*; Loader, *Sexuality*, 7–34.

no-one, Jew nor Greek, can "boast" (3:27) in the presence of God: "since all have sinned, and fall short of the glory of God," all stand equally in need of the gift of redemption through God's grace (3:23–24). Homosexual practices are also included in the vice-lists of 1 Cor 6:9; 1 Tim 1:9–10: the lists include idolatry, adultery, robbery, greed, drunkenness, rapacity, murder, kidnapping, and slander.

How should we approach this material? A responsible exegesis will pay attention to questions of *context* and *canon*, and will start with questions of *philology and translation*.[24] Four terms in the vice-lists in 1 Cor 6:9 and 1 Tim 1:9–10 relate to sexual sin: *pornoi, moichoi, malakoi, arsenokoitai*. *Moichoi* refers to (heterosexual) adulterers. *Pornoi* may be male prostitutes or rent-boys (the feminine form is used of a female prostitute in 6:16)— though the same word is used more generally of sexually immoral persons (both within and without the church) in 5:9–11. *Malakos* literally means "soft" and may refer in a general way to "effeminacy" (a quality frowned on among first-century males) or more specifically to the passive partner in male same-sex activity. *Arsenokoitēs* (literally, "bedding a male") echoes the language used by the Septuagint (the ancient Greek translation of the Hebrew Bible) in Lev 18:22 and 20:13, and probably refers to the active partner in a male same-sex encounter.

Though the precise meaning of these terms has occasioned some dispute, there is no real doubt that they identify various forms of culturally unacceptable sexual activity, both heterosexual and homosexual. But the language used reveals a first-century social construction of same-sex relations as a shameful distortion of "natural" gender roles, in which one male partner takes a "female" (i.e., passive, submissive, inferior) role. To use the word "homosexual" in these texts is to impose on Paul a modern concept that belongs to our world, not to his. Paul's ethical instructions are addressed to first-century men (very rarely to women) using first-century moral categories that reflect his own hybrid cultural identity as an observant Jew, with a Greek education, growing up in the Roman Empire.

The next question we need to ask is the question of *canon*. Taken as a whole, the Bible actually says very little about homosexual activity, even in the ancient sense: and it is important to put the negative texts in a broader biblical context. The debate is often conducted purely in terms of "what the Bible says": but which parts of the Bible? Do "biblical values" embrace the primitive value-system of the patriarchal narratives, in which women are seen as legitimate objects of male sexual violence? Or the affectionate

---

24. Nissinen, *Homoeroticism*, 113–18.

friendship between David and Jonathan? We need to ask, why *these* texts, and what is their position in relation to the biblical canon as a whole?

We might ask, for example, why does Leviticus figure so large in this discussion? Are Christians bound by all the prohibitions of Leviticus (and if not, why just this one)? Traditional Christian teaching has held that Christians are bound by the moral Law embodied in the Ten Commandments, but not by the rest of the 613 *mitzvoth*: and the Ten Commandments say nothing about homosexual practice. Leviticus 19 also forbids the interbreeding of cattle, sowing two kinds of seed in one field, and wearing cloth made of mixed fibers (19:19); eating flesh with blood in it (19:26); "rounding off the hair on your temples or marring the edges of your beard" (19:27); or getting a tattoo (19:28). Are all these equally forbidden for Christians today? It also, of course, includes the sublime principle, "You shall love your neighbor as yourself" (19:18), cited by Jesus as a one-line summary of the second half of the law (Matt 22:39). Reading the law for Christians has always been a matter not of simple appropriation but of canonic interpretation: we are called to read the law in light of the gospel, not the other way round.

When we come to the New Testament, it is important to observe that the Gospels contain no explicit teaching on same-sex relationships. In a canonic context, this silence is significant. Many find it odd that a church that has found it quite possible to ignore a hard dominical saying on divorce (on which Jesus is quite explicit) struggles to accommodate same-sex relationships (on which Jesus says nothing at all). Even in the Pauline Epistles, we have to note that in none of these passages is sexuality the main point at issue: all three cite homosexual practice as a passing example in a much longer standardized list of sinful practices. Paul's view of homosexual behavior is uniformly negative: it is cited as a sin typical of the gentile world. But it is not intrinsic to the argument: other sins are listed, and others could have been chosen without diminishing the force of the argument.

That brings us to the question of *culture*: how does Paul fit into the cultural patterns of his day? In the debate about biblical ethics, it is often assumed that the Bible and "culture" are diametrically opposed. But the fact is that the Bible reflects the cultural contexts of its writers just as much as we reflect our own—and with just the same range of dissonance and congruence that we find in contemporary debates. This means that in order to understand Paul, we have to take the time and trouble to understand him in his own context, to hear what he is saying in his own terms and not rush to assimilate him to the concepts of a very different world.

How was same-sex activity constructed in Paul's social world? Paul shares the moral perception of other Jewish writers of his day that homosexual practice was a specifically gentile vice, which was peculiarly abhorrent to Judaism. This perception may well go back to the Babylonian exile and to the need to preserve religious and ethnic purity for a people in exile; it is linked with the commendation of fertility in the creation narrative (Gen 1:28) and the prohibition of mixed marriages in Ezra (Ezra 9–10), where intermarriage both pollutes the holy race (Ezra 9:2) and offers an opening to the "abominations" of the peoples of the land (Ezra 9:11). The rejection of same-sex activity as a quintessentially "gentile" vice is a theme developed by post-biblical Jewish writers. Paul's language in Romans is strongly reminiscent of the words of the Wisdom of Solomon, tracing all the corruptions of gentile society (including its sexual corruption) to the basic sin of idolatry (Wis 14:22–27). Paul's anthropology of desire is shaped by his particular cultural location as a first-century Diaspora Jew living in a gentile world.[25]

Even in the Greco-Roman world, attitudes to homosexual behavior were more complex and ambivalent than we might think. Greek culture (as is well known) was much more tolerant of same-sex relationships than Jewish culture. The Platonic dialogues envisage a loving and formative relationship between the adolescent beloved (*erōmenos*), typically a young boy aged between eleven and seventeen, and the adult lover or *erastēs*, typically (though not solely) an adult male in his twenties. But these relationships were strongly controlled by cultural codes designed to protect the honor of both parties and ensure that they did not forfeit their status as elite males in a heterosexual society. The relationship was not equal: it was framed on the assumption that the older partner took the "active" (i.e., masculine) role and the younger the "passive" (i.e., feminine) role. It was not permanent: as the adolescent matured he was expected to graduate into the role of *erastēs* and seek out his own, younger *erōmenos*. And it was not exclusive: the adult elite male was expected, as a civic duty, to marry a woman of his own social class, to father children, and keep his wife safe at home. Same-sex relationships belonged not to this domestic, dynastic world, but to a parallel world of masculine sociality from which wives were excluded, where elite married men could continue to enjoy a variety of extra-marital social and sexual relationships, with concubines, slaves, and courtesans—and with boys.[26]

The Platonic dialogues belong to classical Athenian society, 400 years before Paul: how much they shaped everyday social reality in Paul's day is another question (this pattern of behavior was not universally accepted even within classical Greek society). Roman attitudes were much less

---

25. Nissinen, *Homoeroticism*, 89–102. See further Loader, *The New Testament on Sexuality*, together with Loader's more detailed studies of sexuality in his Eerdmans series on sexuality in ancient Jewish writings: in the Jesus Tradition (2005), in the LXX and Philo (2004), in the Pseudepigrapha (2011), and in the Dead Sea Scrolls (2009).

26. Nissinen, *Homoeroticism*, 57–88.

tolerant. The elite Roman male was expected to marry and bear children, but continued to enjoy a range of sexual relationships, within and without marriage. Adultery was a legal offence: that is, having a sexual relationship with a woman who belonged to another elite male. Sexual intercourse with social inferiors (male or female slaves, dependents, or prostitutes) did not count as adultery: many regarded it as a normal expression of adult male power, especially within the household. Musonius Rufus is making a conscious stand against accepted mores when he writes:

> So no-one with any self-control would think of having relations with a courtesan or a free woman apart from marriage, no, nor even with his own maid-servant, . . . a thing which some people consider quite without shame, since every master is held to have it in his power to use his slave as he wishes. In reply to this I have just one thing to say: if it seems neither shameful nor out of place for a master to have relations with his own slave, particularly if she happens to be unmarried, let him consider how he would like it if his wife had relations with a male slave.[27]

Conservative Roman morality frowned on same-sex relationships, especially for adult men who were regarded as taking a "passive" ("feminine") role that belonged to social inferiors.[28] Slaves and rent-boys (by implication) had no choice, but for a free adult male to take such a role was regarded as "unnatural": it was seriously damaging to his elite status.

These cultural patterns form the underlying framework of the Pauline same-sex texts. Starting from the fundamental perception that same-sex proclivity is a voluntary moral choice exercised by heterosexual people, ancient moralists saw it as an expression of violent and excessive sexual desire (*pathos*)—itself morally reprehensible, and frequently used as an expression of domination over social inferiors or subjugated enemies. It represented an "unnatural" confusion of gender roles, and thus a distortion of the social hierarchies built into marriage and household. Paul's distinction between "active" and "passive" partners in a same-sex relationship, and his distaste for the "effeminate" male, reflect the perceptions of Roman culture—as does his conviction that long hair on a man is "unnatural" (1 Cor 11:14). But Paul also takes over cultural perceptions from his Jewish environment, like the argument that sexual immorality is a result of idolatry. Even if Paul knew of the "Platonic" pattern from classical times, it would not offer a model of

---

27. Cited from Malherbe, *Moral Exhortation*, 153.

28. Musonius Rufus regards sexual relations of men with men as "contrary to nature," and "no more tolerable" than those involving adultery, which are "the most unlawful" sexual relations (ibid., 153).

faithful and stable same-sex relationships. Such relationships were inherently unequal, impermanent, and non-exclusive. They belonged to the shadow-world of extra-marital sexual relations, and (especially in the mercantile/artisan urban circles in which Paul moved), were most likely to occur with rent-boys or household slaves.

TOWARDS A CHRISTIAN SEXUAL ETHIC

Does this cultural embeddedness mean that we cannot use Paul's letters for the construction of a Christian sexual ethic? Far from it (*mē genoito*, as Paul would say). If we have come to understand homosexuality as a matter of sexual identity, rather than a free moral choice, that doesn't mean that it doesn't raise moral issues. Of course it does—just as heterosexuality does. All our sexuality raises moral issues, not because sex is intrinsically "bad," but because all sexuality is capable of being a vehicle for the most appalling abuse and degradation as well as for the most sublime altruism and grace. If we could stop using Paul's letters to fight our gender wars, we might be able to make much better use of them for constructing a genuinely Christian sexual ethic—something our confused generation desperately needs.

But in order to do that, we have to read the Bible *historically,* paying proper attention to the moral and cultural frameworks in which it was written; and we have to read it *dialogically,* paying proper attention to the way theological insight emerges out of the dialectic of experience and debate. And in that dialogue we shall want to pay especial attention to the points where Paul is *counter*-cultural: that is, where his wrestling with genuine moral dilemmas (issues concerning real people, not cardboard cut-outs) allows us to glimpse something of the genuinely new and enduring possibilities of living into God's kingdom.

Paul was not a systematic ethicist (or theologian for that matter). The closest we get to a sustained and coherent treatment of sexual ethics is in the long and complicated series of *responsa* to incidents and questions arising in the life of the Corinthian community that we find in chapters 5–7 of 1 Corinthians (a passage surprisingly little exploited in the current debates). What I find fascinating about this whole letter is that we can hear Paul thinking on his feet, forced by his own congregation—and the new situation in which they find themselves—to face up to a whole series of ethical issues and ask what it means to rethink them from a distinctively *Christian* perspective—a kingdom perspective formed by the mind of Christ. Paul's teaching reflects the double strand running through early Christian sexual ethics: what we might call the world-affirming and world-denying strands, this-worldly and other-worldly, Lincoln's "Now" and "Not Yet." 1 Corinthians 5–7 offers an extended reflection on "bad sex" and "good sex": how can Christians tell which forms of sexual activity are destructive and unholy and which are affirmative and consistent with the life of God's kingdom ("holy")? Paul is clearly seeking to mediate between two extremes: a "liberal" view that "anything goes" (6:12 "All things are lawful") and a restrictive view that Christians should abstain from sexual activity altogether (7:1 "It is well for a man not to touch a woman").

Sex and Marriage in the Gospels

Jesus' teaching affirms marriage as a God-given, creation institution (Mark 10:2–12). In a world where it was easy—at least for men—to obtain a divorce on relatively trivial grounds, Jesus affirms the importance of fidelity, commitment, and exclusivity in marriage (Matt 5:27–32). But Matthew's version of the saying allows an exception in the case of adultery (Matt 19:9); and the disciples' question already shows that this was regarded as an impossibly high ideal: "If such is the case of a man with his wife, it is not expedient to marry" (Matt 19:10). It looks as if Jesus' radical standards were already causing debate and revision within the church at the time when the Gospels were being written down.[29]

But marriage is not the only option for Jesus' followers. Jesus goes on to say that only "those to whom it is given" can receive his saying (Matt 19:11). Whatever we make of the puzzling saying about "eunuchs" (Matt 19:12), it seems to imply that there are those for whom heterosexual marriage is not an option, whether from birth, because of castration, or "for the sake of the kingdom."[30] For Jesus himself, the single lifestyle was probably a prophetic choice; he also downplays family ties (Mark 3:31–35), and insists that "marrying and giving in marriage" will not be part of the "new creation" in the world to come (Mark 12:24–25).[31]

---

29. For a full discussion, cf. Loader, *Sexuality and the Jesus Tradition*, chapters 1–2.

30. Nissinen, *Homoeroticism*, 120.

31. Osiek and Balch, *Families*, 123–43; Loader, *Sexuality and the Jesus Tradition*, ch. 3. Lindars provides a useful discussion of Jesus' celibacy in "The Bible and the Call," 228–45.

1 Corinthians 5–7: Good Sex, Bad Sex[32]

Like Jesus, Paul goes back to Gen 2:24 to provide a base for a Christian sexual ethic: "Do you not know that he who joins himself to a prostitute becomes one flesh with her?" (1 Cor 6:16). For Paul, the "one flesh" principle applies not only to marriage but to all sexual encounters—a radical (and profoundly counter-cultural) stance that decisively affirms the importance of the body ("the body is for the Lord"). On this view, there is no such thing as "casual sex." All sexual acts are significant: but their significance can be either destructive or affirmative. How can we tell which is which?

In this passage Paul deals with two examples of "bad sex" (*porneia*), i.e., sexual relations that compromise the holiness of the Christian community. Both of these, we should note, are heterosexual. The first is a case of abuse within the household: "a man is sleeping with his father's wife" (1 Cor 5:1). This is almost certainly not biological incest: in a culture where girls were married young, and many women died in childbirth, a young adult son could easily have a stepmother who was younger than himself. But in almost any culture this would be a "taboo" relationship, violating the trust on which the intimacy of family life depends (cf. 5:2). The other example is a sexual relationship with a prostitute (6:16)—commercial sex, sex without commitment, as common and everyday in Paul's world as it is today. Neither of these is a homosexual relationship: but (as we have observed), in Paul's world most same-sex relationships would fall under one or the other of these broad categories. Same-sex activity is not Paul's concern in this passage: it is mentioned only in passing as another example of *porneia*, "bad sex," i.e., abusive, exploitative, casual sexual activity (6:9).

Paul's real concern in these chapters—because it is a question raised by the Corinthians—is the question of marriage between a Christian and a non-Christian. Doesn't this also qualify as a case of "bad sex," violating the boundaries of the holy community? It seems clear that some Christians thought that way: that's why they were seeking to divorce their pagan spouses (7:12–16). This seems to be the thinking behind Ezra's prohibition on marriage to non-Jews in Ezra 9–10, which might have provided a precedent for the Corinthians. But Paul here springs a surprise: his concept of holiness is much more robust than Ezra's. In the case of a union between a Christian and a prostitute, the sexual act is unholy and has the potential to pollute the whole body of Christ (6:15–18). But where a Christian is married to

---

32. I have dealt with this passage in more detail in "Better to Marry," 235–56. Deming locates Paul's arguments within the context of the ancient *peri gamou* debate, with full citation of philosophical texts in *Paul on Marriage*.

a non-Christian, the sexual act is "holy" and has the capacity to sanctify (make holy) both the non-Christian partner and their children (7:14).

What has reversed the holiness force-field? What makes sex within marriage "good sex," even with a non-Christian partner? Paul is not (we must be clear) talking about a "Christian" marriage, celebrated in church and blessed by a Christian priest. No such marriages existed in Paul's day (or for several centuries afterwards). In any case, it is clear that these were marriages entered into before the conversion of one of the partners. They are "secular" marriages, following the civil laws of whatever community they belonged to—Jewish, Greek, or Roman.

Is it procreation that legitimizes the sexual act within marriage? Many of Paul's contemporaries thought so. Musonius Rufus and other Stoic philosophers held that even within marriage sexual activity should only be undertaken for the sake of begetting children—otherwise it was "unlawful": "Men who are not wantons or immoral are bound to consider sexual intercourse justified only when it occurs in marriage and is indulged in for the purpose of begetting children, since that is lawful, but unjust and unlawful when it is mere pleasure-seeking, even in marriage."[33] A similar view is upheld by Jewish thinkers such as Philo.[34] But Paul does not mention procreation anywhere in this chapter as an essential component of "good sex"—another counter-cultural move.

Nor (equally surprising) is it a matter of maintaining the hierarchies built into ancient concepts of marriage. This was (again) an important component in contemporary philosophical thinking about marriage. Elsewhere in the letter, Paul knows and accepts these hierarchies (though with a hint that "in the Lord" things might be different: 1 Cor 11:11–12).[35] But they are not evident in this passage. Unlike most ancient philosophers, Paul goes out of his way in this chapter to address both husbands and wives ("It reads

33. Cited from Malherbe, *Moral Exhortation*, 153. Cf. Ocellus Lucanus 44–45 (cited from Deming, *Paul on Marriage*, 230–31): "We have sexual intercourse not for the sake of pleasure, but the procreation of children. For, in fact, the reproductive powers themselves, and the sexual organs, and the yearnings that were given to human beings by God in order to bring on sexual intercourse happen not to have been given for the sake of pleasure, but the ever-lasting continuation of the race. . . . For those who have intercourse not at all for the sake of having children do [no] justice to the most revered systems of partnership. And if, in fact, such persons as these give birth, by means of wantonness and lack of self-control, then those born will be wretched and pitiful, and loathsome in the sight of gods, and divine beings, and men, and households, and city-states."

34. Nissinen, *Homoeroticism*, 95–96.

35. For the "household codes" in the later Paulines, see Andrew Lincoln's lengthy treatment of Ephesians 5:21–33 in Lincoln, *Ephesians*.

like he's swallowed a manual on political correctness," as one of my students once remarked in disgust). For the ancient philosophers, the question "Should the wise man marry?" is addressed solely to men: women had little choice, and were not treated as moral subjects.[36] In contrast, a careful reading of 1 Cor 7 makes it clear that Paul's concept of "one flesh" is inherently reciprocal, both in the studied and careful mutuality of his language, and in the priority he gives to "pleasing" the other (not the self! 7:4, 33–34). Rowan Williams highlights this "remarkable passage" where Paul speaks of "mutual rights and mutual belonging: neither partner owns or governs their own body, but makes it over to the other, a very startling idea indeed in Paul's culture."[37] *The Message* brings out this reciprocity very well in 7:3–4: "The marriage bed must be a place of mutuality—the husband seeking to satisfy his wife, the wife seeking to satisfy her husband. Marriage is not a place to 'stand up for your rights.' Marriage is a decision to serve the other, whether in bed or out."[38] So (in sum) for Paul, "good sex" is a physical act of mutual respect and self-giving love set within a faithful, committed, stable relationship recognized by the law of the land.

Alternative Lifestyles: Singleness, Celibacy, and Divorce

Nevertheless, Paul's attitude to marriage in 1 Cor 7 is ambivalent to say the least (much more ambivalent than the highly selective readings of the *Pilling Report* allow). Marriage is good—but it is not the only option. Paul's preferred sexual option is celibacy. It is too easy to dismiss this as a purely pragmatic response to "the present necessity" (7:26). Celibacy also fits with Paul's apocalyptic worldview of adopting the lifestyle of the age to come (a worldview he shared with Jesus).[39] And it was celibacy, not marriage, that became the distinctive lifestyle option of early Christianity, and gave young Christians (especially young Christian women) a platform to exercise their refusal to be conformed to the world.[40]

---

36. For the *peri gamou* topos, cf. Alexander, "Better to Marry," 240–50; Deming, *Paul on Marriage*, ch. 2. The question was typically posed in the form, "When ought *a man* to marry?" (Diogenes Laertius VI.6); or, "Should the wise *man* marry and bear children?" (Diogenes Laertius X.119; Seneca, *Letters* 116.5).

37. R. Williams, "Sexual Ethic," 165.

38. Peterson, *The Message*, 346.

39. Loader, *Sexuality and the Jesus Tradition*, 185.

40. The classic study is Brown, *The Body and Society*. For patristic exegesis of 1 Cor 7 "as an inspiration [for] ascetic practice," cf. Kovacs, "Servant"; Hunter, "Reclaiming Biblical Morality."

Nevertheless, Paul recognizes that celibacy is not a practical option for everyone, and states clearly that it is not to be imposed on those who have not the gift for it (7:7)—a point to be remembered by those who would impose lifelong celibacy on same-sex couples. It is better that sexual desire should be "quenched" (i.e., satisfied) in marriage than left to "burn" as unrequited passion (7:9).[41] For Paul, therefore, marriage itself could be seen as a kind of pastoral accommodation to human sexual needs. It is not the ideal ("I would that all were as I am")—but it is not a sin (7:28, 36: "Let them marry—it is no sin").

Paul shows a similar readiness to make pastoral accommodations in allowing the possibility of divorce in certain cases, even though he knows it was forbidden by the Lord (7:10–11). Divorce was relatively straightforward in many Greek and Roman civil codes. The statement that "the brother or sister is not bound" (7:15) is an implicit ruling that they are legally free to remarry, just as a wife is free to remarry if her husband dies (7:39)—even though Paul's personal opinion is that "she is happier if she remains as she is" (7:40).[42] Finally, we should also note that Paul valorizes singleness in both men and women (again, a deeply counter-cultural stance: 7:32–35). The possibility of a meaningful life as a single woman was almost unheard-of in ancient society.

WHAT ARE THE PASTORAL CONSEQUENCES FOR THE CHURCH TODAY?

How does this biblical material help us to resolve the questions posed by the *Pilling Report*? First of all, we have to recognize the ambiguity of the biblical material—and its embeddedness in its own social context. *All* Scripture is contextual (not just the bits we don't like).[43] Within the church, it is also accepted as the word of God—but we have to use our God-given powers of discernment ("reason") to interpret what it means for our own context. That hermeneutical activity is common to all readers of the Bible—not just the "liberal" side of the debate.

In the *Pilling Report*, both sides affirm their commitment to resisting homophobia and welcoming "LGBTI" people into the church. This implies that both sides are working with a construction of sexuality that is radically different from that of Paul and the biblical world. Where they differ is in the

---

41. Alexander, "Better to Marry," 253.

42. Note that this viewpoint is reversed in the Pastorals, where widows are positively encouraged to re-marry (1 Tim 5:14).

43. Alexander, "God's Frozen Word," 241.

practical conclusions they draw from that disjunction for Christian sexual ethics today. For the conservative viewpoint represented by the dissenting report, the consequence is a distinction between "homosexual orientation" (a modern construction which Paul does not condemn as such) and homosexual practice (which Paul does condemn). Therefore (it is argued) the mere fact of experiencing same-sex desire is not morally culpable: but those who experience it must abstain from homosexual practice.

This sounds clear and logical—but is it? It overlooks the fact that the Bible is not a culture-free zone. Ethics and anthropology are inextricably linked. Paul's ethical condemnation of homosexual acts is a logical consequence of his anthropology of desire, his construction of sexuality—and that construction is derived from his own first-century cultural world. Sever the connection, and the moral condemnation is left without foundation. How can it be right to construct a sexual ethic for people of homosexual orientation today based on an anthropology of desire that does not recognize such orientation? It would be like basing our medical treatment of epilepsy on the Gospel story of the epileptic child in Mark 9:17–27, a description belonging to a cultural world in which epilepsy was understood as a form of demon-possession—a first-century medical diagnosis that, if taken at face value today, would be deeply damaging to people who suffer from epilepsy.

What we need is a sexual ethic for people of homosexual orientation that starts from the same premise as our rejection of homophobia: that is, from the recognition (shared by both sides in the Pilling debate) that sexual orientation is neither immoral nor defective *per se*, but a "given" of sexual identity. We can acknowledge that homosexual relationships (like all sexual relationships) have enormous potential for good or ill. Many examples of homosexual practice (then and now) fall under Paul's concept of "bad sex," *porneia:* but then, so do many examples of heterosexual practice. We need to disentangle the *ethics* of sexuality from the question of *sexual identity* or "who you sleep with" (as Paul begins to do in 1 Cor 7). The question then is, what should be our response to a homosexual relationship that corresponds in all other respects to the pattern of "good sex" that Paul sets out in 1 Cor 7—that is, a permanent, faithful, stable relationship that is legally sanctioned by the law of the land? Can we construct a biblically based theology that would allow LGBTI people to engage in committed sexual relationships and to find in them a source of grace?

Cranmer's 1549 marriage service (followed by the 1662 *Book of Common Prayer*) sets out three "causes for which matrimony was ordained": the procreation of children, "a remedy against sin," and "the mutual society, help and comfort that the one ought to have of the other."[44] In placing the procreation of children first, Cranmer is following what had become the established view of marriage among Christian theologians, following Augustine.[45] As we have seen, this was the standard view among ancient philosophers. The linkage between marriage and procreation is certainly an element of Gen 2:24—it is part of the cultural framework of this ancient story. Indeed, marriage was always inextricably linked with procreation until the arrival of easy and effective contraception in the 1960s (another twentieth-century cultural shift that has radically affected all our construction of sexuality). Nevertheless, the imperative to procreate has never been quite as central in Christian marriage as in traditional Jewish society (where a wife's failure to conceive is still a legitimate cause for divorce): and it is conspicuously absent in Paul's definition of "good sex" in 1 Cor 7.

Cranmer's second cause picks up on the fact that for Paul, marriage itself can be seen as a form of "pastoral accommodation" for those unable to endure the rigors of the celibate life. Paul's "Better to marry than to burn"—i.e., to be tormented with unrequited passion—is the direct precursor of Cranmer's view of marriage as a "remedy for sin." Unfashionable as it is, there is a practical pastoral insight here that has a very obvious relevance to the pre-1980s gay scene, where the lack of recognition made it impossible to create stable relationships.

Cranmer's third cause ("for the mutual society, help, and comfort that the one ought to have of the other") picks up on the counter-cultural assumptions of the Genesis creation story ("It is not good for man to be alone"). For the writer of Genesis, marriage entails both an act of separation ("leaving") and an act of commitment ("cleaving") that creates a new biological unit ("one flesh") that is at the same time a new covenant, a new space for companionship with God. It is easy to forget how counter-cultural this conception of the dynamics of the marriage relationship is in the ancient Mediterranean world, where it was normal for the woman (rather than the man) to "leave" her parents' home and move in with her husband's family. This "cleaving" (as we have seen) is the aspect of the Genesis text that both Jesus and Paul focus on: it is this mutual trust and commitment that creates the definitive framework for "good sex." For Rowan Williams, the combination of fidelity, commitment, and mutuality opens up the possibility for a

---

44. For the texts, see Cummings, *The Book of Common Prayer*, 64, 434–35. The Swiss reformer Martin Bucer comments, "and I should prefer what is placed third among the causes for marriage might be in the first place, because it is first": cited from *To Set Our Hope on Christ*, §2.27.

45. Though Augustine's adoption of this view is later and more circumspect than we might expect: Hunter, "Reclaiming Biblical Morality."

sexual relationship to be *sacramental*: "God's surrender to us in the weakness and nakedness of Christ, especially Christ crucified, is what generates in us the courage to put ourselves into God's hands. What God has done for our life and joy, we learn to do for God's joy, the joy there is in heaven over the return of the lost. A sexual relationship that lives from this gift and joy is properly 'sacramental.'"[46]

This perspective is echoed in an earlier statement of the House of Bishops:

> A true marriage reflects Christ's own love for us all. He too gave himself to others, "for better, for worse, till death." In it we learn to break down our pride and self-concern, to be open to our partner as he or she really is, to treasure what is good, and forgive faults, to be loyal, whatever the price.... A good marriage creates for each partner the same kind of environment which we recognize as promoting growth to maturity in the case of children: a combination of love and challenge within an unbreakably reliable relationship.[47]

Given the recognition of LGBTI orientation implicit in the *Pilling Report* (and in agreed statements already issued by the Church of England), it seems perverse to deny these benefits to those same-sex couples who aspire to live a life of fidelity, mutuality, and commitment. Where LGBTI couples *want* to reach out to this recognizably Christian ideal, why should the church deny them?

---

46. R. Williams, "Sexual Ethic," 165.
47. John, *Permanent, Faithful, Stable*, 30–31.

18

Spirituality, Ethics, and Memory

JOHN GOLDINGAY
Fuller Theological Srminary

REMEMBERING IS OF KEY importance to spiritual and ethical life. In a class on Old Testament Ethics, one of my students commented that there did not seem to be much written about the link between ethics and memory. He rightly implied that there surely was a link, not least because both Old and New Testaments make one. The dearth of books that look directly at the question[1] seems especially odd given the way memory has become a topic of interest in a wide range of disciplines over recent decades.

Whereas what set me thinking, then, was the question of the connection between memory and ethics, I soon realized that Scripture relates memory at least as much to spirituality. Admittedly, neither ethics nor spirituality is a category that the Bible itself uses, any more than is theology. These categories came out of Western thinking, rather than biblical thinking. That fact does not make it illegitimate to work with them; when Europeans in the centuries after biblical times thought about biblical faith, it was not wrong for them to seek to understand its questions in their categories. But that translation has its dangers, and categories such as ethics, spirituality, and theology are inclined to conceptualize things and divide things up in a way that loses aspects of the way biblical thinking works and holds things

---

1. One exception is Margalit, *The Ethics of Memory*.

together. In Scripture, spirituality and ethics are both aspects of relating to God, to one another, and to life. One cannot think about spirituality without thinking about ethics; or about ethics without thinking about spirituality. And in the twenty-first century in the West, it is particularly important not to let spirituality and ethics be separate.

In this paper I note four aspects of the relationship between spirituality, ethics, and memory—four things to be remembered.

REMEMBERING THE STORY ON WHICH THE FAITH IS BASED

First, spirituality involves remembering the story on which the faith is based. The Hebrew word זכר (*zākar*) has a broader meaning than the English verb "remember," its common translation. In Hebrew one can "remember" a future event (for instance, Isa 47:7; Lam 1:9), because זכר means something more like "be mindful of" or "think about." The Old Testament thus sees remembering as a deliberate business; and spirituality and ethics are mindful acts. Paul declares that people are transformed by the renewing of their minds (Rom 12:1–2), and that point in his argument in Romans illustrates how it is so. "I urge you therefore, brothers and sisters, by the mercies of God, to present your bodies as a sacrifice, living, holy, and acceptable to God," he says.[2] He has spent eleven chapters expounding the operation of God's mercies, and now says, "Therefore," implying that the application of the mind to the argument of these eleven chapters is the way to spiritual well-being. The renewing of the mind is the key to transformation. The Romans are not to make the mistake Ezekiel draws attention to, when Israel did not remember the sad state it was in when Yahweh took up with it (Ezek 16:22, 43).

In connection with applying the mind to the past, considering the use of the actual verb "remember" is instructive, but focusing on how a text uses an individual word often does not get to the heart of a subject. The first indicator that remembering is an important biblical theme is the fact that Scripture is dominated by the story of what God did with Israel over the centuries and what God did in Jesus and in the early church. Neither Genesis nor Matthew begins, "Remember this story," but it is the implication of their telling their story, and of the Jewish and Christian communities' letting these stories dominate their Scriptures.

So the Scriptures tell the story on which the faith is based, but they do so a way that writes into it the story's significance for the people who tell

---

2. Translations here and elsewhere in this paper are my own.

it and listen to it. "Memory is the place where faith resides; consequently, memory is related to the present."[3] I recently heard two Christian singer songwriters playing in an ordinary Hollywood club. One of them had made a song out of the story of Jesus' stilling the storm, but the song simply paraphrased the story, without making any point of contact with twenty-first-century California. The other singer introduced her song by telling us that her aim was to give people hope, but she made no reference to the fact that Jesus is the reason for hope. It seemed to me that expressing the gospel in song required bringing together the strength of retelling with the strength of contemporary linkage—not just retelling, and not just contemporary application, but the two combined. Both "the work of memory and the work of hope" are aspects of "the two-sided hermeneutical process in the history of a person's life."[4]

Such is the nature of memory as the Scriptures understand it, to judge from the way they tell their story. In the Old Testament, the clearest example comes in the books of Samuel and Kings, on one hand, and the books of Chronicles, on the other. Both tell Israel's story from Saul and David to the fall of Jerusalem, but they tell different stories because they envisage audiences in different situations. Samuel and Kings tell the story for the people who experienced the destruction of Jerusalem and the exile of many of its people, and tell it in such a way as to draw their audience into acknowledging that these events had happened because people had turned away from Yahweh. Chronicles is a new version of the story, written in the time when God has made it possible for the people to rebuild the temple but when life is still discouraging, so it tells the story in such a way as to encourage its audience. In both versions, there is memory and there is also insight on how the story of the past relates to where people are now in their relationship with God.

Something similar is true about the Gospels. They are concerned with passing on what Christ was and taught, but they pass on this story in different ways that show the significance of Jesus for different audiences. Mark puts the emphasis on how God's reign arrived in Jesus. Matthew makes Jesus Act II to the Old Testament's Act I and has Jesus interpreting Torah. Luke makes Jesus Act I to an Act II in the church's life. John presupposes the way the Holy Spirit interprets Jesus in the life of the church.

> [T]he words and deeds of Jesus ... transmitted to us depend upon and involve the active role of people who heard and witnessed Jesus. More than that, however, what was remembered

---

3. Gutiérrez, *The God of Life*, 5.
4. Moltmann, *The Church in the Power of the Spirit*, 281.

was remembered because it was significant for the people who remembered it.... "What lives on in memory is what is necessary for present life."[5]

The study of theology can drive people into something like the first songwriter's manner, into investigating the past story of Jesus but not getting to what it means to people's lives in their own context. They may then live their life on a wholly other basis, on the basis of the natural instincts of someone in the United States in the third millennium. They then end up in the same place as the other songwriter, who was good at relating to the lives of her contemporaries but did not investigate how the story of Jesus connected with those lives. It is easy for spirituality then to conform to a culture. For instance, it is often noted that Westerners tend to be concerned with themselves as individuals and with a desire to look inside themselves, and to make spirituality conform to those interests. The application of memory to the story on which the faith is based has the capacity to rescue people from the limitations of their context.

If people are to live in hope, as the second songwriter wanted them to do, and to act in the conviction that they may achieve something, may "make a difference," then remembering is again of foundational importance. Richard Horsley comments about the context of Jesus' ministry, that

> ... the memory of God's promises of blessings to the people, particularly of the great divine acts of deliverance from foreign bondage and domestic exploitation and of their earlier independence in their own land, informed the apocalyptic imagination.[6]

That is, memory formed people's vision of the way God's purpose could turn things upside down. Remembering what God had done for Israel in the past enabled them to have a vision for the future, because

> ... if life had not always been lived in subjection, then it need not remain in subjection for ever.... In placing the then-current situation in historical perspective the apocalyptic imagination ... also involved a *critical demystifying* of the pretensions and practices of the established order. Emperors were not divine, and high priests were not sacrosanct.[7]

Remembering how God defeated Egypt and Babylon reminded them that God could defeat Rome. Passover brought that fact home each year.

5. Horsley, *Jesus and the Spiral of Violence*, 165, quoting Kelber, *The Oral and Written Gospel*, 15.
6. Horsley, *Jesus and the Spiral of Violence*, 143–44.
7. Ibid., 144.

Many peoples' festivals "functioned mainly to integrate human life into the sacred annual natural cycle"; one may consider the festivals of New Year, the Superbowl, Valentine's Day, Spring Break, Mother's Day, Memorial Day, Independence Day, Labor Day, Halloween, and Thanksgiving. In contrast, Horsley continues,

> ... the Jewish Passover celebrated the people's historical liberation.... Thus the memory informing the people's fantasy of new liberation came face-to-face with the very imperial order from which they hoped for deliverance.[8]

For the church, the equivalent is observing Advent Sunday, Christmas, Epiphany, Ash Wednesday, Maundy Thursday, Good Friday, Easter Day, Ascension Day, and Pentecost.

In Jesus' time, people were under the oppression of the power of Rome and also of their own religious establishment. How could they know whether there was any escape from that bondage? They could know because they used their community memory of what God had done with them in the past. It was the corporate memory preserved in the Scriptures that told them how they had not always been a subject people and thus opened up the possibility that they might not always be in subjection. But it was not only the Scriptures that told them; the Passover story, for example, was brought home to them in the celebration each year. Remembering is not just something that happens in the mind. "Do this in remembrance of me," Jesus said at his last dinner with his disciples, when they celebrated Passover. Memory involves doing as well as thinking. Worshipers celebrate the Eucharist so that it becomes part of them—it involves eating, drinking, and moving, as well as thinking. The outward expression of coming to belong to Christ is baptism, and that event brings home the memory of Christ's baptism in water and the baptism involved in his dying.

The Israelites had other *aides-mémoire*. They wore garments that had tassels with purple cords to help them remember Yahweh's commands, to stay faithful to Yahweh, and thus to give themselves to holiness (Num 15:37–40). One aspect of these garments' significance lay in the tassels' purple color, which reminded Israelites of their royal status as a people. Another lay in the garments' combining wool and linen, which was generally forbidden in the Torah but was allowed in some priestly garments, so that these garments reminded Israelites of their priestly status as a people.[9] Christian faith has analogous *aides-mémoire* such as the sign of the cross,

---

8. Ibid., 143–44.
9. So Milgrom, *Numbers*, 401–14.

the distribution and the later burning of palm crosses, and the washing of feet, as well as baptism and Eucharist. They turn remembering the story on which the faith is based into an aspect of bodily life.

REMEMBERING GOD'S PREVIOUS ACTS

Spirituality and ethics also require people to remember the way God has related to them personally in the past.

To take an illustration from a movie, *Fair Game* is about a C.I.A. agent and her ex-ambassador husband who accidentally get involved in exposing the untruths about the intelligence concerning weapons of mass destruction on which the invasion of Iraq was based. Here, as often in thrillers, the central character has everyone against her: people in the White House, her former colleagues in the C.I.A., the reporters camping on her doorstep, the people who send her death threats, the friends to whom she cannot explain things, the husband from whom she splits for a while. Unlike many other thrillers, however, this particular movie was "based on true events," rather than being pure fiction. Now to say a story is "inspired by true events" also implies that it is not pure history, so one cannot press the story's details. But the claim to some form of historical actuality brings home that a sense of persecution can be very real, as the psalmists also knew.

Many of the psalms are written for people who have everyone against them and who are seeking to cope with that experience before God. One of the coping mechanisms they presuppose is that one can remind oneself, and God, and any listeners, of the truths about God that can slip from the mind in a crisis. One recalls God's power and faithfulness, the way God listens to prayers, and the way God acts. But are those convictions about God simply fancies that someone thought up? Memory is one of the bases to which those psalms then appeal—not only remembering the story on which the faith is based, but also the memory of personal past experience. Crises can make people forget everything that has gone before, and the Psalms know the importance of being mindful of what God has previously done with the people who are praying. "I remember the days of old" (Ps 143:5), the occasions when God acted on our behalf, and this remembering encourages prayer now. Psalms retell the story of such acts, and imply that people need to shape their thinking more by the story and less by what has happened to them just now.

The point emerges in the first psalm in the book of Psalms that is actually a prayer. Psalm 3 starts by telling God how many people are attacking the psalmist. It talks about the way people are saying to one another, "God is not going to rescue *him*." Psalms like this can have the effect of expressing what the psalmist, or the reader, may actually be thinking, and this brings them into an argument with themselves. While the psalm does affirm some key truths about God's being a shield and someone who lifts one's head high, the fact that it goes on to talk about how things have been in the past, in the person's own experience, implies an unease about whether these statements are true.

> With my voice I would call to Yahweh,
>   and he has answered me from his holy mountain.
> I myself have lain down and slept;
>   I have woken up, because Yahweh sustains me.
> So I'm not afraid of a company of myriads
>   that has taken its stand against me all around.

The person praying has been through crises before; the psalm looks like a prayer for the king to pray, or for a leader like Nehemiah, and it is easy to see how that would be true for such a person. So the psalm gets him to recall how he has known in the past what it's like to call out and have God respond. He has had the experience of going to bed not knowing whether he may get killed in the night, but then waking up in the morning alive and well. He goes on to remember how he has not had to smash his enemies on the jaw; he has been able to watch God do so. He can turn the other cheek. He can pray for God's deliverance with confidence.

It has been said that no biblical command is as persistent as the command to "remember,"[10] and though this is overstated, it is not greatly so. My wife, Kathleen (who has contributed in various ways to this paper), reminds me that actually the most common command in Scripture is, "Do not be afraid." There is, indeed, a link between these two commands. The person who remembers the wrong things, who remembers how much the enemy has achieved, and forgets what God has done before, may be the person who is afraid. The person who remembers the right things may be the person who can overcome fear. Faced by the Canaanites, Moses tells the Israelites to remember what God did to the Egyptians (Deut 7:18). In the wilderness, they had failed to remember the wonders God had done, and had resolved to return to Egypt (Neh 9:17; compare Pss 78:42; 106:7). Failing to remember imperiled their vocation as God's people. They needed to remember God as the one who had acted in their lives, and thus to safeguard against turning to other deities (Judg 8:33–34); but they failed so to remember. There are other forms of misguided remembering of the past. In the wilderness they did remember the fish and the leeks, onions, and garlic that they had in Egypt

---

10. Wiesel, *Kingdom of Memory*, 9, as quoted by Volf, *Exclusion and Embrace*, 235.

(Num 11:5); this shows they knew about cooking, but it meant they were remembering their time in Egypt in selective fashion. "Remember that I am your own flesh and blood," says Abimelek when he is planning a coup and trying to hijack people's memories to his own ends (Judg 9:2).

So it is important not merely to remember things, but to remember selectively. Many therapists encourage people to relive their memories, and such reliving can indeed be a means of healing. Yet a continual reliving of past memories can be a means of prolonging trauma rather than moving beyond it. It's said that depression comes from living too much in the past, while anxiety comes from living too much in the future, but maybe the aphorism requires reformulation. Depression comes from living in the wrong aspects of the past, anxiety comes from living in the wrong aspects of the future, or from living in the future in a way that ignores certain kinds of fact about the present and the past.

Memory is always selective. The song *The Way We Were*[11] looks back on a relationship and talks about memories as misty watercolors, scattered images. Was it all so simple then, as it seems when you think about it, the song asks, "or has time rewritten every line?" In Jer 2:2, God remembers how things were at a more idyllic stage in the relationship between God and Israel, when they were first married: "I remember the commitment of your youth," God says. That remembering is an example of the kind that is selective; "a history of [one's] emotions tends to become revisionist history."[12] Evidently even God's memory is selective, because sometimes God's recall of the early days of the relationship with Israel makes for a more aggressive memory than the one just noted. Memories may be beautiful, the lyric of that song says, but "What's too painful to remember we simply choose to forget." We'll choose to remember the laughter, not the tears, when we remember "the way we were." The challenge is to train the memory to be selective in a wholesome way. An alcoholic told me that alcoholics are inclined to remember the good things about drinking, and they have to be trained to remember the bad things.

That selectivity is complicated. In Isa 46 God tells the Israelites, "Remember the former events, long ago, because I am God, there is no other" (Isa 46:9). Fifty years previously, God had abandoned Jerusalem and let the Babylonians destroy the city, and some of the survivors of that event and their descendants are still living in Judah, while some are living in Babylon. But a turning-point in history is now here. The army of Cyrus, the king

---

11. Written by Alan Bergman, Marilyn Bergman, and Marvin Hamlisch, and performed in the movie *The Way We Were* by Barbra Streisand.
12. Margalit, *The Ethics of Memory*, 110, 111.

of Persia, is about to conquer Babylon. For the average Babylonian this is threatening news, and it is hard for Judahites to see it as good news, still less to believe that it might be God's way of bringing about a new era in which God will return to Jerusalem and free them to go back, a new era in which the temple will be rebuilt. They need to have their faith built up so that they can believe that such an event might be possible. For the prophet, one of the keys to that upbuilding is memory. There are events in their past that establish that Yahweh is God, and that there is no other, and therefore that God can be and is behind the political events taking place now. The prophecy is not explicit about which earlier events God wants them to think about. Maybe it refers to the wonders of God's creation of the world—elsewhere it does refer to these events. Or maybe the earlier events are God's delivering the Israelites from Egypt and rescuing them at the Reed Sea. Or maybe they are other wonders in Israel's history. Perhaps it is not necessary to choose. The point is that the people's past provides evidence that Yahweh is God, and that looking to what God has done in their past as a people is key to faith in the present.

That point might seem clear. The trouble is that Isa 43 has already bidden people,

> Do not remember the former events,
> Do not think about earlier events.
> There: I am doing something new. (Isa 43:18–19).

Memory can hold people back, discourage them from expecting God to do something new, or disable them from recognizing something new when God does it.

If the earlier events in their story as a people that the prophecy has in mind are God's delivering them from Egypt and rescuing them at the Reed Sea, it is shocking to tell them to forget about these events. It's almost like a preacher telling people to forget about Jesus' resurrection. But maybe the preacher might do so to get them to focus on the fact that Jesus is coming again. The prophet might tell people to forget about God's delivering people from Egypt centuries ago, in order to get them to focus on the new act of deliverance that God intends to do, in freeing them from the power of Babylon. People can fail to focus enough on what God has done for them before, or they can focus on it in such a way that they cannot imagine God acting now.

There are other senses in which the prophet might want people to forget earlier events. The earlier events might be the first stages of Cyrus' creating his empire, so that the prophecy is saying to the Israelites, "You ain't seen nothin' yet." Or maybe it is going behind that event to that time fifty years previously when God had abandoned Jerusalem and let the Babylonians destroy the city. It would not be surprising if many Judahites could not imagine God returning and the temple being rebuilt. Jerusalem remembers the precious things she once had (Lam 1:7); she cannot imagine a future. In that kind of connection, the prophet says, "Do not think about the past." Whether it is the distant past or the recent past, God's acts of blessing or God's acts of destruction, people are not to let the past limit what they can believe could happen in the future.

REMEMBERING THE OBLIGATIONS THAT THE PAST IMPOSES

While remembering what God has done for us is thus of key importance to our looking to the future, it is also of key importance to our living a good life, a holy life. Human relationships involve remembering one another. Joseph challenges his fellow prisoner to remember him when he gets released, but he fails to do so (Gen 40:14, 23). Abigail urges David to remember her when God has fulfilled his good purpose for him (1 Sam 25:31). Joash fails to remember Jehoiada's commitment and kills his son (2 Chr 24:22). The wicked person does not remember to act with commitment to other people (Ps 109:16). Edom did not remember the covenant of brotherhood (Amos 1:9). People who want to be holy have to cultivate their memory.

In this connection, while there is something to be said for forgetting the sufferings of the past, there is something to be said for remembering them, too. Israelites are urged to remember their past suffering. They are to remember that they were servants in Egypt, so as to be able to take this experience into account in the way they treat their servants and other needy people (Deut 5:12–15; 15:15; 16:12; 24:18, 22). They are to remember the long way Yahweh led them on their forty-year journey through the wilderness to test them, teach them, and discipline them (Deut 8:2–6). They are to remember how Yahweh provided for them through the wilderness, so that they still look to Yahweh as provider and do not think they can look after themselves or look to other gods (Deut 8:11–20).

The same issue arises when Isa 58 talks about loosing faithless chains, untying the cords of the yoke, letting the broken go free, and smashing yokes (Isa 58:6). God has acted in this way for the community in liberating it from Babylon. But what is Judah doing now? Instead of modeling and thus perhaps facilitating that liberation for other peoples, it does not even embody it in its own life. People fail to recognize how their behavior contrasts with the way Yahweh had treated the community in releasing it from bondage to Babylon. There needs to be a connection between the experience of such acts of deliverance and the lives people then live. "As people who had an experience and a memory of 'the yoke' of exile themselves and who, further, had felt that yoke broken by God in their release from captivity, they should have been the people committed to maintaining and extending the freedom of others, especially the freedom of their neighbors."[13] But they are not. There is a parallel at Corinth, where people are supposed to be remembering the Lord at their communal meal, but their celebration rather too closely follows social convention in the ways in which the richer and poorer people take part, which suggests they are not remembering at all.

As there is something to be said for forgetting the suffering of the past but also something to be said for remembering it, so it is with the shame of the past. Isaiah 54 exhorts people,

> Do not be afraid, because you will not be shamed;
>   Do not be humiliated, because you will not be disgraced.
> Because you will forget the shame of your youth,
>   and the reproach of your widowhood you will not remember any more.
> Because your maker is your lord. (Isa 54:4–5)

The prophecy looks back to the time to when Jerusalem was young. As a people, Israel was young in the time of Moses and in the subsequent century or two, a period when Israel was often unfaithful to God and paid for it. But the prophecy is addressing Jerusalem, so perhaps it is referring especially to the time when it was young, the time of the kings, which was also a period of recurrent unfaithfulness and of invasion and defeat—so a time of shame for the unfaithfulness and for the humiliation. The prophet then refers to the time of Jerusalem's widowhood, the time when Yahweh divorced the city, walked out on it because of that unfaithfulness, and let it be destroyed. You can forget all that now, the prophet says. It is not going to be like that anymore.

So there is something to be said for forgetting the sin and the shame. But there is also something to be said for remembering them. "Remember how you provoked God in the wilderness," Moses urges the Israelites (Deut 9:7). In response to Yahweh's remembering, Israel is to remember its wrongdoing and feel the shame of it (Ezek 16:63; compare 20:43; 36:31). "It is hard to remember a past humiliation without reliving it,"[14] which can be a

---

13. Gray, *Rhetoric and Social Justice in Isaiah*, 77.
14. Margalit, *The Ethics of Memory*, 120.

good thing. The memory of shame for wrong actions can have the effect of restraining from further such actions.

The obligation of memory extends to people who are themselves past. After my death I would quite like to be remembered; to remember me will be an act of love. After my first wife died, I wrote a memoir about her, which I called *Remembering Ann*,[15] partly because I thought the significant ministry she had exercised deserved to be remembered—for her sake, and for the sake of people who might be blessed by reading her story. Hebrews 11 speaks of Abel as someone who was dead, but still speaks; and it had been observed to me that the same was true of Ann.

Avishai Margalit opens his book on the ethics of memory with an anecdote about the outrage expressed at an army commander who had forgotten the name of one of his soldiers who had been killed. To forget the name is to forget the person. It is not to care.[16] The Jewish or Armenian community's commitment to keeping alive the memory of their destroyed past communities is an act of love. It denies the destroyers the fulfillment of their aim. Further, whereas it might be thought that these two communities should now put out of mind the genocide of their people in the first half of the last century, it is noteworthy that the two communities are prominently active in supporting anti-genocide activists in the present century, such as people seeking to make known the needs of the people of Darfur. Another link between memory and ethics emerges.

Remember the Amalekites' wrongdoing, Moses tells Israel (Deut 25:17). Admittedly, preserving the memory of the people who were destroyed also preserves the memory of the destroyer; but the first is an act of love, the second an act of judgment. Maybe remembering also reduces the possibility of a repetition of the event, though it is less clear whether this is so when you are remembering someone else's wrongdoing than when you are remembering your own. Further, such an argument turns the remembering into a utilitarian act, as happens when people argue for capital punishment on the basis of its being a deterrent to murder or other serious crimes. If there is an argument for capital punishment, it is not that it is a deterrent, but that it punishes the person who has acted, honors the victim of the action, and honors the values and standards of the offender's society.

There is a biblical concern with blotting out people's name and also a concern with causing the name to be remembered (for instance, Deut 29:20; 1 Sam 24:21; 2 Sam 18:18). It suggests that there can be two stages to an act of murder: the destruction of the person and then the destruction of the

---

15. Goldingay, *Remembering Ann*.
16. Margalit, *The Ethics of Memory*, vii, 18–19.

name. The Jerusalem Holocaust memorial is called Yad Vashem, A Monument and a Name (the phrase comes from Isa 56:5), because it seeks to ensure a remembering of the names of the victims, and thus of the people themselves. Yet there is something in the phrase "forgive and forget." Individuals who spend years seeking to recover their lost memories of the past may find healing in doing so, but may not. I have noted that people who keep reliving traumas from the past may perpetuate their trauma rather than escaping it. It is sometimes said that awareness of the Holocaust holds back the state of Israel in its relationships in the Middle East, rather than protecting it, and that for some people, at least, South Africa's Truth and Reconciliation Commission may be based on a false premise, in that for them its proceedings prolong the memory of the horror of the past that people were trying to forget.

These examples show how remembering is not merely individual. My mostly African American congregation was founded nearly a century ago as a result of the first great migration of African Americans out of the South, which mostly took people to northern cities, but also brought them to California. Some sought to join three Episcopal churches in the Los Angeles area, but were rebuffed one way or another, and in our city, the members of the big Episcopal parish arranged for the building of a small Episcopal church in the part of town where African Americans had settled, so that the white people in the church could send their black servants there. Hardly anyone now alive is old enough to have been involved in those events, but they are part of the collective memory, the shared memory of Episcopalians in our city and in our diocese, and in 2011 we had a service of repentance in our cathedral center for the way we had behaved in relation to the African American community. Although I was not born when this story began and I have lived in Los Angeles for only seventeen years, I am part of the white "we" that needed to remember and repent, as well as part of the African American community that remembers because I am the priest in charge of the parish. I have a similar memory of growing up in a British city in the 1950s, when people from the Caribbean were immigrating into Britain with our encouragement, but, as I learned decades later, were turned away from the white churches and driven into founding their own. Churches, dioceses, religious communities, seminaries, families, clans, are communities of memory.[17] Memory depends on relationship and relationship depends on memory. People who are content to be isolated individuals need not concern themselves with memory.[18] But if they want to be fully human, they

---

17. Ibid., 69.
18. Ibid., 106.

will need to remember the way God has related to them in the past, and related to them both individually and as members of communities.

REMEMBERING THAT GOD REMEMBERS

The Bible's first explicit allusions to memory refer to God's remembering: after the flood, "God remembered Noah" (Gen 8:1). Then, when God made a commitment to Noah and the new humanity after the flood, God promised, "I will remember my covenant between me and you" (Gen 9:15–16). God remembers the afflicted (Ps 9:12 [13]). God has remembered his commitment, remembered his covenant, remembered his holy word of promise (Pss 98:3; 105:8, 42). God has remembered us and will bless us (Ps 115:12). The story of Hannah shows how prayer involves appealing to God's capacity to remember (1 Sam 1:11). When human beings make commitments, they may find it easy to put them out of mind later, and may think they are right to do so. The classic example is that of marriage; when half the people in our culture who make a lifelong commitment to someone realize that they cannot keep it, they have to go back on it. The biblical witness tells us that God does not act in that way. God remembers.

The fact that God remembers things does have a bad side. God remembers Israel's wrongdoing, remembers its turning to other deities (Jer 44:21; compare Hos 7:2). In that connection God's memory is selective. When the Babylonians destroyed Jerusalem, God did not remember his footstool (Lam 2:1). The heavens are God's throne and the earth is his footstool, and God, sitting in the heavens in glory, puts his feet up on the earth; specifically, Jerusalem is the place where he puts his feet up. But when its people turned to other deities and declined to keep God in mind, God returned the compliment. God put Jerusalem out of mind. If God remembers you, you are secure; if God decides to forget you, you are finished.

But God cannot finally forget Israel. "He turned into an enemy to them; he himself fought against them," but then "he remembered the days of old, remembered Moses, his people" (Isa 63:10–11). In the account of God's words at Sinai, God anticipates the catastrophe that Hosea, Jeremiah, and Lamentations talk about, and makes a similar statement about how he will remember his commitment (Lev 26:42, 45). Evidently forgetting will not be final. God makes another similar statement when the exile has happened (Ezek 16:60). There the background is the prospect of the Israelites failing to keep their side of the covenant, and the prospect of God's taking them into exile, and then the actuality of those happenings. When they face the facts about their relationship with God, God will remember the covenant with their ancestors. The encouraging aspect to these references to God's memory is that it operates in a positive way in connection with people's wrongdoing. God made commitments that were impossible to escape even if Israel spurned God. So God is still committed to the Jewish people and still committed to the church and still committed to us as individuals despite the way we fail to keep our side of the commitment.

Therefore Israel can pray, "Do not remember waywardness forever" (Isa 64:9 [8]); and part of God's response is to say,

> The former troubles will have been put out of mind;
>   they will have been hidden from my eyes.
> Because here I am, creating
>   a new heavens and a new earth.
> The former things will not be remembered;
>   they will not come to mind. (Isa 65:17)

God will have forgotten the sins that led to the exile and the calamity that these sins led to. God's memory is indeed selective. God's mind is now all on the future. When God speaks of a new heavens and a new earth, the reference is not to a new cosmos; there is nothing wrong with the cosmos. The context indicates that God is talking about a new Jerusalem, a new city, a new community there. God will forget the nasty aspects of the past and give people a new future.

The fact that God remembers may be the most important aspect of the link between spirituality and memory. It is important to remember the story on which the faith is based. It is important to remember the way God has related to us ourselves in the past. It is important to remember the obligations that the past places on us. But it is most important that God remembers, which is in small ways a solemn fact, but in big ways an encouraging fact.

19

Pacing the Cage

BRIAN J. WALSH
Wycliffe and Trinity Colleges

PACING THE CAGE

Sunset is an angel weeping
Holding out a bloody sword
No matter how I squint I cannot
Make out what it's pointing toward
Sometimes you feel like you've lived too long
Days drip slowly on the page
You catch yourself
Pacing the cage

So BEGINS ONE OF Bruce Cockburn's finest songs.[1] The artist finds himself struggling to read the signs of the time, squinting to interpret the apocalyptic portent that is before him. For Cockburn, that sunset is an angel weeping. It doesn't *look like* such an angel, nor does it *remind* the artist of such a thing. No, "sunset *is* an angel weeping." Of that he is sure. And that

---

1. Bruce Cockburn, "Pacing the Cage," from the album *The Charity of Night* ©1996 True North Records.

this angel is holding a bloody sword is also not in doubt. But what does it mean? And where is that sword pointing? "No matter how I squint I cannot/ make out what it's pointing toward."

It has been another day of bloodshed, another day of violence. There is a bloody sword and it seems to have been wielded by that angel. But where is it pointing? And if we could discern an answer to that question, would that tell us only where the sword has struck already, or where it is about to strike again? Whatever the answer, the artist feels the weight of interpretation upon him. It matters that he interpret this portent well. Without such an interpretation he won't be able to warn those who are in danger of being struck next. He will not know the meaning of what is before him.

Caught in this interpretive crisis, the artist wonders if he's lost the gift of prophecy. "Sometimes you feel like you've lived too long/days drip slowly on the page." Maybe he's just getting too old for the hard work of interpretation. But advancing age or not, the weight of this interpretive moment has set him to "pacing the cage." Constricted in his imagination, perhaps held captive within the hegemony of a cultural ethos, this artist starts pacing the cage. Pacing back and forth, he is impatient with his own interpretive inability.

But there is more going on here. There is more that has set the artist to pacing. "I've proven who I am so many times/the magnetic strip's worn thin." He's played the game, he's done what was asked of him, he's proven himself as an able interpreter, but even with the accolade of his peers this has grown tiresome. None of that will carry him through his interpretive uncertainty. Moreover, "powers chatter in high places/stir up eddies in the dust of rage." This chatter in the hierarchies of his world seem to render rage a necessity, and this, too, sets him to pacing the cage. This chatter is full of words, but devoid of meaning. This chatter conveys the rarefied language game of "high places," but is inept at reading the signs of the times. Indeed, the more this interpreter thinks about it, the more it seems to him that "it's as if the thing were written/in the constitution of the age/sooner or later you'll wind up/pacing the cage." This may not be an answer to the question of where that bloody sword is pointing, but it has at least got the artist to a place where he perceives that "pacing the cage" is constitutive to the times. And that is, itself, an important interpretive conclusion.[2]

What does all of this have to do with Andrew Lincoln? And why would I begin this essay, written in honor of my dear friend and esteemed colleague, with the evocative lyrics of Bruce Cockburn? Am I saying that

---

2. For some of Cockburn's own thoughts about this song see his autobiography, *Rumours of Glory*, 412–13.

Lincoln has lived so long that "days drip slowly on the page"? Of course not. Am I saying that Lincoln has found himself, more than once, pacing the cage in his struggle to be a faithful interpreter? Yes, and more. Indeed, I would suggest that an interpreter who never finds him- or herself in a place akin to Cockburn's "pacing the cage" is likely not taking the interpretive calling seriously enough.

Cockburn's song sets off certain resonances. A song about an artist squinting to interpret what is before him resonates well with a biblical scholar who bears the weight of interpretation, and who just might react with some rage to the vacuous chattering going on in high places, perhaps even the high places of the academy. Such a scholar might well grow weary of the incessant need to prove himself within such high places. So I've got to wondering whether my friend Andrew Lincoln's career might bear some of the tread-worn marks of a man who has been pacing the cage.

TESTIMONY, TRUTH, AND LINCOLN'S PACING OF THE CAGE

I do not intend my essay to be overly biographical.[3] Rather, I bring attention to just a few indications of a professional and personal pacing of the cage in Andrew's remarkable book *Truth on Trial*.[4] The way in which Lincoln pushes the bounds of his discipline in this book seems consonant with his career as a whole, and his pedagogical presence in the classroom.

The sheer breadth of the book bears witness to a scholar who sees the connections, notices the tensions, and feels called to bring his erudite exposition of the lawsuit motif in the Fourth Gospel into dialogue with the issues that Christian faith must face in a postmodern cultural and intellectual context. Not only does Lincoln push his discussion beyond the textual analysis of the Fourth Gospel to questions of theology and historical and social context, he also devotes the last 150 pages to how the lawsuit motif resonates in the contemporary context. In these pages we find ourselves in dialogue with Ricoeur's notion of testimony, A. J. Greimas's structural semiotics,

---

3. One brief biographical note on this song and my friendship with Andrew. The recording of "Pacing the Cage" features an exquisite bass solo by the celebrated bassist Rob Wasserman. The only time that Cockburn and Wasserman performed this song live in Toronto (with the aforementioned solo) Andrew Lincoln was in the audience. I was not. I confess that I continue to break the tenth commandment in relation to Andrew's musical experience that day.

4. In this section I will quote liberally from this book, allowing Lincoln's own eloquent writing to carry the argument and to set up my more "testimonial" response in the second half of the essay.

Nietzsche's reduction of truth to power, and Jacques Derrida's deconstruction as justice in service of hospitality. The book continues to ask how a text with a scope as grand as the Fourth Gospel could be heard in a world that has developed a profound incredulity towards all metanarratives, how this text authorizes and calls for an advocacy for justice and truth, and how we can read the Fourth Gospel in light of the Holocaust.

Why? Why is Lincoln compelled to bring his exegetical insight into an ancient text into conversation with such a complex and wide range of contemporary issues?

On one level the issue is appropriation. "Contemporary Christians... need to reflect not simply on the power of the metaphor [of the lawsuit motif] for Christian living, but on its public status. Does it still work as a way for Christians to explain not only to themselves but also to others how to make sense of life, how to construe reality?"[5] There is, then, an apologetic mandate. If we are to engage this ancient text in a way that takes seriously the motif of a lawsuit in which truth is on trial, then we need to ask whether the truth that is vindicated in this narrative remains compelling in a very different historical context. Lincoln's project is to "analyze the motif [of the trial] in such a way that, despite its historical and cultural conditionedness, its limitations and potential for abuse, we can return to it at the level of its narrative power and hear its claims afresh."[6] We can hear in these words not just an apologetic intention, but a pastoral and evangelistic thrust to Lincoln's work as well.

The testimony of the Fourth Gospel "aims at drawing its readers into its narrative world in such a way that they will be convinced of its witness to the realities of such a world and return to their own world to believe and live in their light."[7] Indeed, "the witness of the Fourth Gospel's narrative functions as a claim to transform the world as its readers know it."[8]

It is the transformative power of the Gospel narrative that gets Lincoln to pacing the cage of the academic guild of biblical studies. If the witness of the Fourth Gospel does indeed draw its readers into its narrative world in order to transform the world as the readers know it, then "any interpretation of this Gospel that remains content with setting it in its historical and social context, elucidating its syntax, or analyzing its plot would not be doing justice to the human words with which such an interpretation is concerned. These words claim to be a testimony. And to take testimony seriously is to

---

5. Lincoln, *Truth on Trial*, 339.
6. Ibid., 353.
7. Ibid., 396.
8. Ibid.

pay attention to that to which it testifies. Therefore, any adequate interpretation of the Fourth Gospel has to be theological interpretation."[9] Lincoln fully understands that a biblical scholarship shaped by biblical commitments would require stepping "outside the rules of the academy" and runs the risk that one will "no longer be taken seriously as a scholar by one's colleagues," but faithful engagement will settle for no less.[10] For Lincoln, the crucial issues are "(a) how someone who has come to believe . . . the key claims of the Fourth Gospel could not be an advocate for its truth in his or her scholarship and (b) why someone who holds that God has a claim on this world and that the Gospel's trial of truth reveals the nature of this claim would be willing to carry out his or her daily work in conformity with a completely contrary claim about truth."[11]

Gone is the pretense of neutral autonomy and the modernist myth of objectivity. Gone is an exegesis that ignores radical truth claims and a biblical scholarship divorced from the life of the church and the call of discipleship. As far as Lincoln is concerned, "Champions of the autonomy of critical reason in interpreting biblical texts are . . . no less fideistic than those they accuse of being uncritical. But the abandonment of belief in the autonomy of critical judgment does not mean the abandonment of critical judgment. The latter now takes place within a perspective that is open to trusting the claims of testimony."[12] While critical judgment and trusting the claims of testimony may not be antithetical, this will certainly require a rethinking of what we mean by "critical." Lincoln pieces this together well when he writes:

> The Gospel narrative discloses a world in which it invites its readers, and this narrative world becomes the context that is able to shape readers' beliefs and actions. Yet this world is not simply read off the text and accepted. Readers are involved in construing the text and constructing the world in the first place. It emerges only as a result of their critical engagement with the text. The authority of such a world lies not in its ability to compel acceptance but in its ability to persuade of its basic trustworthiness in the course of engagement with it.[13]

But how is such trustworthiness established? The narrator of the Fourth Gospel writes of the beloved disciple that "we know that his testimony is

---

9. Ibid., 418.
10. Ibid., 472.
11. Ibid., 473.
12. Ibid., 357.
13. Ibid., 368.

true."[14] Why does the community to whom he writes find his testimony to be persuasive? Lincoln argues that "this testimony about Jesus and its vision of life in the world are convincing to the community because it trusts and agrees with the perspective of the beloved disciple, because it finds it plausible and in line with what it already knows about the traditions of Jesus' life and death, and because this version of the significance of that life and death matches its experience of the state of affairs in the world as it affects the community as a particular group of Christian believers."[15] Of these three grounds of persuasiveness it is the third, I suggest, that has the most power to render the testimony of the Fourth Gospel as trustworthy in the contemporary context. Profoundly shaped by Paul Ricoeur's hermeneutics of testimony, Lincoln argues that testimony "points primarily to an alternative world by providing a different construal on reality in the light of a conviction on which one is willing to stake one's life."[16] The Fourth Gospel is clearly such a testimony. "The truth claim of the witness of the Fourth Gospel's narrative functions as a claim to transform the world as the readers know it." Therefore, "readers will reach a verdict on its truth by discovering whether the testimony's reconfigurations of that past world now has power in their present world."[17]

But how does that happen? What form does such a testimony take in the present world that will lead readers to see its truthfulness? Lincoln asks, "How does the world come to know that the God of the trial is uniquely disclosed in Jesus and that this God is love?" and answers, "through seeing and experiencing the advocacy of a community united in loving acceptance of one another."[18] Lincoln elaborates further: "The truth to which the Fourth Gospel's narrative bears witness is known and experienced to be true when it is encountered in a community that lives by the narrative's metaphor of a trial and all that this entails." "Just as that truth was embodied in the Logos becoming flesh, so the truth about the achievement of God's verdict of life for the world has to be enfleshed in a community whose witness takes the form not only of proclamation but also of love."[19]

The testimony is known to be true when it takes on flesh and moves into the neighborhood. And since any truth that is to be enfleshed is always

---

14. John 21:24.
15. Lincoln, *Truth on Trial*, 389.
16. Ibid., 396.
17. Ibid.
18. Ibid., 455.
19. Ibid., 456.

... a particular truth, it becomes accessible through particular channels—the inscripturated witness of this Gospel and the testimonies of those who constitute the community of Jesus' followers and who ... articulate the significance of the decisive verdict of God in Jesus' death and resurrection. It could not be otherwise. A witness that was not embodied in a particular cultural tradition and in a specific place and time would not be able to influence human activity in history.[20]

Let there be no doubt. The truth that is at stake in the cosmic trial that we meet in the Fourth Gospel is universal in scope. But our access to this truth "depends on others who bear witness, and their witness is embodied in, and expressed through, the language of a tradition and a community. The trial is on a cosmic scale, but its verdict is made known through specific people in concrete relationships employing particular language."[21]

This is a truth that is enfleshed in a community of love, manifest in specific people in concrete relationships and employing a particular language that resonates deeply and transformatively with real life in the twenty-first century. Sounds great. Where do I sign up?

Here, I suggest, we meet the deepest of Andrew Lincoln's pacing of the cage. The deepest place of his longing and disappointment. Lincoln may well have paced the cage of the academic guild, but my hunch is that he has been pacing the cage of the church all of his life. His scholarship, in *Truth on Trial* and throughout his significant body of work, has been animated most profoundly and most painfully by a longing that the truth would indeed be made flesh in the church. Lincoln is a faithful churchman. But the failure of the church to enflesh the radical gospel that it proclaims, to be shaped by the liturgy that it practices, to offer and embody an alluring and credible testimony to the truth that it confesses has set my friend to pacing the cage for most of his adult life.

A TESTIMONY: THE FOURTH GOSPEL, 1969

It is all about an embodied hermeneutics of testimony. This is at the heart of Lincoln's appropriation of the Fourth Gospel in *Truth on Trial*. And so to such testimony I now turn. As a sixteen-year-old kid raised in Toronto, I found myself pacing the cage of suburban mediocrity, mass-culture numbness, and spiritual homelessness. While the happy "Father Knows Best" narrative of my childhood had been proven to be a lie in my personal life, the

20. Ibid., 464.
21. Ibid.

modernist mythology of civilizational progress was collapsing in Vietnam, a decade of assassinations, and race riots. But then, in the autumn of 1969, I read the Gospel of John. To be precise, it was a paraphrase of that text called *Good News according to John*. Raised in a secular household I had never read the Bible before. Indeed, I wasn't much of a reader at all, and this was the longest text that I had ever read in one sitting. And it changed my life. In this story I encountered a Jesus who was more radical than the student politics of the day and more subversive than anything that the counter-culture had been able to dream up. On that evening back in 1969, I met a man of audacious claims.

> I am the bread of life.
> I am the light of the world.
> I am the good shepherd.
> I am the resurrection.
> I am the way.
> I am the truth.
> I am the life.

And somehow I found myself in prayer. Somehow I found myself wanting to follow this great "I am." It didn't matter that I missed most of the nuances of John's masterful narrative, with its multiple allusions and references to the Hebrew Scriptures. The audacity of it all simply captured my imagination.

I may not have picked up on the cosmic lawsuit at the heart of the narrative, but it was easy to see that this Jesus was on a collision course with both the religious and political authorities of his day. And I could also see that he would be on the same collision course in the religious and political environment of my own time, at the end of the 60s.

I also had an intuitive grasp from the very first words that this was a story about the whole universe even as it was a story about Jesus of Nazareth. Those opening words, "in the beginning was the Word, and the Word was with God, and the Word was God" had me from the get-go. I met in this story neither the proto-gnostic readings of this Gospel as somehow promoting a mystical Jesus who leads us on a path to enlightenment, nor a dualistic evangelical piety of heavenly escapism. If I had, the little booklet would have ended up in the trash. I somehow knew, as unschooled in biblical literature as I was (or perhaps *because* I was so unschooled), that this was a story about the restoration of all things through this enigmatic, though deeply compelling and alluring, figure of Jesus. Years later Andrew Lincoln wrote what I knew that very first evening with the Fourth Gospel: "Eternal life is not the abandonment of creation but the establishment of God's claim through the renewal of the created world."[22] Precisely.

I read a testimony and found myself drawn into the truthfulness of that testimony and into the world construed by that witness. That's called conversion. But to employ the language of Greimas, I had no prior "fiduciary contract" with either the narrator of the Fourth Gospel or the one to whom he bore witness.[23] I had little reason on my own to trust this testimony, no predisposition to a hermeneutics of trust in relation to this ancient text. Yet I received this little booklet, *Good News according to John* from someone with whom I had enough of a fiduciary relationship to take the time to read it, and perhaps even to have a very slight predisposition to believe it. I had been hanging out in a Christian coffee house in the inner city of Toronto for a number of months. And somehow in a dingy basement of a soup-kitchen mission to the poorest of the poor in my city, drinking terrible coffee and listening to barely passable Christian folk music, I found myself face-to-face with something that I later recognized to be nothing less than the truth of Jesus embodied in a community of love. Here developed the crucial fiduciary relationship. Within the faithfulness of a particular Christian community in a specific time and place the conditions were set for the development of a struggling and stumbling hermeneutics of trust. And here was the beginning of my own calling to bear witness to the truth of Jesus through the fostering and nurturing of such communities of trust.

ST. JOHN BEFORE BREAKFAST

Shortly after Andrew Lincoln left Wycliffe College in Toronto I founded a worshipping community at the University of Toronto called Wine Before Breakfast. Born on September 18, 2001, while the smoke was still rising from the World Trade Center in New York, this community has grown over the years to include students and faculty, young and older professionals, local street pastors, shelter workers, and some homeless neighbors. They come from many denominational backgrounds or no faith background at all. We are a community of diverse ethnicity, race, sexual orientation, education, and economic location. At 7:22 on Tuesday mornings we come to bear witness, to listen to testimony, and to be drawn into the narrative world of the Scriptures so that the biblical world will transform our own. And that testimony takes many forms. Bread and wine are shared, as is a large breakfast after our worship. We find ourselves drawn into the alternative

---

22. Lincoln, *Truth on Trial*, 258.
23. Ibid., 362.

worldview of the Scriptures through evocative liturgy, preaching, prayer litanies written within the community each week, lament and confession, thanksgiving and joy.[24]

The heart of our worship, however, is the music. The prayers and reflections, litanies and homilies of our community find much of their meaning in the context of what our musical sisters and brothers bring to us every Tuesday morning. What we seek in our music is not so much "relevance" as "resonance." For example, on a morning where we are reading the story of Jesus' confrontation with the temple in John 2:13–23 it makes sense that the band would perform Bruce Springsteen's "Rocky Ground."

> Forty days and nights of rain have washed this land
> Jesus said the money changers in this temple will not stand
> Find your flock, get them to higher ground
> The floodwater's rising, we're Canaan bound.[25]

Leonard Cohen's "Heart with No Companion"[26] and "Come Healing"[27] resonate deeply with the story of healing on the Sabbath in John 5:1–24. Peter Gabriel's "Washing of the Water"[28] sets off resonances with the invitation to living waters in John 7:37–52. Imagine what happens when Ani DiFranco's "Wish I May,"[29] with its refrain, "don't tell me it's gonna be alright/you can't sell me on your optimism tonight" is set in the context of Martha and Mary's complaint "Lord, if you had been here my brother would not have died" when we are in John 11. And then we bring DiFranco's voice back the next week singing:

> I do it for the joy it brings
> Because I'm a joyful girl
> Because the world owes me nothing
> And we owe each other the world
> I do it because it's the least I can do
> I do it because I learned it from you

---

24. A glimpse into the life of this community, specifically during the year that we spent in John (2013/14) can be found in Walsh et al., *St. John Before Breakfast*.

25. Bruce Springsteen, "Rocky Ground" from the album *Wrecking Ball* ©2012 Columbia Records.

26. Leonard Cohen, "Heart with No Companion," from the album *Various Positions* ©1984 Columbia Records

27. Leonard Cohen, "Come Healing," from the album *Old Ideas* ©2012 Columbia Records.

28. Peter Gabriel, "Washing of the Water," from the album ©1992 Geffen Records.

29. Ani DiFranco, "Wish I May," from the album *To the Teeth* ©1999 Righteous Babe.

> And I do it just because I want to
> Because I want to.[30]

resonating with the exquisite beauty of Mary anointing Jesus in John 12:1–11. And as we approach Holy Week, doesn't Sting's "The King of Pain"[31] ("it's my destiny to be the king of pain . . .") suggest itself, or Cockburn's "Strange Waters"[32] ("you may run or you may stand/everything is bullshit but the open hand"), or Cohen's "Show me the Place"?

> Show me the place, help me roll away the stone
> Show me the place, I can't move this thing alone
> Show me the place where the word became a man
> Show me the place where the suffering began.[33]

    A testimony is received as true both when the witness is trusted and when the testimony has interpretive power to illuminate the experience of those who receive the testimony. The testimony is persuasive when it has transformative power in the present world. But how does that ancient testimony have access to the present world? How can the testimony be heard speaking in our own tongue? There are, of course, many ways that this happens, but we have found that well-chosen contemporary music opens up the possibility for resonance to happen between the testimony and the contemporary lives of the readers/hearers. Now some of the songs that I just listed are composed by artists who have an intentionally spiritual (and often profoundly Christian) tone to their work. But not all. For example, whether Ani DiFranco is thinking of God in either of her songs "Wish I May" or "Joyful Girl" really doesn't matter. What matters is what happens when these songs are placed in the context of a liturgy that is inviting the community into the stories of the death and resurrection of Lazarus and the anointing of Jesus respectively. The songs will occasion certain resonances (whether noted in the liturgy or homily or left unstated) that bring this testimony to life. Such resonances, I suggest, have persuasive power. Indeed, music and liturgy are themselves profound forms of testimony. Or to pick up on something that Lincoln says later in the book, theological interpretation is itself a form of advocacy and "advocates need to be competent readers if they

---

    30. Ani DiFranco, "Joyful Girl," from the album *Dilate* ©1996 Righteous Babe.

    31. The Police, "King of Pain," from the album *Synchonicity* ©1983 A&M Records.

    32. Bruce Cockburn, "Strange Waters," from the album *The Charity of Night*, ©1996 True North Records,.

    33. Leonard Cohen, "Show Me the Place," from the album *Old Ideas* ©2012 Columbia Records.

are to be persuasive theological interpreters."[34] Some engagement with and understanding of the world of contemporary music, I contend, is crucial to competent advocacy.

Lincoln also notes that "if witness is inevitably associated with suffering, theological interpretation ought to value, in particular, readings of Scripture that come from those who have experienced the pain of marginalization and oppression, not least those who have experienced such pain from oppressive theological interpretations."[35] Such an experience of pain and marginalization describes many in our community. For many of our members, Wine Before Breakfast was their last shot at staying in the Christian story, their last attempt to belong, the last time that they would give this testimony the chance of being heard. As a result, many of them would resonate with these lines from Bruce Cockburn, "derailed and desperate/how did I get here/hanging from this high wire/by the tatters of my faith."[36] Derailed, desperate, and often hanging by the tatters of their faith, our community come from places of different degrees of suffering, pain, and disappointment.

Lesbian, gay, bisexual, transgender, and queer sisters and brothers who have found little but condemnation and disgust in the church have found an open, affirming community at Wine Before Breakfast. Women who continue to experience the oppressive weight of patriarchy find a place of full ministry and leadership. First Nations brothers and sisters know that the kind of theology that legitimated the cultural genocide of their people will find no voice in our midst. So also will our black sisters and brothers know that in this community racism will be named and repented of as the sin that it is. But perhaps more generally, we are a community in which many of our members suffer from "Post Evangelical Traumatic Stress Disorder," or as one sister put it, "Post Born Again Traumatic Stress Disorder." The dualistic and theologically dogmatic distortion of the Fourth Gospel, especially by its "John 3:16" placard-waving evangelists, has caused deep pain and suffering in the lives of untold millions of people who are at best "post-evangelical" and, sometimes more tragically, post-Christian. Wine Before Breakfast has been a place of renewed faith, restored trust, and vibrant discipleship for folks suffering under the oppression of that placard.

Lincoln testifies that the "positive verdict of life in the cosmic trial was an assurance that in Jesus God was at work in this world against all that

---

34. Lincoln, *Truth on Trial*, 478.

35. Ibid.

36. Bruce Cockburn, "Whole Night Sky," from the album *Charity of Night* ©1995 True North Records.

threatened created life, including injustice, violence, and death, and was restoring the conditions that make for human well-being, even though these would be experienced at present in the midst of continuing hostility and death."[37] In such an assurance, with tear-filled eyes wide open to continuing hostility and death, people in our community have heard this testimony anew, been reconverted to this vision of human well-being and found an increasing liberation from the tyranny of the empire through the truth of the one who was crucified and rose from the dead.

Don't get me wrong. We're still pacing all kinds of social, ecclesial, economic, cultural, academic, and personal cages. Testimony may well require a hermeneutics of trust, but this does not erase and invalidate a hermeneutics of suspicion. Sometimes that suspicion is the continuing baggage of past oppression and suffering. Sometimes that suspicion is occasioned by deep struggles with the story itself.

In the Fourth Gospel, Thomas appears as the disciple who struggles most deeply with the truthful testimony of the other disciples to the resurrection. And yet his doubt and suspicion is woven into the narrative and are integral to the persuasiveness of John's testimony. Our narrator creates space for doubt. Any contemporary community that will give embodied testimony to the power of the resurrection must also give such a space for an ongoing hermeneutics of suspicion on the way to trust. I offer my concluding sermon of our year together in St. John as a testimony to the truth of resurrection that I have met in this community. Such a word is also, I think, a fitting tribute to the testimony that I have met through the years in the writing and friendship of Andrew Lincoln.

THOMAS AND PRACTICING RESURRECTION[38]

> Thomas wanted proof.
> He had heard the testimony of the other disciples,
>   he had heard the witness of Mary Magdalene,
> but he wanted proof.
>
> He heard his friends talk with dumbstruck amazement
>   about Jesus appearing to them in that house,
>   even though the doors were locked.
>
> He had heard their tale of resurrection

---

37. Lincoln, *Truth on Trial*, 432.

38. This sermon also appears in *St. John Before Breakfast*, 225–33. It is reproduced here with permission.

and nothing less than new creation.
He listened as they told him about Jesus breathing on them
  as the Creator had breathed on that first human at the dawn of time.
He paid attention as they talked about being sent as missionaries
  of this new creation.

And he may even have wanted to believe it all.
  But it was too good to be true.
All of this may well have been the fulfillment of his deepest longings,
  but when you have lived with disappointment for generations,
    when you saw it all come crashing down with a hammer and a spear
      just days earlier,
    when you had seen with your own eyes
     the death of your greatest hope,
       well, it is going to take more than words
        to turn things around for you.

I won't believe it, unless I see it, Thomas insists.

And then . . . a week later.
The doors were shut.
And there he is again.
There is Jesus in their midst.

But it was a week later.

I wonder what that week was like.

What was it like for the others to be with Thomas,
  when he didn't believe?

What was it like for them to recount over and over
  the amazing experience they had,
  with someone in the room,
     who hadn't been there,
     and who wasn't believing a word of it?

What was it like for them to begin to piece it all together,
  this resurrection,
  this new creation,
  this new commission,
  this call to forgiveness,

what was it like for all this to be happening
  with Thomas as part of the conversation?

What was it like to spend that week with a disbeliever,
  with a friend who wouldn't accept your testimony,
  with a fellow disciple who stubbornly wanted proof?

And what was it like for Thomas?

What was it like to be listening to a tale that
  he desperately wanted to be true,
  but just couldn't believe?

What was that week like?

How alienated did Thomas feel from his friends?
How guilty did he feel?
How upset were they with him?
How awkward was it all?

You ever been there?
  You ever been with a friend whom you love,
  but who just can't bring herself to believe
  in something like the resurrection?

You ever been there?
  You ever been the religiously odd guy out?
  You ever found yourself with friends who believe
      but you just can't?

My hunch is we've all been there.
  We've all been Thomas to someone else's belief,
  and we've all been with someone who was Thomas to our belief.

And you know, if there wasn't much at stake,
  we could just kind of shrug it all off with a sense of cheap tolerance.
      "You believe what you believe,
      and I'll believe what I'll believe,
      and we won't get too worked up about it all."

The problem is that too much is at stake to just shrug it off.
I mean this is life and death stuff that we are dealing with here.

Thomas wants proof before he is going to believe.

So Jesus gives him proof.
   Take a look and come and touch, Thomas.
   Check out the hands and the side.
   I invite you to believe and no longer doubt.

Well, it works,
   it works real good.
So good that Thomas realizes
   for the first time in this whole Gospel,
   that Jesus isn't just his Lord, but also his God.

But Jesus wants to push him on the matter of belief and seeing.
   "You believe because you saw;
   well, blessed are they who have not seen,
   but have still come to believe."

Umm . . . that's us.

Here we are, some 2,000 years later,
   celebrating the resurrection of Jesus
   and none of us have seen him.

And, truth be told, some of us,
   many of us,
   okay, pretty much most of us,
   can relate to Thomas's disbelief.

But for us it isn't so much a matter of not seeing
the risen Jesus in the flesh,
   as it is a matter of not seeing the new creation that he inaugurated,
      not seeing the resurrection life
      that was born on Easter Sunday,
      not seeing a community suffused with forgiveness,
      not seeing the shalom that he pronounced in that locked
      room so long ago.

This is a "not seeing" that makes Thomas of all of us.
This is a "not seeing" that means that we end up embracing the hope of resurrection against most of the evidence.

So, my dear brothers and sisters,
I want to end this year of journeying with St. John,
   by bearing witness to the reality of resurrection,
   a reality that I have seen with my own eyes,

in this very room, week after week.

I want to bear witness to the reality of resurrection in our midst,
　through the practice of resurrection in our lives.

Do you want evidence, do you want proof of the resurrection?
Then look at the resurrection practices all around you.

Walk with members of this community
　as they are on street patrol in the middle of the winter,[39]
　caring for our most vulnerable neighbours.
Go with some of our folks to the Gateway Shelter[40]
　where homeless men are treated with respect,
　and doors are opened for a life beyond the streets.
Check out Switchback Cyclery[41] or Gateway Laundry,[42]
　social enterprises that Wine Before Breakfast folks have launched.
Follow an undergraduate member of the community
　who founded an Out of the Cold program.[43]

This is resurrection power in our midst,
this is called practicing resurrection.

Listen as our wordsmiths dig deep to craft words that are worthy of our prayers.
Watch as some of our members limp after wrestling with the Word
　so that it will bless us in a sermon.
Tap your toe as the bandhood of all believers finds gospel resonances
　in the music of Ani DiFranco, Leonard Cohen,
　Bruce Springsteen, Joe Pug, and Joni Mitchell.

---

39. People on "street patrol" are checking the alleyways, under the bridges, and other places where the homeless live to make sure that our neighbors are safe and know of warm alternatives to rough living that night.

40. The Gateway is a shelter for homeless men founded by one of our community members where a number of our folks have worked over the years.

41. A social enterprise bicycle store run out of the Sanctuary ministry in Toronto and founded by one of our community members. Switchback employs folks with experiences of the street and homelessness and offers training in bicycle repair and retail.

42. Gateway Laundry is a social enterprise-based industrial laundry, cleaning the linens of homeless shelters and luxury hotels alike.

43. Out of the Cold is a program that provides overnight emergency shelter for the homeless. Different from shelters like the Gateway where people could stay for a number of weeks, Out of the Cold is a program offered on different nights in different locations—usually church halls and synagogues.

Receive bread and wine from each other,
  served up by our faithful priests and sacristans.

This too is resurrection power in our midst,
this is called practicing resurrection.

Come out on a Thursday night and meet
a vibrant community of students
  who know how to ask the big questions with respect and love,
  while also knowing how to make every night
into a resurrection party.

Sit in the study with one of our sisters
writing an ethnographic study of the Gateway;
  scholarship in service of the staff and residences of that community.
And then look over the shoulder of another sister
  writing on healing in the lives of female political prisoners
and refugees.

Read a thesis on the Occupy Movement
as an alternative social imaginary,
check out some research and therapy with struggling adolescents,
follow one of our members as he animates youth in a high school
classroom.

Now watch our law students struggle with the meaning of justice,
  while others advocate for the rights of Roma refugees.
Then join the campaign of another community member,
  now running for city council.
Resurrection, friends, that's what all of this about!

Follow one member as he forges new paths
in an ecological spirituality,
  while another studies energy consumption
and systems of conservation,
  and then come on up to Russet House Farm[44] and plant a garden.
Take a look at another member's work towards a theology of disability,
  go with one of our members to L'Arche[45]

---

44. Russet House Farm is where I live with Sylvia Keesmaat and our family. This off-the-grid organic farm is integral to the life of the Wine Before Breakfast community, with folks coming for days of work, food, relaxation, and reflection.

45. L'Arche is an international movement of communities of intellectually disabled adults founded by Jean Vanier. There are two L'Arche communities in Toronto and Wine Before Breakfast folks have been serving in these communities for many years.

       where the disabled are core members.
Witness the alternative and holistic care of our nurses
   and occupational and music therapists.
Everywhere I look, I'm seeing resurrection.

I see it in our sister churches,
   forming alternative communities,
   hanging out with sex trade workers,
   living amongst the poorest of the poor.

I see it in the courage of two of our members
   accepting the call to ordained ministry
   in the profoundly dysfunctional institution of the church.
I see it in the youth ministry of some of our folks.

Resurrection, my friends, that's where all of this comes from.

It can't be missed in this year's Lenten study group,
   in reaffirmation of faith and baptism this morning.

I tell you, my friends, there is resurrection power
   in this room and in this community today.

But there is no resurrection without wounds.
There is no resurrection without death.
There is no resurrection joy without the tears of sorrow.
There is no resurrection peace without violent enmity.
And there is no resurrection faith without profound doubt.

There's been a lot of death this year.
I've lost track about how many have died in the Sanctuary community.
There was Mark, and Fred, and Cliff.
There was a member killed in a fight,
and the incarceration of his assailant.

No wonder Iggy asks whether God must really hate this community.
Iggy, who sat and did bead work during one of our services some months ago.

So where is resurrection in all of this?
How do you practice resurrection
in the face of such an avalanche of death?

You go to a hospital room or to the hospice and sit with the dying.
You go on the street and let your tears
       and the tears of your friends mix with the cold rain.
You organize another funeral with dignity and care.
You rage at God because he is the God of life
       and this is too much damn death!

And all of this,
  with tears and anger,
  with pain and sorrow,
  with rage and doubt,
all of this . . . is practicing resurrection.
Against the odds, against the evidence.

And so, if I may be very personal for a moment,
I believe in the resurrection because you live it.
I believe in the resurrection because you practice it.

Thomas wanted proof.
Jesus said, blessed are those who believe but do not see.

Well, my sisters and brothers, I believe and I actually do see.
I see the resurrected body of Jesus every Tuesday morning.
I taste it in the bread and the wine.
I am embraced by it during the passing of the peace.

I see resurrection practiced in this community
in so many different ways,
and that is why I can still say, sometimes through my tears,
  Alleluia. Christ is risen.

Bibliography

Adams, Edward. *The Earliest Christian Meeting Places: Almost Exclusively Houses?* London: T & T Clark, 2013.
Adams, Samuel L. *Social and Economic Life in Second Temple Judea.* Louisville: Westminster John Knox, 2014.
Aichele, G. *The Control of Biblical Meaning.* Harrisburg, PA: Trinity, 2001.
Alexander, Loveday. "Better to Marry than to Burn: St. Paul and the Greek Novel." In *Ancient Fiction and Early Christian Narrative*, edited by Ron Hock, 235–56. SBLSymS. Atlanta: Scholars, 1998.

———. "Canon and Exegesis in the Medical Schools of Antiquity." In *Le Canon Biblique: La formation du recueil de la Bible juive, de l'Ancien Testament chrétien et du Nouveau Testament*, edited by J.-D. Kaestli, 115–53. Genève: Labor et Fides, 2005.

———. "God's Frozen Word: Canonicity and the Dilemmas of Biblical Studies Today." *ExpTim* 117:6 (2006) 237–42.

———. "'This is That': The Authority of Scripture in the Acts of the Apostles." In *History and Exegesis: New Testament Essays in Honor of Dr. E. Earle Ellis for His 80th Birthday*, edited by Aaron Son, 55–72. London: T & T Clark, 2006.
Appold, M. L. *The Oneness Motif in the Fourth Gospel.* WUNT 2.1. Tübingen: Mohr Siebeck, 1976.
Ashton, John. *Understanding the Fourth Gospel.* Oxford: Clarendon, 1991.

———. *Understanding the Fourth Gospel.* 2nd ed. Oxford: Oxford University Press, 2007.
Asumang, A. "Be Filled with the Spirit and Not with Wine: Echoes of the Messianic Banquet in the Antithesis of Ephesians 5:18." *Conspectus* 5 (2008) 21–38.
Balentine, Samuel E. *The Hidden God: The Hiding of the Face of God in the Old Testament.* Oxford: Oxford University Press, 1983.
Ballard, Paul, and John Pritchard. *Practical Theology in Action: Christian Thinking in the Service of Church and Society.* 2nd ed. London: SPCK, 2006.
Barrett, C. K. "Christocentric or Theocentric? Observations on the Theological Method of the Fourth Gospel." In *Essays on John*, 1–18. London: SPCK, 1982.

———. "'The Father is greater than I' (John 14:28): Subordinationist Christology in the New Testament." In *Essays on John*, 19–36. London: SPCK, 1982.

———. *The Gospel according to St. John: An Introduction with Commentary and Notes on the Greek Text.* 2nd ed. London: SPCK, 1978.

———. *The Gospel of John and Judaism*. London: SPCK, 1975.

———. "What is New Testament Theology? Some Reflections." In *Jesus and the Word*, 241–58. Edinburgh: T & T Clark, 1995.

Bar-Tal, Daniel. *Group Beliefs: A Conception for Analyzing Group Structure, Processes, and Behavior*. Springer Series in Social Psychology. New York: Springer Verlag, 1990.

———. "Group Beliefs as an Expression of Social Identity." In *Social Identity: International Perspectives*, edited by Stephen Worchel, J. Francisco Morales, Darío Páez, and Jean-Claude Deschamps, 93–113. London: Sage, 1998.

Bartelt, Andrew H. *The Book around Immanuel: Style and Structure in Isaiah 1-12*. Biblical and Judaic Studies 4. Winona Lake, IN: Eisenbrauns, 1996.

Barth, Fredrik. "Introduction." In *Ethnic Groups and Boundaries: The Social Organization of Culture Difference*, edited by Fredrik Barth, 9–38. London: Allen and Unwin, 1969.

Barth, Karl. *Church Dogmatics* I/1. Edinburgh: T & T Clark, 1975.

———. *The Epistle to the Romans*. Translated by Edwyn C. Hoskyns. 1922. Reprint. London: Oxford University Press, 1933.

———. *The Göttingen Dogmatics: Instruction in the Christian Religion*. Grand Rapids: Eerdmans, 1991.

———. *Theology and Church*. London: SCM, 1962.

Barth, M. *Ephesians: Introduction, Translation, and Commentary on Chapters 4-6*. New York: Doubleday, 1974.

Barton, Caitlin. "The Roman Blush: The Delicate Matter of Self-Control." In *Constructions of the Classical Body*, edited by James I. Porter, 212–33. Ann Arbor, MI: University of Michigan Press, 1999.

Barton, Stephen C. "Spirituality and the Emotions on Early Christianity: The Case of Joy." In *The Bible and Spirituality: Exploratory Essays in Reading Scripture Spiritually*, edited by Andrew T. Lincoln, J. Gordon McConville, and Lloyd K. Pietersen, 171–93. Eugene, OR: Cascade, 2013.

Bauckham, Richard. *God Crucified: Monotheism and Christology in the New Testament*. Carlisle, UK: Paternoster, 1998.

———. *The Gospels for All Christians*. Grand Rapids: Eerdmans, 1998.

———. *The Testimony of the Beloved Disciple: Narrative, History, and Theology in the Gospel of John*. Grand Rapids: Baker Academic, 2007.

Bauckham, Richard, and Benjamin Drewery. *Scripture, Tradition and Reason: A Study in the Criteria of Christian Doctrine*. Edinburgh: T & T Clark, 1988.

Bauckham, Richard, and C. Mosser, eds. *The Gospel of John and Christian Theology*. Grand Rapids: Eerdmans, 2008.

Bauer, G. L. *Biblische Theologie des Neuen Testaments*. 4 vols. Leipzig, 1800–1802.

Bauer, W., F. A. Arndt, F. W. Gingrich. *A Greek-English Lexicon of the New Testament and Other Early Christian Literature*. 3rd ed. [BDAG] Chicago: University of Chicago Press, 2000.

Baur, F. C. *The Church History of the First Three Centuries*. 2 vols. 1853. ET. London: Williams and Norgate, 1878–79.

———. *Kritische Untersuchungen über die kanonischen Evangelien*. Tübingen, 1847.

———. *Paul the Apostle of Jesus Christ: His Life and Work, His Epistles, and His Doctrine*. 2 vols. 1845. ET. London: Williams and Norgate, 1875.

———. *Vorlesungen über neutestamentliche Theologie*. 1864. Reprint. Darmstadt: Wissenschaftliche Buchgesellschaft, 1973.
Bavinck H. *Reformed Dogmatics. 1: Prolegomena*. Grand Rapids: Baker, 2003.
Beale, G. K. *A New Testament Biblical Theology: The Unfolding of the Old Testament in the New*. Grand Rapids: Baker Academic, 2011.
———. *We Become What We Worship: A Biblical Theology of Idolatry*. Downers Grove, IL: IVP Academic, 2008.
Belfiore, E. "Wine and *Catharsis* of the Emotions in Plato's *Laws*." *Classical Quarterly* 36 (1986) 421–37.
Bennett, Zoë, and Christopher Rowland. "'Action is the Life of All': New Testament Theology and Practical Theology." In *The Nature of New Testament Theology*, edited by Christopher Rowland and Christopher Tuckett, 186–206. Oxford: Blackwell, 2006.
Berger, K. "Rhetorical Criticism, New Form Criticism, and New Testament Hermeneutics." In *Rhetoric and the New Testament: Essays from the 1992 Heidelberg Conference*, edited by Stanley E. Porter and Thomas H. Ulbricht, 390–96. JSNTSup 90. Sheffield, UK: Sheffield Academic Press, 1993.
Berkouwer, G. C. *Holy Scripture*. Grand Rapids: Eerdmans, 1975.
Bernoulli, C.A. *Die wissenschaftliche und die kirchliche Methode*. Freiburg: 1897.
Berry, Wendell. *What Matters? Economics for a Renewed Commonwealth*, Berkeley, CA: Counterpoint, 2010.
Bertram, G. "ὑψόω, ὑπερυψόω." In *TDNT* 8:606–13.
Best, E. *A Critical and Exegetical Commentary on Ephesians*. Edinburgh: T & T Clark, 1998.
Beutler, Johannes. "Greeks Come to See Jesus (John 12, 20f)." *Biblica* 71 (1990) 333–47.
Billings, J. Todd. *The Word of God for the People of God: An Entryway to the Theological Interpretation of Scripture*. Grand Rapids: Eerdmans, 2010.
Blenkinsopp, Joseph. *Isaiah 1–39*. AB 19. New York: Doubleday, 2000.
Blowers, Paul M. "Theology as Integrative, Visionary, Pastoral: The Legacy of Maximus the Confessor." *Pro Ecclesia* 2 (1993) 216–30.
Bockmuehl, Markus. *The Epistle to the Philippians*. BNTC. Peabody, MA: Hendrickson, 1998.
Bonhoeffer, Dietrich. *Ethics*. Translated by Ilse Tödt et al. Minneapolis: Fortress, 2009.
Bonnie J. Miller-McLemore. "Five Misunderstandings about Practical Theology." *International Journal of Practical Theology* 16 (2012) 5–26
Boyer, James L. "Relative Clauses in the Greek New Testament: A Statistical Study." *Grace Theological Journal* 9 (1988) 233–56.
Bredin, Mark. "Gentiles and the Davidic Tradition in Matthew." In *A Feminist Companion to the Hebrew Bible in the New Testament*, edited by Athalya Brenner, 95–111. Sheffield, UK: Sheffield Academic Press, 1996.
Brooke, George J. *Exegesis at Qumran*. JSOTSup 29. Sheffield, UK: JSOT, 1989.
Brooke, S. A. *Life and Letters of Fred. W. Robertson, M. A.* London: Kegan Paul, Trench, Trübner & Co., 1906.
Brown, Peter. *The Body and Society: Men, Women, and Sexual Renunciation in Early Christianity*. New York: Columbia University Press, 1988.
Brown, Raymond E. *The Birth of the Messiah*. Rev. ed. London: Chapman, 1993.
———. *The Community of the Beloved Disciple*. London: Chapman, 1979.
———. *The Gospel according to John*. AB 29. 2 vols. New York: Doubleday, 1966.

Bruce, F. F. "Scripture in relation to Tradition and Reason." In *Scripture, Tradition and Reason: A Study in the Criteria of Christian Doctrine*, edited by Richard Bauckham and Benjamin Drewery, 35–64. Edinburgh: T & T Clark, 1988.

Brueggemann, Walter. *Isaiah*. 2 vols. Westminster Bible Companion. Louisville: Westminster John Knox, 1998.

———. *Israel's Praise: Doxology Against Idolatry and Ideology*. Minneapolis: Fortress, 1988.

———. "Land: Fertility and Justice." In *Interpretation and Obedience*, 235–60. Minneapolis: Fortress, 1991.

———. *Prophetic Imagination*. Minneapolis: Fortress, 1989.

———. "Reflections on a Biblical Understanding of Property." In *A Social Reading of the Old Testament: Prophetic Approaches to Israel's Prophetic Life*, edited by Patrick J. Miller, 276–84. Minneapolis: Fortress, 1994.

———. *Theology of the Old Testament: Testimony, Dispute, Advocacy*. Minneapolis: Fortress, 1997.

Bühner, J.-A. *Der Gesandte und sein Weg im 4. Evangelium*. WUNT 2.2. Tübingen: Mohr Siebeck, 1977.

Bultmann, R. *The Gospel of John: A Commentary*. Louisville: Westminster John Knox, 1971.

———. "The History of Religions Background of the Prologue to the Gospel of John." In *The Interpretation of John*, edited by J. Ashton, 27–46. 2nd ed. Edinburgh: T & T Clark, 1997.

———. "The Significance of 'Dialectical Theology' for the Scientific Study of the New Testament." 1928. In *Faith and Understanding*, 145–64. London: SCM, 1969.

———. *Theology of the New Testament*. 2 vols. London: SCM, 1952, 1955.

———. "Zur Geschichte der Paulus-Forschung," *TRu* 1 (1929) 26–59.

Burtchaell, J. T. *Catholic Theories of Biblical Inspiration since 1810: A Review and Critique*. Cambridge: Cambridge University Press, 1969.

Butterfield, H. *Writings on Christianity and History*. Edited by C. T. McIntyre. New York: Oxford University Press, 1979.

Cadbury, Henry J. "The Relative Pronouns in Acts and Elsewhere." *JBL* 42 (1923) 150–57.

Caird, G. B. *Paul's Letters from Prison in the Revised Standard Version*. NCB. Oxford: Oxford University Press, 1976.

Campbell, Constantine R. *Paul and Union with Christ: An Exegetical and Theological Study*. Grand Rapids: Zondervan, 2012.

Carson, D. A. "Theological Interpretation of Scripture: Yes, But . . . ." In *Theological Commentary: Evangelical Perspectives*, edited by R. Michael Allen, 187–207. London: T & T Clark, 2011.

Carter, W. *John and Empire: Initial Explorations*. London: T & T Clark, 2008.

Catchpole, David R. *Jesus People*. London: DLT, 2006.

Charlesworth, J. H. "The Dead Sea Scrolls and the Gospel according to John." In *Exploring the Gospel of John: In Honor of D. Moody Smith*, edited by R. A. Culpepper and C. C. Black, 65–97. Louisville: Westminster John Knox, 1996.

Childs, Brevard S. *Isaiah*. OTL. Louisville, KY: Westminster John Knox, 2001.

———. *The Struggle to Understand Isaiah as Christian Scripture*. Grand Rapids: Eerdmans, 2004.

Cockburn, Bruce. *Rumours of Glory: A Memoir*. Toronto: Harper Collins, 2014.

Cole, Jonathan. *About Face*. Cambridge: MIT, 1998.
Conzelmann, H. *Theologie als Schriftauslegung*. Munich: Kaiser, 1974.
Crawford, M. R. *Cyril of Alexandria's Trinitarian Theology of Scripture*. Oxford: Oxford University Press, 2014.
Cross, F. M. *Canaanite Myth and Hebrew Epic: Essays in the History of Religion*. Cambridge: Harvard University Press, 1973.
Culpepper, R. A. *John: The Son of Zebedee; The Life of a Legend*. Edinburgh: T & T Clark, 2000.
Cummings, Brian. *The Book of Common Prayer: The Texts of 1549, 1559, and 1662*. Oxford: Oxford University Press, 2011.
Danker, Frederick William. *A Greek-English Lexicon of the New Testament and Other Early Christian Literature*. 3rd ed. Chicago: University of Chicago Press, 2000.
Davies, Margaret. "New Testament Ethics and Ours: Homosexuality and Sexuality in Romans 1:26–27." *Biblical Interpretation* 3 (1995) 315–31.
Davies, W. D., and D. C. Allison. *A Critical and Exegetical Commentary on the Gospel according to St. Matthew*. Volume 1. ICC Commentary. Edinburgh: T & T Clark, 1988.
Davis, Ellen F. "Critical Traditioning: Seeking an Inner Biblical Hermeneutic." In *The Art of Reading Scripture*, edited by Ellen F. Davis and Richard B. Hays, 163–80. Grand Rapids: Eerdmans, 2003.
———. "Learning our Place: The Agrarian Perspective of the Bible." *Word and World*. 29:22 (Spring 2009) 109–20.
———. *Scripture, Culture, Agriculture: An Agrarian Reading of the Bible*. Cambridge: Cambridge University Press, 2009.
———. "Surprised by Wisdom: Preaching Proverbs." *Interpretation* 63 (2009) 264–77
Davis, Ellen F., and Richard B. Hays, eds. *The Art of Reading Scripture*. Grand Rapids: Eerdmans, 2003.
Delitzsch, F. *Die Genesis Ausgelegt*. Leipzig: Dörffling und Franke, 1852.
Deming, Will. *Paul on Marriage and Celibacy*. SNTSMS 83. Cambridge: Cambridge University Press, 1995.
Dodd, C. H. *The Interpretation of the Fourth Gospel*. Cambridge: Cambridge University Press, 1953.
Doney, Malcolm. *How Healthy is the C of E? The Church Times Health Check*. Norwich, UK: Canterbury, 2014.
Doniger, Wendy. "The Mythology of the Face-lift." *Social Research* 76:1 (2000) 99–125.
Douglas, Mary. *Natural Symbols*. London: Barrie and Rockliff, 1970.
Drinkwater, Joel F., Jr. "Face." In *ABD* 7:743–44.
Driver, S. R. *The Book of Genesis*. Westminster Commentaries. London: Methuen, 1904.
Dunderberg, J. "The School of Valentinus." In *A Companion to Second-Century Christian 'Heretics,'* edited by A. Marjanen and P. Luomanen, 64–99. VCSup 76. Leiden: Brill, 2005.
Dunn, J. D. G. *Christianity in the Making*. Vol. 1: *Jesus Remembered*. Grand Rapids: Eerdmans, 2003.
———. *Christology in the Making*. 2nd ed. London: SCM, 1989.
———. *Jesus and the Spirit*. London: SCM, 1975.
———. "Let John be John." In *The Gospel and the Gospels*, edited by P. Stuhlmacher, 293–322. Grand Rapids: Eerdmans, 1991.

———. *Unity and Diversity in the New Testament: An Inquiry into the Character of Earliest Christianity*. 3rd ed. London: SCM, 2006.

Dwyer, Timothy. *The Motif of Wonder in the Gospel of Mark*. Sheffield, UK: Sheffield Academic Press, 1996.

Eastman, Susan Grove. "Philippians 2:6–11: Incarnation as Mimetic Participation." *JSPL* 1 (2010) 1–22.

Ebeling, G. "The Meaning of 'Biblical Theology.'" In *Word and Faith*, 79–97. London: SCM, 1963.

Ehrman, B. D. *The Orthodox Corruption of Scripture: The Effect of Early Christological Controversies on the Text of the New Testament*. Oxford: Oxford University Press, 1993.

Ekblad, Eugene Robert. *Isaiah's Servant Poems according to the Septuagint: An Exegetical and Theological Study*. Biblical Exegesis and Theology 23. Leuven: Peeters, 1999.

Elliott, John H. "Jesus the Israelite Was Neither a 'Jew' Nor a 'Christian': On Correcting Misleading Nomenclature." *Journal for the Study of the Historical Jesus* 5 (2007) 119–54.

Elliott, Neil. *The Arrogance of Nations: Reading Romans in the Shadow of Empire*. Minneapolis: Fortress, 2008.

———. "Disciplining the Hope of the Poor in Ancient Rome." In *A People's History of Christianity Volume 1: Christian Origins*, edited by Richard A. Horsley, 177–97, 301–4. Minneapolis: Fortress, 2005.

Ellis, E. Earle. *The Old Testament in Early Christianity*. WUNT 54. Tübingen: Mohr Siebeck, 1991.

Esler, Philip F. "Beware the Messiah! Psalm of Solomon 17 and the Death of Jesus." In *To Set at Liberty: Essays on Early Christianity and Its Social World in Honor of John H. Elliott*, edited by Stephen K. Black, 179–93. Sheffield, UK: Sheffield Phoenix, 2014.

———. *Conflict and Identity in Romans: The Social Setting of Paul's Letter*. Minneapolis: Fortress, 2003.

———. "The Early Christ-movement in Its Mediterranean Context: Texts, Groups and Identities." In *Ehe—Familie—Gemeinde: Theologische und Soziologische Perspektiven auf Frühchristliche Lebenswelten*, edited by Dorothee Dettinger and Christof Landmesser, 179–93. ABG 46. Leipzig: Evangelische Verlagsanstalt, 2014.

———. *The First Christians in Their Social Worlds: Social-Scientific Approaches to New Testament Interpretation*. London: Routledge, 1994.

———. "From *Ioudaioi* to Children of God: The Development of a Non-Ethnic Group Identity in the Gospel of John." In *In Other Words: Essays on Social Science Methods and the New Testament in Honor of Jerome H. Neyrey*, edited by Anselm C. Hagedorn, Zeba A. Crook and Eric Stewart, 106–37. Sheffield, UK: Sheffield Phoenix, 2007

———. *Galatians*, New Testament Readings. London: Routledge, 1998.

———. "Intergroup Conflict and Matthew 23: Towards Responsible Historical Interpretation of a Challenging Text." *Biblical Theology Bulletin* 45 (2015) 38–59.

———. "Judean Ethnic Identity and the Matthean Jesus." In *Jesus—Gestalt und Gestaltungen: Rezeptionen des Galiläers in Wissenschaft, Kirche und Gesellschaft: FS Für Gerd Theissen*, edited by Petra von Gemünden, David G. Horrell, and Max Küchler, 193–210. NTOA. Göttingen: Vandenhoeck & Ruprecht, 2013.

———. "Judean Ethnic Identity and the Purpose of Hebrews." In *Method & Meaning: Essays on New Testament Interpretation in Honor of Harold A. Attridge*, edited by Andrew B. McGowan and Kent Harold Richards, 469-89. Atlanta: Society of Biblical Literature, 2011.

———. "Judean Ethnic Identity in Josephus' *Against Apion*." In *A Wandering Galilean: Essays in Honour of Sean Freyne*, edited by Zuleika Rodgers, with Margaret Daly-Denton and Anne Fitzpatrick McKinley, 73-91. Leiden: Brill. 2009.

———. "Paul's Contestation of Israel's (Ethnic) Memory of Abraham Galatians 3." *Biblical Theology Bulletin* 36 (2006) 23-34.

Evans, Craig A. "Ephesians 5:18-19 and Religious Intoxication in the World of Paul." In *Paul's World*, edited by S. E. Porter, 181-200. Leiden: Brill, 2008.

———. "Obduracy and the Lord's Servant: Some Observations on the Use of the Old Testament in the Fourth Gospel." In *Early Jewish and Christian Exegesis: Studies in Memory of William Hugh Brownlee*, edited by Craig A. Evans and William F. Stinespring, 221-36. Atlanta: Scholars, 1987.

Evans, Donald. *The Logic of Self-Involvement*. London: SCM, 1963.

Fitzmyer, Joseph A. "Glory Reflected on the Face of Christ (2 Cor 3:7—4:6) and a Palestinian Jewish Motif." *TS* 42:4 (1981) 630-44.

Foerster, W. *Gnosis: A Selection of Gnostic Texts. Vol. 1: Patristic Evidence*. Oxford: Clarendon, 1972.

———. *Gnosis: A Selection of Gnostic Texts. Vol. 2: Coptic and Mandaic Sources*. Oxford: Clarendon, 1974.

Ford, David F. *Self and Salvation: Being Transformed*. Cambridge: Cambridge University Press, 1999.

Forrester, Duncan. "The Scope of Public Theology." *Studies in Christian Ethics* 17 (2004) 5-19.

Fowl, Stephen E. *Engaging Scripture: A Model for Theological Interpretation*. Oxford: Blackwell, 1998.

———. *Philippians*. THNTC. Grand Rapids: Eerdmans, 2005.

———. "Theological and Ideological Strategies of Biblical Interpretation." In *Scripture: An Ecumenical Introduction to the Bible and Its Interpretation*, edited by Michael J. Gorman, 163-75. Peabody, MA: Hendrickson, 2005.

———. *Theological Interpretation of Scripture*. Cascade Companions. Eugene, OR: Cascade, 2009.

Fraser, Mariam, and Monica Greco, eds., *The Body: A Reader*. London: Routledge, 2005.

Fretheim, Terence. "The Plagues as Ecological Signs of Historical Disaster." *JBL* 110 (1991) 385-96.

———. "The Reclamation of Creation: Redemption and Law in Exodus." *Int* 45 (1991) 354-56.

Frey, Jörg. *Die johanneische Eschatologie III*. WUNT 117. Tübingen: Mohr Siebeck, 2000.

———. "Die '*theologia crucifixi*' des Johannesevangeliums." In *Kreuzestheologie im Neuen Testament*, edited by Andreas Dettwiler and Jean Zumstein, 169-238. WUNT 151. Tübingen: Mohr Siebeck, 2002.

———. "'Wie Mose die Schlange in der Wüste erhöht hat . . .': Zur frühjüdischen Deutung der 'ehernen Schlange' und ihrer christologischen Rezeption in Johannes 3,14f." In *Schriftauslegung im antiken Judentum und im Urchristentum*, edited by Martin Hengel and Hermut Löhr, 153-205. WUNT 73. Tübingen: Mohr Siebeck, 1994.

Fulford, B. *Divine Eloquence and Human Transformation. Rethinking Scripture and History through Gregory of Nazianzus and Hans Frei*. Minneapolis: Fortress, 2013.
Fulton, Deirdre N. "Genealogies." In *The Eerdmans Dictionary of Early Judaism*, edited by John J. Collins and Daniel C. Harlow, 662–63. Grand Rapids: Eerdmans, 2010.
Gabler, J. P. "On the Proper Distinction between Biblical and Dogmatic Theology and the Correct Delimitation of Their Boundaries," 1787. German translation of the original Latin in O. Merk, *Biblische Theologie in ihrer Anfangszeit*. Marburg: Elwert, 1972. Reprinted in *Das Problem der Theologie des Neuen Testaments*, edited by G. Strecker. Darmstadt: WBG, 1975. ET *SJT* 33 (1980) 133–58.
Gaventa, Beverly Roberts. "Reading for the Subject: The Paradox of Power in Romans 14:1—15:6." *JTI* 5:1 (2011) 1–11.
Girardet, Herbert. "Rome and the Soil." In *Far from Paradise: The Story of Man's Impact on the Environment*, edited by John Seymour and Herbert Girardet, 54–62. London: BBC, 1986.
Goldingay, John. *Isaiah*. NIBCOT 13. Peabody, MA: Hendrickson, 2001.
———. *Remembering Ann*. Carlisle, UK: Piquant, 2011.
Goodacre, Mark. *The Case against Q*. Harrisburg, PA: Trinity, 2002.
Gorman, Michael J. *Becoming the Gospel: Paul, Participation, and Mission*. Grand Rapids: Eerdmans, 2015.
———. *Cruciformity: Paul's Narrative Spirituality of the Cross*. Grand Rapids: Eerdmans, 2001
———. *The Death of the Messiah and the Birth of the New Covenant: A (Not So) New Model of the Atonement*. Eugene, OR: Cascade, 2014.
———. *Inhabiting the Cruciform God*. Grand Rapids: Eerdmans, 2009.
———. "Romans: The First Christian Treatise on Theosis." *JTI* 5:1 (2011) 13–34.
———. "The Self, the Lord, and the Other: The Significance of Reflexive Pronoun Constructions in the Letters of Paul, with a Comparison to the 'Discourses' of Epictetus." PhD diss., Princeton Theological Seminary, 1989.
Gosnell, P. W. "Ephesians 5:18–20 and Mealtime Propriety." *Tyndale Bulletin* 44 (1993) 363–71.
Gray, Mark. *Rhetoric and Social Justice in Isaiah*. London: T & T Clark, 2006.
Green, Joel. "Re-thinking 'History' for Theological Interpretation." *JTI* 5 (2011) 159–74.
Griffin, Susan. *Women and Nature: The Roaring Inside Her*. New York: Harper, 1980.
Gruenwald, I. *Apocalyptic and Merkavah Mysticism*. AGJU 14. Leiden: Brill, 1980.
Güpfest, H. ed. *Gotthold Ephraim Lessing Werke*, vol. 8. Darmstadt: Wissenschaftliche Buchgesellschaft, 1996.
Gutiérrez, Gustavo. *The God of Life*. Maryknoll, NY: Orbis, 1991.
Güttgemanns, Erhard. *Offene Fragen zur Formgeschichte des Evangeliums; eine methodologische Skizze der Grundlagenproblematik der Form- und Redaktionsgeschichte*. München: Kaiser, 1970. Translated as *Candid Questions Concerning Gospel Form Criticism: A Methodological Sketch of the Fundamental Problematics of Form and Redaction Criticism*. Pittsburgh Theological Monograph Series. Pittsburgh: Pickwick, 1979.
Haenchen, E. *John: A Commentary on the Gospel of John*. 2 vols. Minneapolis: Fortress, 1984.
Hahn, F. *Theologie des Neuen Testaments*. 2 vols. Tübingen: Mohr Siebeck, 2002.
Halperin, D. J. *The Faces of the Chariot: Early Jewish Responses to Ezekiel's Vision*. Tübingen: Mohr Siebeck, 1988.

Harrer, G. A. "Saul who also is Called Paul." *HTR* 33 (1940) 19–33.
Harrington, Daniel J. *The Gospel of Matthew*. Sacra Pagina 1. Collegeville, MI; Liturgical, 1991.
Harris McCoy, Daniel E. *Artemidorus' Oneirocritica: Text, Translation, and Commentary*. Oxford: Oxford University Press, 2012.
Hart, Ray L. *Unfinished Man and the Imagination: Toward an Ontology and Rhetoric of Imagination*. New York: Seabury, 1979.
Harvey, A. E. *Jesus on Trial: A Study in the Fourth Gospel*. London: SPCK, 1976.
Hauerwas, Stanley. *Approaching the End: Eschatological Reflections on Church, Politics, and Life*. Grand Rapids: Eerdmans, 2013.
———. *Matthew*. Brazos Theological Commentary. Grand Rapids: Brazos, 2006.
———. *The Peaceable Kingdom: A Primer in Christian Ethics*. 2nd ed. London: SCM, 2003.
———. *Unleashing the Scripture: Freeing the Bible from Captivity to America*. Nashville: Abingdon, 1993.
Hawkin, David J. "The Critique of Ideology in the Book of Revelation and Its Implications for Ecology." *Ecotheology* 8:2 (2003) 161–72.
Hays, Richard B. *Echoes of Scripture in the Letters of Paul*. New Haven: Yale University Press, 1989.
———. "Spirit, Church, Resurrection: The Third Article of the Creed as Hermeneutical Lens for Reading Romans." *JTI* 5:1 (2011) 35–47.
Healy, Nicholas M. *Hauerwas: A (Very) Critical Introduction*. Interventions. Grand Rapids: Eerdmans, 2014.
Heath, Jane M. F. *Paul's Visual Piety: The Metamorphosis of the Beholder*. Oxford: Oxford University Press, 2013.
Hendel, Ron. "Farewell SBL: Faith and Reason in Biblical Studies." *BAR* (July/August 2010) 70–74.
Hendriksen, W. *Exposition of Ephesians*. Grand Rapids: Baker, 1967.
Hengel, M. *The Four Gospels and the One Gospel of Jesus Christ*. London: SCM, 2000.
———. *The Johannine Question*. London: SCM, 1989.
———. "Reich Christi, Reich Gottes und Weltreich im Johannesevangelium." In *Königsherrschaft Gottes und himmlischer Kult in Judentum, Urchristentum und in der hellenistischen Welt*, edited by M. Hengel and A. M. Schwemer, 163–84. Tübingen: Mohr Siebeck, 1991.
Heppe, H. *Reformed Dogmatics*. Grand Rapids: Baker, 1978.
Hill, C. E. "The Orthodox Johannophobia Theory." In *The Johannine Corpus in the Early Church*, 11–72. Oxford: Oxford University Press, 2004.
Hollis, H. "The Root of the Johannine Pun— ΥΨΩΘΗΝΑΙ." *NTS* 35 (1989) 475–78.
Homan, M. M. "Beer and Its Drinkers: An Ancient Near Eastern Love Story." *Near Eastern Archaeology* 67 (2004) 84–95.
Hooker, Morna D. *From Adam to Christ: Essays on Paul*. Cambridge: Cambridge University Press, 1990.
Horrell, David G. "'Race,' 'Nation,' 'People': Ethnic Identity Construction in 1 Peter 2.9." *NTS* 58 (2012) 123–43.
Horrell, David, et al. *Greening Paul: Rereading the Apostle in a Time of Ecological Crisis*. Waco, TX: Baylor University Press, 2010.
Horsley, Richard A. *Galilee: History, Politics, People*. Valley Forge, PA: Trinity, 1995.
———. *Jesus and the Spiral of Violence*. Reprint. Philadelphia: Fortress, 1993.

Houlden, J. L. *Paul's Letters from Prison: Philippians, Colossians, Philemon, and Ephesians*. Harmondsworth, UK: Penguin, 1970.

Hovey, Craig. *Unexpected Jesus: The Gospel as Surprise*. Eugene, OR: Cascade, 2012.

Hughes, Donald J. *Environmental Problems of the Greeks and Romans: Ecology in the Ancient Mediterranean*. 2nd ed. Baltimore: John Hopkins University Press, 2014.

Humphries-Brooks, Stephenson. "The Canaanite Women in Matthew." In *A Feminist Companion to Matthew*, edited by Amy-Jill Levine (with Marianne Blickenstaff), 138–56. The Feminist Companion to the New Testament and Early Christian Writings 1. Sheffield, UK: Sheffield Academic Press, 2001.

Hunter, David G. "Reclaiming Biblical Morality: Sex and Salvation History in Augustine's Treatment of the Hebrew Saints." In *In Dominico Eloquio—In Lordly Eloquence*, edited by Paul M. Blowers et al., 317–35. Grand Rapids: Eerdmans, 2002.

Hurtado, Larry W. "Jesus as Lordly Example in Philippians 2:5–11." In *From Jesus to Paul: Studies in Honour of Francis Wright Beare*, edited by Peter Richardson and John C. Hurd, 113–26. Waterloo, ON: Wilfred Laurier University Press, 1984.

Hutchinson, John, and Anthony Smith. *Ethnicity*. Oxford: Oxford University Press, 1996.

Ilan, Tal. "'Man born of Woman . . .' (Job 14:1) The Phenomenon of Men bearing Metronyms at the Time of Jesus." *Novum Testamentum* 34:1 (1992) 23–45.

Jensen, Derrick. *Endgame: Vol 1: The Problem of Civilization & Endgame: Vol II: Resistance*. New York: Seven Stories, 2006.

Jenson, Robert W. "Christian Civilization." In *God, Truth, and Witness: Engaging Stanley Hauerwas*, edited by Robert N. Bellah et al., 153–63. Grand Rapids: Brazos, 2005.

———. "Identity, Jesus, and Exegesis." In *Seeking the Identity of Jesus: A Pilgrimage*, edited by Beverly Roberts Gaventa and Richard B. Hays, 43–59. Grand Rapids: Eerdmans, 2008.

———. "The Strange New World of the Bible." In *Sharper than a Two-Edged Sword: Preaching, Teaching, and Living the Bible*, edited by Michael Root and James F. Buckley, 22–31. Grand Rapids: Eerdmans, 2008.

Jewett, Robert. "The Corruption and Redemption of Creation: Reading Romans 8.18–23 with the Imperial Context." In *Paul and the Roman Imperial Order*, edited by Richard A. Horsley, 25–46. Harrisburg, PA: Trinity, 2004.

John, Jeffrey. *Permanent, Faithful, Stable*. 2000. Reprint. London: DLT, 2013.

Johnson, Luke Timothy. *Scripture and Discernment: Decision Making in the Church*. Nashville: Abingdon, 1996.

Jonas, H. *The Gnostic Religion: The Message of the Alien God and the Beginning of Christianity*. 2nd ed. Boston: Beacon, 1958.

Jongman, William M. "The Early Roman Empire: Consumption." In *The Cambridge History of the Greco-Roman World*, edited by Walter Scheidel et al., 592–618. Cambridge: Cambridge University Press, 2007.

Kaftan, J. *Das Wesen der christlichen Religion*. Basel: 1881.

Kanyinga, Karuti. "The Legacy of the White Highlands: Land Rights, Ethnicity and the Post-2007 Election Violence in Kenya." *Journal of Contemporary African Studies* 27 (2009) 325–44.

Käsemann, Ernst. "A Critical Analysis of Philippians 2:5–11," *JTC* 5 (1968) 45–88 (translation of "Kritische Analyse von Phil. 2, 5–11," *ZTK* 47 [1950] 313–60).

———. *The Testament of Jesus*. London: SCM, 1968.

Kaufman, Gordon D. *The Theological Imagination: Constructing the Concept of God.* Philadelphia: Westminster, 1981.

Keener, Craig S. *The Gospel of John: a Commentary.* Peabody, MA: Hendrickson, 2003.

———. *Matthew.* IVPNTS. Downers Grove, IL: IVP, 1997.

Keesmaat, Sylvia C. "Crucified Lord or Conquering Saviour? Whose Story of Salvation?" *HBT* 26:2 (2004) 69-93.

———. *Paul and His Story: (Re)Interpreting the Exodus Tradition.* Sheffield, UK: Sheffield Academic Press: 1999.

———. "The Psalms in Romans and Galatians." In *The Psalms in the New Testament*, edited by Steve Moyise and Maarten J. J. Menken, 139-61. London: T & T Clark, 2004.

———. "Reading Romans in the Capital of the Empire." In *Reading Paul's Letter to the Romans*, edited by Jerry L. Sumney, 47-64. Atlanta: SBL, 2012.

Kehoe, Dennis. "The Early Roman Empire: Production." In *The Cambridge History of the Greco-Roman World*, edited by Walter Scheidel et al., 543-69. Cambridge: Cambridge University Press, 2007.

Kelber, W. H. *The Oral and Written Gospel.* Philadelphia: Fortress, 1983.

Kingsley, C. *The Gospel of the Pentateuch.* London: Parker, Son, and Brown, West Strand, 1863.

Klink, Edward, III. *The Audience of the Gospels.* LNTS 353. Edinburgh: T & T Clark, 2010.

Knöppler, Thomas. *Die theologia crucis des Johannesevangeliums: Das Verständnis des Todes Jesu im Rahmen der johanneischen Inkarnations—und Erhöhungschristologie.* WMANT 69. Neukirchen-Vluyn: Neukirchener Verlag, 1994.

Koestenberger, A. I. *Encountering John: The Gospel in Historical, Literary and Theological Perspective.* Grand Rapids: Baker, 1999.

Koester, Craig. "Why Was the Messiah Crucified?" A Study of God, Jesus, Satan, and Human Agency in Johannine Theology." In *The Death of Jesus in the Fourth Gospel*, edited by Gilbert Van Belle, 163-80. Leuven: Peeters, 2006.

Koester, H. *Ancient Christian Gospels: Their History and Development.* London: SCM, 1990.

Kovacs, Judith. "Servant of Christ and Steward of the Mysteries of God." In *In Dominico Eloquio—In Lordly Eloquence*, edited by Paul M. Blowers et al., 147-71. Grand Rapids: Eerdmans, 2002.

Kovacs, Judith, and C. Rowland. *Revelation.* Oxford: Blackwell, 2004.

Kugel, James. *The Idea of Biblical Poetry: Parallelism and Its History.* Baltimore: Johns Hopkins University Press, 1981.

Kümmel, W. G. *Introduction to the New Testament.* Rev. ed. London: SCM, 1975.

———. *The New Testament. The History of the Investigation of its Problems.* London: SCM, 1973.

Kvalbein, H. "The Kingdom of God and the Kingship of Christ in the Fourth Gospel." In *Neotestamentica et Philonica: Studies in Honor of Peder Borgen*, edited by David E. Aune, Torrey Seland, and Jarl Henning Ulrichsen, 215-32. Leiden: E. J. Brill, 2003.

Labahn, Michael. "Bedeutung und Frucht des Todes Jesu im Spiegel des johanneischen Erzählaufbaus." In *The Death of Jesus in the Fourth Gospel*, edited by Gilbert Van Belle, 431-56. BETL 200. Leuven: Leuven University Press, 2007.

Legaspi, Michael. *The Death of Scripture and the Rise of Biblical Studies*. Oxford: Oxford University Press, 2010.
Lessing, Gotthold Ephraim. *The Education of the Human Race*. Translated by F. W. Robertson. London: Kegan Paul, 1872.
Levering, Matthew. *Participatory Biblical Exegesis: A Theology of Biblical Interpretation. Reading the Scriptures*. Notre Dame, IN: University of Notre Dame Press, 2008.
Levin, Yigal. "Jesus, 'Son of God' and Son of David': The 'Adoption of Jesus into the Davidic Line.'" *JSNT* 28 (2006) 415–42.
Levine, Amy-Jill. "Matthew." In *Women's Bible Commentary*, edited by C. A. Newsom and S. H. Ringe, 252–63. Louisville, KY: John Knox, 1992.
Lincoln, Andrew T. *Born of a Virgin? Reconceiving Jesus in the Bible, Tradition and Theology*. London: SPCK, 2013.
———. *Colossians*. In *NIB* 11:551–669.
———. *Ephesians*. WBC 42. Waco, TX: Word, 1990.
———. *The Gospel according to Saint John*. BNTC. London: Continuum, 2005.
———. *Hebrews: A Guide*. London: T & T Clark, 2006.
———. "'I Am the Resurrection and the Life': The Resurrection Message of the Fourth Gospel." In *Life in the Face of Death: The Resurrection Message of the New Testament*, edited by Richard N. Longenecker, 122–44. Grand Rapids: Eerdmans, 1998.
———. "The Spiritual Wisdom of Colossians." In *The Bible and Spirituality: Exploratory Essays in Reading Scripture Spiritually*, edited by Andrew T. Lincoln et al., 212–32. Eugene, OR: Cascade, 2013.
———. "Spirituality in a Secular Age: From Charles Taylor to Study of the Bible and Spirituality." *Acta Theologica Supplementum* 15 (2011) 61–80.
———. *Truth on Trial: The Lawsuit Motif in the Fourth Gospel*. Peabody, MA: Hendrickson, 2000.
Lincoln, Andrew T., and Angus Paddison, eds. *Christology and Scripture: Interdisciplinary Perspectives*. London: T & T Clark, 2007.
Lincoln, Andrew T., et al., eds. *The Bible and Spirituality: Exploratory Essays in Reading Scripture Spiritually*. Eugene, OR: Cascade, 2013.
Lindars, Barnabas. "The Bible and the Call: The Biblical Roots of the Monastic Life in History and Today." *BJRL* 66:2 (1984) 228–45.
———. *The Gospel of John*. London: Oliphants, 1972.
———. *New Testament Apologetic*. London: SCM, 1961.
Lindbeck, George A. *The Nature of Doctrine: Religion and Theology in a Postliberal Age*. Philadelphia: Westminster, 1984.
Litwa, M. David. "Transformation through a Mirror: Moses in 2 Cor. 3.18." *JSNT* 34:3 (2012) 286–97.
Loader, William. *The New Testament on Sexuality: Attitudes Towards Sexuality in Judaism and Christianity in the Hellenistic Greco-Roman Era*. Grand Rapids: Eerdmans, 2012.
———. *Sexuality and the Jesus Tradition*. Grand Rapids: Eerdmans, 2005.
———. *Sexuality in the New Testament: Understanding the Key Texts*. London: SPCK, 2010.
LoCascio, Elio. "The Early Roman Empire: The State and the Economy." In *The Cambridge History of the Greco-Roman World*, edited by Walter Scheidel et al., 619–47. Cambridge: Cambridge University Press, 2007.

Locher, C. *Die Ehre einer Frau in Israel: Exegetische und Rechtsvergleichende Studien zu Deuteronomium 22,13–21*. OBO 70. Freiburg: Universitätsverlag, 1986.
Lohse, Eduard. "πρόσωπον κτλ." In *TDNT* 6:768–80.
Longenecker, B. W., and M. C. Parsons, eds. *Beyond Bultmann*. Waco, TX: Baylor, 2014.
Lust, J., et al. *A Greek-English Lexicon of the Septuagint*, Part II. Stuttgart: Deutsche Bibelgesellschaft, 1996.
Luz, Ulrich. *Matthew 1–7: A Commentary*. Translated by Wilhelm C. Linss. Edinburgh: T & T Clark, 1989.
MacDonald, Margaret Y. "Slavery, Sexuality and House Churches: A Reassessment of Colossians 3:18–4.1 in Light of New Research on the Roman Family." *NTS* 53 (2007) 94–113.
Macquarrie, John. *Godtalk*. London: SCM, 1967.
MacRae, G. W. "The Jewish Background of the Gnostic Sophia Myth." *NovT* 12 (1970) 86–101.
Malherbe, Abraham. *Moral Exhortation: A Greco-Roman Sourcebook*. Philadelphia: Westminster, 1989.
Malina, Bruce J. "Mediterranean Sacrifice: Dimensions of Domestic and Political Religion." *Biblical Theology Bulletin* 26 (1996) 26–44.
———. *The New Testament World. Insights from Cultural Anthropology*. 3rd ed. Louisville: Westminster John Knox, 2001.
———. "Religion in the Imagined New Testament World: More Social Science Lenses." *Scriptura* 51 (1994) 1–26
Malina, Bruce J., and Richard L. Rohrbaugh. *Social-Science Commentary on the Synoptic Gospels*. Minneapolis: Fortress, 1992.
Marcus, Joel. "Crucifixion as Parodic Exaltation." *JBL* 125 (2006) 73–87.
———. "Idolatry in the New Testament." *Int* 60:2 (April 2006) 152–64.
Mardaga, Hellen. "The Repetitive Use of ὑψόω in the Fourth Gospel." *CBQ* 74 (2012) 101–17.
Margalit, Avishai. *The Ethics of Memory*. Cambridge: Harvard University Press, 2002.
Marohl, Matthew J. *Joseph's Dilemma: "Honor Killing" in the Birth Narrative of Matthew*. Eugene, OR: Cascade, 2009.
Martin, Dale B. "Heterosexism and the Interpretation of Romans 1:18–32." *Biblical Interpretation* 3 (1995) 332–55.
Martin, F. "*Sacra Doctrina* and the Authority of its *Sacra Scriptura* according to St. Thomas Aquinas." In *Sacred Scripture: The Disclosure of the Word*, 1–19. Naples, FL: Sapientia, 2006.
Martin, Ralph P. *Ephesians, Colossians, and Philemon*. Atlanta: John Knox, 1991.
———. *A Hymn of Christ: Philippians 2:5–11 in Recent Interpretation and in the Setting of Early Christian Worship*. Downers Grove, IL: InterVarsity, 1997 (orig. *Carmen Christi: Philippians 2:5–11 in Recent Interpretation and in the Setting of Early Christian Worship* [Cambridge: Cambridge University Press, 1967]). 2nd ed. Grand Rapids: Eerdmans, 1983.
Martyn, J. Louis. "Epistemology at the Turn of the Ages." In *Theological Issues in the Letters of Paul*, 89–110. Edinburgh: T & T Clark, 1997.
———. *History and Theology in the Fourth Gospel*. 2nd ed. Nashville: Abingdon, 1979.
McHugh, J. F. *John 1–4*. ICC. London: T & T Clark, 2009.
McKinlay, Judith E. *Reframing Her: Biblical Women in Post-Colonial Focus*. Sheffield, UK: Sheffield Phoenix, 2004.

McKnight, S. *A Community Called Atonement*. Nashville: Abingdon, 2007.
McNamara, Martin. "The Ascension and the Exaltation of Christ in the Fourth Gospel." In *Targum and New Testament*, 450–59. WUNT 279. Tübingen: Mohr Siebeck, 2011.
Meeks, Wayne A. "The Man from Heaven in Johannine Sectarianism." In *The Interpretation of John*, edited by John Ashton, 169–205. 2nd ed. Edinburgh: T & T Clark, 1997.
———. "The Man from Heaven in Paul's Letter to the Philippians." In *The Future of Early Christianity: Essays in Honor of Helmut Koester*, edited by Birger Pearson, 329–36. Minneapolis: Fortress, 1991.
———. "Why Study the New Testament?" *NTS* 51 (2005) 155–70.
Meggitt, Justin J. "Artemidorus and the Johannine Crucifixion." *Journal of Higher Criticism* 5 (1998) 203–8.
Metzger, B. M. *A Textual Commentary on the Greek New Testament*. 2nd ed. London: United Bible Societies, 1994.
Meyer, P. W. "'The Father': The Presentation of God in the Fourth Gospel." In *Exploring the Gospel of John: In Honor of D. Moody Smith*, edited by R. A. Culpepper and C. C. Black, 255–73. Louisville: Westminster John Knox, 1996.
Middleton, Richard J. *The Liberating Image*. Grand Rapids: Brazos, 2005.
———. "The Liberating Image? Interpreting *Imago Dei* in Context." *CSR* 24 (1994) 8–25.
Milgrom, Jacob. *Numbers*. Philadelphia: JPS, 1990.
Miller-McLemore, Bonnie J. "Five Misunderstandings about Practical Theology." *International Journal of Practical Theology* 16 (2012) 5–26.
Mitchell, Claire. "The Religious Content of Ethnic Identities." *Sociology* 40 (2006) 1135–52.
Moberly, R. W. L. *Old Testament Theology: Reading the Hebrew Bible as Christian Scripture*. Grand Rapids: Baker Academic, 2013.
———. "What is Theological Interpretation of Scripture?" *Journal of Theological Interpretation* 3 (2009) 161–78.
Moloney, Francis J. *The Johannine Son of Man*. Biblioteca di Scienze Religiose 14. 2nd ed. Rome: Libreria Ateneo Salesiano, 1975.
———. "Recent Johannine Studies: Part Two: Monographs." *ExpTim* 123:9 (2012) 424–26.
Moltmann, Jürgen. *The Church in the Power of the Spirit*. London: SCM, 1977.
Moore, Stephen D. *Empire and Apocalypse: Postcolonialism and the New Testament*. Sheffield, UK: Phoenix, 2006.
———. "Que(e)rying Paul: Preliminary Questions." In *Auguries: The Jubilee Volume of the Sheffield Department of Biblical Studies*, edited by D. J. A. Clines and Stephen D. Moore, 250–74. JSOTSup 269. Sheffield, UK: Sheffield Academic Press, 1998.
Morgan, R. "C. K. Barrett and New Testament Theology." *JSNT* 37:4 (2015) 432–57.
———. "Gabler's Bicentenary." *ExpTim* 98 (1987) 164–68.
———. *The Nature of New Testament Theology*. London: SCM, 1973.
Morley, Neville. "The Early Roman Empire: Distribution." In *The Cambridge History of the Greco-Roman World*, edited by Walter Scheidel et al., 570–91. Cambridge: Cambridge University Press, 2007.
Morris, L. *The Gospel according to John: The English Text with Introduction, Exposition and Notes*. Grand Rapids: Eerdmans, 1971.

Moule, C. F. D. "Further Reflections on Philippians 2:5–11." In *Apostolic History and the Gospel: Biblical and Historical Essays Presented to F. F. Bruce on his 60th Birthday*, edited by W. Ward Gasque and Ralph P. Martin, 264–76. Grand Rapids: Eerdmans, 1970.
Muddiman, J. *The Epistle to the Ephesians*. London: Continuum, 2001.
Muller, R. A. *Post-Reformation Reformed Dogmatics 2: Holy Scripture: The Cognitive Foundation of Theology*. Grand Rapids: Baker, 1993.
Nagel, T. *Die Rezeption des Johannesevangeliums im 2. Jahrhundert*. Leipzig: Evangelische Verlagsanstalt, 2000.
Niebergall, F. *Praktische Auslegung des Neuen Testaments*. Tübingen: Mohr Siebeck, 1909.
Nisbett, H. B. *Lessing. Eine Biographie*. Munich: Beck, 2008.
Nissinen, Marti. *Homoeroticism in the Biblical World: A Historical Perspective*. Minneapolis: Fortress, 1988.
Oakes, Peter. *Reading Romans in Pompeii: Paul's Letter at Ground Level*. London: SPCK, 2009.
O' Brien, Peter T. *The Epistle to the Philippians*. NIGTC. Grand Rapids: Eerdmans, 1991.
———. *The Letter to the Ephesians*. Leicester, UK: Apollos, 1999.
Odeberg, H. *The Fourth Gospel*. Stockholm: Almqvist & Wiksells, 1929.
Orlov, A. A. *Heavenly Priesthood in the Apocalypse of Abraham*. Cambridge: Cambridge University Press, 2013.
Osiek, Carolyn, and David L. Balch. *Families in the New Testament World: Households and House Churches*. Louisville: Westminster John Knox, 1997.
Oswalt, John N. *Isaiah 1–39*. NICOT. Grand Rapids: Eerdmans, 1986.
Overbeck, Franz. *How Christian is Our Present-day Theology?* Translated by Martin Henry. 1873. Reprint. London: T & T Clark, 2005.
Paddison, Angus. *Scripture: A Very Theological Proposal*. London: T & T Clark, 2009.
———. *Theological Hermeneutics and 1 Thessalonians*. SNTSMS. Cambridge: Cambridge University Press, 2005.
Pagels, E. H. *The Johannine Gospel in Gnostic Exegesis: Heracleon's Commentary on John*. Nashville: Abingdon, 1973.
Pancaro, S. *The Law in the Fourth Gospel: The Torah and the Gospel, Moses and Jesus, Judaism and Christianity According to John*. Leiden: Brill, 1975.
Peacock, James L., Patricia M. Thornton, and Patrick B. Inman, eds. *Identity Matters: Ethnic and Sectarian Conflict*. New York: Bergahn, 2007.
Pesch, Otto. "Exegese des Alten Testament bei Thomas." In *Deutsche Thomas Ausgabe* vol. 13, 682–716. Salzburg: Anton Pustet, 1934.
Peterson, Eugene. H. *The Message: The New Testament in Contemporary English*. Colorado Springs: NavPress, 1993.
Phoenix, Ann. "Ethnicities." In *The Sage Handbook of Identities*, edited by Margaret Weatherell and Chandra Talpade Mohanty, 297–320. Los Angeles: Sage, 2010.
Pierce, Madison N. and Benjamin E. Reynolds. "The Perfect Tense-Form and the Son of Man in John 3.13: Developments in Greek Grammar as a Viable Solution to the Timing of the Ascent and Descent." *NTS* 60 (2014) 149–55.
Pilling Report: Report of the House of Bishops Working Group on human sexuality. London: Church House, 2013. Also available online at www.churchofengland.org/pilling.

Porter, Stanley E. "Ephesians 5:18-19 and Its Dionysian Background." In *Testimony and Interpretation: Early Christology in Its Judeo-Hellenistic Milieu: Studies in Honor of Petr Pokorný*, edited by J. Mrázek and J. Roskovec, 68-80. London: T & T Clark, 2004.

———. "What Exactly is Theological Interpretation of Scripture and Is It Hermeneutically Robust Enough for the Task to Which It has Been Appointed?" In *Horizons in Hermeneutics: A Festschrift in Honor of Anthony C. Thiselton*, edited by Stanley Porter and Matthew Malcolm, 234-67. Grand Rapids: Eerdmans, 2013.

Portier-Young, A. *Apocalypse against Empire: Theologies of Resistance in Early Judaism*. Grand Rapids: Eerdmans, 2011.

Powell, M. A. "Wine and the Vine in Ancient Mesopotamia: The Cuneiform Evidence." In *The Origins and Ancient History of Wine*, edited by P. E. McGovern, S. J. Fleming, and S. H. Katz, 97-131. Abingdon, UK: Routledge, 1996.

Preus, R. D. *The Inspiration of Scripture: A Study of the Theology of the Seventeenth Century Lutheran Dogmaticians*. Edinburgh: Oliver and Boyd, 1955.

Radner, Ephraim. *Hope among the Fragments: The Broken Church and its Engagement with Scripture*. Grand Rapids: Brazos, 2004.

Rahner, K. "Inspiration in the Bible." In *Studies in Modern Theology*, 7-86. London: Burns and Oates, 1965.

Reinhartz, Adele. *Befriending the Beloved Disciple: A Jewish Reading of the Gospel of John*. London: Continuum, 2001.

Reno. R. R. "Series Preface." In *Matthew*, Stanley Hauerwas, 9-14. Brazos Theological Commentary. Grand Rapids: Brazos, 2006.

Rensberger, D. *Johannine Faith and Liberating Community*. Philadelphia: Westminster, 1988.

Reumann, John. *Philippians: A New Translation with Introduction and Commentary*. AYB 33B. New Haven: Yale University Press, 2008.

Richey, L. B. *Roman Imperial Ideology and the Gospel of John*. Catholic Biblical Quarterly Monograph Series 43. Washington, DC: The Catholic Biblical Association of America, 2007.

Ricoeur, Paul. "The Bible and the Imagination." In *Figuring the Sacred: Religion, Narrative, and the Imagination*, 144-66. Minneapolis: Fortress, 1995.

———. *The Rule of Metaphor: Multi-disciplinary Studies in the Creation of Meaning in Language*. Translated by Robert Czerny, K. McLoughlin and J. Costello. Toronto: Toronto University Press, 1977.

Robertson, A. T. *A Grammar of the Greek New Testament in the Light of Historical Research*. Nashville: Broadman, 1934.

Robertson, F. W. *Lectures, Addresses and Other Literary Remains*. London: Kegan Paul, Trench, 1882.

———. *Notes on Genesis*. London: Kegan Paul, 1879.

———. *Sermons on Bible Subjects*. Everyman Library. London: Dent, 1906.

———. *Sermons Preached at Brighton*. First Series. London: Kegan Paul, Trench, Trübner, 1893.

Rogers, C. L. "The Dionysian Background of Eph. 5:18." *Bibliotheca Sacra* 136 (1979) 249-57.

Rogerson, J. W. *Old Testament Criticism in the Nineteenth Century: England and Germany*. London: SPCK, 1984.

———. "What Difference Did Darwin Make?" In *Reading Genesis after Darwin*, edited by S. C. Barton and D. Wilkinson, 75–91, esp. 84–85. Oxford: Oxford University Press, 2009.

———. "Wrestling with the Angel: A Study in Literary Hermeneutics." In *Hermeneutics, the Bible and Literary Criticism*, edited by A. Loades et al., 131–44. London: Macmillan, 1992.

Rosenberg, Joel. *King and Kin: Political Allegory in the Hebrew Bible*. Bloomington, IN: Indiana University Press, 1986.

Rosner, Brian S. *Greed as Idolatry: The Origin and Meaning of a Pauline Metaphor*. Grand Rapids: Eerdmans, 2007.

Rudolph, K. *Gnosis: The Nature and History of an Ancient Religion*. Edinburgh: T & T Clark, 1983.

Sallers, Robert. "Ecology." In *The Cambridge History of the Greco-Roman World*, edited by Walter Scheidel et al., 15–37. Cambridge: Cambridge University Press, 2007.

Sanders, J. N. *The Fourth Gospel in the Early Church: Its Origin and Influence on Christian Theology up to Irenaeus*. Cambridge: Cambridge University Press, 1943.

Sarisky, Darren. *Scriptural Interpretation: A Theological Exploration*. Challenges in Contemporary Theology. Chichester, UK: Wiley-Blackwell, 2013.

Scheidel, Walter. "Demography." In *The Cambridge History of the Greco-Roman World*, edited by Walter Scheidel et al., 38–86. Cambridge: Cambridge University Press, 2007.

Schleiermacher, F. D. E. *Brief Outline on the Study of Theology*. 1810, 1830. ET. Richmond, VA: John Knox, 1966.

Schnackenburg, R. *Ephesians: A Commentary*. Edinburgh: T & T Clark, 1991.

———. *The Gospel according to St. John*. Vol. 1. New York: Herder & Herder, 1968.

Schneiders, Sandra. *The Revelatory Text: Interpreting the New Testament as Sacred Scripture*. 2nd ed. Collegeville, MN: Liturgical, 1999.

Schnelle, U. *Antidocetic Christology in the Gospel of John*. Minneapolis: Fortress, 1992.

———. *The History and Theology of the New Testament Writings*. Minneapolis: Augsburg, 1998.

Schröter, J. "Trinitarian Belief, Binitarian Monotheism, and the One God: Reflections on the Origin of Christian Faith in Affiliation to Larry Hurtado's Christological Approach." In *Reflections of the Early Christian History of Religion*, edited by C. Breytenbach and J. Frey, 171–94. Ancient Judaism and Early Christianity 81. Leiden: Brill, 2013.

Schwindt, Rainer. *Gesichte der Herrlichkeit: Eine exegetisch- traditionsgeschichtliche Studie zur paulinischen und johanneischen Christologie*. HBS 50. Freiburg: Herder, 2007.

Scruton, Roger. *The Face of God*. London: Continuum, 2012.

Seitz, Christopher R. *Figured Out: Typology and Providence in Christian Scripture*. Louisville: Westminster John Knox, 2001.

———. *Isaiah 1–39*. Interpretation. Louisville: John Knox, 1993.

Silva, Moisés. *Philippians*. 2nd ed. BECNT. Grand Rapids: Baker, 2005.

Simian-Yofre, H. "*pānîm*." In *TDOT* XI: 589–615.

Smart, Ninian. *The Concept of Worship*. London: Macmillan, 1972.

Smith, D. E. *From Symposium to Eucharist: The Banquet in the Early Christian World*. Minneapolis: Fortress, 2003.

Smith, Wilfrid Cantwell. *The Meaning and End of Religion*. Minneapolis: Fortress, 1991 [1962].
Soares Prabhu, George. *The Formula Quotations in the Infancy Narrative of Matthew*. Rome: Biblical Institute, 1976.
Stäudlin, C. F. "Über die blos historische Auslegung der Bücher des Neuen Testaments." *Kritisches Journal der neuesten Literatur* 1 (1814) 321–48.
Steinmetz, David. "The Superiority of Pre-Critical Exegesis." In *Theological Interpretation of Scripture: Classic and Contemporary Readings*, edited by S. Fowl, 26–38. Oxford: Blackwell, 1997.
Stendahl, Krister. "Biblical Theology: Contemporary" In *Meanings: The Bible as Document and as Guide*, 11–44. Philadelphia: Fortress, 1984.
Strathmann, H. "*laos*." In *TDNT* 4:29–39.
Strecker, G. *Das Problem einer Theologie des Neuen Testaments*. Darmstadt: WBG, 1975.
Stuhlmacher, P. *Biblische Theologie des Neuen Testaments*. 2 vols. Göttingen: Vandenhoeck, 1992, 1999.
Suphan, B., ed. *Herder Sämmtliche Werke* VI. Berlin: Weidmannsche Buchhandlung, 1883.
Swain, S. *Trinity, Revelation and Reading: A Theological Introduction to the Bible and Its Interpretation*. London: T & T Clark, 2011.
Swain, Simon. ed., *Seeing the Face, Seeing the Soul: Polemon's Physiognomy from Classical Antiquity to Medieval Islam*. Oxford: Oxford University Press, 2007.
Swinton, John, and Harriet Mowat. *Practical Theology and Qualitative Research*. London: SCM, 2006.
Tang Nielsen, Jesper. "The Lamb of God: The Cognitive Structure of a Johannine Metaphor." In *Imagery in the Gospel of John: Terms, Forms, Themes, and Theology of Johannine Figurative Language*, edited by Jörg Frey et al., 217–56. WUNT 200. Tübingen: Mohr Siebeck, 2006.
Tarrant, H. "Wine in Ancient Greece: Some Platonist Ponderings." In *Wine & Philosophy: A Symposium on Thinking and Drinking*, edited by F. Allhoff, 15–29. Oxford: Blackwell, 2008.
Temple, W. *Readings in St. John's Gospel (First and Second Series)*. London: Macmillan, 1945.
Thatcher, T. *Greater than Caesar: Christology and Empire in the Fourth Gospel*. Minneapolis: Fortress, 2008.
Theissen, G. *Polyphones Verstehen. Entwürfe zur Bibelhermeneutik*. Berlin: Lit, 2014.
Theobald, Michael. "Gott, Logos und Pneuma: 'Trinitarische' Rede von Gott im Johannesevangelium." In *Studien zum Corpus Iohanneum*, 349–88. WUNT 267. Tübingen: Mohr Siebeck, 2010.
———. *Herrenworte im Johannesevangelium*. HBS 34. Freiburg: Herder, 2002.
Thiselton, Anthony C. *New Horizons in Hermeneutics: The Theory and Practice of Transforming Biblical Reading*. Grand Rapids: Zondervan, 1992.
———. *The Two Horizons: New Testament Hermeneutics and Philosophical Description with Special Reference to Heidegger, Bultmann, Gadamer, and Wittgenstein*. Exeter, UK: Paternoster, 1980.
Thompson, M. M. *The Humanity of Jesus in the Fourth Gospel*. Philadelphia: Fortress, 1988.
To Set Our Hope on Christ: A Response to the Invitation of Windsor Report ¶135. New York: The Episcopal Church, 2005.

Townsley, Jeramy. "Paul, the Goddess Religion, Queer Sects: Roman 1.23–28." *JBL* 130:4 (2011) 707–28.
Tracy, David. *The Analogical Imagination: Christian Theology and the Culture of Pluralism.* New York: Crossroad, 1981.
Turner, Bryan S. *The Body and Society.* Oxford: Blackwell, 1984.
Utzschneider, Helmut. *Gottes Vorstellung; Untersuchungen zur literarischen Ästhetik und ästhetischen Theologie des Alten Testaments.* BWANT 15/175. Stuttgart: Kohlhammer, 2007.
Van der Watt, Jan. "The Cross/Resurrection Events in the Gospel of John with Special Emphasis on the Confession of Thomas (20:28)." *Neotestamentica* 37 (2003) 123–41.
Vanhoozer, Kevin J. *The Drama of Doctrine: A Canonical-Linguistic Approach to Christian Theology.* Louisville: Westminster John Knox, 2005.
Van Kooten, George H. "Man as God's Spiritual or Physical Image? Theomorphic Ethics versus Numinous Ethics and Anthropomorphic Aesthetics in Early Judaism, Ancient Philosophy, and the New Testament." In *Anthropologie und Ethik im Frühjudentum und im Neuen Testament*, edited by Matthias Konradt und Esther Schläpfer, 99–138. Tübingen: Mohr Siebeck, 2014.
———. *Paul's Anthropology in Context.* Tübingen: Mohr Siebeck, 2008.
Van Unnik, W. C. "The Purpose of St. John's Gospel." *SE* I (1959) 382–11
Verkuyten, Maykel, and Ali Aslan Yildiz. "National (Dis)identification and Ethnic and Religious Identity: A Study among Turkish-Dutch Muslims." *Personality and Social Psychology Bulletin* 33 (2007) 1448–62.
Via, Dan O., and Robert A. J. Gagnon. *Homosexuality and the Bible: Two Views.* Minneapolis: Fortress, 2003.
Village, Andrew. "The Bible and Ordinary Readers." In *Exploring Ordinary Theology: Everyday Christian Believing and the Church*, edited by Jeff Astley and Leslie J. Francis, 127–36. Farnham, UK: Ashgate, 2013.
Visotzky, B. L. "Methodological Considerations in the Study of John's Interaction with First-Century Judaism." In *Life in Abundance: Studies of John's Gospel in Tribute to Raymond E. Brown*, edited by J. R. Donahue, 91–107. Collegeville, MN: Liturgical, 2005.
Volf, Miroslav. *Exclusion and Embrace.* Nashville: Abingdon, 1996.
———. "Theology, Meaning, and Power." In *The Future of Theology: Essays in Honor of Jürgen Moltmann*, edited by Miroslav Volf, Carmen Krieg, and Thomas Kucharz, 98–113. Grand Rapids: Eerdmans, 1996.
Walsh, Brian J. *Kicking at the Darkness: Bruce Cockburn and the Christian Imagination.* Grand Rapids, Brazos, 2011.
Walsh, Brian J., and Sylvia C. Keesmaat, *Colossians Remixed: Subverting the Empire.* Downers Grove, IL: IVP Academic, 2005.
Walsh, Brian J., et al. *St. John Before Breakfast.* Toronto: Books Before Breakfast, 2014.
Walton, Heather. *Writing Methods in Theological Reflection.* London: SCM, 2014.
Watts, John D. W. "Babylonian Idolatry in the Prophets as a False Socio-Economic System." In *Israel's Apostasy and Restoration: Essays in Honour of Roland K. Harrison*, edited by Abraham Gileadi, 115–22. Grand Rapids: Baker, 1988.
———. *Isaiah 1–33.* WBC, 24. Waco, TX: Word, 1985.
Webster, John. *The Domain of the Word: Scripture and Theological Reason.* London: T & T Clark, 2012.

———. "The Human Person." In *The Cambridge Companion to Postmodern Theology*, edited by Kevin J. Vanhoozer, 219–34. Cambridge: Cambridge University Press, 2003.

———. "'In the Society of God': Some Principles of Ecclesiology." In *Perspectives on Ecclesiology and Ethnography*, edited by Pete Ward, 200–22. Grand Rapids: Eerdmans, 2012.

———. "Theologies of Retrieval." In *The Oxford Handbook of Systematic Theology*, edited by John Webster, et al., 583–99. Oxford: Oxford University Press, 2007.

Wengst, Klaus. *The Pax Romana and the Peace of Jesus Christ*. Translated by John Bowden. London: SCM, 1987.

Wenham, G. J. "*betûlāh*: a Girl of Marriageable Age." *VT* 22 (1972) 326–48.

Westermann, Claus. *Genesis 12–36*. Translated by John J. Scullion. London: SPCK, 1986.

Wiesel, Elie. *Kingdom of Memory*. New York: Summit, 1990.

Williams, Catrin H. "Abraham as a Figure of Memory in John 8.31–59." In *The Fourth Gospel in First-Century Media Culture*, edited by Anthony Le Donne and Tom Thatcher, 205–22. LNTS 426. London: T & T Clark, 2011.

———. *I am He: The Interpretation of 'Anî Hû' in Jewish and Early Christian Literature*. WUNT 2.113. Tübingen: Mohr Siebeck, 2000.

Williams, Rowan. "Is there a Christian Sexual Ethic?" In *Open to Judgement: Sermons and Addresses*, 161–67. London: DLT, 1994.

———. "Making Moral Decisions." In *The Cambridge Companion to Christian Ethics*, edited by Robin Gill, 3–15. Cambridge: Cambridge University Press, 2001.

Wink, W. *Naming the Powers: The Language of Power in the New Testament*. Philadelphia: Fortress, 1984.

Witherington, B., III *The Letters to Philemon, the Colossians, and the Ephesians: A Socio-Rhetorical Commentary on the Captivity Epistles*. Grand Rapids: Eerdmans, 2007.

Wolf, H. "A Solution to the Immanuel Prophecy in Isaiah 7:14—8:22." *JBL* 91 (1972) 449–56.

Wolff, Stefan. *Ethnic Conflict: A Global Perspective*. Oxford: Oxford University Press, 2006.

Work, T. *Living and Active: Scripture and the Economy of Salvation*. Grand Rapids: Eerdmans, 2002.

Wrede, W. "The Tasks and Methods of 'New Testament Theology.'" In *The Nature of New Testament Theology*, edited by Robert Morgan, 68–116. London: SCM, 1973.

———. *Über Aufgabe und Methode der sogenannten neutestamentlichen Theologie*. Göttingen, 1897. Reprinted in G. Strecker, *Das Problem einer Theologie des Neuen Testaments*, 81–154. ET R. Morgan, *The Nature of New Testament Theology*. London: SCM, 1973.

Wright, N. T. *How God Became King*. London: SPCK, 2012.

———. *The Kingdom New Testament: A Contemporary Translation*. New York: HarperCollins, 2011.

———. *The New Testament and the People of God*. London: SPCK, 1992.

———. *Paul and the Faithfulness of God*. London: SPCK, 2013.

Yeago, D. S. "The Bible, the Church and the Scriptures: Biblical Inspiration and Interpretation Revisited." In *Knowing the Triune God. The Work of the Spirit and the Practices of the Church*, edited by J. J. Buckley and D. S. Yeago, 49–93. Grand Rapids: Eerdmans, 2001.

Yoder-Neufeld, T. R. *Ephesians.* Scottdale, PA: Herald, 2002.
Young, Frances M. *Biblical Exegesis and the Formation of Christian Culture.* Cambridge: Cambridge University Press, 1997.
Zachhuber, J. *Theology as Science in Nineteenth-Century Germany: From F. C. Baur to Ernst Troeltsch.* Oxford: Oxford University Press, 2013.
Zagefka, Hanna. "The Concept of Ethnicity in Social Psychology Research: Definitional Issues." *International Journal of Intercultural Relations* 33 (2009) 228–41.
Zelyck, L. R. *John among the Other Gospels: The Reception of the Fourth Gospel in the Extra-Canonical Gospels.* WUNT 2.347. Tübingen: Mohr Siebeck, 2013.

Index of Ancient Documents

OLD TESTAMENT

Genesis

	72, 224–35
1–3	227
1:1—2:3	228
1	102, 227
1:3	150
1:27	143
1:28	263
2:4	228
2:7	141
2:10–14	79
2:15	91
2:24	267, 272
3	94, 229
3:8	139
4–11	230
4:16	140
5:6	26
7:17	60
8:1	287
9:15–16	287
12	230
14:18	130
17:1–16	162
17:3	139
19	259
20	11
22	232
22:12	232
24:15–61	163
24:43	5
27:28	130
32:22–32	232
32:25	234
32:30	139, 146
35:10	25
40:13	61
40:14	283
40:19	61
40:20	61
40:23	283

Exodus

	72
2:8	5
29:40	130
31:8	148
33:11	139, 146
33:14	139
33:20	139
34	142
34:29–35	149
34:29	149

Leviticus

18:22	260–61
19	262
19:18	262
19:19	262
19:26	262

19:27	262	**Joshua**	
19:28	262		24
20:13	260–61		
26:3–6	94	**Judges**	
26:10	94	6:14–15	167
26:18–20	94	8:33–34	280
26:42	287	9:2	281
26:45	287	11:34–38	163
		13:5	167
Numbers		19	260
6:24–26	139		
11:5	281	**1 Samuel**	
12:6–8	146		276
12:8	146	1:11	287
15:37–40	278	2:3	239
21:4–9	63	24:21	285
21:4–7	65	25:31	283
21:8–9	64		
		2 Samuel	
Deuteronomy			276
2:13–15	96	7:11b–16	4
4:25–34	101	7:12–14	84
5:12–15	283	7:18–26	171
7:18	280	11:4	27
8:2–6	283	15:12	27
8:11–20	283	18:18	285
9:7	284	23:34	27
9:10–11	148		
10:12–22	101	**1 Kings**	
15:15	283		276
16:12	283	18:20–38	101
20:19	91	21	94, 96
22:4	91		
22:6–7	91	**2 Kings**	
22:13–21	163		276
24:18	283	11	90
24:22	283	16	4
25:4	91	17:15	94, 97
25:17	285		
28:2–5	94	**1 Chronicles**	
28:11–12	94		276
28:15–18	94		
29:20	285	**2 Chronicles**	
32:20	139		276
32:36–43	101	24:22	283
33:23–29	101		

Ezra

9–10	263, 267
9:2	263
9:11	263

Nehemiah

9:17	280

Job

1–2	39

Psalms

	72, 97
2	9, 84–85
2:7	84, 168
3	279–80
3:7[3:8LXX]	101
5:9	96
7:6[7:7LXX]	101
8:4–9	102
9:12[13]	287
9:19[9:20LXX]	101
10[9LXX]	97
10:3	96
10:7	96
10:12[9:33LXX]	101
14[13LXX]	97
17:13[16:13LXX]	101
17:47[LXX][18:48EV]	60
27:6	139
27:8	140
27:9	139
36:3	96
42:2	140
44:26[43:27LXX]	101
45:11[LXX][46:10EV]	60
65	94
68:1[67:2LXX]	101
71[70LXX]	97
72	85, 94
78:42	280
82[81LXX]	101
82:8[81:8LXX]	101
89	85
95:2	140
96:9[LXX][97:9EV]	60
97	95
97:7	94
98:3	287
102:2	139
102:13[101:14LXX]	101
104:15	130
105:4	140
105:8	287
105:42	287
106:7	280
106:20[105:20LXX]	93–94
106:24	93
109:16	283
115	95, 101
115:3–8	94
115:8	94
115:12	287
119:33	240
119:73	240
132:8[131:8LXX]	101
135	101
135:1–7	95
140[139LXX]	97
140:3	96
143:5	279
143:7	139
146	95

Proverbs

3:10	130
15:25	96
16:19	96
20:1	132
22:8	97
23:31	126–27
30:19	5

Ecclesiastes

3:19	97

Isaiah

	72, 79
1–55	9
1–12	9, 12
1:21–26	9
1:27–31	9
2–12	12, 13
2:6–8	94
2:7–11	96
2:11	60

4:2	62	30:18	60
5:11–12	132	31:1–5	10
5:16	62	31:1–3	90
6:9–10	68	31:16	139
6:9	248	33:10	62
7	4	35	94
7–8	7, 9–12	37	10
7:1—9:1	xv, 8	37:23	60
7:1–6	4	40–48	101
7:1–16	10	40	12
7:2	4	40:13–14	239
7:3	4	41:17–20	95
7:9	10	42:8	94
7:9	4	43:10	68
7:12	8	43:18–19	282
7:13	4	44:9	94, 97
7:14	xv, 3, 4, 6, 11, 163–64	44:10–20	94
7:14–16	7, 8, 11, 13, 15–16	45:1–8	95
7:15–16	4, 11	45:1	10
7:17–25	10	45:5	44
7:17	8	45:18–19	95
8:1–4	7, 8, 10–11, 13	46	281
8:5–8	8, 10	46:9	281
8:9–10	8	47	90
8:9–11	10	47:7	275
8:11–15	9–10	52–53	68
8:16–23a	9–10	52:12—53:1	68
8:16	8	52:13—53:12	63
8:18	9, 11	52:13–15	62
8:23a	9	52:13	62–63
9:2	150	52:14–15	62–63
9:5–6[6–7]	10	52:15	63, 68
10:5–6	87	53:1–11	63
10:15	62	53:1	68
10:22	97	54:4–5	284
11	85	56–66	9
11:10	97	56:5	286
12	12	58	283
12:1	12	59:20–21	97
13:11	96	63:10–11	287
13:19	90	64:9[8]	288
14:12	80	65:17	288
14:28	10	67:1	139
20:1–6	90		
23	90	**Jeremiah**	
24:1–13	91	2:2	281
28:7	132	2:5	93, 94, 97
29:1–8	10	2:7	93

2:11	93–94
2:18–19	90
4:23–28	91
5:7–9	94
6:6	96
6:9	96
7:6	97
7:9	97
8:10	95
9:3–14	95
10:1–15	101
10:2	94
10:3	94, 97
10:14	94–95
10:15	94, 97
22:9–17	94
22:17	96
31:33	148
50–51	90
51:17–18	94
51:17	94

Lamentations

1:7	283
1:9	275
2:1	287

Ezekiel

16:22	275
16:43	275
16:60	287
16:63	284
18:1–19	94
20:7–8	90
20:43	284
22:1–16	94
22:22	94
22:27–29	96
36:26	148
36:31	284
47:1–12	79

Daniel

	83, 88
7	77
7:14	102

Hosea

2:23	97
4	94
4:1–3	91, 96
4:2–3	93
4:2	93
4:6	94–95
4:7–19	94
4:7	93, 94
4:8	94
5:11	94, 97
7:2	287

Amos

1	91
1:9	283
2:6–8	94
4:1–4	91
5:2	91
9:14	130

Micah

5:1	29
6:9–16	94, 96
7:1–13	96–97
7:1–3	96

Habakkuk

1–3	91
1:5–6	87
2	95
2:4–5	96
2:4	92
2:6–17	96–97
2:6	92
2:8	92
2:9–10	94
2:9	92, 96
2:10	92
2:11	93
2:17	92
2:18–19	92, 101
2:18	94
2:20	93

NEW TESTAMENT

Matthew

	215, 276
1–2	xv, 19, 30, 164
1	26
1:1	26
1:1–17	26
1:2–17	34
1:3	27
1:5	27
1:6	27
1:16	163
1:18—12:23	27
1:18–25	27–28, 162–65
1:18	163, 16
1:19	164
1:20–21	28
1:20	163–64
1:21	30, 164
1:22–23	164
1:22	163
1:23	3, 6
1:24	164
1:25	164–65
2	29
2:1	29
2:2	29, 30
2:5	29
2:1–23	27
2:6	28, 30
2:20	29
2:21	29
2:22–23	29
3:7b–9	34
4:10	25
4:15	31
5:9	33
5:27–32	266
5:45	33
5:47	31
6:32	31
6:7	31
7:28	161
8:5–13	30
8:11	31
10:5–6	30
10:5	31
10:18	31
11:2	37
11:19	37, 127
11:23–24	260
11:23	60
12:17–21	31
12:18	31
12:21	31
12:24	76
15:24	30
15:21–28	30
18:15–20	31–32
18:20	164
19:9	266
19:10	266
19:11	266
19:12	266
19:28	30
20:19	31
20:25	31
21:43	31
22:39	262
23	xv, xvi, 19, 31–32
23:7	32
23:8–12	32
23:9	32
23:1–12	33
23:12	60
23:29–36	33
23:29	33
23:30–32	33
23:30	33
23:33	34
24:7	31
24:9	31
24:14	31
24:49	127
25:32	31
27:42	30
28:18–20	31
28:19	31
28:20	164

Mark

	46, 276
1:22	160
1:27	160
1:41	161

Index of Ancient Documents   337

3:20-35	160	3:23	168
3:31-35	266	4:6	78
4:3-20	160	4:16-30	168
5:33	161	4:22	168
5:41	161	7:34	127
5:42	161	9:20	168
6:1-6	168	9:43	161
6:2-3	159	10:15	60
6:2	160-61	10:18	80
6:3	160-61	12:45	127
6:4	160	14:11	60
7:11	115	18:14	60
7:21-22	123	21:34	127
7:34	161		
7:37	161		

John

	203, 292-97, 301
1:1-18	36
1:1-2	44
1:1	37
1:3-4	44
1:3	44
1:4-5	41
1:14	36-38, 41, 44-46
1:12-13	32
1:17	41, 50
1:18	38, 40, 84
1:29	55
2	79
2:1-10	125
2:4	77
2:10	127
2:13-23	298
2:13-20	44
3:3-4	58
3:6	37
3:13-21	68
3:13-15	59
3:13	39, 65, 67
3:14-15	64, 65
3:14	58, 63-65, 67
3:15	64, 65
3:16-21	66
3:19-21	41, 50, 55
3:31-36	66
3:34	41
4:1-42	44
4:10-14	126
4:10-11	58

Mark (continued):
8:29	168
8:31	58, 64
9:17-27	271
9:31	58
10:2-12	266
10:33-34	58
11:8	161
12:24-25	266
15:42	115

Luke

1:5-25	169
1:15	126
1:26-38	167, 169-70
1:26-35	172
1:30-35	170
1:31-33	171
1:32-35	172
1:32	170-71
1:33	171
1:35	171-72
1:36-37	169-70
1:38	172
1:52	60
2	168
2:1-7	168
2:5	168
2:7	168-69
2:22-24	169
2:22	169
3-4	168
3:21—24:30	168
3:22	168

4:25	42	9:29	53
4:46–54	44	9:32	54
5:1–24	298	9:34	54
5:19–29	66	9:37	54
5:19	41	9:38	54
6	80	9:39	54
6:38	39	9:40	52, 55
6:40	65	9:41	55
6:53–58	38	10	78, 86
6:54–58	126	10:4–5	42
6:62	39	10:14	42
6:63	37	10:16	64
6:69	42	10:30	40, 45
6:70	80	10:38	42
7	78	11	77, 298
7:28	41	11:48	77
7:28–29	42	11:50	77
7:35	44	11:51	64
7:37–52	298	11:52	77
7:37–39	126	12	76–77, 81–82
7:38	79	12:1–11	299
8	78	12:19	77, 82
8:12	41	12:20–43	68
8:26	41, 66	12:20–36	xvi, 81
8:28–29	59	12:20–26	44, 76–77, 81
8:28	40, 58, 65–67	12:20–22	67
8:29	66	12:20	77
8:31	51	12:21	65
8:32	41, 42	12:23	68, 77, 80
8:34–36	55	12:24	67, 77
8:34	51	12:27–38	82
8:39–59	80	12:27–36	68
8:40	51	12:31–34	59
8:42	41	12:31–32	78
8:58	40, 51	12:31	83
9	xvi, 21, 42, 49, 54, 56, 78	12:32	58, 67–69
9:2	54	12:34	58, 64, 68
9:3	50	12:30–36	xvi, 66,
9:4	51	12:37–40	68
9:8–34	54	12:31	66, 75–76, 80, 82
9:8–9	51	12:32	67
9:10	52	12:33	67
9:11	52	12:36	41
9:12	52	12:45	40, 65
9:19	52	12:46–50	66
9:22	52	12:46	41
9:24	53	12:49	41, 241
9:27–28	21, 53	13–17	xvii, 78, 82

Index of Ancient Documents 339

13	86	19:12	84
13:1	85	19:14	83
13:2	80, 81	19:15	83–84
13:19	40	19:19	83
13:27	80–81	19:21–22	83
13:30	80	19:34	45
13:31	80	19:36–37	65
14	xvi, 79, 81	20:21	87
14:2	45	20:31	38
14:6	41, 45	21:22	89
14:7	42	21:25	89
14:9	40, 65		
14:10	241		

Acts

2:13–15	126, 133
2:16	258
2:33	59, 60
2:39	115
5:30	60
5:31	59
5:39	126
9	243
9:15	243
13:9	116
13:12	161
15	258
16:26	126
17:22	26
24:19	26
26:5	25
26:14	126
26:24–25	126

14:17	42
14:20	42
14:26	241
14:28	41
14:30–31	81, 83
14:30	72, 76, 81
14:31	79
15:1–5	126
15:18	72
16:2	25, 72
16:8–11	81, 83, 87
16:11	76
16:33	72, 82–83
17	79, 82
17:3	40, 42
18–19	xvii, 82
18	72, 80, 81
18:3	81
18:10–11	85
18:12	81
18:26—19:16	83
18:31–32	67
18:33	83
18:36	85
18:37	86
18:38	73, 86
19–20	70
19	72, 80, 81
19:1–3	83
19:3	83
19:5	86
19:7	84
19:8	84
19:10	87
19:11	87

Romans

1	xvii, 92–95
1:1–18	92
1:1	243
1:29–31	123
1:3–4	84, 171–72
1:4	102
1:16	92
1:18–23	260
1:18	92, 94, 101
1:19–20	93
1:20–21	94
1:21–22	94, 240
1:21	93, 97
1:22	93
1:23	94, 102

340 Index of Ancient Documents

1:24–31	94
1:24–25	260
1:25	93–94
1:26–31	93
1:26–27	260
1:28–31	260
1:28	96
1:29	92–93, 96
1:30	96
1:31	96
3:10–18	96
3:23–24	261
3:27	261
4	97
5:2	101
5:8	101
5:12–21	97
5:12	91
5:17	101
6–8	97
8	xvii, 91, 98, 102
8:1–2	97
8:1	120
8:3–4	84
8:3	xvi, 39
8:5	112
8:6	112
8:7	112
8:9–10	120
8:19–23	91
8:19–21	102
8:19	91, 102
8:20	91, 97
8:21	102
8:22	91
8:23	102
8:26	102
8:27	112
8:29	102
8:30	101–2
8:23	98
8:35	98
9:4	25
9:25	97
9:27	97
11:20	112
11:25	112
11:26	97
11:32	239
11:34	239
12–15	112
12:1–2	275
12:1	25
12:2	152
12:3	112, 119
12:16	101, 112
13:1–7	87
13:13	123, 127
14:6	112
15:5	112, 114
15:12	97

1 Corinthians

	130
1:1	243
2	245
2:7	245
2:8	82
2:9–10	245
2:10–11	245
2:12	245
2:13	245
2:16	239
4:16	120
5–7	xx, 265–67
5:1	267
5:2	267
5:9–11	261
5:10–11	123
5:11	127
5:16	124
6:9–10	123
6:9	261, 267
6:10	127
6:12	266
6:15–18	267
6:16	261, 267
7	269, 271–72
7:1	266
7:3–4	269
7:4	269
7:7	270
7:9	270
7:10–11	270
7:12–16	267
7:14	268

Index of Ancient Documents   341

7:15	270
7:26	269
7:28	270
7:32–35	270
7:33–34	269
7:36	270
7:39	270
7:40	270
8:1–3	147
8:3	147
10:11	14
11–14	122, 125, 129–30
11	129, 134
11:1	120
11:11–12	268
11:14	264
11:17	129
11:18	129
11:20	129
11:21	124–25, 127, 129
11:33	129
11:34	129
12–14	129, 134, 145
12:13	126, 129
13:2	147
13:9	147
13:12	xvii, 138, 145–46
14:23	126, 129
14:26	129
15:10	146
15:24–28	145
15:28	145

2 Corinthians

1:1	243
2:14—14:6	147–48
2:17	148
3	153
3:1–3	148
3:3	148
3:6	148
3:7–11	149
3:7	150
3:12–18	149
3:12	149
3:13	149–50
3:14	149
3:15	149
3:16–18	150
3:16	149
3:17	149
3:17–18	149
3:18	xvii, 138, 145, 147, 149–51
4	119, 153
4:3–6	150
4:4	78, 151
4:6	xvii, 138, 145, 148, 151
4:16	152
5:17	151
10:10	151
11:7	60
11:13	148
11:22	148
11:23–29	151
12:7–9	152
12:20–21	123

Galatians

1:1	243
1:15	243
2:19–20	120
4:4	xvi, 39
4:9	147
5:19–21	123
5:21	127

Ephesians

	130
1:1	243
1:4	243
2:1	243
2:2	78
2:10	243
3	133
3:7	243
4:1	133
4:2	133
4:18	240
4:24	133
4:25	133
4:31	123
4:32	133
5:3–5	123
5:3	133
5:4–20	134
5:21–33	268

5:4	xvii, 134
5:8	123
5:18–19	122, 126, 130, 133
5:18	xvii, 122, 126–27
5:19	129
5:19–20	125
6:12	78

Philippians

1:3–6	111
1:5	113
1:6	111, 113
1:7	110–13
1:8	113, 118
1:9	111, 113
1:19	111
1:22	111
1:25	111
1:27—22:4	104, 110, 121
1:28	111
2	105, 119, 121
2:1–4	108, 111, 113, 115, 120
2:1	111, 113, 118, 121
2:2–4	112
2:2	110, 112, 118
2:3–4	118–19
2:4	114
2:5	xvii, 104–5, 108–9, 111–13, 115–21
2:6	121
2:6–11	104, 108–9, 113, 115, 119–20
2:6–8	112, 115, 118–19
2:6–7	xvi, 39
2:7	120
2:9	59–60
2:12–16	121
2:12	120
2:13	113, 121
3	121
3:3–14	111
3:7	112
3:15	111–12
3:19	112
4:2	112, 118
4:8	112
4:9	112
4:10	112

Colossians

1:1	243
1:15–20	87
1:21	240
2:9	37
2:14–15	82
2:18	25
3:5–8	123
3:10	102
3:16	129

1 Thessalonians

5:7	127

1 Timothy

1:9–10	123, 261
3:3	127–28
5:14	270
6:4–5	123

2 Timothy

1:1	243
1:5	115
3:2–4	123

Titus

1:1–3	244
1:7	128
3:3	123

Hebrews

4:12	223
7:2	115
7:4–10	15
7:9–10	27
9:1	25
9:6	25
11	285
12:25–26	115

James

1:26–27	25
4:4	78
4:10	60

1 Peter

2:1	123

4:3	123, 128
4:15	123
5:6	60

2 Peter
1:21	242

1 John
	37–38, 203
2:20	241
3:2	241
4:4	78
5:19	78

Jude
7	260

Revelation
	83
1:11	245
1:19	245
9:21	123
12:8–9	80
13	82
13:2	xvi, 81
21:8	123
22:15	123

APOCRYPHA AND SEPTUAGINT

IV Kingdoms
19:22	60
25:27	60

Baruch
3:37	41
4:1	37

Sirach
	72
23:22–24	158
23:22	158
24:23	37
24:43	43
25:24	168
26:10–12	158
31:25–31	132
38:24—39:15	159
42:9–11	158
42:10	159, 163
49:15–16	168

Wisdom of Solomon
	72
10–11	36
13:4–5	161
14:22–27	263
16:6–7	64
18:14–16	36

OLD TESTAMENT PSEUDEPIGRAPHA

1 Enoch
42	41

2 Enoch
44:1–3	143

Letter of Aristeas
263	60

3 Maccabees
	132, 133
6:30–36	130–31

Psalms of Solomon
1:5	60
17–18	167

Sibylline Oracles
3.583	60

Testament of Judah
21.8	60

DEAD SEA SCROLLS

1QH
4:5–6	142
4:27–29	142

APOSTOLIC FATHERS

Martyrdom of Polycarp
10.2	87

NAG HAMMADI CODICES

Trimorphic Protennoia
13:47.15–16	45
13:50.12–15	45

GREEK AND LATIN WORKS

Artemidorus
Oneirocritica
2:53	61
4:49	61

Athenaeus
Deipnosophistae
1.61	127
15.675b–c	135

Augustine
Dr Doctrina Christiana
	179

Evangelium Johannis Tractatus
49.14	124

Caesarius of Arles
Sermons
46.1	124

Chrysostom
Homiliae in Epistulam ad Ephesios
19	124

Clement of Alexandria
Excerpta ex Theodoto
1:6	44
1:7	44
1:41.3–4	44
55:3	44
61:1–4	45

Paedagogus
2.2	124

Diogenes Laertius
VI.6	269
X.119	269

Epiphanius
Panarion
31:9.1–27	43
51:3–4	43

Irenaeus
Adversus Haereses
1:1.1–8	43
1:1.1–3	44
1:1.8.5	44
1:2.2	44
1:4.1	44
1:5.1–6	44
1:5.1	44
1:5.4	44
1:6.1	44
1:6.2	44
1:6.4	44
1:7.5	44
1:8.2–4	45
1:9.3	45
3:11.2–3	45
3.11.7	43
3:16.2	45
3:16.5–8	45
3:17.4	45
3:18.1	45

3:18.7	45
3:19.1	45
5:18.2–3	45

Josephus
Bellum Judaicum

2.219	60
5.523	60
7.153–57	85

Contra Apionem

	28, 33
1.179	25
2.199–202	164

Origen
Commentarii in Evangelium Joannis

2:15	44

De Principiis

	179

Letter to Gregory in Patrologia Graeca

11.88–89	182

Philo
De Abrahamo

100	37

De Cherubim

9–10	37
40–52	165
42	166
43	166
44	166
45	37
48	166
40–50	37
50	166

De Congressu Eruditionis Gratia

9	37
13	37
22	37
79–80	37

129	37

De Ebriatate

147–48	134

De Mutatione Nominum

79–80	37
151–53	37

De Posteritate Caini

2	140

De Specialibus Legibus

4.123	141
3.9, 113	164

De Virtutibus

217	141

De Vita Mosis

2.70	141

Legum Allegoriarum

1.39	141
2.82	37

Questiones et Solutiones in Genesim

2.62	40

Quod Deterius Potiori Insidiari Soleat

124	37

Plato
Laws

	132, 133
2.666a–c	128

Republic

	128
389d–e	131
475a	132

Pliny the Elder
Natural History

14.29.149	127

Plutarch
De Garrulitate
4   134

Seneca
Epistles
11.2   144
116.5   269

Strabo
Geography
17.2.5   127

Other
The Prayer of Joseph   37

Author Index

Adams, Edward, 21 n.6
Adams, Samuel L., 100 n.48
Aichele, G., 14 n.22
Albertz, Rainer, 14 n.22
Alexander, Loveday, xx; 257 n.6; 258 and nn.12,13; 259 n.19; 267 n.32; 269 n.36; 270 nn.41,43
Allison, D. C., 27 n.31
Appold, M. L., 41 n.19
Ashton, John, 40 n.15; 198; 199
Asumang, A., 122 and n.1

Balch, David L., 266 n.31
Balentine, Samuel E., 139 n.4
Ballard, Paul, 218 n.35
Barclay, John, 151 n.19
Barrett, C. K., 38 n.10; 41 nn.18,19; 43 n.28; 78 n.24; 189 n.4; 209
Bar-Tal, Daniel, 21 n.8
Bartelt, Andrew H., 12 and n.20
Barth, Fredrik, xv; 21 and n.10; 22 and nn.11,13; 27;
Barth, Karl, 194 and nn.15–17; 197 n.21; 201 and n.26; 202; 204; 205 and nn.34,35; 206 and n.39; 246 and nn.4–7
Barth, M., 124 n.4; 125
Barton, Caitlin, 143; 144 nn.11,12
Barton, Stephen C., xvii; 112 n.29
Bauckham, Richard, 62 n.16; 63 n.20; 73 and nn.2,3; 175 n.4; 257 nn.7,10; 258 and n.11
Bauer, G. L., 188 n.2; 189 and n.6; 192 n.12

Baumgarten, Michael, 226 and n.12
Baur, F. C., 200 and n.23; 201; 204 and n.33; 206 and n.40
Bavinck, H., 247 n.9
Beale, G. K., 93 n.11; 94 n.18; 95 n.21; 188 n.2
Belfiore, E., 128 n.18; 129 n.19
Bennett, Zoë, 220 n.42
Berger, K., 175 n.3
Berkouwer, G. C., 247 n.9
Bernoulli, C. A., 201 n.24
Berry, Wendell, 90 n.1
Bertram, G., 59 n.6
Best, E., 125 n.6
Beutler, Johannes, 68 n.33
Beyschlag, W., 191 n.10
Billings, J. Todd, 214 n.14
Blenkinsopp, Joseph, 5 n.4; 6–7 n.11
Blowers, Paul M., 213 n.8
Bockmuehl, Markus, 108 and nn.14–18; 109; 116; 120 n.45
Bonhoeffer, Dietrich, 220 n.41
Boyer, James L., 115 nn.32,34,35
Bredin, Mark, 27 nn.30,31
Brooke, George J., 259 n.18
Brooke, S. A., 225 and nn.4–9; 226 n.10
Brown, Malcolm, 254 n.2
Brown, Peter, 269 n.40
Brown, Raymond E., 42 n.23; 43 nn.28,31; 45 n.41; 53 n.19; 56 n.24; 69 and n.35; 159 n.2; 163 n.13; 164 n.17; 169; 170 and nn.22,23; 171 and nn.25,26

Author Index

Bruce, F. F., 257 and n.8
Brueggemann, Walter, xvii; 14 n.22; 16 and nn.31,32; 17; 92 n.7; 96 n.26; 101 nn.52,53
Bühner, J.-A., 39 n.13
Bultmann, R., 40 and n.15; 42 and nn.24,25,26; 43 n.28; 46 n.47; 192 n.13; 194 n.15; 197 n.21; 201 and n.27; 203 and n.30; 204; 206 and n.40; 207 n.41
Burtchaell, J. T., 249 n.10
Butterfield, H., 193 n.14

Cadbury, Henry J., 116 n.39
Caird, G. B., 116 and n.38
Campbell, Constantine R., 118 n.42
Carson, D. A., 212 and n.6
Carter, W., 74 and n.13; 75
Catchpole, David R., xviii; 159 n.5
Chadwick, Henry, 257 n.10
Charlesworth, J. H., 43 n.28
Childs, Brevard S., 5 nn.2,5; 6 n.6; 7 and n.13; 14 and nn.23,24,25; 15 and nn.28,29; 16 and nn.32,33; 188 n.2
Cockburn, Bruce, xx; 289 and n.1; 290 and n.2; 291 and n.3
Cole, Jonathan, 136 n.2
Colenso, J. W., 224
Cölln, Daniel G. C. von, 188 n.2
Conzelmann, H., 194 n.17
Crawford, M. R., 238 n.1
Culpepper, R. A., 43 n.31
Cummings, Brian, 272 n.44

Danker, F. W., 26 n.26
Davies, Jamie P., xvi
Davies, Margaret, 260 n.23
Davies, W. D., 27 n.31
Davis, Ellen F., 91 and nn.3,4,5; 94 and n.19; 220 n.42; 256 n.4; 258 n.11; 259 n.17
Delitzsch, F., 226 and n.11
Deming, Will, 267 n.32; 268 n.33; 269 n.36
Derrida, Jacques, 292
Dodd, C. H., 43 n.28; 44 n.32; 63 n.20; 198; 199

Doney, Malcolm, 256 n.5
Doniger, Wendy, 152 n.24
Douglas, Mary, 152 and n.23
Drewery, Benjamin, 257 nn.7,10; 258 n.11
Drinkwater Jr., Joel F., 138 n.3
Driver, S. R., 234 and n.42
Dunderberg, J., 45 n.40
Dunn, J. D. G., xvi; 36 n.2; 38 n.11; 39 n.12; 47 n.50; 124 n.4
Dwyer, Timothy, 161 n.10

Eastman, Susan Grove, 109 n.19
Ebeling, G., 188 n.1
Ehrman, B. D., 38 n.10
Ekblad, Eugene Robert, 62 n.19
Elliott, John H., 25 and n.24
Elliott, Neil, 95 and n.22; 96 n.30
Ellis, E. Earle, 259 n.17
Esler, Philip F., xv; 20 n.3; 21 nn.7,9; 25 n.23; 29 n.34; 30 n.35; 31 nn.36,37; 32 n.39; 34 n.40; 35 n.41
Evans, Craig A., 68 n.33; 125 n.5; 126 and nn.13,14
Evans, Donald, 207 n.41

Fitzmyer, Joseph A., 142 and nn.8,9; 151 and nn.18,20
Foerster, W., 43 n.30; 44 nn.36,37,39
Ford, David F., 136 n.2; 153 and n.25
Forrester, Duncan, 217; 218 n.34
Fowl, Stephen E., xviii; 105 n.3; 107 and n.7; 112 and nn.27,28; 177 n.8; 182 n.14; 211 and n.3; 216 and nn.26,28; 218; 219; 259 nn.15,16
Fraser, Mariam, 152 n.22
Fretheim, Terence, 98 n.36
Frey, Jörg, 59 n.1; 64 nn.22,23; 65 nn.24,28; 67 n.32; 68 n.33
Frick, H., 193
Frye, Northrop, 12 n.17
Fulford, B., 238 n.1
Fulton, Deirdre N., 158 n.1

Gabler, J. P., 189 and nn.3,4,6; 196
Gadamer, Hans-Georg, 202

Gagnon, Robert A. J., 260 n.23
Gaventa, Beverly Roberts, 195 n.18
Girardet, Herbert, 99 nn.42,43
Goldingay, John, xx; 16 n.30; 285 n.15
Goodacre, Mark, 176 n.5
Gorman, Michael J., xvii; 105 n.2; 119 n.44; 120 n.47; 121 nn.48,49; 195 n.18
Gosnell, P. W., 125 n.6
Gray, Mark, 284 n.13
Greco, Monica, 152 n.22
Green, Joel, 178 n.11; 180 n.13
Greimas, A. J., 291; 297
Griffin, Susan, 96 n.26
Gruenwald, I., 37 n.8
Güpfest, H., 227 n.17
Gutiérrez, Gustavo, 276 n.3
Güttgemanns, Erhard, 175 n.2

Haenchen, E., 76 n.21
Hahn, F., 203 n.31
Halperin, D. J., 37 n.8
Harrer, G. A., 117 n.41
Harrington, Daniel J., 6 and n.9
Harris McCoy, Daniel E., 61 nn.11,14
Hart, Ray L., 18 n.41
Harvey, A. E., 86 n.32
Hauerwas, Stanley, xix; 212; 213 n.12; 214; 215 and nn.18,20,22; 216 n.27; 217 and n.33; 221 n.45
Hawkin, David J., 99 n.43
Hays, Richard B., 92 n.10; 148 and n.15; 149 and n.16; 150 and n.17; 151 n.18; 195 n.18; 256 n.4
Healy, Nicholas M., 213 and n.9; 215 and nn.19,21; 222 n.51
Heath, Jane M. F., 63 n.21
Hegel, G. W. F., 200
Heidegger, M., 201 n.27
Hendel, Ron, 178 n.10
Hendriksen, W., 125 n.5
Hengel, M., 45 n.44; 73 and n.5; 87
Hengstenberg, E. W., 226 and n.12
Heppe, H., 246 n.4
Herder, J. G., 227
Hill, C. E., 45 n.44
Hofmann, J. C. K. von, 188 n.2
Hollis, H., 61 n.10

Homan, M. M., 127 n.17
Hooker, Morna D., 109 n.19
Hooker, Richard, 257 n.10
Horrell, David G., 25 n.22; 91 n.6; 97 n.35; 98 n.38
Horsley, Richard A., 88; 100 n.48; 277 and nn.5–7; 278 and n.8
Houlden, J. L., 124 n.4
Hovey, Craig, 221 and n.44
Hübner, H., 188 n.2
Hughes, J. Donald, 100 and nn.46,47,49
Humphries-Brooks, Stephenson, 27 n.31
Hunter, David G., 269 n.40; 272 n.45
Hurtado, Larry W., 108 and n.13
Hutchinson, John, xv; 22; 23 and n.14; 25

Ilan, Tal, 160 n.7; 162 and n.12
Inman, Patrick B., 20 n.1

Jensen, Derrick, 96 n.26
Jenson, Robert W., 214 nn.13, 15; 216 n.27; 219
Jervis, L. Ann, xvi
Jewett, Robert, 99 n.39
John, Jeffrey, 273 n.47
Jonas, H., 45 n.41
Jongman, William M., 99 n.40

Kaftan, J., 201 n.25
Kant, I., 193
Kanyinga, Karuti, 20 n.2
Käsemann, Ernst, 40 n.15; 42 and n.27; 43; 46 and nn.46,48; 107 and n.12; 109
Kaufman, Gordon D., 18 n.41
Keener, Craig S., 7 n.12; 73; 81 and n.26
Keesmaat, Sylvia C., xvii; 92 n.8; 98 n.36; 99 n.39; 102 nn.55,57; 306 n.44
Kehoe, Dennis, 99 n.41
Kelber, W. H., 277 n.5
Kingsley, Charles, 224 and n.2; 225 n.3; 234
Klink III, Edward, 176 n.4

Knöppler, Thomas, 65 n.24; 67 n.32
Koestenberger, A. I., 73 and n.4
Koester, Craig, 65 and n.25
Koester, H., 43 n.28
Kovacs, Judith, 205 nn.36,37; 269 n.40
Kümmel, W. G., 43 n.28; 191 n.9
Kvalbein, H., 73; 73 n.5; 87

Labahn, Michael, 61 nn.12,14
Lakey, Michael, 136 n.1
Legaspi, Michael, 177 n.7
Lessing, Gotthold Ephraim, 193; 226; 227 and nn.17,18; 229
Levering, Matthew, 215; 216 n.23; 238 n.1
Levin, Yigal, 159 n.3
Levinas, Emmanuel, 136 n.2
Levine, Amy-Jill, 27 n.31
Lietzmann, Hans, 194 n.15
Lincoln, Andrew T., xiii; xvi; xvii; xviii; xx; xxi; 6 and nn.7,8; 19; 36 and n.1; 37 n.6; 39 n.14; 41 n.18; 43 n.28; 48 and nn.1-4; 49 and nn.5-13; 50 and n.15; 52 n.17; 55 n.21; 59 nn.2,3; 69 and n.36; 75 n.20; 86; 88; 105 n.4; 121 and n.50; 122; 123 and n.2; 125 n.8; 126 and n.15; 133 n.24; 134; 136 n.1; 157; 159 and n.4; 160 and nn.6,8,9; 163 n.14; 164 n.15; 165 and nn.18,19; 167 and nn.20,21; 171 and n.24; 173; 174; 176 n.6; 202; 203; 207 n.42; 209; 210 and n.1; 211; 213 n.10; 224 n.1; 253; 268 n.35; 290; 291 and nn.3,4; 292 and nn.5-8; 293 and nn.9-13; 294 and nn.15-19; 295 and nn.20-21; 296; 297 and nn.22,23; 300 and nn.34,35; 301 and n.37
Lindars, Barnabas, 76 n.21; 258 and n.14; 266 n.31
Lindbeck, George A., 216 and n.25; 219 and n.38
Litwa, M. David, 146 n.14
Loader, William, 260 n.23; 263 n.25; 266 nn.29,31; 269 n.39
LoCascio, Elio, 99 n.40
Locher, C., 5 n.5

Lohse, Eduard, 138 n.3; 140 n.5
Longenecker, B. W., 201 n.28
Lossius, J. C., 188 n.2
Lust, J., 59 n.5
Luz, Ulrich, 26 and n.27; 205 n.37
Lyell, Charles, 228

MacDonald, Margaret Y., 95 n.24
Macquarrie, John, 207 n.41
MacRae, G. W., 42 n.24
Malherbe, Abraham, 264 nn.27,28; 268 n.33
Malina, Bruce J., 20 n.5; 26 n.28; 161 n.11
Marcus, Joel, 61 n.15; 95 n.21
Mardaga, Hellen, 59 n.6
Margalit, Avishai, 274 n.1; 281 n.12; 284 n.14; 285 and n.16; 286 nn.17,18
Marohl, Matthew J., 28 n.32
Martin, Dale B., 260 n.23
Martin, Ralph P., 107 and n.12; 109; 123 n.3
Martyn, J. Louis, 52 and n.18; 56 n.24; 141 n.7; 145 and n.13
Maurice, F. D., 224; 232 and n.32
McConville, J. Gordon, xiv; xv
McHugh, J. F., 37 n.6; 38 n.10
McKinlay, Judith E., 27 n.31
McKnight, S., 89 n.36
McNamara, Martin, 61 n.9
Meeks, Wayne A., 69 n.37; 108 n.14; 112 n.26; 194 n.17; 197
Meggitt, Justin J., 61 nn.12,13
Metzger, B. M., 38 n.10
Meyer, P. W., 41 n.19
Middleton, Richard J., 95 n.25; 102 n.56
Milgrom, Jacob, 278 n.9
Miller-McLemore, Bonnie J., 222 n.52
Mitchell, Claire, 23 and n.17; 24 and nn.18,19,20; 28
Moberly, R. W. L., 7 n.13; 136 n.1; 220 n.43
Moloney, Francis J., 65 nn.24,27; 74 and nn.11,15; 75
Moltmann, Jürgen, 276 n.4

Moore, Stephen D., 73 and nn.5–8; 74 and nn.9,10; 75; 81 n.25; 83 and n.27; 88; 260 n.23
Morgan, Robert, xviii; 189 nn.3,4; 190 n.7; 191 n.11; 194 n.17
Morley, Neville, 99 n.40
Morris, L., 78 n.24
Mosser, Carl, 73 n.2
Moule, C. F. D., 111 n.23; 209
Mowat, Harriet, 218 n.36
Muddiman, J., 124 n.4; 125 and n.7
Muller, R. A., 244 n.3

Nagel, T., 45 n.44
Niebergall, F., 193; 194 n.15
Nietzsche, Friedrich, 292
Nisbett, H. B., 226 and nn.14,15; 227 n.16
Nissinen, Marti, 255 n.3; 260 nn.20–23; 261 n.24; 263 nn.25,26; 266 n.30; 268 n.34

Oakes, Peter, 96 and n.31; 98 n.37; 100 n.50
O'Brien, Peter T., 104 n.1; 109 n.19; 111 n.23; 123 n.3
Odeberg, H., 39 n.14
Orlov, A. A., 37 n.8
Osiek, Carolyn, 266 n.31
Oswalt, John N., 7 n.12; 16 n.30
Overbeck, Franz, 191 and n.8; 194 and n.16

Paddison, Angus, xiv; xix; 210; 211; 214 n.17; 238 n.1
Pagels, E. H., 43 n.29; 44 nn.32,39
Pancaro, S., 50 n.14; 56 n.25
Parsons, M. C., 201 n.28
Peacock, James L., 20 n.1
Pelikan, Jaroslav, 212
Pesch, Otto, 14 and n.25
Peterson, Eugene H., 269 n.38
Phoenix, Ann, 21 n.10
Pierce, Madison N., 65 n.26
Pietersen, Lloyd K., xiv; xvii
Porter, Stanley E., 125 and nn.5,11; 126 and n.12; 180 n.13; 212 and nn.5,6

Portier-Young, A., 76 n.23
Powell, M. A., 127 n.16
Preus, R. D., 244 n.3; 246 n.8; 249 n.11
Pritchard, John, 218 n.35

Radner, Ephraim, 216 and n.24
Rahner, K., 249 n.10
Reinhartz, Adele, 199
Rensberger, D., 76 n.21
Reno, R. R., 212 and n.4
Reumann, John, 107 and n.8
Reynolds, Benjamin E., 65 n.26
Richey, L. B., 74 and n.12; 75 and n.16
Ricoeur, Paul, xv; 17 and nn.34–39; 18; 202; 294
Ritschl, A., 201
Robertson, A. T., 115 n.35
Robertson, F. W., xix; 224–35
Rogers, Cleon L., 125 and nn.5,9,10
Rogerson, John W., xix; 226 n.12; 233 n.35; 234 n.41
Rohrbaugh, Richard L., 26 n.28
Rosenberg, Joel, 11; 12 and nn.17,18,19; 13 and n.21; 15 and n.27
Rosner, Brian S., 95 n.21
Rowland, Christopher, 205 and nn.36,37; 220 n.42
Rudolph, K., 45 n.41

Sallers, Robert, 99 nn.44,45
Sanders, J. N., 45 n.44
Sarisky, Darren, 214 n.16; 217 n.28
Scheidel, Walter, 100 nn.50,51
Schelling, F. W. J., 200
Schleiermacher, F. D. E., 191; 192 and n.13; 194; 200; 201; 205
Schmid, H., 188 n.2
Schnackenburg, R., 43 n.28; 123 n.3
Schneiders, Sandra, xv; 18 and nn.40–44
Schnelle, U., 37 n.9; 43 n.28
Schröter, J., 41 n.19
Schwindt, Rainer, 62 n.19
Scruton, Roger, 136 n.2
Seitz, Christopher R., 5 n.1; 7 n.13; 11 n.15; 14; 15 n.26

Silva, Moisés, 114 and n.31; 119 n.43
Simian-Yofre, H., 138 n.3
Smart, Ninian, 207 n.41
Smith, Anthony, xv; 22; 23 and n.14; 25
Smith, D. E., 129 and nn.20,21; 135 n.27
Smith, Wilfrid Cantwell, 20 n.4
Soares Prabhu, George, 159 n.2; 164 n.16
Staszak, Gary, 121 n.50
Stäudlin, C. F., 191 n.9
Steinmetz, David, 174 n.1
Stendahl, K., 189 n.5
Strathmann, H., 28 and n.33
Strecker, G., 191 n.11; 194 n.17
Stuhlmacher,P., 41 n.18; 188 n.2
Suphan, B., 227 n.19
Swain, Scott R., 238 n.1
Swain, Simon, 151 n.21
Swinton, John, 218 n.36

Tang Nielsen, Jesper, 62 n.16
Tarrant, H., 130 n.23
Temple W., 78 n.24
Thatcher, T., 74 and n.14; 75 and n.17; 87
Theissen, Gerd, 198 and n.22
Theobald, Michael, 41 n.19; 65 n.29
Thiselton, Anthony C., 176 n.6; 201 n.27; 202
Thompson, M. M., 46 n.49
Thornton, Patricia M., 20 n.1
Tonstad, Sigve, 73
Townsley, Jeramy, 95 and n.23
Tracy, David, 18 n.41
Troeltsch, E., 193; 201 and n.24
Tuch, Friedrich, 226 and n.12
Turner, Bryan S., 152 n.22

Ussher, James, 228
Utzschneider, Helmut, 7 and n.14

Van der Watt, Jan, 69 n.34
Vanhoozer, Kevin J., 216 n.28
Van Kooten, George, 44 n.32; 136 n.1; 140 n.6; 143 n.10; 151 n.21
Verkuyten, Maykel, 24 n.21
Via, Dan O., 260 n.23

Village, Andrew, 221 n.48
Visotzky, B. L., 52 n.18; 56 n.24
Volf, Miroslav, 211 n.2; 218 n.37; 219 and n.39

Walsh, Brian J., xx; xxi; 99 n.39; 298 n.24; 301 n.38
Walton, Heather, 219; 220 n.40
Warner, Rob, 256 n.5
Watts, John D. W., 5; 6 n.6; 91 n.2
Webster, John, xix; xx; 213 n.11; 214 and n.16; 216 and n.28; 217 and nn.29-32; 221 n.46; 222 and n.50
Wedderburn, A. J. M., xiv
Weidner, R. V., 188 n.2
Weinel, H., 188 n.2
Weiss, B., 188 n.2; 191 n.10
Wengst, Klaus, 99 nn.42,43
Wenham, G. J., 5 n.5
Westermann, Claus, 11 n.16
Whitelaw, Thomas, 234
Wiesel, Elie, 280 n.10
Williams, Catrin H., xvi; 66 nn.30,31; 70 n.38
Williams, Rowan, 221 nn.47,49; 269 and n.37; 272; 273 n.46
Wink, Walter, 76; 76 n.23
Witherington III, B., 125 n.5
Wolf, H., 7 n.12
Wolff, Stefan, 23 and n.16
Woodhead, Linda, 256 n.5
Work, T., 238 n.1
Wrede, W., xviii; 177 n.8; 190 and n.7; 191 and n.11; 192 and n.13; 193; 194 and n.17; 197; 203; 204
Wright, N. T., xvi; 72 n.1; 84 nn.28-30; 85 n.31; 88 n.35; 106 and n.6; 121 n.50

Yeago, D. S., 238 n.1
Yildiz, Ali Aslan, 24 n.21
Yoder-Neufeld, T. R., 123 n.3
Young, Frances, 257 n.9

Zachhuber, J., 201 n.25
Zagefka, Hanna, 22 and nn.11,12; 23; 23 n.15
Zelyck, L. R., 43 n.28

www.ingramcontent.com/pod-product-compliance
Lightning Source LLC
Chambersburg PA
CBHW021338300426
44114CB00012B/999